Harvard English Studies 2

Twentieth-Century Literature in Retrospect

HARVARD ENGLISH STUDIES 2

Twentieth-Century Literature in Retrospect

Edited by Reuben A. Brower

Harvard University Press, Cambridge, Massachusetts 1971

Editorial Note

This volume, the second of the *Harvard English Studies,* is focused on a reconsideration of literature of the twentieth century. With the century now past the seventy-year mark, it seems appropriate to take a backward glance at the achievement of writers and critcs who have given the literature of the age its special character. The essays collected here are divided into two groups: the first, concerned mainly with poets and novelists who have reached an almost canonical status; the second, dealing with earlier writers whose position has been radically altered through interpretation and criticism of the past forty years. The twentieth-century Donne, Milton, and Pope are no longer quite the Donne, Milton, and Pope of their own periods or of the last century. A poet so recent as Wordsworth is today barely recognizable as the "poet of nature" beloved by the "Wordsworthians" of Arnold's generation. It is safe to say that the twenty-first century will give us fresh versions of both the older and the newer classics. R.A.B.

The third volume in this series, "Varieties of Humor," will be edited by Harry Levin; the fourth, "The Uses of Literature in the United States," by Monroe Engel.

Contents

Contents

I. Writers and Critics

MONROE ENGEL

Dubliners and Erotic Expectation

Very near the beginning of the first story in *Dubliners,* "The Sisters," there is an obscure joke. The extent of the joke may be uncertain, but its effect in any case is ironic — to cast doubt on the authority of the first-person narrator (a boy of about thirteen, since the story takes place in July 1895, Joyce was born on 2 February 1882, and with the boy-narrator Joyce intends some version of himself even as the uncle is some version of John Joyce, his father). The narrator, troubled by an unconfirmed rumor of the death of an old priest with whom he has consorted, returns home to find a man known to him as Old Cotter discussing the priest's death with his family, his aunt and uncle.[1]

Old Cotter is doing most of the talking, rambling on ellipti-

1. Neither here nor in "Araby," where the same domestic situation pertains, is there explanation of why the boy lives with his aunt and uncle, why his parents are neither visible nor referred to. Presumably he is an orphan, and by thus orphaning the boy (and, imaginatively, himself) Joyce accentuates the lovelessness of his existence.

All quotations from *Dubliners* are from the Viking edition (New York: copyright © 1967 by the Estate of James Joyce; originally published by B. W. Huebsch, Inc., in 1916), reprinted by permission of The Viking Press, Inc., and Jonathan Cape Ltd.; all rights reserved.

3

cally, the crucial facts always missing — a style of discourse
that is recurrently, for Joyce, the epiphany of the banal. The boy
finds Old Cotter an excruciating bore, but as narrator he com-
municates this judgment in problematic fashion: "Tiresome old
fool! When we knew him first he used to be rather interesting,
talking of faints and worms; but I soon grew tired of him and
his endless stories about the distillery." What are these "faints
and worms" that the narrator distinguishes from Old Cotter's
"endless stories about the distillery"? Each of the two words has
a number of possible meanings,[2] but the meanings appropriate
here are ascertainable if not obvious. Faints: "the crude, impure
spirits given off in the first and last stages of the distillation of
liquors." Worms: "something thought of as being wormlike because of the spiral shape, etc., as . . . the coil of a still" (*Web-
ster's New World Dictionary, College Edition*, 1968).

I don't know for how many contemporary readers, even Irish
readers, these meanings would have been present; everything
suggests that they would not have been many. But my recent
informal sampling of good English and American readers has
turned up nobody aware of them — which may only mean real-
istically that next to nobody is. The interesting question is
whether the boy-narrator in the story is aware of them though
the author most certainly is. The working relationship between
the boy narrator in the first-person stories and the author, the
retrospective narrator, is by no means clear. Does the boy think
of the more ordinary meanings of "faints and worms" and attribute to them a morbid glamor — not unrelated to the glamor he
attributes to the paralytic, snuff-covered priest — at a far re-
move from shop talk about a distillery? Or does he know that
Old Cotter had used these as distillery terms — which the context of even that old man's elliptical conversation must have suggested — but hear in them nonetheless a sufficient overtone of
their common meaning to give them some distinguishing interest? In either case, since Old Cotter obviously has talked about
nothing but the distillery, the distinction the narrator makes can
operate really only against himself. The irony is greater or lesser
depending on what understanding is attributed to the boy, but it

2. I doubt that I should have noticed this without extraordinarily generous guidance from John V. Kelleher.

produces the same kind of effect in either case: to make romantically dubious the value the boy attributes to some corners of his world in contrast to the drab emptiness he finds elsewhere.

It casts more or less severe doubt, too, on the criteria by which he establishes his realities: thinking he can best discover whether the priest is dead by looking for "the reflection of candles on the darkened blind" rather than by more direct evidence or communication; associating the strangeness of the sound of the word *paralysis* with the sound of "the word *gnomon* in the Euclid and the word *simony* in the Catechism." This is or would be its effect, that is, if the irony could register. But if the irony was even a fraction as private when it was conceived as it is now, why is it there at all? Did Joyce expect his readers to forage it out? Or was it rather that in this instance he was and knew himself to be his own chief audience and that the irony functioned primarily as a warning to separate himself from his narrator's romanticism which, given his connection with that narrator, might have seemed a real hazard. Was the chief function of the irony then to keep Joyce straight in writing the story?

The "faints and worms" themselves are of little consequence in the story. Nor, for that matter, is Old Cotter himself of any great consequence. And yet the irony of "faints and worms" might suggest that we are not to dismiss too easily Old Cotter's contention that it is bad for children to associate with types like the priest "because their minds are so impressionable. When children see things like that, you know, it has an effect." The substantive question of the story is whether the boy's romantic imagination is not in fact being judged pejoratively as morbid and distorting. The question is of particular moment because this potentiality of the boy's imagination has been fed by the priest and not, so far as one can tell, by anyone else. In other words, the priest has possibly had a unique reinforcing effect on that aspect of the boy's cast of mind that the story forces us to judge, or at least to estimate.

The nature of the old priest's influence on the boy, the nature of the imaginative stimulation he provides, is suggested by the dream rendered in two parts: the first part in its proper chronological sequence in the story, the second part in recollection. In the dream the boy sees "the heavy grey face of the paralytic" following him, murmuring, and he understands "that it desired to confess something. I felt my soul receding into some pleasant and vicious region." The logic of the dream is not absolutely apparent, but it is apparent enough, I think, that the dream is covertly auto-erotic. It is a childish precursor of the overtly auto-erotic dreams and reveries that Stephen enjoys in the *Portrait* and Bloom in *Ulysses.*

In this "pleasant and vicious region" the old priest is waiting, and he begins to murmur a confession to the boy, who wonders why he smiles "continually" and why his lips are "so moist with spittle." The boy's sense of puzzlement is curiously dissolved, though, when he remembers that the old man "had died of paralysis and I felt that I too was smiling feebly as if to absolve the simoniac of his sin." This is of the class of explanations that satisfies the dreamer without easily satisfying anyone to whom the dream is described. None of the other descriptions of the priest, living or dead, suggests that he drooled; nor do the circumstances of his disgrace (at least as recounted by his sister Eliza) carry any suggestion of simony, the buying or selling of ecclesiastical pardons, offices, or emoluments. But *simony* and *paralysis* are two of the three words to which, the narrator has told us, he is peculiarly attracted (the third, *gnomon,* is not, so far as I can discern, present in the dream). *Paralysis,* he says, "sounded to me like the name of some maleficent and sinful being. It filled me with fear, and yet I longed to be nearer to it and to look upon its deadly work." This unexplained verbal bond seems to be the chief organizing force of the dream (not inappropriately, perhaps, for the boy who was to become the author of *Finnegan's Wake*). The narration of the dream is concluded as recollection, after a break of some hours, but the recollection is incomplete. The boy cannot remember "the end of the dream," but he remembers its atmosphere: "long velvet curtains and a swinging lamp of antique fashion . . . very far away, in some land where the customs were strange." He thinks this land might be Persia, a largely imaginary place not unlike the Araby of the third story in *Dubliners,* the last of the triad of first-person stories that constitute a crucial first entity in the collection.

But the priest is not simply a dream figure. He has existed. The narrator gives two views of him alive — not discrete instances, but rather quintessential views each of which must subsume many instances. In the first it is established that the priest is in the back room behind his sisters' drapery shop. The shop is on Great Britain Street (the name of the street is an emblem of what is sad about the shop) and it deals chiefly in "children's bootees and umbrellas" and carries a notice "in the window, saying: *Umbrellas Re-covered.*" The insistence on genteel desiccation is unmistakable.

But "the little dark room behind the shop," where the priest sits by the fire "nearly smothered in his great-coat," has a very different aura. The boy rouses the priest from "his stupefied doze" with the gift of a packet of snuff, empties the packet into his snuff-box for him, and then watches the snuff grains dribble from his trembling hands in "little clouds of smoke," falling over his clothing and remaining there because "the red handkerchief, blackened, as it always was, with the snuff-stains of a week . . . was quite inefficacious" to brush them away. What is being described has a grotesque glamor: the somnolent palsied moribund priest who cannot take snuff without dribbling it on himself is addicted to snuff as his last pleasure. The habit has become eroticized for him, its affect accentuated probably by his life of celibacy as well as by his age. And the boy apprehends the back room as erotically infused even as he apprehends the utter absence of eros in the drapery shop at the front of the house.

This character of the priest is supplemented by the other living view we have of him, a view that makes the nature of his influence on the narrator far more explicit, far less simply impressionistic. In his converse with the narrator, the priest had talked about the catacombs and Napoleon and had revealed to him "how complex and mysterious were certain institutions of the Church which I had always regarded as the simplest acts." The institutions specified are "the duties of the priest towards the Eucharist and towards the secrecy of the confessional." He also habitually questioned the boy on a wide range of matters having to do with the Church and listened to his answers, nodding, "pushing huge pinches of snuff up each nostril alternately," smiling, uncovering "his big discoloured teeth and [letting] his tongue lie upon his lower lip."

The specificity of the description here and elsewhere in *Dubliners* requires one to see as well as hear, to visualize a scene.[3]
And the scene is brilliantly grotesque. It should be no wonder,
save to the boy himself, that his response to the priest's death
is not entirely what he thinks it should be, that he is not "in a
mourning mood" and that he feels "freed." Some part of what
the priest has taught him is close to terror, the terror of mystery,
but he is apparently the only living person to whom the old man
has been able to convey this education. For the rest of Dublin
he was simply dotty, broken, pitiful. The boy has learned a les-
son from him that the others do not comprehend. He will not,
for example, accept the cream crackers he is offered because he
does not wish to "make . . . noise eating them" in the house
that still contains the dead priest's body. Moreover, while his
aunt, the priest's two sisters, and the woman who has washed
the body think the priest looks "peaceful and resigned" in death,
the boy sees him rather as "solemn and truculent."

It is not possible to adjudicate these divergent views with certainty. But the assertion that the priest looks "peaceful and resigned" is so absolutely conventional, socially conventional, as
to be suspect, particularly when it is supported by no concrete
observation. In contrast, the boy's more individual impression is
supported by keen, coherent observation: "I saw that he was not
smiling. There he lay, solemn and copious,[4] vested as for the
altar, his large hands loosely retaining a chalice. His face was
very truculent, grey and massive, with black cavernous
nostrils and circled by a scanty white fur." What is absolutely
consistent here and in the next two stories, both also first-person
stories of childhood, is how the child's eroticized expectations
separate him from the ordinary world and from all adults save
certain outcasts from that ordinary world (there are after all remarkable similarities, whatever the obvious differences, between
the priest in "The Sisters" and the homosexual derelict in "An
Encounter"). What distinguishes "The Sisters," though, from

3. There is far more natural opportunity for the film-maker's art in
these stories than in *Ulysses* or *Finnegan's Wake*. Any one of them might
make a fine film and "The Dead" a great film.
4. The word "copious" in unexpected usage is a Joycean favorite, as in
the description of the easy chair in the whore's room at the end of chapter ii of *Portrait*.

the two stories that follow it is the extent to which the boy's eroticized sense of the world is still allowed dignity. The joke about "faints and worms" is so obscure, perhaps even problematic, as to count for little more than an indication or caution that Joyce may be directing more to himself than to the reader. The boy's loose association of exotic words, related to his auto-eroticism,[5] is perhaps also a caution. But caution scarcely seems to be in order in this story, since the boy experiences no comeuppance at the end as he does in the climactic actions of the two succeeding stories. I could suggest two reasons — speculations, though I hope in time to indicate their reasonableness — for this: first, that the boy does not actively seek any form of gratification; second, that in addition to being passive, his eroticism takes its nutriment from the grotesque and morbid and does not apparently hunger for those more simply wholesome erotic objects in which Joyce's belief seems to have been strained at best.

Each of the two succeeding stories, though, concerns a search for such objects — a search subjected to strong irony at the outset and coming to no ultimate good. So in "An Encounter," the imaginative ideal of "the Wild West" is found in magazines with such self-eradicating names as *The Union Jack, Pluck,* and *The Halfpenny Marvel* and promoted chiefly by a boy who turns out paradoxically to have a "vocation for the priesthood." For all the boys in the school the stories of the Wild West represent escape, but they embrace this alternative to their daily incarceration in very different spirits: "some boldly, some in jest and some almost in fear." The narrator (much the same narrator as in "The Sisters") numbers himself among the fearful group and says that in the line of escape he "liked better some American detective stories which were traversed from time to time by unkempt fierce and beautiful girls" [6] — revealing what is already evident enough, that for these pubescent boys the Wild West is an erotic substitute.

Seeking an escape, "real adventures," the narrator plans "a day's miching" (playing truant) with two companions, Leo Dil-

5. The relationship is of course a continuing issue in Joyce's work, as well perhaps as in his life.
6. The conjunction of adjectives constitutes a cliché and has therefore an ironic thrust.

lon and Mahony. They decide "to go along the Wharf Road until we came to the ships, then to cross in the ferryboat and walk out to see the Pigeon House." A modest enough plan it would seem, but not sufficiently modest even so to be realizable. The narrator sleeps badly the night before the adventure. Then in the morning Mahony turns up but Leo Dillon doesn't. The two set off without him, appropriating the sixpence he had contributed to the common treasury; and "school and home" do seem to "recede" from them — which the narrator had earlier established as the precondition for adventure. But the ship they watch unloading, perhaps "a Norwegian vessel," disappoints the narrator in a curious fashion that becomes crucial in the ultimate scheme of the story. He wishes some of the sailors to have green eyes, but their eyes are only "blue and grey and even black." Everything thereafter is downhill. The boys tire of watching the ship unload, the biscuits they buy to eat with chocolate are so old that they have to be eaten "sedulously," Mahony chases a cat but the cat gets away, they realize that the hour and their fatigue make it impossible for them to continue on to the Pigeon House, and the only adventure they meet is provided by an elderly fag who presumably goes through some exhibitionistic sexual ritual in their sight, asks them about their sweethearts, and confesses to the narrator (Mahony has found and begun to chase the cat again) a rather feverish interest in the beating of small boys — a confession not unrelated to the old priest's confession in "The Sisters." What the narrator finds, then, on his day's outing is a thwarting or corruption of all his erotic expectations, whether of the Wild West he fears or of the "unkempt fierce and beautiful girls" he really desires. But significantly, the derelict-invert has the "bottle-green eyes" the narrator was looking for among the sailors (though the boy does not himself make this connection), and he responds to him with the "fear" out of which he had originally "banded . . . together" with the other boys in "a spirit of unruliness."

In the third of the first-person stories, "Araby," the view of the relationship of the eroticized expectation of the narrator to the world is so much less ambiguous than in the two previous stories as to approach the formulaic. Consequently, though "Araby" may well be the greatest very short story in English, it lacks some of the richness of the two preceding stories. The division of ironic force seems to have changed. The thrust of the irony is directed very little against the banality of the world, preponderantly against the narrator's belief that the world can be other than banal. Unlike its two predecessors (or, at least, to an extent far beyond them) the story has an encompassing scheme which directs its reading — an interesting early instance of a peculiarly Joycean tyranny and a simpler instance, I think, than he will allow himself again. "North Richmond Street, being blind," the story opens: "blind" meaning literally that it is a dead end, a cul-de-sac. But the ordinary psychological meaning of blind takes on commanding resonance as the story proceeds and concerns itself with seeing and not seeing, or with what is seen in the light and what in the dark.

The first paragraph of the story seems exact, circumstantial, unassailable. But our confidence in the narrator's understanding of the story he is telling is already being eroded in the second paragraph and it never wholly recovers. The books which the boy singles out from among the old priest's effects are obviously joined by the variant forms of romanticism they represent, including a romantic religiosity which is crucial to the end of the story. Of the three books, the narrator likes best *The Memoirs of Vidocq* only "because its leaves were yellow." The narrator is being subjected to irony too when, a few lines farther along, he describes the old priest as "charitable." Most readers will, I think, judge that the priest would have been more genuinely charitable had he left some of his money and not simply his old furniture to his sister.

But it is in the third paragraph that the romantic adolescent temperament begins to be described as a form of willed blindness that depends for its continuance on dark or dusk. Winter is apparently the narrator's favorite season, when "dusk fell before we had well eaten our dinners." The band of boys — some fragment presumably of the group joined in "An Encounter" by their varied forms of enthusiasm for the Wild West — play in the "dark muddy lanes," "the dark dripping gardens," "the dark odorous stables," places for which the dark alone makes possible the peculiar dominance of their romantic elements. The boys hide in the shadows from the adult intruders who appear in the light that comes through the kitchen windows. From the shadows too they watch Mangan's sister, who, because she is midway between the adolescent and adult worlds, stands in a curious relation to the light: in one appearance her figure is defined "by the light from the half-opened door," but in the next, far more pointedly, she is a figure of chiaroscuro, divided into light and dark: "The light from the lamp opposite our door caught the white curve of her neck, lit up her hair that rested there and, falling, lit up the hand upon the railing. It fell over one side of her dress and caught the white border of a petticoat, just visible as she stood at ease."

The narrator, straining at his own adolescent limits, watches the girl, Mangan's sister, from behind a "blind . . . pulled down to within an inch of the sash so that I could not be seen." "Accompanied" by her image, he finds romance "even in places the most hostile to romance" and sees himself romantically in these places, bearing his "chalice safely through a throng of foes." On a "dark rainy evening" in "the back drawing-room in which the priest had died," he is "thankful that [he can] see so little," his "senses [seem] to desire to veil themselves," and he presses "the palms of [his] hands together until they trembled, murmuring: *O love! O love!* many times." Again, only the exact extent of the irony resists specification. The narrator's judgment, or in the most general way his vision, is being made to seem defective, and the reader is being prepared for his comeuppance.

The working out of the rest of the story requires little detailing. The fair, Araby, becomes the emblem of the boy's romantic illusions. The play on night or dark and adolescent blindness continues — the night air is bad for Mrs. Mercer (the oldest of the adults) and the image of Mangan's sister comes between the narrator and the page of the book he is trying to read. Painful change is at work in him, so that child's play, which is what is after all being described with romantic fervor at the beginning of the story, comes to represent what is contemptible to him: his schoolwork, as it stands "between me and my desire" [7] seems "child's play, ugly monotonous child's play." The other formalized change is even more crucial, for it is in the darkness of the

7. Though it is rather that his "desire" seems to stand between him and his schoolwork.

hall at the very end of the story that the boy's sense of romantic possibility collapses, though the "anguish and anger," so disproportionate to the occasion, suggest that his romantic temperament has in fact not changed.

I have detailed certain recurrent tendencies in these three first-person stories that begin *Dubliners,* not because the stories individually present any great problems to any reasonably conscientious reader, but rather to indicate the ways in which they constitute a coherent progressive unit in *Dubliners* — a unit that can inform one's reading not only of the other stories in this collection, but of much of the rest of Joyce's work as well. All three stories concern the thwarting of the eroticized life expectations of their adolescent narrator. This is consistent. But the irony to which the narrator is subjected is progressive: he is subject to some irony from the beginning, but the extent increases radically from the first to the second to the third story. In "The Sisters" the irony is only intermittent. In "Araby," it is virtually relentless. This becomes a crucial issue and a crucial estimate of possibility. The boy narrator is after all a partial portrait of Joyce himself, whose first published novel, closely following the long-delayed publication of *Dubliners,* is an ironicized (among other changes) rewriting of an earlier, more literally and simply autobiographical novel (a novel about, among other things but importantly, erotic possibility) that he seems never to have considered publishing.

But it is not only for this first person narrator, this surrogate for himself, that Joyce envisages such narrowness of erotic possibility. No greater possibility is allowed any of the other characters in *Dubliners* until we come to "The Dead," which is really a separate enterprise. Except in "The Dead" the restriction of possibility (not simply of achievement but of possibility) is withering. Only the meanest or most callow Dubliners flourish at all, and not much at that — Corley in "Two Gallants" or Ignatius Gallaher in "A Little Cloud." Any attempt to move out, to seize some portion of happiness, exacerbates a hunger that cannot be fed and leads therefore to disaster. Witness Mrs. Sinico in "A Painful Case." Even the minimal expectation that Maria brings to the Hallow Eve party in "Clay" earns her a handful of wet garden mud. Possibly the most direct, the least modified authorial sympathy allowed any character in *Dubliners* is given to Eveline, whose belief in her "right to happiness" is insufficient to enable her to leave Dublin for Buenos Aires, "a distant unknown country," even when she has gone to the North Wall with her fiance and they have purchased their tickets. About to quit her "hard life," she no longer finds it "a wholly undesirable life," and she apprehends the new happier life that she has imagined as a form of drowning. The implied statement is about as coherent as the collective statement of a group of largely independent stories could be.

In the fall of 1905, Joyce divided the stories of *Dubliners* into four categories: stories of "my childhood," "adolescence," "mature life," and "public life in Dublin," specifying the stories in each category and designating "Grace" as "the last story of the book." [8] Omitted in this account are "Two Gallants," "A Little Cloud," and "The Dead," all written later. But "Two Gallants" and "A Little Cloud" are very much of a piece with the other stories in *Dubliners,* whereas "The Dead" is in a different mood (as well as of a different scope). By September 1906, when the publisher Grant Richards had already been stalling over a manuscript of the stories for some time, Joyce could write to his brother Stanislaus that he sometimes felt he had been "unnecessarily harsh" in writing about Ireland, and that he had "not reproduced its ingenuous insularity and its hospitality" nor "been just to its beauty" (Ellmann, 239). It was only after another year, and his move from Trieste to Rome and then back to Trieste, that he came to write "The Dead," which takes a much less harsh view of Dublin than do the other stories and does render "its ingenuous insularity and its hospitality" as well as its "beauty." But by this time Joyce was three years out of Ireland and could move from his earlier harshness not only by way of the greater equanimity that temporal and spatial distance made possible, but most pointedly too by way of whatever satisfaction he had gained from the first years of his common-law marriage to Nora Barnacle — a problematic satisfaction encouraged by stratagems which, though still in their earliest stages of develop-

---

8. Richard Ellmann, *James Joyce* (New York: Oxford, 1959), p. 216; hereafter designated parenthetically as Ellmann. Note the "my" used with the childhood stories and not with the other categories.

ment and usefulness, seem to have been vital both to the relationship and to a good part of the imaginative writing (drama and verse as well as fiction) of the rest of Joyce's career.

Joyce met Nora Barnacle first on 10 June 1904, though he did not "walk" with her until June 16, Bloomsday, the day on which the action of *Ulysses* takes place. On this day also or sometime close to it, Joyce first entertained the theory (which Stephen expounds on this day in *Ulysses*) that Shakespeare identified himself not with Prince Hamlet but with his betrayed father — a theory that not only sets in advance a model to which Joyce will force his apprehension of his own experience to conform, but also legitimizes the reader who is disposed to look for thematic correspondence between Joyce's fiction and his life.

What little evidence we have suggests that Joyce's courtship of Nora must have been a curious affair. The courtship is not reconstructable, but the letters Joyce wrote to Nora in the course of it are significant. The most interesting of them, those in which Joyce tries to explain himself to Nora, indicate that she was at least puzzled by his wooing — by, for example, his insistence on telling her his sexual and religious histories, but the trouble he had finding an appropriate way to sign his letters to her and the fact that he could never tell her he loved her. On 19 September he wrote to reassure her: "You ask me why I don't love you, but surely you must believe I am very fond of you and if to desire to possess a person wholly, to admire and honour that person deeply, and to seek to secure that person's happiness in every way is to 'love' then perhaps my affection for you is a kind of love. I will tell you this that your soul seems to me to be the most beautiful and simple soul in the world and it may be because I am so conscious of this when I look at you that my love or affection for you loses much of its violence." [9] Despite her puzzlement, and surely not entirely relieved by his explanations, Nora Barnacle left Dublin with Joyce on 8 October 1904 without even the conventional reassurance of marriage.

9. All quotations from Joyce's letters, unless otherwise specified, are from Richard Ellmann, ed., *Letters of James Joyce,* vol. II (New York: Viking, copyright © 1966 by F. Lionel Monro, administrator of the estate of James Joyce). Reprinted by permission of The Viking Press, Inc.; all rights reserved.

Only a couple of months later (3 December) Joyce was writing about her to Stanislaus with detachment at least, as someone who "admits the gentle art of self-satisfaction. She has had many love-affairs, one when quite young with a boy who died. She was laid up at news of his death." In the same letter also he tells Stanny of "a curate in Galway" who, when Nora was sixteen, "took her on his lap and said he liked her . . . put his hand up under her dress which was shortish," and afterwards "told her to say in confession it was a man not a priest did 'that' to her."

The myth of Nora has begun, but at this point the edge of discontent is more in evidence than is the staying power of any imaginative self-dramatization; and by the summer of 1905 the durability of the arrangement between Joyce and Nora seems very questionable. On 12 July Joyce writes to Stanislaus that Nora, who is within two weeks of being delivered of their first child, "is not of a very robust constitution . . . more than this I am afraid that she is one of those plants which cannot be safely transplanted." Then, after a continued narration of Nora's unhappiness and its depressing effect on him, he does not "desire any such ending for our love-affair as a douche in the Serpentine.[10] At the same time I want to avoid as far as is humanly possible any such apparition in our lives as that abominable spectre which Aunt Josephine calls 'mutual tolerance.'" The temporary solution, he thinks, is that after Nora's confinement he and Nora and their child should return to Dublin and set up joint residence there with Stanislaus. But this decampment did not take place. Instead, Stanislaus came to Trieste in October and joined a household to which, over a period of some years, he gave much, but from which he took chiefly abuse.

By midwinter, despite Stanislaus' arrival, the marriage seems very much on the rocks. Joyce writes (4 December 1905) to the Aunt Josephine he has quoted to Stanislaus:

I have hesitated before telling you that I imagine the present relations between Nora and myself are about to suffer some alteration.

10. Ellmann considers the import of the reference to be Harriet Shelley's suicide in the Serpentine in 1816; *Letters of James Joyce*, vol. II (New York: Viking, 1966), p. 96 n. 2.

I do so now only because I have reflected that you [are] a person who is not likely to discuss the matter with others. It is possible that I am partly to blame if such a change as I think I foresee takes place but it will hardly take place through my fault alone. I daresay I am a difficult person for any woman to put up with but on the other hand I have no intention of changing. Nora does not seem to make much difference between me and the rest of the men she has known[11] and I can hardly believe that she is justified in this. I am not a very domestic animal — after all, I suppose I am an artist — and sometimes when I think of the free and happy life which I have (or had) every talent to live I am in a fit of despair. At the same time I do not wish to rival the atrocities of the average husband and I shall wait till I see my way more clearly. I suppose you will shake your head now over my coldness of heart which is probably only an unjust name for a certain perspicacity of temper or mind. I am not sure that the thousands of households which are with difficulty held together by memories of dead sentiments have much right to reproach me with inhumanity.

There is little evidence to suggest what did hold the household together for the next several years unless it was absence of money. Not wishing "to rival the atrocities of the average husband" and being absolutely impoverished as well was a combination to keep separation out of reach. A son Giorgio was born on 27 July 1905 and two years later shy a day, 26 July 1907, a daughter Lucia. However much Joyce may have considered such arrangements an "abominable spectre," it must have been in considerable part "mutual tolerance" (with perhaps intermittent intervals of something more fervid) on which the household survived for the several years during which *Dubliners* and *Stephen Hero* were completed and the conversion of *Stephen Hero* into *A Portrait of the Artist as a Young Man* was begun.

Then in 1909, with his son Giorgio in tow, Joyce visited Dublin for the first time since his departure. There an old friend, Vincent Cosgrave (perhaps egged on by Joyce's enemy Gogarty), told him that he, Cosgrave, had also been "walking" with Nora in the summer of 1904, presumably on more or less alternate evenings. Joyce was shattered. To J. F. Byrne he "wept and

11. It seems unlikely that "the rest of the men" Nora had known was much of a category save in Joyce's imagination.

groaned and gesticulated in futile impotence as he sobbed out
. . . the thing that had occurred." [12] For the first time in any
of the letters either to or about Nora there is the sound of a man
in love, an infatuated, deeply injured man:

My eyes are full of tears, tears of sorrow and mortification. My
heart is full of bitterness and despair. I can see nothing but your
face as it was then raised to meet another's. O Nora, pity me for
what I suffer now.   (6 August 1909)

Is Georgie my son? The first night I slept with you in Zurich was
October 11th and he was born July 27th. That is nine months and
16 days. I remember that there was very little blood that night.
                                                      (7 August 1909)

The primitive suffering of these calculations is worse than the
assertions of suffering, more absolute. It is painful also, I think,
to juxtapose Joyce's assumption (presumably correct) that Nora
was a virgin when she left Dublin with him with his remarks to
Stanislaus less than two months after their departure that Nora
not only admitted to "the gentle art of self-satisfaction" but had
had many love affairs.

Within about two weeks however, Joyce had allowed himself
to be persuaded by Byrne that Cosgrave was lying, out of malice,
and that Nora had not betrayed him. He writes to her then
asking her to "forgive me for my contemptible conduct" and
"take me again to your arms," and tells her: "A whole life is
opening for us now. It has been a bitter experience and our love
will now be sweeter" (19 August 1909). Presumably the repetitions of "now" here and below are significant. Two days later he
tells Nora that she was "not in a sense the girl for whom I had
dreamed and written the verses [*Chamber Music*] you find now
so enchanting," but that she surpasses that earlier love image
and is "the fulfilment of that desire" (21 August 1909). The
following day he writes to tell her how much he desires her —

12. J. F. Byrne, *Silent Years* (New York: Farrar, Straus, and Young,
1953), p. 156. Byrne, gallantly, does not reveal what "the thing that had
occurred" was.

"I see you in a hundred poses, grotesque, shameful, virginal, languorous" — and reminds her of

the three adjectives I have used in *The Dead* in speaking of your body. They are these: "musical and strange and perfumed."

My jealousy is still smouldering in my heart. Your love for me must be fierce and violent to make me forget *utterly*.

Do not let me ever lose the love I have for you now, Nora. If we could go on together through life in that way how happy we should be.

On 31 August he writes to her that she was "to my young manhood what the idea of the Blessed Virgin was to my boyhood," and a few lines farther on: "How I would love to surprise you sleeping now! There is a place I would like to kiss you now, a *strange* place Nora. *Not* on the lips, Nora. Do you know where?" We proceed by way of the Blessed Virgin into the notorious erotic letters proper. In a letter written two days later, Joyce tells Nora he would "like to be flogged by" her and to see her eyes "blazing with anger." This is the province of Sacher-Masoch, a province which gets extensive epistolary exploration in the ensuing winter[13] when Joyce returns to Dublin once more, this time on an ill-fated entrepreneurial scheme having to do with the establishment of a motion-picture theatre. But the first trip to Dublin is the important moment, commemorated by a gift Joyce brought back to Trieste for Nora, a necklace of ivory pieces or dice with an inscribed ivory tablet, the five dice signifying "the five years of trial and misunderstanding" (1904–1909). The letter written (3 September 1909) to Nora from Dublin to describe his gift in advance ends: "Save me, my *true* love! Save me from the badness of the world and of my own heart!"

The burden of this commemorative gift as well as of the letters that precede it is, I think, unavoidable: Joyce's love for Nora came to keen, clear life presumably for the first time in 1909, after five years of marriage, under stimulus of his conviction that he had been betrayed. The great carrying power of this convic-

13. The province of Sacher-Masoch is largely exploited of course in *Ulysses*.

tion, though he soon learned that it was without substance, must derive from the circumstance that it had been imagined in advance[14] anticipated, perhaps even desired (for it was later obviously encouraged), and that it was so useful to Joyce as to jutify being called essential. Moreover, if the situation of betrayal was long anticipated, perhaps desired — believed in at first suspicion, then used even when discredited — it seems likely that the love for Nora that inflamed Joyce and informed his work was in good part the product of a meeting of his own needs and "cunning," and that the character he attributed to Nora was similarly created.

It is certainly an earlier version of betrayal that does much, perhaps most, to eroticize "The Dead" (written two years before this incident) and set it apart from all the other stories in *Dubliners*. Gabriel Conroy thinks of Gretta's body as "musical and strange and perfumed" ("the three adjectives I have used in *The Dead* in speaking of your body") just before she tells him of her early love for Michael Furey — Michael or "Sonny" Bodkin, Nora's boy lover who died — who "used to sing that song, *The Lass of Aughrim*" (in a letter to Nora of 31 August 1909 Joyce refers to "The Lass of Aughrim" as "your song"). For it is not an essential difference in materials but rather a difference in intention and sensibility, in point of view toward the fictive materials, that distinguishes "The Dead" from the earlier stories. The character of Gabriel Conroy is in part an amalgam of Joyce himself and his father (Ellmann, 255ff), the narrator and uncle of the three childhood stories; and the other guests at "the Misses Morkan's annual dance" provide reasonable analogies to all but the very most riff-raff of the characters in *Dubliners*. Mary Jane holds her annual pupils' concerts in the same "Antient Concert Rooms" that figure in "A Mother"; Freddy Malins is no more or less difficult than most of the other heavy drinkers in *Dubliners*; and so on. Moreover, Joyce could and did skew the social and economic placement of his charac-

14. Not only archetypically: in one of the letters to Nora written during their courtship (29 August 1904), he talks of his betrayal, largely imagined, by a friend (Byrne) as the example of what he fears from her. It is therefore especially interesting that it is Byrne who persuades him that Nora did not betray him.

ters — and, relatedly, their respectability — more or less at will, as can be seen by comparing the surviving fragment of *Stephen Hero* with the comparable portion of *A Portrait of the Artist.*

The distance at which Joyce discovers his love for Dublin (Trieste to Dublin) is the very distance at which he discovers his love for Nora, though the orientation is reversed. That the distances are the same in both cases is, of course, a trivial coincidence. But that each love finds life at a considerable distance from its object is not coincidental at all. And though "The Dead" was written in 1907 and the crucial long-distance exchange with Nora does not occur until 1909, it is by way of a betrayed (less betrayed? or is betrayal an absolute?) lover with whom he identifies himself that Joyce is able to express tenderness for Dublin. The setting of "The Dead" — the entirely female household, a setting unlike that of any of the other stories — is conducive to tenderness. But it is the sensibility attributed to Gabriel Conroy, some fraction of Joyce's own more complicated and various sensibility, that conveys the tenderness; and Gabriel is from his first appearance in the story a lover who loves more than he is loved, in this sense at least betrayed from the outset. His mind is on his wife at his first appearance and even more strongly at the last, distracted from her in between only by the immediate demands and annoyances of the party. He enters excusing his lateness with a joking reference to the length of time it takes Gretta to dress. His casual, almost automatic remark to Lily the maid ("I suppose we'll be going to your wedding one of these fine days with your young man, eh?") and "the gloom cast over him" by her "bitter" answer ("the men that is now is only all palaver and what they can get out of you") both show, I think, this same direction of mind. Lily's retort moreover, and the situations of the other guests so far as they are specified, establish Gabriel and Gretta as nontypical Dubliners. Save for them, we are unrelievedly in a familiar city of bachelors, old maids, and widows.

Gretta's consistent femaleness is unique in *Dubliners,* and Joyce never allows the reader's consciousness of it to waver; but the value of this femaleness is not simple, is subject to some scrutiny. Gretta's immediate contrast, of course, is Miss Ivors, a woman of roughly the same age but educated — which makes

her Gabriel's peer as his wife is not, and in a story in which
Gabriel thinks most of the guests' "grade of culture differed from
his." We are told at once, however, that Miss Ivors "did not
wear a low-cut bodice." And though her hand on Gabriel's arm
is both warm and eager, she badgers him in a sufficiently un-
feminine fashion that when she later refuses his offer to escort
her home she can very credibly say: "I'm quite well able to take
care of myself." Gretta's response to this points to the opposition
of their characters: "Well, you're the comical girl, Molly," she
says. For Gretta is obviously incapable of taking herself anywhere. She is a dependent woman, and her attachment to Gabriel
may, by the end of the story, seem more surely founded on dependence than on any other aspect of love. Though she joins
herself to Miss Ivors' suggestion that Gabriel take a trip to the
west of Ireland, she makes her case in a very different fashion,
an almost parodically feminine fashion: "His wife clasped her
hands excitedly and gave a little jump. — O, do go, Gabriel, she
cried. I'd love to see Galway again."

The entire last portion of "The Dead," in the hotel room, is
suffused with what is presumably essential or most profound in
Gretta's femaleness, her capacity for passion. If the value of this
is subject to any question it has to be serious question — perhaps in its connection with death and its neglect of the living.
But at the party, Gabriel's sense of the pathos, the dignity, and
the generosity of his aunts is shadowed by his memory of the
"sullen opposition to his marriage" expressed by their dead sister, his mother: "Some slighting phrases she had used still
rankled in his memory; she had once spoken of Gretta as being
country cute and that was not true of Gretta at all." This memory immediately precedes the incident with Miss Ivors; and in
the contrast with Miss Ivors, both overt and implied, Gretta's
femaleness does in fact sometimes seem "country cute."

"The Dead" doesn't distinguish itself from the other stories in
Dubliners only by its more generous view of Dublin. Its scale,
too, makes it most apparently a different order of enterprise. It
is twice the length of "Grace," the next longest story, and about
seven times the length of "Araby" or "After the Race," the
shortest of the stories. Relatedly, its structure is also very different. The final incident in the hotel room becomes almost a sepa-

rate but related story, or a final chapter in a short novel. The break comes[15] when Freddy Malins and his mother and Mr. Browne leave the party in a cab. The scene turns suddenly quiet. Gabriel, "gazing up the staircase," sees his wife, a figure of mystery, unaware that she is being watched, listening to Bartell D'Arcy (who in turn does not see her) singing "The Lass of Aughrim." From here to its conclusion "The Dead" fastens more or less exclusively on its major theme, the affinity of love and death. And it is this, of course, rather than the more indulgent picture of Dublin (though the two cannot be entirely separated), that makes for the story's greatness.

The theme is not introduced for the first time in this last portion of the story, though. It has been building all through, and in ways that may be meant inter alia to cast doubt on the absolute spiritual or even animal superiority of Gretta to Gabriel no matter how ready Gabriel is to concede her superiority. It is important though perhaps difficult to see that Gabriel's view at this point is simpler than Joyce's. To Gretta's telling of the story of Michael Furey, there is an overtone of Aunt Julia singing "Arrayed for the Bridal" — an overtone too faint to be considered irony, but there nonetheless. The reader is intended also I think to remember Gabriel's remarks in his after-dinner speech about "living duties and living affections" (with the emphasis on "living") and even to see his rejection of vacations in the west of Ireland, his preference for holidays on the continent, as an option for life. Then too there is the remark by Mr. Browne, the story's good Protestant, that the monks of Mount Melleray who "slept in their coffins" might have done as well with a "comfortable spring bed." But once into the thrust of the latter portion of the story, no reader is disposed to register such overtones very forcibly.

The essentials of this last part of "The Dead" are continuous, it is only the reader's and Gabriel's sense of what has happened that changes. Gabriel thinks of Gretta, as he sees her on the stairs, as "a symbol of something." By the end of the story one can almost say of what she is a symbol — though neither Gab-

15. Though no break is indicated here by Joyce, as one is indicated near the very end of the story — between the time Gabriel leaves Gretta to her grief and the time he sees that she is asleep, a time break.

riel not Joyce does, fortunately, say it. As Gretta comes down
the stairs, Gabriel sees "that there was colour on her cheeks and
that her eyes were shining. A sudden tide of joy went leaping out
of his heart." He associates her appearance with the "moments
of ecstasy" that have punctuated "the years of their dull existence together." But of course what has kindled her has nothing
to do with him. Instead, Bartell D'Arcy's song has reminded her
of Michael Furey. In the hotel room, Gabriel finally forces her
attention back to himself by way of his solicitude for her and by
telling her of the good deed he has done for Freddy Malins: a
form of courtship that he feels to be fully as demeaning as it is.
Nonetheless, in his "fever of rage and desire," he tries to construe as evidence of the complement to his own feelings her un-
promising "you are a very generous person, Gabriel."

In the process of discovering his mistake, Gabriel moves from
speaking in "a kinder note than he had intended" to a "dull
anger" in which "the dull fires of his lust . . . glow angrily in
his veins" to humiliation for a vulgar assumption[16] to a gentle
generosity once more — a generosity adequate perhaps to everyone but himself: "He had never felt like that himself towards
any woman but he knew that such a feeling must be love." But
Gabriel's acknowledgment is not just what the story acknowledges.

Gretta, in talking about Michael Furey — "I was great with
him at that time . . . I think he died for me" — achieves the
genuine, uniquely Irish simplicity that Joyce ascribed to Nora
Barnacle[17] and is relieved of any touch of being "country cute."
But the qualities that Gretta remembers of Michael Furey are
very much the qualities that Gabriel himself possesses and demonstrates: "he was very fond of me," she says of Michael Furey,
"and he was such a gentle boy." What distinguishes Gabriel's
love for Gretta from Michael Furey's seems chiefly to be that it
is more fully erotic love, and that he is dying for her by incre-
ments rather than all at once.

16. That Gretta had wished to go to Galway in order to see Michael
Furey once more.

17. For example in the previously quoted letter of 19 September 1904:
"your soul seems to me to be the most beautiful and simple soul in the
world." It is this quality incidentally, Joyce tells Nora, that makes his
love for her lose its violence.

Moreover, Michael Furey did not literally die for Gretta. He was, she says, already "in decline . . . or something like that. I never knew rightly." But it is his death that fixes her love: "O, the day I heard that," she says, "that he was dead!" His death seems also in some crucial way to have arrested the development of her capacity for love, for it is inescapably suggested that Gabriel's desire for Gretta has been thwarted more often than met.

In some curious and, for this collection of stories, significant way then, Gretta and Gabriel are not so utterly removed from the life possibilities — and in particular from the erotic possibilities — of the other Dubliners as might at first be supposed. And in this sense, possibility means limitation of possibility. Gabriel thinks the point very explicitly: "so she had had that romance in her life: a man had died for her sake . . . He [Gabriel] watched her while she slept as though he and she had never lived together as man and wife."

Death triumphs over life at the end of "The Dead," and thereby at the end of *Dubliners*. Gabriel can no longer understand or believe in "his riot of emotions of an hour before." But in effect he had known this doubt already, or he would likely not have thought of Gretta on the stairs as "a symbol of something":

He stood still in the gloom of the hall, trying to catch the air that the voice was singing and gazing up at his wife. There was grace and mystery in her attitude as if she were a symbol of something. He asked himself what is a woman standing on the stairs in the shadow, listening to distant music, a symbol of. If he were a painter he would paint her in that attitude. Her blue felt hat would show off the bronze of her hair against the darkness and the dark panels of her skirt would show off the light ones. *Distant Music* he would call the picture if he were a painter.

The snow that is falling at the end of the story is an obliterating snow; "falling . . . upon all the living and the dead," it tends to obliterate even that distinction.

The apparent complement to this concluding portion of "The Dead" is the concluding portion of *Ulysses,* in which another married couple for whom Joyce creates strategic connections with himself and Nora are also in bed, moving on the edges of sleep. The end of *Ulysses* is generally read as a resounding affirmation of life. Lionel Trilling finds that Joyce "consciously intended Molly's ultimate 'Yes' as a doctrinal statement, a judgment in life's favor made after all the adverse evidence was in." [18] I do not doubt the essential correctness of that view, and yet I find the affirmation seriously qualified nonetheless — qualified as Molly's authority for affirmation is qualified. For it is as necessary to see Molly's pathos as it is to see Bloom's (which is more immediately evident) and to understand that her soliloquy is, as often as anything else, an expression of unrealized aspiration. The end of "The Dead," too, may be seen as an affirmation by apprehending what had happened years back between Gretta and Michael Furey in the very same terms in which Gabriel apprehends it. But this would, I think, be a misreading of a story which, however much less harsh it may be than the other stories with which it appears, is nonetheless not utterly apart in its limited confidence in erotic fulfillment. Whatever capacity for passion is indicated by Gretta's grief, neither her dead lover nor her living husband has had much access to her passion. The conflict between high erotic aspiration and a low estimate of the possibility of erotic fulfillment is very near the dynamic center of Joyce's literary production. The conflict manifests itself formally in the erosive irony of *Dubliners* and *Portrait,* but equally formally and far more dramatically in the deployment of complementary characters in *Exiles* and *Ulysses.*

18. "James Joyce in His Letters," *Commentary* (February 1968), p. 53.

HELEN GARDNER

T. S. Eliot

It is perhaps too early for anyone to attempt an assessment
of the achievement of T. S. Eliot as poet, critic, and man of
letters. His correspondence has not been published; there seems
little prospect of an authoritative biography; and the discovery
of the supposedly lost manuscript of *The Waste Land,* the publication of extensive quotations from the drafts of the plays, and
the knowledge that comparable material exists for the study of
the growth of *Four Quartets*[1] make this an unpropitious moment
for the discussion of Eliot as an artist. We need time to come
to terms with this new image of a fluent writer who pared down
his first drafts and learned what he had to say in process of saying it. If it is said that all this missing and new information is
strictly irrelevant to discussion of the value of Eliot's poetry and

All quotations from Eliot's verse are from *Collected Poems 1909–1962*
(New York, 1963), and are reprinted here by permission of Harcourt
Brace Jovanovich, Inc.

I have to thank the editor of the *New Statesman* for permission to
print in a revised and expanded form material that appeared in that journal on 28 November 1969.

1. At the invitation of Mrs. Eliot I am at present working on a book
on the composition of *Four Quartets.*

27

criticism, the pure critic, if such a creature can be said to exist, is uneasily aware that it is difficult at the moment to get Eliot in focus. He is suffering the fate that overtakes every famous writer on death: a reaction that has in it a good deal of malice, like the malice of schoolboys when the master has just left the room. What truth there is in the anti-Eliot movement will have to be digested in time. At the moment he is neither a living presence nor a historic figure. Yet, even if the time for a reassessment had come, I could not attempt it. His poetry is too much a part of my own experience, from the time when, as an undergraduate, I read *The Waste Land,* and knew "Prufrock" and the quatrain poems by heart, to the moment when, in the dreary spring of 1940, I read *East Coker* on its appearance in the *New English Weekly,* and realized that a poet I had rather written off in the political thirties was still the poet, above all others then writing, who could make me feel "Yes, this is where I am." A prime source of Eliot's power is that again and again he touches the raw nerve of experience, experience that is often painful and disturbing but which is transformed by his expression of it into something that can be contemplated and understood. His poetry is a poetry that "questions the distempered part" and in doing so resolves, or at least moves towards resolving, enigmas. For me it has worn well, and I think it always will.

It has to be conceded that Eliot's poetry appears to have little influence at present, and that his plays, far from having inaugurated a new era of poetic drama, have been made to appear old-fashioned by the arrival of the "new" drama of the fifties. Only the fragmentary *Sweeney Agonistes* seems "modern" today; it might, as has justly been said, have very well been called "Waiting for Pereira." [2] His critical revaluations have been revalued, many by himself, and the questions his criticism was most concerned with are not at the centre of critical concern today. One no longer expects to find critics taking one of Eliot's sentences or phrases as almost a sacred text to be expounded or glossed. The sociological writings on which he spent so much time and thought are largely ignored. Yet I cannot change my sights and

2. See William V. Spanos, " 'Wanna Go Home, Baby?' ": *Sweeney Agonistes* as Drama of the Absurd," *PMLA,* 85 (January 1970), 8–20.

try to look at Eliot from some supposed standpoint of the seventies. He remains the poet who made sense to me of my own experience of life and of the age I lived in. I do not mean by this that I accepted all his views, religious, political, or literary. I mean that, of all the poets writing in the period between the two wars, he most seriously and persistently took upon himself the burden of his time, and laboured to express his sense of it as exactly and truthfully as he could. He submitted himself to experience, including the experience of growing old, and attempted to discover in personal distress and world catastrophe a way of life. His career was a long quest of the mind and spirit to discover a pattern in living that would give unity and meaning to the flux of feelings, events, and experiences that make up the disorder of daily life. He did not rest content with the expression of personal distress or disgust, or with recording fleeting moments of delight, but attempted to discover the meaning of his experience, and in so doing discovered grounds for faith and hope. Where others took refuge in fables and myths, he went deeper and deeper into history.

In so doing he was extending to the art of living his convictions about the art of poetry. From the beginning Eliot realized that no poet starts from scratch. Whether he is aware of it or not, the material of his art — words and their meanings, rhythms of speech and those artificial arrangements of natural rhythms we call metres — and the techniques of his art are things he has not made but inherits; and what he in turn makes of them he does not make for himself alone or for his generation alone. Eliot saw very early as a poet what came to be the great theme of his later poetry: the involvement of past and future in the present. The famous essay on "Tradition and the Individual Talent" saw every true poet as altering the map of poetry, changing our view of what went before and creating conditions for what is to come after. In his later life and in his later poetry Eliot viewed the life of individual man and the life of mankind in the same way. Nobody can now miss in the early poetry the pressure of a distress that can only be called religious. There hangs over it an "overwhelming question" that Prufrock dare not even phrase as he thinks of

> Streets that follow like a tedious argument
> Of insidious intent
> To lead you to an overwhelming question . . .
> Oh, do not ask, "What is it?"
> Let us go and make our visit.

The Waste Land ends with longing for the rain to fall, with the invitation to "The awful daring of a moment's surrender," with the dream that the key that turned in the lock might turn again — that there might be a release from the prison of the self — with the memory of controlling a boat, and the hint that, in obedience to "controlling hands," the heart would respond as gaily as a boat. In the parodic wit of "The Hippopotamus," and the irony of "Mr. Eliot's Sunday Morning Service" — which plays as much over the priggish Mr. Eliot as over the polyphilo-progenitive "sutlers of the Lord" and their spotty young, whom he views with such distaste — religious satire springs from religious need. The poet who deliberately made himself a poet, by submission to the tradition of European poetry, submitted himself in the same way to the religious tradition of Europe. If there were any answer for him to the overwhelming question, it was to be looked for where others had found it through the centuries: the religious man must go to school to the saints as the poet must to the poets. As the poet learned his individual craft from the masters of the past, so the man found his individual way of life within the communion of the church of the country he had settled in, the Church of England. The poet accepted for transformation into his unique idiom the idiom of his own day, believing that the developments of a language in "vocabulary, in syntax, pronunciation and intonation — must be accepted by the poet and made the best of." [3] In the same way, he "made the best of" the church of his time and place. The leader of the modern movement, which was paradoxically an attempt to recover the values of the past in the present, did not change course when he accepted baptism and confirmation.

The rapidity with which Eliot established himself as leader of the modern movement is remarkable. It is possible that but for the outbreak of war, which caught him in Europe, he would

3. "The Music of Poetry," *On Poets and Poetry* (1957), 37.

have returned to Harvard in 1914, submitted his doctoral thesis on F. H. Bradley, and accepted the position waiting for him in the Harvard department of philosophy. Instead he went to Oxford, fell in love and married, and decided his vocation was poetry. In the following year he met Ezra Pound in London and showed him the poems he had written while at Harvard and in Paris. Pound, with that passion for good letters and that generosity that makes one forgive his follies and sins, recognized at once the brilliant originality of "Prufrock" and devoted his energies to the building of Eliot's reputation. *Prufrock and Other Observations,* a drab little volume of forty pages priced at one shilling, was published in June 1917. Five hundred copies were printed and the edition took four years to sell out. After a spell of schoolmastering, Eliot found employment at a bank and in his evenings lectured to adult education classes, while writing for Middleton Murry's *Athenaeum* the famous essays he collected in 1920 under the enigmatic title *The Sacred Wood.* It was a hard life, made harder by his wife's ill health and nervous instability. Two years later, in 1922, he became editor of a newly founded journal, the *Criterion,* whose first number contained *The Waste Land.*

With publication of *The Waste Land* Eliot became at once *the* modern poet, idolized by some, dismissed and derided by others; but recognized by admirers and detractors alike as having made a decisive break with the late Romantic tradition. His admirers saluted him as an innovator comparable to Dryden, who revolted against the decadent metaphysical tradition, and to Wordsworth, who broke with decadent neoclassicism; his detractors saw him as a pretentious seeker after novelty and a literary Bolshevik. From publication of *The Waste Land* Eliot dominated the literary scene in England and indeed, to some extent, in the world. He is one of the few English poets who have won a continental reputation in their lifetime. His companions are Byron and Oscar Wilde, who both had the advantage of scandal to help them. Eliot won his world reputation in spite of the handicap of his extreme respectability. He was not only respectable in old age, when he became a grand old man of letters. The author of *The Waste Land* was a bank clerk and looked like one, with his stiff white collar, bowler hat, well-rolled umbrella,

and exquisite formal manners. The idol of the avant-garde had
no touch of the Bohemian in his appearance; he left to Ezra
Pound such flourishes as a Texan sombrero and earrings. Although the poets of today do not acknowledge Eliot as their
master, and many of the younger critics are occupied in taking
him down several pegs, I do not believe that my generation was
wrong to see him as a master and think that even those who
repudiate his influence and dislike his poetry have inherited free-
doms that he won. I believe the literary historians of the future,
however they rank Eliot among the English poets, will have to
speak of the years between the two wars as "The Age of Eliot."

It was not only as a poet that he was at the centre. He followed up the essays in *The Sacred Wood* with a series of essays,
many originally written as full-page reviews and articles for the
Times Literary Supplement. In these he boldly redrew the map
of English literary history, exalting Donne and the metaphysicals, "dislodging" Milton from his pre-eminence, paying homage
to John Dryden, reviving the Jacobean dramatists, rejecting
Shelley as incomprehensible and Tennyson and Browning as
"ruminators." These essays were remarkable for other things
beside immensely influential revaluations, many of which Eliot,
to the dismay of some of his admirers and followers, subsequently "revalued." There was first their extraordinarily confident tone: a tone of authority. There was also the pertinacity
with which they assaulted certain fundamental critical problems
concerning the nature of poetry. They raise fundamental questions, questions that are not capable of receiving permanently
satisfying answers but which have to be asked again and again:
such questions as the nature of a poet's beliefs qua poet. Last,
and perhaps most striking, was the critic's marvelous gift for
quotation, the product of wide reading combined with a wonderfully sensitive ear.

Then again, as editor of the *Criterion* from 1922 to 1939,
Eliot carried on, or revived, the tradition of the Victorian man
of letters as critic of society. In the preface to the second edition
of *The Sacred Wood* in 1928 he said that, when he wrote the
essays he had collected in the first edition in 1920, he was concerned with the "integrity of poetry": that when we are considering poetry "we must consider it primarily as poetry and

not another thing" — but that now he had passed on to another problem, "the relation of poetry to the spiritual and social life of its time and other times." This is very apparent in the essays he wrote and the lectures he gave in the twenties: in the famous discussion of the "dissociation of sensibility" supposed to have taken place in the late seventeenth century, and in the discussion of Shakespeare and Dante in the lecture on "Shakespeare and the Stoicism of Seneca," where the poet is virtually reduced to a mere mouthpiece for the ideas of his age. The *Criterion,* from the beginning, aimed at being more than a literary magazine. It was a review in the old-fashioned sense, an organ of opinion; and Eliot's long editorials were more concerned with cultural and social than with purely literary issues. He was here the heir of Coleridge and Arnold as a critic of industrial democracy. His position has, I think, been misunderstood and the range of his thought undervalued. He has been unjustly accused of sympathy with fascism because of his sympathy with certain French thinkers, notably Maurras, whose ideas contributed to fascist ideology. It would be juster to say that he was troubled by the problems for which fascism provided a false solution. He was primarily concerned with the preservation of human values, intellectual, cultural, and spiritual, in a society in which the human scale was disappearing. As was natural in a poet who wrote with such power on the terrible loneliness of great cities, who had "watched the smoke that rises from the pipes / Of lonely men in shirt-sleeves, leaning out of windows," who saw the crowd of automatons flowing over London Bridge to work, "And each man fixed his eyes before his feet," who was haunted at the thought that "Weeping, weeping multitudes / Droop in a thousand A.B.C.'s" and noted the "strained time-ridden faces" in the London tube, he feared and dreaded the morbid growth of great urban conglomerations, or "conurbations" — places where no man knows his neighbour and local pride, patriotism, and affections can find no soil to grow in. In these vast ant-heaps, replacing towns and cities of men, what is the role of the intellectual or the artist? What place has an artist in an industrial society, organised to make money, or in a society organised to secure the material well-being of its members? The question became linked in Eliot's mind with the question of the role of a church in secular society. None of the problems, religious, cultural, social, educational, which Eliot discussed in his editorials, and in books such as *The Idea of a Christian Society,* has been solved; but he did not attempt to evade them by nostalgic longing for an earlier age, a rural or aristocratic society gone forever. He did not "ring the bell backward" or "follow an antique drum." His concern was deep and serious, and it was a concern with the fundamental problem of the quality of life. It flowed into his later poetry and is one of the strands in the web of *Four Quartets.*

Lastly, as the director of Faber and Faber for forty years, from 1925 to his death, Eliot exercised with great discrimination and generosity the role of patron to the next generation of poets. Many of them held religious and political views far from his own; but to them he was universally known as "Uncle Tom," and the rather cramped little office upstairs which he inhabited at Fabers was the mecca of young poets in the thirties. The care and pains he took in criticising poetry that was sent to him appear in the recently published letters to Keith Douglas,[4] a foretaste of what his published correspondence will show.

The first essay in *The Sacred Wood,* "The Perfect Critic," originally published in the *Athenaeum* in 1920, bore as a motto a text from Remy de Gourmont: "Eriger en lois ses impressions personelles, c'est le grand effort d'un homme s'il est sincère." It is an appropriate motto for Eliot's lifelong "wrestle with words and meanings" or, to use the words of Heraclitus which he set above *Burnt Norton,* his effort not to rest in a wisdom of his own but to arrive at the logos common to all. His work is dominated by the desire to achieve "sincerity" in de Gourmont's sense, or, in his own words, "a condition of complete simplicity." It may seem paradoxical to speak of sincerity in characterising the work of a poet so lacking in spontaneity, who has been dubbed the Invisible Poet, whose nickname was Possum, and who, as much when he was the idol of the avant-garde as when he was the distinguished elder statesman of the literary world, preserved so impeccably discreet a demeanour, displaying what I. A. Richards has described as a "formality, a precision, a con-

4. *Times Literary Supplement,* 2 July 1970.

cern for standards in dress and deportment, a kind of consciousness of conduct" which had about it "the ghostly flavour of irony
. . . as though he were preparing a parody." [5] It may seem even
stranger to speak of complete simplicity as the aim of a poet
whose notorious obscurity has given occupation to whole tribes
of scholiasts offering conflicting guidance on the identity of
Pipit,[6] the number of persons involved in the drama of "Sweeney
Among the Nightingales," the symbolism of the rose-garden, and
the allegorical significance of Mrs. Guzzard. But Eliot's personal
reserve, his "deliberate disguises," the fence he set about his
private life and most intimate feelings, were necessary defences
for a poet aiming at truth more profound than mere frankness
offers, to be won by the disciplining of the feelings and the submission of immediate impressions to other impressions to discover their meaning through experience and the power of memory. And the simplicity he aimed at was a simplicity "costing not
less than everything," to be arrived at by the absorption of disparate and conflicting experiences, not by a simplification.

This way of thinking about the meaning of words is something
that Eliot both as a poet and a critic forces on his readers. "Trying to learn to use words" was his own description of his occupation *entre deux guerres.* He taught a whole generation a new
awareness of language as the material of the poet's art and
trained his readers to read the poetry of the past with a new
alertness, diverting us from hasty and ill-considered raids on a
poet's "thought" or a poem's "meaning" to the gradual absorption of it by concentration on the language embodying it. Pound,
who divided the art of poetry into the use of words to evoke
visual phenomena, the use of words to register or suggest auditory phenomena, and "a play or dance among the concomitant
meanings, customs, usages and implied contexts of the words
themselves," thought that he exceeded Eliot in the second but
that Eliot surpassed him in the third. The huge bulk of Eliot
criticism and the concentration on the exegesis of his thought
and symbolism is in danger of depriving a new generation of

5. "On T. S. E.," *Sewanee Review,* January–March 1966, p. 26.
6. In a letter to me Eliot wrote that he thought the discussion in *Essays
in Criticism* on the identity of Pipit was "the nadir" in criticism of his
poetry.

readers of the profound poetic pleasure that Eliot's earlier poetry offered to my generation. We delighted in such witty dandyisms as "Reorganised upon the floor," and the contrast of a stale pietism with modish jargon in "Flesh and blood is weak and frail, / Susceptible to nervous shock;" we were moved by, and paused on, the unexpectedly cold word "cogitations" at the close of "La Figlia che Piange," were haunted by the "insidious intent" of the streets in "Prufrock" and the "handful" of dust in *The Waste Land*. Striking felicities are much rarer in the later poetry, though it can still astonish and arrest us on a word — the "*disconsolate* chimera," the "*oppression* of the *silent* fog," the "parched *eviscerate* soil," a word that came late in the writing — but Eliot came to feel that poetry demanded a more "severe keeping," aiming at the ideal he expressed in the final section of *Little Gidding*. He outgrew the virtuoso brilliance of his earlier poetry, where meaning concentrated itself in the image and developed, beyond symbolist theory, a style that was not afraid of statement. But the later poetry, though it develops from the earlier, is not either an improvement on it or a falling-off. The earlier has its own perfection. Today we need to read it for its own sake and less with Eliot's later poetry in mind, to pay more attention to its surface and less to fishing in its depths.

It is a poetry of the twenties, and many of its allusions, once commonplaces, now need elucidation. I found recently that it was necessary to explain to the young in the sixties what a "cooking egg" is. But I cannot believe that they will be helped to read the poem with this title by the suggestion that the name "Pipit" may carry a "learned and obscure 'egg' joke." "Pipi," one is informed in a recent *Student's Guide,* "is the Greek misrendering of the Hebrew *Yahweh,* regarded by the occultists as a word of power: written on a shelled hard-boiled egg, it is said to open the heart to wisdom."

Such a note seems unlikely to open anybody's heart or mind to whatever wisdom is contained in this poem, and likely to militate against response to the wit and the sadness and the humanity of a poem which, trivial though it may seem, and even flippant, revolves around a permanently recurring mood of distress: "Is this really all that being 'grown-up' has to offer?" Having myself contributed to the mountains of commentary heaped on Eliot's poetry, I am not in a position to cast stones; and Eliot himself set us all a bad example, as he later ruefully owned, when at his New York publisher's request he eked out the scanty number of pages of *The Waste Land* by the addition of some unhelpful and perfunctory notes and "sent inquirers off on a wild-goose chase after Tarot cards and the Holy Grail." But at the moment we need less explication of the earlier poetry and to recover appreciation of its highly original, indeed unique, combination of a melancholy, even a depressing, subject matter with intellectual high spirits. Its true seriousness is destroyed by too solemn an approach. Its author, writing in 1928, defined poetry as "a superior amusement," adding that this was not a true definition, but that "if you call it anything else you are likely to call it something still more false." [7]

What persisted in Eliot was his devotion to his vocation as a poet, which appears as a ceaseless process of experiment, a kind of sacred discontent with what had been achieved. He wrestled all his life with the material of his art, words and meanings, attempting to be as truthful as he could. It is a long way from "Portrait of a Lady," his first fully achieved poem, to *Little Gidding,* his last. Both are in their way masterpieces of art, absolutely assured, with no uncertainty or weakness in diction or style. They are fully realised as poems. The attitudes are very different, in the one youthful and dandified, in the other mature; the first is semidramatic, the second is meditative, philosophic, and didactic. The technique in both is fully adequate to the author's purpose; the diction has the same blend of an apparent naturalness and ease with fastidious exactness. In each poem Eliot seems to have said exactly what he had to say at the time and no more. Each respects its own limits.

Unlike many poets, Eliot did not repeat his successes. He is the opposite of a writer who, after a period of experiment, finds his style and then goes on turning out competent repeats. The two early Jamesian monologues would, one feels, with any other writer have been only the first of a long series. He turned from them to the evocative "Preludes" and "Rhapsody on a Windy Night," and then from fluid free verse to the diamond-hard qua-

7. Preface to the second edition of *The Sacred Wood.*

train poems. The mythical monologue "Gerontion" in Jacobean blank verse led to the inspired ventriloquism of *The Waste Land,* with its dramatic "many voices." From this he moved to the opposite extreme of "The Hollow Men," a ghostly poem, stripped down to images without connexion, in lines that extend themselves into silences. From the inarticulacy of "The Hollow Men" he moved to the intensely personal, loose, relaxed, meditative style of *Ash Wednesday.* None of these provided a style to rest in, or a formula for a poem. One might say that for longer poems the five-part structure of *The Waste Land,* with its lyric fourth section, achieved by Pound's ruthless surgery, provided a model for *Four Quartets*; but the verse and method of the later poems are so different that it seems mere pedantry to point out that their ground plan is the plan of *The Waste Land.*

Each new poem or group of poems was "a wholly new start," or "a fresh beginning," a "raid on the inarticulate" from a different point of attack and employing new tactics. From "The Hollow Men" onwards each new venture was greeted with dismay by many of the most fervent admirers of the poem it succeeded. (One sometimes wonders how Eliot had the heart to go on in face of the groans of disappointment at his failure to continue doing the same thing.) Having written a poem, he seems to have felt that he had done with it, made it as good as he could, got it out of his system. He notoriously refused to discuss or comment on his poetry, and though he showed much more willingness to discuss his plays it was mainly their technical aspect he commented on. He declared more than once that a poem meant what the reader made of it. This was not affectation, but the way in which a humble and modest man confessed his belief in poetic inspiration. He neither suppressed nor rewrote his earlier poetry. Other poets in this century, notably Yeats and Auden, revised their early work, Yeats from dissatisfaction with his earlier style, Auden for more complicated reasons; and each new edition of Graves's *Collected Poems,* while it adds new poems, omits old. One poem that Eliot sent to press he withdrew at the proof stage, economically using some lines from it in *The Waste Land.* One published poem he did not reprint: "Ode" in the 1920 volume. Apart from this, each new volume of poems prints the earlier volumes with only minor revisions of style and corrections of misprints and punctuation. Eliot seems to have felt no urge to go back on what he had written.

Now that the early notebook and the original drafts of *The Waste Land* have turned up and large portions of the drafts of the plays are available, the notion of Eliot as a costive writer painfully squeezing out a few lines of verse is shown to be false. He wrote fluently; but he published little. He wove whole yards of cloth; out of it he cut and made up his poem. Having done so he took a remarkably objective view of it, concentrating on the "making," willingly entertaining criticism and suggestions. He thought of poetry as an art and not as a means of self-expression, and of the poet as a "maker" of a poem, not the giver of a personal testimony beyond criticism. It has long been known that Pound radically criticised *The Waste Land,* advising extensive cutting but strongly urging that the beautiful lyric on Phlebas the Phoenician, which Eliot wanted to drop, be kept. Much detailed criticism of phrases and words in *The Dry Salvages* and *Little Gidding* came from John Hayward, who was proud of having supplied the phrase "the laceration of laughter," with its echo of Swift's epitaph. Arnold Bennett was asked to help an inexperienced dramatist to write the play of which we have only the two fragments in *Sweeney Agonistes,* and Martin Browne has told how pliable Eliot was as a dramatist, and how willing to accept suggestions and criticism from his producer and from the actors in his plays.

At times, of course, he dug in his heels. He refused to cut on Pound's advice the "No, I am not Prince Hamlet" passage in "Prufrock," saying it was essential — as indeed it is, for the heroism of Hamlet in daring to formulate the "overwhelming question" contrasts his indecision with Prufrock's, who is no hero. The fact that he neither revised nor suppressed his early poems suggests that however much he had changed he respected their integrity as poems. There had been a time for them; it was now time for another way of writing. Change and continuity is the theme of his last great poem on Time the preserver and Time the destroyer. In discussing Eliot one has to stress both.

This devotion to his vocation as a poet, to poetry as an art to be learned from the study and assimilation of the work of its great practitioners, made Eliot, as Robert Lowell has recently declared, the hero of many in the next generation of poets. Others, and they were by no means only Philistines, were unattracted by a poetry so much the product of will and conscious choice and intellectual decisions. To them the poetry of Eliot seemed to display a factitious originality, to be a pseudoscholarly excogitation of a highly selective version of the European tradition, containing good lines and good passages but lacking in creative energy and imaginative sympathy, overcerebral and overliterary: a patchwork poetry made up of scraps pieced together and eked out by parody. The debate continues, and I suspect that it always will. For Eliot is a poet of a particular kind, a kind that divides opinion, rousing a strong response in some who treasure his poetry for its deliberation and as strong a distaste in others who, while owning his skill and his seriousness, feel his poetry to be fatally narrow in range and lacking in the "roll, the rise, the carol, the creation." They also, and this applies to many who admire aspects of his work, find antipathetic that strongly Puritan strain in his personality as man and poet which links him so oddly with Milton, whom he attacked, and Wordsworth, whom he virtually ignored. Like them he is a poet of "the egotistical sublime," with a powerful poetic personality, the opposite of Keats's poet, who has, as poet, "no Identity."

   Eliot, by deliberate and conscious choice and effort of will, first made and then remade himself as a poet. Starting from the late Romantic tradition in England and America, he broke from it radically and made himself a European poet by a bold assimilation of very varied styles. Only one poet remained as an influence with him throughout his life: Dante, whom he read first at Harvard. In his middle life he remade himself, as a man and a poet, with great courage, discipline, and pain. He did so by going back to his original foundations — to his childhood and youth — and attempted in his last great poem to include and bring into a pattern all his experience as child, young man, American, and European, refusing nothing that had happened to him as man and artist. He brought back into his poetry what he had earlier repudiated, his nineteenth-century heritage, and developed a new style all his own, expressive in its variety and remarkable for its accent of personal truth. This new style could accommodate the brilliant images, and the haunting phrases — for Eliot is one of the great masters of the unforgettable poetic phrase — that marked his poetry from the beginning; but it also allowed him to modulate from personal reflection to philosophic exploration of ideas and meanings, and to include in his poetry general statements.

This new style first appeared in *Ash Wednesday,* where the poet drops his mask, forgets his cherished doctrine of impersonality and speaks to us candidly as "I":

> Because I do not hope to turn again
> Because I do not hope
> Because I do not hope to turn
> Desiring this man's gift and that man's scope
> I no longer strive to strive towards such things

Its appearance coincides with the final breakdown of his tragic first marriage and with his baptism and confirmation. These two experiences, the long-drawn-out agony of his first marriage and his acceptance of the discipline of religious commitment, are the twin subject of his later poetry and plays. They are concerned with the attempt to find "somewhere on the other side of despair" that which "forever renews the earth," with the leap in the dark, the venture of faith, the deliberate choice of hope against despair, the decision to rejoice, "having to construct something / Upon which to rejoice," or, to use his own image from *Marina,* with the struggle to "build a boat."

> Bowsprit cracked with ice and paint cracked with heat.
> I made this, I have forgotten
> And remember.
> The rigging weak and the canvas rotten
> Between one June and another September.
> Made this unknowing, half conscious, unknown, my own.
> The garboard strake leaks, the seams need caulking.

They are concerned also with the effort to learn how to love; with the effort of the will and the conscience to practise what ways of love are possible when loving has brought pain and agony and the sense of failure and guilt; and with learning how to live with the burdens on one's conscience.

All Eliot's poetry from "Portrait of a Lady," his first master-piece, is concerned with deeply troubling, and also with precious but rare, experiences. For all the range of his observation, its width and shrewdness, the breadth of his intellectual interests and culture, the depth and variety of his friendships — he was a conspicuously loyal friend — his subject matter is confined. He recurs again and again to the same situations, situations that involve some kind of moral distress, as he does to the same images. I am not referring simply to his fondness for certain symbols that are obviously symbols — lilacs, hyacinths, the rose-garden, yew trees, the desert — but his obsessive interest in times and seasons, times of day, the quality of months, the process of the year from spring to winter, and also what Leonard Unger has recently pointed out: his recurrent use of images of stairs and doors, stairs one ascends or descends or stands on, stairs on which one hesitates or stumbles, doors to be opened or looked through: "I mount the stairs and turn the handle of the door / And feel as if I had mounted on my hands and knees."

He began as a poet of observation, attempting to escape from the personal and confessional, concentrating on the evocation of a scene or a mood, eschewing all reflection in the attempt to catch the moment as it was. He avoided the expression of general ideas, and found for himself deliberate disguises, adopting various quasi-dramatic roles: Prufrock, Gerontion, the little old man, or Tiresias, the blind bisexual consciousness behind *The Waste Land*. He ended as a great poet of memory and desire and aspiration, who had learned to speak with his own voice. I find the voice of the later Eliot very moving in prose as well as poetry. The remarkable note of authority in the early critical essays corresponds to the brilliant surface of the earlier poetry. The later criticism is tentative and relaxed, the voice of a man who is ready to confess that he has changed his mind. Its gentle-ness and dry self-deprecating humour have been attacked as timidity, and its qualifications mocked at. I find it refreshing to listen to a critic not so much in love with himself as to be unable to do anything but repeat the insights of his youth. "Gentleness and justice, these are the marks of his later criticism," wrote

I. A. Richards, adding: "The only writer he is rough with in these later pages is himself . . . I doubt if another critic can be found so ready to amend what he had come to consider his former aberrations. There was more to this, I think, than just getting tired of long-occupied positions. These reversals and recantations strike me as springing from an ever deepening scepticism, a questioning of the very roots of critical pretensions." [8] The same scepticism, integrated into faith,[9] gives its peculiar quality of unauthoritative authority to the later verse.

Eliot was endowed with brilliant intellectual gifts, the power to work hard and develop them, and an acute sensibility. He responded deeply to certain rare and fleeting moments. He also recoiled from ugliness, shabbiness, ignobility, and vulgarity, recoiling with a violence that revealed a fascination. "You attach yourself to loathing as others do to loving," Agatha says to Harry in *The Family Reunion,* in what is surely a piece of profound self-criticism. He was also gifted with gaiety, charm, wit, and humour. But it was not for nothing he came of Puritan New England stock. He was from the beginning a poet of the conscience. He was capable of great moral suffering and developed the moral strength and the integrity of purpose to live with pain and explore its roots without self-pity or indulgence in self-disgust. He entered very deeply into the still unresolved crisis of this century, a crisis of unbelief, failure of purpose, loss of hope, in which "the best lack all conviction." His earlier poetry, under its dazzling wit, conveys a sense of desolate meaninglessness, of pointless, purposeless activities, social and cultural, lives "measured out with coffee spoons" in rooms where women "come and go" indulging in cultured conversation, overlaying the basic realities of human existence, "birth, copulation, and death." His Waste Land is a land of sterile desires and panic fears and futile illusions and dreams of happiness, set in a present context of the loneliness of great cities and of the breaking of nations, the collapse of civilisations into anarchy. Through entry into himself to find the sources of his own pain, and his own sense of loss and despair, through exploration of his own past, and through sub-

8. *Ibid.,* p. 28.
9. See the essay on "The *Pensées* of Pascal," *Essays Ancient and Modern* (1936), 150–151.

mission to the religious tradition of Europe, as he had earlier as
a poet submitted himself to its poetic tradition, he came to a
sense of meaning in personal experience and in human history. I
cannot believe that future ages — if mankind has a future on this
planet, and those who accused Eliot of too gloomy a view of
human history now look rather foolish — will not respect in
Eliot's poetry the voice of the conscience of civilised man speaking out of an age of anxiety and despair, and that even those who
reject the formulations of his faith will not respond to the accent
of faith, and honour him as a man and a poet who chose not to
despair.

FRANK KERMODE

The English Novel, circa 1907

Around 1907 great changes, we may confidently announce, were either occurring or pending, both in English society and in the English novel. Joyce and Lawrence were already at work; so was Gertrude Stein. James was publishing his Prefaces, and Ford, who had worked with Conrad, was excogitating a new theory of the novel. Arnold Bennett was writing *The Old Wives' Tale* on what seemed to him sound French principles. 1907 wasn't a bad year for novels, for it saw the publication of both *The Secret Agent* and *The Longest Journey*. Who would read them? Three years earlier a public had been found for both *Nostromo* and *The Golden Bowl*; the next year they would accept, though at first without enthusiasm, Bennett's novel, as well as *The Man Who Was Thursday, The War in the Air,* and *A Room with a View*. There were Wagnerites and Ibsenites in the audience: William Archer's translations started to appear in 1907 and so, as I've suggested, did the New York edition of James. Many people had read some Flaubert and Tolstoy, Nietzsche and Whitman; a few had encountered *The Interpretation of Dreams*. Husserl was little known, but Russell was famous. The climate, at first glance, seems one in which there

might have been an audience for fictions aspiring to art and
seriousness.

Of the society more generally, it is necessary to say only that
there were signs of a more critical attitude to the past, a developing habit of national self-examination. The fragility of the Empire had become more evident after the Boer War. The educated
conscience had discovered the poor, whose plight, like that of
women, troubled the liberal mind as much as the low standard
of national health disturbed those whose property might, before
long, be dependent on the country's ability to find fit men for
the army. There was a powerful sense of transition, accompanied as always by mixed reactions to all the new evidence of
decadence or of renovation, according to how one interpreted
such signs of relaxation as the criticism of capitalism, conventional sexual morality, and the treatment in literature of previously forbidden subjects. The early years of Edward's reign
showed a real loss of nerve, which was in some measure recovered before its end. There was some feeling of crisis, that there
was no telling how things might go; and this is caught in James's
tragic retrospect at the outbreak of war in 1914: "the plunge
of civilisation into this abyss of blood and darkness . . . is a
thing that so gives away the whole long age in which we have
supposed the world to be, with whatever abatement, gradually
bettering, that to have to take it all now for what the treacherous
years were all the while really making for and *meaning* is too
tragic for any words." [1]

How do such concerns affect the works of the time? There
ought to be a relation between the Condition of England and the
condition of the English novel. Such a relation would be not
merely a matter of what novelists say about the state of the nation, and specific aspects of it — but how they go about doing
so. Is there, so to say, a period lexicon? If so it should be easier
to describe than a period syntax. Successful novels normally use
language understood by many people. Let us glance first at a

---

1. *Letters of Henry James,* ed. Percy Lubbock (1920), ii, 384; quoted
by Samuel Hynes, *The Edwardian Turn of Mind* (Princeton, N.J.: Princeton University Press, 1969), p. 358. Hynes's book not only characterises
the general mood of the period but provides much helpful detail on the
whole "Condition of England."

little group of novels that did well with the readers of 1907. In one way or another they might tell us something about the lexicon, and the grammar, of mid-Edwardian fiction. Of course we should remember that many of these readers were not fully extended by the works here discussed, since they could also read *The Secret Agent,* a work — to continue the figure — that made much severer linguistic demands.

Elinor Glyn's *Three Weeks* is, if not read, remembered still as a sexual fantasy, and in a way this is just; though the American preface defends the book against the charge that it is merely "a sensual record of passion," and so, in its fashion, it is. The lovers are a young Englishman of great beauty and stupidity and the Imperatorskoye, a royal adventuress whose sensuality, at once mystical and practical, uplifts and exalts the young man, so that after the three weeks he spends with her — ending at the full of the moon — he finds himself transformed into a man of intellect and embarks on a career of distinguished public service. The Imperatorskoye separates love from all else, including domestic convenience and learning and art and "feverish cravings for the impossible new," blaming such mixtures for the "ceaseless unrest" now generally felt. (" 'Yes,' said Paul, and thought of his mother.") The consequence of all this is that the Empress bears Paul a son, but is murdered by her husband. He in turn falls to the hand of an avenging Kalmuck loyal to the Empress, and the child becomes, apparently, Czar or Czarevitch. Paul is able to attend his fifth birthday celebrations in the cathedral of the capital and sees his son, "a fair, rosy-cheeked, golden-haired English child, future ruler by right."

This curious and successful dream appealed to an increasingly felt need to abandon not only official morality but also cultural isolation. English virtue could reasonably be exchanged for alien virtuosity. The bedroom scenes, like the foreignness of the lady's manners, catch the exotic in an unserious way, or anyway in dreamlike fashion. The lady is "beyond the ordinary laws of morality," and the novel offers the satisfaction of a solution in which this Nietzschean wickedness is paid for by death, yet contributes to the advancement of the real, that is the British, Empire. Paul is saved from his hearty English fiancée but nevertheless produces an heir, and a pure English heir for an empire previously the domain of foreigners; while he, purged by an admittedly unrepeatable sexual experience, returns to the true imperial centre, London. He is able to give it the benefit of all the knowledge and experience it had lost sight of during its protracted estrangement from Europe, for this is what he had acquired during his three weeks in an exotic but undeniably imperial bed.

Miss Glyn's rejection of middle-class English women may be seen as a measure of the urge her female contemporaries may have been feeling to liberate themselves from the old roles, much as her rejection of the provincialism of the British Empire reflects a growing mood of the time. But she does not consider the possibility of asking the very considerable audience which was somehow ready for this kind of thing to abandon social and national assumptions inconsistent with the changes currently proposed. Her new man is a boring Englishman transformed and liberated by coming into the knowledge, conveniently subsumed under sexuality, which his own society denied him. He remains an upper-middle-class Englishman whose powers had been concealed, not destroyed, by the barrenness of his life, and he continues to behave in conformity with class conventions. The new Emperor is wholly English, apparently without genetic inheritance or early training from his foreign mother, who simply educated the husband, produced the son, and died. Thus the growing uneasiness lest imperialisms clash, a new awareness that British arrangements would have to be changed, defended, and perhaps even suffer overthrow, that stupidities of education and rank urgently required correction, and that sexual repression might be dangerous, are eased and calmed in a dream, in a bestseller. Taking it seriously is likely to seem odd or offensive because the text is not of a kind that advertises its connexions with reality. They exist, perhaps inevitably; only sometimes the discrepancies are so huge as to conceal them.

The sense that one was entering a new age, in which some transformation of the British might be necessary if they were to maintain their hitherto effortless supremacy, inspired a whole range of invasion novels; and as the period wore on the outcome of these novels tended to change, first from easy victory to hard struggle, then to disaster. Erskine Childers, in the best of them, still showed some confidence in British racial superiority;[2] Wells, in a book serialised in 1907,[3] showed the coming world conflict through the eyes of an undereducated English mechanic, but transferred the capital of the world to New York. But conscious enquiry into contemporary problems — as in Wells, or in *Major Barbara* (1905), or even in Galsworthy — isn't perhaps as good a guide to the capacities and needs of the audience as fiction which has no such explicit purpose. Florence Barclay's *The Rosary,* of 1908, will serve as an example of such fiction. This extraordinarily bad book was still being reprinted in my youth, and I read it somewhere around 1933 in a cheap edition; apparently it went on satisfying a public, albeit an unsophisticated one, for a quarter of a century.

The American publishers claimed that it was a modern book; ("modern" was already a hard-sell word); it is in fact a dream of the new woman, in this case represented as having been a nurse in the Boer War, a golfer, and very strong and healthy. She gives up an affair with an exquisite painter because she is too old and plain for him. The setting is a ducal home, and the upper-class dialogue works because the author has learned how to do it from, among others, Oscar Wilde. The poor are represented by a railway porter who when heavily tipped by the heroine imagines her an angel sent from heaven to provide delicacies for his sick wife. This fantasy about the poor is contemporary, it should be remembered, with the conscience-stricken sociological enquiries into their lot that were well under way with Fabianism and with the fear of rioting mentioned by Shaw in *Major Barbara.* Galsworthy surrounded his rich with a frieze of poor in attitudes of misery and sickness. Chesterton professed to regard them as the champions of a gay Christendom. Conrad knew they were exactly what the police existed to control. But Miss Barclay's new woman still treats them as beneficiaries of upper-class generosity, and this social imperceptiveness fairly represents the general level of her imagination.

Her artist goes blind and, incognito, she nurses him, pulls him through his worst time, and not only marries him but assists his completely effortless translation from painter into composer.

2. *The Riddle of the Sands,* 1903.
3. *The War in the Air,* 1908.

Problems of art become, in this imaginative light, as simple as those of poverty. The impassioned dénouement, incidentally, is visible a mile off, and is an emblem of the easy gratifications expected of popular fiction.

Yet the success of the book transcended that of the ordinary cheap romance; it was taken more seriously. What is of some interest is the coexistence of decent, even accomplished, upper-class dialogue and an immense vulgarity of imagination and technique. It was possible to learn to do certain things, which probably sounded quite modern, without the slightest notion that there was a crisis in the relations between fiction and society which had already elicited much more radical modernisation. And to have them taken seriously; one American reviewer, gratefully quoted by the publisher, called *The Rosary* a book that "strengthens faith in the outcome of the great experiment of putting humanity on earth" and held that it was one of those unusual stories that appealed to "all classes of readers of fiction." This credits it with powers which were at the time much sought after, for example by Conrad. There existed a real desire to maintain the popularity of fiction while modernising it.

But the urgency of technical innovation as a means to modern truth is felt by novelists rather than their readers. In general people probably wanted then, as in a measure they still do, old techniques applied to genial, or anyway familiar, materials. 1907 produced one novel worth examining in this light, William de Morgan's *Alice-for-Short*. De Morgan had been an associate of Morris in the pottery business and was himself a distinguished artist; only when at sixty-five he lost his studio did he turn to writing long novels, the first and most successful being *Joseph Vance* (1906).

De Morgan's manner was deliberately archaic. In a message to his readers at the end of *It Can Never Happen Again* (1909) he says, excusing himself for a particularly cosy, omniscient chat: "I know that gossiping with one's readers is a disreputably Early Victorian practice, and far from Modern, which everything ought to be . . . " In *Alice-for-Short* he does much the same thing: "We are dwelling (to your disgust, we doubt not) on these points because we really want to take you into our confidence about Charles and Alice, and what they thought and felt.

Never you mind how we come to know these things! We answer for their accuracy. Be content with that!" (p. 464). The jocose unease of these interpolations suggests that the Modern was a trouble to de Morgan, and its presence in his thoughts produces some odd twists in his novels. *Alice* is about a waif brought up as an adopted daughter by a good family; eventually, despite their long adherence to the notion that their feelings are purely fraternal, she and the son of the house marry. The facetious chapter heads and the waggishly archaic tone don't quite gloss over the fact that much of the story is about death, broken marriage, drink, and slums, "the great hells of civilisation," the stunted, abandoned children of the very poor. The time of the action is the early Victorian period, and there are obvious sources in Dickens; but to anybody who is interested, de Morgan is talking about Edwardian slums — his date and his tone exempt whoever does not want them from disagreeably topical reactions.

That he was conscious of doing more than producing a pastiche is indicated by the subtitle of his book, "a dichronism." Not content with a complicated Victorian plot, he makes unusual play with a character called Mrs. Verrinder, whose basic narrative function is to bring the lovers together. But Mrs. Verrinder is also the agent of further festoons of plotting. Having been knocked on the head at the age of twenty, sixty years before, she has only now come to; there is a good scene when she first sees herself in a looking glass, but the interest really lies in her being a sort of human time machine. Also we are told of her views on the art of fiction. She is surprised to learn that the poet Scott has turned to novel writing and, since the lovers cannot persuade her of the merits of Dickens and Thackeray, she reverts, in her search for entertainment, to *The Vicar of Wakefield*.

Since de Morgan was a man of intellect and imagination, this novel poses some odd questions. Nowhere else, so far as I know, can one point to narratives that please by a deliberate thematic and technical archaism, yet at the same time carry within them an awareness of technical change and the complex action of time on the authenticity of narrative. De Morgan doesn't of course propose these as the main interests of his book; but his object is to give to readers who feel about the Victorian novel what Mrs. Verrinder felt about *The Vicar of Wakefield* more of what they wanted, with as little change as time and conscience permitted. *Alice-for-Short* is therefore an example of a number of complex relationships — of changes in the life of forms in art, changes in the relations of writer to reader — all of which, given practised intelligence and practised conscience, continue to occur even in situations where they are for other reasons not wanted. A book caught like this, reluctantly but consciously, in an inevitable change of *discours,* may well be something of a monster, and probably a short-lived one; but it has its interest.

The three books I've mentioned so far all illustrate, in different ways, the pressure of the times — of the Condition of England — on popular fiction. None of them was written on the assumption that serious changes in technique might be required to accommodate the dimly perceived new shape of the world; de Morgan's awareness that this might be so was deliberately dulled by his archaism. Yet this was also a time in which the technique of fiction was a matter of intense concern, not only because men wanted, as artists, to refine the instruments they had inherited, but because they felt with much urgency that the condition of the world required kinds of understanding which could not be provided otherwise than by technical innovation. There was even a characteristically patriotic motive, since it was not thought right to allow the English novel to remain technically inferior to the foreign. This was the age of the dreadnought; one needed to overgo Flaubert and Maupassant as one needed to keep ahead of the German navy.

There are, I think, discriminations to be made. The whole history of the novel in the present century is dominated by the notion that technical changes of a radical kind are necessary to preserve a living relation between the book and the world. Yet the effect then was to turn the attention of serious practitioners to the nature of the instrument itself; the novel grew very introspective about its own technology and has subsequently been quite capable of inventions that one might find it hard to account for in terms of that relation.

At present I refrain from looking too far ahead, and limit myself to the earlier stages of this technical research. Serious writers lived with the knowledge not only of the problems of naturalism but also of James. The marvelous Prefaces were appearing. James had failed to interest a large popular audience, but had written, and commented upon, novels of great importance to technicians, who certainly did not believe that their interest was limited to the area of professional know-how. *What Maisie Knew* was especially venerated and not only for its "technique." It was a model of how technique is necessary to imaginative apprehension of the times. And James's audience was not confined to practitioners; he could not, in the early years of the century, have repeated his complaint of 1884 that "the 'serious' idea of the novel appeals apparently to no one." In 1897 the *Academy* reviewer greeted *Maisie* with "amazement and delight." In the opinion of the *Edinburgh Review,* James so far succeeded in his determination to achieve "an immense correspondence with life" as to have "added a new conception of reality to the art of fiction." The *Saturday Review* said that this novel was "very easily followed"; and many echoed the views of Oliver Elton in his fine essay of 1903 associating James with a specifically *modern* beauty and significance; Elton was a professor of English, and we would not ordinarily associate him with desperately adventurous opinions.[4]

These and similar observations imply a newly developed interest, confined no doubt to a smallish circle of readers, in the technical and theoretical aspects of fiction. Brownell, in a remarkable long essay published in the *Atlantic Monthly* in 1905, observed acutely that "the present time may fairly be called the reign of theory in fiction . . . and Mr. James's art is in nothing more modern than in being theoretic." Admittedly he goes on to complain that James is obsessed with theory to a damaging degree, "palpably withholding from us the expected, the needful exposition and explanation." [5] But this is the normal reaction against technical developments which proceed from an understanding that the routine product often has features which, on rigorous inspection, turn out to be archaic, redundant, and falsifying. Those features served no purpose relevant to the nature of the novel as it was coming to be understood, but they did give

4. These quotations are all from Roger Gard, *Henry James: The Critical Heritage* (London: Routledge & Kegan Paul, 1968), pp. 149, 269, 347, 382, 349ff.
5. Gard, *Henry James,* pp. 401–407.

assurances to the normally inactive reader that whatever was going on matched his own comfortable and quite arbitrary expectations, so that he, unlike the new novelist, mistook them for the main business of the art. In short, the more reflexive, the more technique- and theory-obsessed the fiction, the more it asked its readers to give up and the more it asked them to supply;[6] so the "new" novel demanded a large increase in that art of collaboration which was of course always needed but by convention mitigated and understated. Hence the assertion that the reader of *What Maisie Knew* or *The Golden Bowl* was called on to develop a sharper and more subtle feeling for *relevance*. This was identified as modern and attributed to a modern increase of "general consciousness." The point was taken, even by opponents of James — by Wells, for example. So the new techniques were firmly associated with the new changed times; both were giving up some certainties, looking into attitudes and devices that had come to seem false, and facing a new situation in which more things had to be thought about and in different contexts of relevance.

And here we have to consider Conrad, who was responsible for much of this radical enquiry. By 1907 he had abandoned hope of popular success, supposing that the public was incapable of the sacrifices he required, for example, in the matter of endings — a most important matter, for the "full close," the "nail hit on the head," was among the most falsifying of the time-honoured conventions, as well as the one that seemed especially dear to ordinary readers "in their inconceivable stupidity." [7] By a freak which astonished and possibly annoyed Henry James, but which is of a kind we have later grown more familiar with, Conrad did in 1913 slip into the best-seller list with *Chance,* a book obsessed with method, theory, technique to the point where even hardened Conradians begin to protest. This is testimony either to a rather rapid evolution of public taste or to the truth of Conrad's own view that the public will swallow anything,

6. With the consequence, as Brownell hinted, that the reader gave up James instead: "I know of nothing that attests so plainly the preponderance of virtuosity in Mr. James's art as the indisposition of his readers to re-read his books" (Gard, *Henry James,* p. 404).

7. Quoted in John D. Gordan, *Joseph Conrad: The Making of a Novelist* (New York: Russell & Russell, 1940), pp. 306–308.

even occasionally and fortuitously something that is properly "done." Earlier, Conrad shared the view of his collaborator Ford that there was a genuine though obscure relation between techniques and the times, the condition of fiction and the Condition of England. Ford regarded James not only as a great technician but also as a great historian of the culture. He may already have been contemplating *The Good Soldier,* which is not only a profoundly researched novel as to its techniques but precisely intended as a history of the culture. Ford's friend Masterman, as Wiley reminds us, had written in his book *The Condition of England* of the need to diagnose "the hidden life of England" and suggested that fiction might be the instrument employed.[8] The development of that instrument, Ford was sure, would require study of alien examples rather than of the indigenous novel — a cosmopolitanism acquired for reasons of national health and security in a manner analogous, though remotely, to that dreamed of by Elinor Glyn.

Techniques developed in order to study so great a subject without looseness and bagginess are likely to be of the sort that can propose without explicitness the symptomatic quality of a fictive event. The circumscribed "affair" used by Ford in *The Good Soldier,* and so much admired by him in *What Maisie Knew,* should reverberate within the chambers of the reader's attention in such a way as to induce him to select, from an indeterminate range of possible inferences, those that have significance. Their number is not to be limited by the conventional coding of the old novel, by, for example, the formal close or by steadiness of tone, or by what James called Bennett's "hugging the shore of the real" or by the vouched-for authenticity of narrator, because these are no longer relevant except insofar as the disappointment of illegitimate expectations on the part of the reader may be a legitimately suggestive device.

It is easy enough to see why other writers who were capable of understanding the new thing — Bennett and Wells, for example — nevertheless rejected it. Finally the difference of opinion comes down to incompatible estimates of the rights and duties of the reading public, and to the question of whether the

8. Paul L. Wiley, *Novelist of Three Worlds: Ford Madox Ford* (Syracuse: Syracuse University Press, 1962), p. 40.

dismantling of all expectation-satisfying devices isn't in the last analysis the dismantling of the novel. The true heirs of Conrad are the modern French, with their demand for full collaboration from the reader in an act — all *lexis,* no *logos* — that can scarcely any longer be called fiction, so that the *roman* slips undifferentiated into *écriture.* But that was a long way off, and both Ford and Conrad cherished some hope of winning the attention of *la cour et la ville,* of a general reading public that might be induced to collaborate in the techniques required by the times. To some extent it was so induced. The outcry over the ending of *Jude* was evidence, as Alan Friedman says,[9] of the fact that tampering with the closed ending was tampering with public morality. But in the years that followed there was a change, and the famous hung ending of *Women in Love* seems not in itself to have upset people. There was a change, a recognition that totality, solidity, *rondure* may falsify the truth, especially when not achieved with the laborious sophistication displayed in *Nostromo* and *The Good Soldier.* Bennett, though perhaps he had more natural endowment than Ford or Conrad, was wrong about what was needed. Whether one thinks of the changes wrought in fiction by the pressure of the need generated by the times in terms of technology or in terms of grammar, they did make possible a modern and in some sense a more truthful fiction.

As an instance of how a writer, one who may be said to be of serious intent but of less natural ability than Bennett and less intelligence than Conrad or Ford, can fail significantly at such a moment, consider Galsworthy's novel *The Country House.* It appeared in 1907, a year after *The Man of Property,* which is rightly, for all its faults, the more celebrated. The easiest way to say what's wrong with *The Country House* is to declare, perhaps unreasonably, that it ought to be a Fordian novel. It is about a single "affair" — the prevention of a divorce suit — but is much concerned with the Condition of England. Galsworthy is writing about an upper-class family and the troubles that come upon it when the son and heir gets involved with a New Woman whose husband threatens to cite him in divorce proceedings. The author knew the divorce law from per-

---

9. Alan Friedman, *The Turn of the Novel* (Oxford: Oxford University Press, 1966), p. 74.

sonal experience and was writing at a moment when campaigns to change it had made it a prominent issue in the understanding of the new England.[10] But Galsworthy's hero escapes all the humiliation and obloquy, and does so by a quite deplorable bit of novelism.

His affair is conducted in a London which certainly contains poor people — they stand outside his club in Piccadilly; sick and weary, they wait on him in the discreet restaurant where he takes his wicked lady; at Newmarket they are jockeys in the pay of unscrupulous masters. But the affair of the book is essentially an affair of the rich, for since divorce was for the rich alone it could hurt only them. They are never focused in relation to the sufferers who crowd around; that there is no sorrow like that of the rich is written into the book's texture. This inability to focus may have disturbed the tenderhearted author — and it certainly makes a hash of his story, which, though rumpled and torn by ineffective ironies, arrives at a conclusion in which almost everything of interest in it is ignored or betrayed. What is certainly true is that there is a relation between the social falsity of the book as a whole and the failure of tone in the text, which proclaims its own inconsistencies throughout.

The boy's father, Mr. Pendyce, is a collector.

His collection of rare, almost extinct birds' eggs was one of the finest in the "three kingdoms." One egg especially he would point to with pride as the last obtainable of that particular breed. "This was procured," he would say, "by my dear old gillie Angus out of the bird's very nest. There was just the single egg. The species," he added, tenderly handling the delicate porcelain-like oval in his brown hand covered with very fine blackish hairs, "is now extinct." He was, in fact, a true bird-lover, condemning cockneys, or rough, ignorant persons who, with no collections of their own, wantonly destroyed kingfishers or other scarce birds of any sort, out of pure stupidity. "I would have them flogged," he would say . . . Whenever a rare, winged stranger appeared on his own estate, it was talked of as an event, and preserved alive with the very greatest care, in the hope that it might breed and be handed down with the property; but if it were personally known to belong to Mr Fuller or Lord Quarryman, whose estates abutted on Worsted Skeynes, and there was

10. See Hynes, *The Edwardian Turn of Mind*, pp. 185ff.

grave and imminent danger of its going back, it was promptly shot
and stuffed, that it might not be lost to posterity.
(All quotations from *The Country House* are from the 1907 edition.)

This is firm enough, a little too sarcastic perhaps, but well
made, down to the "very fine blackish hairs." There is no posterity save one's own; if Pendyce cannot possess the egg or the bird
the species may die. The delicacy with which his animal hand
touches the egg, his privileged knowledge of it, do not in the end
distinguish his barbarity from that of the vandals. In itself it is
not inconsistent with a desire to flog such people. This, though
not subtle, is clear and sharp enough. Later we see him as a
Justice of the Peace:

There were occasions . . . when they brought him tramps to deal
with, to whom his one remark would be: "Hold out your hands, my
man," which, being found unwarped by honest toil, were promptly
sent to gaol. When found so warped, Mr Pendyce was at a loss, and
would walk up and down, earnestly trying to discover what his duty
was to them. There were days too . . . when many classes of of-
fender came before him, to whom he meted justice according to the
heinousness of the offence, from poaching at the top down to wife-
beating at the bottom; for though a humane man, tradition did not
suffer him to look on this form of sport as really criminal — at any
rate not in the country.
    It was true that all these matters could have been settled in a
fraction of the time by a young and trained intelligence, but this
would have wronged tradition, disturbed the Squire's settled conviction that he was doing his duty, and given cause for slanderous
tongues to hint at idleness. And though, further, it was true that
all this daily labour was devoted directly or indirectly to interests
of his own, what was that but doing his duty to the country and as-
serting the prerogative of every Englishman at all costs to be pro-
vincial?

Here again the sarcasm produces tired locutions, even very
clumsy sentences; but the focus is again sharp enough, both as
to the way the poor are judged and as to the assumption that the
preservation of his own property is the sole important task the
world sets a man. And the only reason for our hearing so much
about the Squire is that his son's behaviour is a threat to his in-

terests and pleasures, but also to the perpetuation of his property; so there is some expectation that this heavy "placing" of him will tell when the plot begins to question him. There are matters within his upper-class competence, as when, with the Parson, he charges like an officer at the head of his troops to put out a fire in a tenant's barn. But the New Amoral Woman and Divorce should confront him with more difficult problems. Galsworthy, however, has a novelist's trick to play. Mrs. Pendyce is a dull lady and no New Woman, but she is as highly bred as her husband; and by acting with ladylike decision she settles everything satisfactorily. She leaves her husband, thereby shaking momentarily his notions of property and propriety, goes to London, interviews her son and his mistress (who has by this time given the boy up), and then visits the lady's husband, who is still threatening proceedings. He is persuaded to drop them on the sole ground that Mrs. Pendyce *is* a lady. So she sorts out the entire imbroglio at no cost save the speaking of a few sentences she would rather not have uttered.

When this has been done we hear no more of the poor or of bullied jockeys, for Mrs. Pendyce returns home, where all is restored to its prelapsarian calm. The cloud has lifted (even the actual weather is fine) and in the garden are the Squire and the Parson looking at a tree; "symbol of the subservient underworld — the spaniel John was seated on his tail, and he, too, was looking at the tree." She notices weeds, but a word to the gardener will put that right. She picks one of her own white roses and kisses it. So the book ends. Later, no doubt, they will sit down to the modest seven-course dinner, served without champagne, which is all the family allows itself when alone.

This conclusion certainly proves that the rich can be lucky. Galsworthy wrote in a preface to *The Country House* that he had got the name of a revolutionary for speaking as he sometimes did about the upper classes, but argued that he was "the least political of men. The constant endeavour of his pen has been to show Society that it has had luck; and if those who have had luck behaved as if they knew it, the chances of revolution would sink to zero." Nothing else is done, and all the promises that something else will be done are frustrated, ignored. The ironies of the concluding tableau, insofar as they are effective at all, belong to a different book; it could have started from the same *données* and contained the passages on Mr. Pendyce's collecting, but its middle would have been less lucky. It may be worth adding that Galsworthy himself owned a spaniel called John and treated him as the lucky should treat the poor; for when his conscience prevented him any longer taking part in bloodsports, he sent John every summer to Scotland for the shooting, that his instincts should not go unsatisfied.[11]

It is curious that in the much more inclusive and more finely imagined *Man of Property* Galsworthy should have made Soames a "great novel reader"; this prompted him to write a somewhat satirical passage on the ways in which novels "coloured his [Soames's] view of life," giving him the false expectation that Irene would eventually come round to him again. Galsworthy, in *The Country House,* takes refuge in Soames's kind of expectation, having created expectations of another kind. His irony creates an amusing problem for interpreters, for its undoubted existence in some places creates a presumption that it may be found in others, whether he wanted it or not; as when Mrs. Pendyce, seeking knowledge of her son, writes a solicitous letter ostensibly concerning the misfortunes of a poor girl in whom she is interested. We hear no more about the girl, whether she got into the home or not, any more than we hear of the worn-out waiters who so adored the adulterous rich young couple. She uses this pitiful case as a cover for the really serious business of her letter, and this is clear to her correspondent. Our hearing no more of the girl is part of the way things are, the way the lucky behave. What we hear about is how upper-class virtues saved the heir of a great estate from the consequences of his own conduct; and we hear it in no such way as to persuade us that the serving poor, the underworld, are still there in the text. The spaniel John does pastoral duty for them.

One sees in Galsworthy how it may be possible for a writer to command to admiration some traditional technical devices without knowing that the sort of honest dealing with the world he wanted to achieve might require him to control much more machinery, some of it very new. It was nine years later that Ford

11. Dudley Barker, *The Man of Principle: A Biography of John Galsworthy* (New York: Stein & Day, 1969), pp. 22–23.

showed the way in another story of adultery; his narration hardly glances at the poor at all — only describing, as he says, the death of a mouse by cancer, but in such a way as to make it imply the sack of Rome.

Most would agree that the best novel of 1907 was *The Secret Agent,* a story with an enormous hole in the plot; so this particular kind of invitation to exceptionally strenuous hermeneutic activity on the part of the reader must be attributed to Conrad and not to Alain Robbe-Grillet, who has an admittedly more difficult hole in *Le Voyeur.* This is not the place to compare these holes, nor to expatiate on *The Secret Agent.* Conrad in his subtitle called it "a simple tale," but its simplicity is precisely of the kind that makes for interpretative difficulty, like the notion of angels as simple in substance. I shall say something instead of a book published in the following year: Chesterton's *The Man Who Was Thursday,* which may have been a response to Conrad's novel and surely, it must be said, a weak one. It is another tale of "those old fears," of anarchist plots and terrorism. In *The Napoleon of Notting Hill* Chesterton set his action in a London of the future identical with that of the present, a protest against social change which would presumably extend to those technical changes advocated by writers of less conservative and optimistic outlook. Chesterton would dislike "cold mechanic happenings" as much in fiction as in life. "The old trade of story-telling is a much older thing than the modern art of fiction," he believed.[12] He did, however, call *Thursday* a "nightmare" — that is his subtitle, and it may be a comment on Conrad's — and thought it worth reminding people of this fact many years later. He was trying, he said, "to describe the world of wild doubt and despair which the pessimists were generally describing at that date." [13] Most of their fears are dissolved in the dream. Saffron (Bedford) Park was the centre for aesthetes of the Godwin kind, but also housed the anarchist Stepniak, who was killed there on a railway line;[14] Chesterton makes it a sort of Cockaigne where the an-

12. Reported in Anonymous [Cecil Chesterton], *G. K. Chesterton: A Criticism* (1909), p. 202.
13. From a late article reprinted in the Penguin edition.
14. Ian Fletcher, "Bedford Park: Aesthete's Asylum?" in Fletcher, ed., *Romantic Mythologies* (London: Routledge & Kegan Paul, 1967).

archist Gregory and the policeman Syme, disguised as a poet,
can meet. A believer in order, poetry, and life, Syme ousts Gregory and gets himself elected to the Central Anarchist Council,
having first explained — it is Conrad's point but differently put
— the similarities between anarchists and policemen, which
make the war between them a holy one. Chesterton gets some
strikingly stagy effects: the seven top anarchists meet on the
glassed-in balcony of a Leicester Square restaurant and observe
on the street below them not only a policeman, "pillar of common sense and order," but also the poor, entertained by a barrel organ and full of the vivacity, vulgarity, and irrational valour
of those "who in all those unclean streets were . . . clinging to
the decencies and charities of Christendom." The sight fills Syme
with "supernatural valour." Compare the extraordinary moment in *The Secret Agent* when the *agent provocateur* Verloc
calls the policeman in the park; it is like the difference between
fancy and imagination, but it is also a way of expressing a contrast between the modes of paradox and poetry. And it helps to
distinguish the kind of inventiveness proper to this new form
from the kind of fantasy permitted in the old.

Conrad's London is the raw, dark, dirty middle of the world,
where there is no structure in space or in time that enables men
to know one another, or even to familiarise themselves with in-
animate objects. In a Soho cafe his policeman knows nobody and
nothing; human contact is arbitrary and fugitive. But Chesterton
finds order and charity in the dirty city and uses a Soho cafe to
bless its alien inhabitants. Conrad's anarchistic aristocrats are
sleazy politicans, Chesterton's are heroes. He is answering Conrad with counterassertions that are belied even by his own text
with its fake ending; and his truth is of nightmare, which the
paradoxes whitewash. Thus in Chesterton it is a joke that anarchists and policemen turn out to be "just the Syme." And the
primary process of his book *is* nightmare. We remember not
what the comically educated policeman says on the Embank-
ment, but the essentially horrible pursuit of Syme through London by an immobile but nightmarishly speedy ancient in a snow-
storm, or the duel with the bloodless Marquis.

The difference between *The Secret Agent* and *The Man Who
Was Thursday* is instructive in the context of the present discus-

sion. Chesterton was convinced of the existence of evil as a permanent feature of life; it was a sort of world-conspiracy represented by Jewish adventurers who, as he believed, began the Boer War "and set two simpler and braver peoples to kill each other for their profit." But the answers were old and paradoxical, unlike those of the "pack of dirty modern thinkers" he declared incompatible with "the mass of ordinary men." [15] Conrad's novel contains specimens of the dirty modern thinker, but he handles them so originally, with such disregard for the mass of ordinary men, that he is in his way a dirty modern thinker himself. Chesterton takes Conrad's mixture of anarchist and policeman, rich and poor coexisting uneasily at the heart of the world; but Chesterton wants it to be ultimately a benign mixture and a good place, and in the pageant with which he ends, time itself takes on a ritual character as the seven policemen anarchists become days of the week and a mimesis of a good and ordered creation. For Conrad the attempt on the Observatory where time and space are zero and the imperial city is the devourer of the world's light is all the more nihilistic in that it is carried out by an idiot at the instigation of an informer whose master is a corrupt and foolish politician. The frescoes in the pub, the journey of the decrepit cab horse, are nightmares that no paradox will tame; the term "mystery" in this novel belongs in the newspapers that further soil the filthy streets and corrupt the mind, not to a traditional theodicy. Empire, the English poor, the impact on Englishness of alien and often horrible thoughts are as much Conrad's concern as Chesterton's, but his way of seeing them belongs to another world.

Thus it was the alien who saw that the Condition of England was but a shadow of a deeper condition, which could only be diagnosed with transformed instruments. So radical is the change that in order to understand it we should have to look back at least to Nietzsche to discover how a text might have to stand in a new relation to reality to be truthful; and forward, half a century or more, to see more fully its technical implications for fiction. All we can say on this evidence is that it is one thing to know about or sense the issues — in a way, Elinor Glyn did that for those who shared her language and her expectations — and another to

15. Cecil Chesterton, *G. K. Chesterton*, p. 142.

research the means by which a text might be caused to illuminate them. The need was felt by de Morgan, but the new novel was still a little too hard for Englishmen of 1907; it was for them too modern a way of rephrasing a proposition they might, at heart, accept: that the critical condition of England was the critical condition of life, if one had the means to know it.

LOUIS L. MARTZ

Iris Murdoch: The London Novels

London in the summer of 1970 is filled with the presence of Charles Dickens. His benevolent, bearded countenance glides by on the Underground escalators; he is advertising his superb Centennial Exhibition (at the Victoria and Albert), which includes everything from his cuff-links to the manuscript of *Bleak House*. Meanwhile, London Transport is advertising its excellent paperback: *The London of Charles Dickens*, an index of one hundred sixty pages describing virtually all the London sites and streets mentioned in Dickens' writings, with nostalgic, evocative quotations and careful accounts of the action that occurred in each place. Thus under "Foster Lane" there is first a quotation from *Martin Chuzzlewit*: "A dim, dirty, smoky, tumble-down, rotten old house it was as anybody would desire to see." And then follows the explanation: "No. 5 Foster Lane (Priest's Court) is pointed out as very likely premises for the Chuzzlewits, father and son, having a side entrance which was found so useful by Jonas when planning the alibi for his murder of Montague Tigg." Under "St. Magnus's Church" we read: "On the night that Nancy had a secret meeting with Rose Maylie and Mr. Brownlow on London Bridge steps, Dickens describes the murky night while the girl, and the sinister figure following her, were still. 'The tower of old Saint Saviour's Church, and the spire of Saint Magnus, so long the giant-warders of the ancient bridge, were visible in the gloom; but the forest of shipping below bridge, and the thickly scattered spires of churches above, were nearly all hidden from sight.' *Oliver Twist* Ch. XLVI." Under "Grosvenor Square" there is a startling contrast with the present-day scene: "Mr. Tite Barnacle resided here at No. 24, Mews Street, Grosvenor Square, 'a hideous little street of dead walls, stables, and dunghills, with lofts over coach-houses inhabited by coachmen's families, who had a passion for drying clothes, and decorating their window-sills with miniature turnpike-gates . . .' *Little Dorrit* Book i, Ch. X." To choose just one more example, under "Bryanston Square" we find simply this long quotation from *Dombey and Son*:

Mr. Dombey's house was a large one, on the shady side of a tall, dark, dreadfully genteel street in the region between Portland Place and Bryanston Square. It was a corner house, with great wide areas containing cellars frowned upon by barred windows, and leered at by crooked-eyed doors leading to dustbins. It was a house of dismal state, with a circular back to it, containing a whole suite of drawing-rooms looking upon a gravelled yard, where two gaunt trees, with blackened trunks and branches rattled rather than rustled, their leaves were so smoke dried.

In this atmosphere of the Centennial Year, it seems appropriate to celebrate also the achievement of the living writer who is, in her London novels, the most important heir to the Dickens tradition. One would not have said this two or three years ago because the Dickensian use of London scenes that marked Iris Murdoch's first novel, *Under the Net* (1954), was not a dominant characteristic in any of the nine novels that so quickly followed; it is only in her last three, and especially the last two, *Bruno's Dream* (1969) and *A Fairly Honourable Defeat* (1970), that the Dickensian vein in her use of London scenes has strongly re-emerged. If Miss Murdoch continues to write in this vein (as I hope she will) it may not be pure fantasy to imagine an exhibition or an index containing entries such as these:

Boltons, The. S.W. 10. An elegant oval, well shrubbed, with Saint Mary The Boltons in the center, which stands as a green and white oasis in the region between the Old Brompton Road and the Fulham Road. In *A Fairly Honourable Defeat* (Ch. VIII), Morgan frantically pursues Julius along "the left hand curve" of the oval toward the Brompton Road, while Julius, invisible to her, is walking along the right hand curve. They meet at the north end, to Julius' irritation.

Brompton Cemetery. S.W. 10. Located between the Old Brompton Road and the Fulham Road. "Big houselike tombs, the dwellings of the dead, lined the wide central walk which showed in a cold sunny glimpse the curve of distant pillars. In quieter side avenues humbler graves were straggled about with grass, with here and there a cleared place, a chained space, a clipped mound, a body's length of granite chips, a few recent flowers wilting beside a name. Above the line of mist-green budding lime trees there rose far off the three black towers of Lots Road power station" *Bruno's Dream* (Ch. XVI). Danby waits feverishly behind the iron fence at the Brompton Road end for Lisa to walk by on her way home to Miles's house in Kempsford Gardens (see below).

Hammersmith Mall. W. 6. Accurately described in *Under the Net* (Ch. III): "a labyrinth of waterworks and laundries with pubs and Georgian houses in between, which sometimes face the river and sometimes back it." Jake, searching for Anna, goes to a certain address here "on that part of the Mall that lies between the Doves and the Black Lion." These two pubs mark the eastern and the western extremities of Upper Mall. "The number to which I had been directed turned out to be a house standing a little by itself, with its back to the river and its front on a quiet piece of street, and an opening beside it where some steps led down to the water . . . It was a brooding self-absorbed sort of house, fronted by a small ragged garden and a wall shoulder high. The house was square, with rows of tall windows, and had preserved a remnant of elegance." At the east end of that part of Upper Mall accessible to motor cars, the house numbered 21 (next to the Doves) answers this description quite well except for the squareness and the tall windows; these details seem to be adapted from William Morris' Kelmscott House,

which faces the river a few yards away. The stairs down to the river
are in front of Kelmscott House.

Holborn Viaduct. E.C. 1. The bridge over Farringdon Street from
which Jake and his companions start their pub tour in search of
Hugo: "We stood beside the iron lions on the Viaduct. The intense
light of evening fell upon the spires and towers of St. Bride to the
south, St. James to the north, St. Andrew to the west, and St. Sepulchre, and St. Leonard Foster and St. Mary-le-Bow to the east. The
evening light quieted the houses and the abandoned white spires.
Farringdon Street was still wide and empty," *Under the Net* (Ch.
VII). The view is now (1971) eclipsed by new construction. From
beside the lions at the four corners of the Viaduct one can see at
most only two towers, Bow Church and Christ Church (which the
novel calls St. Leonard Foster — a church destroyed in the Great
Fire and never rebuilt).

Lots Road. S.W. 10. In *Bruno's Dream* the site of the power station
whose chimneys loom (protectively or menacingly?) over Danby's
house on Stadium Street. There are only two chimneys; the novel's
"trinity of towers" (Ch. IV) is perhaps a symbolic touch.

And so on, page after page. The kinship with Dickens is, I
hope, evident from all the above citations; but more important
than any particular scene is the underlying kinship in basic function. Both Dickens and Miss Murdoch need this particularity of
detail because they present so many of these London characters
as inseparable from the London setting. Houses, streets, and
squares become part of the personalities living in each particular location. "Like all true Earls Courters, Ducane despised
Chelsea. The bounder [Biranne] would live in a place like this,
he said to himself, as he turned into Smith Street and began to
pass along the line of smartly painted hall doors." [1] Thus in
Dickens Mrs. Todgers is inseparable from her boarding house

1. *The Nice and the Good,* opening of chap. xxiv.
Miss Murdoch's novels are published in New York by The Viking
Press and in England by Chatto and Windus. Quotations from *Bruno's
Dream* (copyright © 1969 by Iris Murdoch; all rights reserved) are re-
printed here by permission of The Viking Press, Inc., as are quotations
from *Under the Net* (copyright 1954 by Iris Murdoch) and *A Fairly
Honourable Defeat* (copyright © 1970 by Irene Alice Murdoch; all rights
reserved).

under the shadow of the Monument; in Murdoch, Bruno and his beloved spiders are inseparable from the damp, decrepit room in which he is breathing so tenaciously his last days.

The London novels of Iris Murdoch have their Dickensian quality of detail because they grow from a deep, instinctive affection for the London setting, whether sordid, shabby, or genteel. And that affection for the outward traces of man's habitation derives from the theme of love that constitutes the redemptive element in the novels of both writers. Danby loves that shabby house in its decaying place:

He loved the little yard outside his window, below ground level, always dark and covered in slippery green moss. It was always called "the yard," never "the garden" although it had a yellow privet bush and a laurel bush and a rose that had reverted to briar. The soil was black and no grass would grow on it, only a few dandelions and weedy marigolds which struggled up each year through the damp crust of the moss. The chimneys of Lots Road power station towered above, suitable extensions of that murky infertile earth (chap. ii).

Somehow Danby's love is inseparable from this earthy atmosphere. Likewise, Danby loves his job at the printing plant: "He loved the works, the clattering noise, the papery dust, the tribal independence of the printers, he loved the basic stuff of the trade, the clean-cut virginal paper, the virile elemental lead." And we learn that "he was fond of the machines, especially the older simpler ones"; he collects with love old printing presses (chap. ii). He loves women too, a good many of them, in various ways; but best of all is his great love for his dead wife, Bruno's "intense and high and spiritual" daughter — who herself died of love in a way, for she jumped off Battersea Bridge and drowned in an effort to save a child who had fallen in the river. This quality of deep, spontaneous affection in Danby accounts for the way in which he proves attractive to the most unlikely women.

Miles, Bruno's son, despises Danby and cannot understand why his own sister (and later the similar character Lisa) could possibly have fallen in love with so ordinary, unintellectual a person. But Miles is severely limited in the range of his own affections. He is so obsessively attached to the memory of his dead

Indian bride, Parvati, that he really cannot apprehend any other
human being. Even his second wife Diana seems neglected and
has to seek an outlet for her affections in the furnishings of the
small house in Kempsford Gardens.

Bruno, above all, is limited in love. He failed his wife first
through infidelity and then he failed her at her death, forty years
before the novel opens; he ignored her death-bed cries, fearing
that she would damn him if he answered. And Bruno failed his
son by not attempting to understand the marriage with Parvati;
he has been utterly cut off from Miles for many years. And yet,
enclosed now in this one moldly room in his last long illness,
Bruno is not wholly cut off from affection. He loves spiders; he
speaks their names as if they were human; to him they are beings
worthy of love. His unwritten books on spiders are his "Books
of Particulars," akin to the "Notebook of Particulars" by which
Miles strives to keep his affections alive while he waits for the
Muse to come. And at the very end of *Bruno's Dream* we note,
by Diana's new grasp of particulars, the signs that she is rescued
from her barren existence by her affectionate care for Bruno:

As she sat day after day holding Bruno's gaunt blotched hand in
her own she puzzled over the pain and what it was and where it
was, whether in her or in Bruno. And she saw the ivy leaves and
the puckered door knob, and the tear in the pocket of Bruno's old
dressing gown with a clarity and a closeness which she had never
experienced before. The familiar roads between Kempsford Gardens
and Stadium Street seemed like those of an unknown city, so many
were the new things which she now began to notice in them: potted
plants in windows, irregular stains upon walls, moist green moss
between paving stones. Even little piles of dust and screwed up paper drifted into corners seemed to claim and deserve her attention.
And the faces of passersby glowed with uncanny clarity, as if her
specious present had been lengthened out to allow of contemplation
within the space of a second. Diana wondered what it meant (chap.
xxxii).

What it means is that Diana has been redeemed through love,
in Danby's house, in Bruno's room, in Bruno's dream. This
scene is one that draws together the whole fine novel into an
effective unity. The streets, the characters, the particulars of

place and scene — all grow together, strands of the consciousness that extends from the dying mind of Bruno. All events of the novel have in one way or another been "caused by some emanation from that awful room in Stadium Street" (chap. xvii).

So, in her twelfth and best novel Miss Murdoch has returned, with greatly enriched powers, to the action of a central consciousness within a London setting and also to the basic, unobtrusive themes of her first novel, *Under the Net*. But one cannot, I think, find the essential relation between these two books by dealing with them as "philosophical novels" and by using, as is sometimes done, frequent references to Sartre, Kant, Simone Weil, Hegel, or Wittgenstein.[2] It is true that Miss Murdoch's first book was a monograph on Sartre (published in 1953, one year before *Under the Net*), and that it throws a great deal of light on her first novel. Moreover, she has given some validity to the relationship between this novel and the thought of Wittgenstein because she has herself said that the title refers to Wittgenstein's "net" of concepts and theories.[3] And it is true that Jake, the protagonist and narrator of *Under the Net,* thinks of himself as a sort of rootless, solipsistic character out of some modern French novel; but the reasons for this are not far to seek. On the opening page of the book Jake is returning from Paris with his suitcases "full of French books and very heavy"; he makes a little money by translating a current French novelist ("Breteuil"), but he is astonished and dismayed when he learns that this novelist has won the Prix Goncourt. The point, I think, is this: Jake has his head and his suitcases full of undigested modern thought, especially French existential thought, but he does not really grasp its meaning. His real self exists elsewhere,

2. Interpretations of this kind are valuable in illuminating some of the latent concepts within the novels, as can be seen from the helpful books by A. S. Byatt, *Degrees of Freedom: The Novels of Iris Murdoch* (London: Chatto and Windus, 1965), and Peter Wolfe, *The Disciplined Heart: Iris Murdoch and Her Novels* (Columbia: University of Missouri Press, 1966). But more needs to be done with the literary aspects of Miss Murdoch's work. For an excellent bibliography of the immense number of essays that have already been written on her novels, see the special issue of *Modern Fiction Studies*, vol. 15, no. 3 (Autumn 1969), devoted to Iris Murdoch.

3. See Byatt, *Degrees of Freedom*, p. 15.

and his problem is to find it. The clue to that essential self lies also on this novel's opening page, in his statement "until I have been able to bury my head so deep in dear London that I can forget that I have ever been away I am inconsolable." Jake's deep affection for and acute consciousness of particular places in the London scene serve ironically to show how securely rooted he really is in his "beloved city," of which he knows every detail from Cannon Street to the Goldhawk Road.

Since this is a novel told in the first person, the response to detail, the memory of places, forms an essential part of the character whose mind is here being created. Jake pursues a dream of love for Anna; he misunderstands *all* the human characters about him; but he is nevertheless rooted and he will be saved, because he is capable of perceiving at last the truth about himself. When at the end, in desperation, he decides to take a job as hospital orderly, he says he is amazed and impressed by the fact that he can do the job so well. But we the readers should not be surprised, for he has shown in all his responses to the London scene a firm grip on detail and a resourceful, unfailing ability to move from spot to spot in search of a goal. The comical pub tour in chapter vii is an indication of his basic grip on external things: "We strode past St. Sepulchre and straight into the Viaduct Tavern, which is a Meux's house . . . There was a sleek Charrington's house called the Magpie and Stump . . . The George is an agreeable Watney's house with peeling walls and an ancient counter with one of those cut-glass and mahogany superstructures." And so on from pub to pub, most of them still standing, though in greatly changed surroundings.

In the process of this tour Iris Murdoch creates the vision of a vanished scene. It is in fact almost as hard to trace this tour of "Iris Murdoch's London" as it is to trace Dickens' London, since the bombed-out City in which this tour occurs has now been so thoroughly rebuilt. That is why such a passage as this has about it the nostalgic quality so often found in Dickens' descriptions:

From the darkness and shade of St. Paul's Churchyard we came into Cheapside as into a bright arena, and saw framed in the gap of a ruin the pale neat rectangles of St. Nicholas Cole Abbey, standing alone away to the south of us on the other side of Cannon Street. In between the willow herb waved over what remained of streets. In this desolation the coloured shells of houses still raised up filled and blank squares of wall and window. The declining sun struck on glowing bricks and flashing tiles and warmed the stone of an occasional fallen pillar. As we passed St. Vedast the top of the sky was vibrating into a later blue, and turning into what used to be Freeman's Court we entered a Henekey's house (*Under the Net,* chap. vii).

Finally, as they make their way down toward a redeeming swim in the Thames, we have a scene that seems even closer to the quality of Dickens:

Across a moonswept open space we followed what used to be Fyefoot Lane, where many a melancholy notice board tells in the ruins of the City where churches and where public houses once stood. Beside the solitary tower of St Nicholas we passed into Upper Thames Street. There was no sound; not a bell, not a footstep. We trod softly. We turned out of the moonlight into a dark labyrinth of alleys and gutted warehouses where indistinguishable objects loomed in piles. Scraps of newspaper blotted the streets, immobilized in the motionless night. The rare street lamps revealed pitted brick walls and cast the shadow of an occasional cat. A street as deep and dark as a well ended at last in a stone breakwater, and on the other side, at the foot of a few steps, was the moon again, scattered in pieces upon the river. We climbed over on to the steps and stood in silence for a while with the water lapping our feet (chap. viii).

By comparison, after all these London details, Jake's subsequent trip to Paris turns out to be a journey into illusion. As he says: "Arriving in Paris always causes me pain, even when I have been away for only a short while. It is a city which I never fail to approach with expectation and leave with disappointment . . . Paris remains for me still an unresolved harmony. It is the only city which I can personify." Yes, he can personify Paris, make the city into a kind of remote goddess; but he cannot do this for London, which, as he says, "I know too well" (chap. xiv). And so the whole long account of Paris, in spite of its frequent detail, takes on the atmosphere of a dream or nightmare, an effect epitomized in the closing scene, where he

pursues what he thinks is the figure of Anna into the darkness
of the Tuileries Gardens. He "loses" her, but it seems likely
that she was never there, for the woman he finally calls to turns
out not to be Anna. This account of Paris is filled with sentimental, overwrought views: "If like myself you are a connoisseur of solitude, I recommend to you the experience of being
alone in Paris on the fourteenth of July. On that day the city
lets down its tumultuous hair, which the high summer anoints
with warmth and perfume. In Paris every man has his girl; but
on that day every man is a sultan. Then people flock together
and sweep chattering about the city like flights of brilliantly coloured birds" (chap. xv). One might add, "Unreal City."

How absurd it is for such a devoted pub crawler to dramatize
himself as "a connoisseur of solitude"! In fact, he hates solitude;
the novel consists of his continual search for companionship,
with Anna, with Hugo, with the dog Mars. And he greatly enjoys being with the nurses and patients at the hospital:

I would sit under one of the trees, while Mars bounded about close
by, giving his attention now to one tree and now to another, and the
young nurses of Corelli would come and gather round me like
nymphs and laugh at me and say that I looked like a wise man sitting cross-legged under my tree, and admire Mars and make much
of him, and defend me against Stitch, who would have liked to have
forbidden me to have Mars in the garden at all. I enjoyed these
lunch times.

It was in the afternoon that I managed at last to see something of
the patients. But this wasn't until the later afernoon. I looked forward to this all day. In my apprehension of it, the Hospital declined
through a scale of decreasing degrees of reality in proportion to the
distance away from the patients. They were the centre to which all
else was peripheral (chap. xvii).

And when he can think of no one else to seek out, he finds
solace in the enigmatic presence of the Soho shopkeeper Mrs.
Tinckham and her cats. Jake loves people, pets, and places: he
is as different from Camus's Stranger or Sartre's Roquentin as
it is possible for a man to be.

Return to London brings the hospital job, along with the
realization of the various truths about Hugo and Anna and Sadie

and Finn. The final taxi ride from Kensington to the Holborn Viaduct marks a return to the source, telling the tale of a man who has never quite been lost and whose individual will has been restored:

> I left the pub. I was somewhere in the Fulham Road. I waited quietly upon the kerb until I saw a taxi approaching. I hailed it. "Holborn Viaduct," I said to the driver. I lay back in the taxi; and as I did so I felt that this was the last action for a very long time that would seem to me to be inevitable. London sped past me, beloved city, almost invisible in its familiarity. South Kensington, Knightsbridge, Hyde Park Corner. This was the last act which would provoke no question and require no reason. After this would come the long agony of reflection. London passed before me like the life of a drowning man which they say flashes upon him all at once in the final moment. Piccadilly, Shaftesbury Avenue, New Oxford Street, High Holborn (chap. xix).

The "dark London boyhood" which Jake mentions early in the novel has become, like Dickens' own boyhood, the sign and the source of his renewal.

What happened in Miss Murdoch's next nine novels, gradually moving away from, weaving in and out of, and finally returning to London, is a story of intense experimentation with many different modes. After this beginning with Dickens-cum-Sartre, she seems to have been impelled toward an extended exploration of the many techniques available to the modern practitioner of fiction. It is a remarkable story, worth sketching briefly in order to show the varying roles that London has played in her career.

Miss Murdoch's second novel, *The Flight from the Enchanter* (1956), also occurs in London except for the fade-out in France and on the shores of Italy, where Rosa forsakes, through fear, the unhappy exile Mischa Fox, whom she might have saved from his empty pursuit of power and his hopeless effort to recover the memory of a lost European childhood. But the novel is only located, it is not really set, in London; the lack of detail is surprising in comparison with *Under the Net*: "Rosa ran down the road towards the factory. The big square building with its square windows grew larger and larger until it was looming over her. A tall chimney held a motionless trail of white smoke over three

streets and the width of the Thames" (chap. iv). "They walked
the length of two streets and then turned into a rather dark
mews, where it seemed to have been raining" (chap. xii). "Mischa had had the fantasy of buying four houses in Kensington, two
adjoining in one road, and two adjoining in the next road, and
standing back to back with the first two" (chap. xv). But what
roads, what streets? One would never ask the question in *Under
the Net* or *Bruno's Dream*.

Only the setting of Rainborough's house and garden is given
anything like the detail of these other novels, and for good reason. "His home was a safe stronghold; it had been the home of
his childhood, and it was full of myths and spirits from the past,
whose beneficent murmur could be heard as soon as he had
stilled his mind and put away the irritations of his day at the
office." As he stands in his garden he discovers his own Book
of Particulars:

Hyacinths, narcissi, primulas, and daffodils stood before him, rigid
with life and crested with stamens, tight in circles, or expanding into
stars. He looked down into their black and golden hearts; and as he
looked the flower-bed seemed to become very large and close and
detailed. He began to see the little hairs upon the stems of the
flowers and the yellow grains of pollen, and where a small snail, still
almost transparent with extreme youth, was slowly putting out its
horns upon a leaf. Near to his foot an army of ants had made a
two-way track across the path. He watched the ants. Each one
knows what it is doing, he thought. He looked at the snail. Can it
see me? he wondered. Then he felt, how little I know, and how little
it is possible to know; and with this thought he experienced a moment of joy (chap. x).

Here and only here Rainborough enjoys a clarification of vision.
He is rooted in this old home, but he is being uprooted, first by
the encroachment of the hospital extension and second by the
aggressions of the intrepid Miss Casement. Fleeing from her
clutches and her red MG, he is provided with a refuge in France
by the cosmopolitan Marcia.

Rosa, who might have saved some of these exiles, saves no
one, not even herself. Rosa represents the kind of welfare
worker whose only welfare lies in her own self-satisfaction. Hav-

ing "saved" the two Polish refugees, the beautiful Lusiewicz brothers, she becomes their willing victim in lust. And the brothers turn out to be vile: cruel to the world that has been cruel to them. Appropriately in this novel of rootless beings, the Dickensian details of a truly London setting do not emerge. The book could as well, or perhaps better, have been set in Los Angeles or Chicago. Yet even here one feels a few traces of Dickens — in the character of that splendid eccentric Mrs. Wingfield, ancient defender of women's rights. The account of her house and person, the scene of the meeting of the board of *Artemis* (ancient magazine of women's liberation) — these are skillful Dickensian touches. But the novel, for all its brilliance, is not as satisfying as *Under the Net*. It lacks the cohesion of a firm setting within a central consciousness and within this "beloved city."

Miss Murdoch's third novel, *The Sandcastle* (1957), has been called by someone a novel best read under the hairdryer. Exactly: it is quite deliberately, I think, designed in the popular mode of fiction for the woman's magazine. Here is the middle-aged couple stuck in their suburban house in Surrey, not a long run from Waterloo Station, with two growing children and a growing boredom in each other's presence. Then in comes a lovely young thing, in the person of a portrait-painter; soon the hero is reluctantly swept away by a strange passion, while Nan, the wife, has to fight for her marriage and wins by bold ingenious action. Trite? Of course, but what Miss Murdoch makes of these conventional materials is unusual, for the chief characters (and some of the minor figures, such as the stammering art teacher, Bledyard) develop into persons of depth and poignancy far beyond the range of the chosen literary model. It is as though the author, somewhat dismayed by the way in which the teeming characters of *Flight from the Enchanter* had refused to cohere, had decided to discipline her powers by working with a small cast within a strictly conventional plot.

The Bell (1958), Miss Murdoch's fourth novel, ranges out again into a large cast. The few London scenes offer a counterpoint to the main setting, an Anglican retreat next to a nunnery in Gloucestershire. This highly successful novel seems to derive from a blending of two models: George Eliot and D. H. Law-

rence, especially the latter. One feels the presence of Lawrence
in certain efforts at lyrical description of nature, but one feels it
more strongly in the two chief characters. Dora, fleeing from her
harsh, demanding, intellectual husband, manages to mature and
win freedom in this country scene. Her act of ringing the great
bell signals her liberation from the arid forces that would deny
her nature. Michael, struggling to subdue his homosexual tendency, reminds one a little of Lawrence's Gerald: an earnest, tormented, and ultimately lost man. This novel deals with a basic
Lawrencian theme: the anguish and death caused by failures "to
touch."

The three-year lapse before the appearance of Miss Murdoch's
fifth novel, *A Severed Head* (1961), perhaps represents a time
of severe reappraisal in her career. This is the period of her
Yale lectures, devoted to the theory of the novel and affirming
her loyalty to the nineteenth-century novel of character. It is all
the more surprising, then, that *A Severed Head* should bear so
little resemblance to the novelists praised in these lectures: Scott,
Jane Austen, George Eliot, Tolstoy. The peculiar mode of the
book emerges clearly from its dramatization by Miss Murdoch
and J. B. Priestley. The revolving stage, with its shifting of bed-
rooms, drawing-rooms, and partners, reveals the basic mode of
Restoration comedy, the comedy of manners — along with a
good many touches of Dickensian caricature. Though it is located for the most part in London, the only significant London
quality is the symbolic (Dickensian) fog representing the muddle in the mind of the narrator, Martin Lynch-Gibbon. The
characters are equally Philadelphian or Bostonian; and indeed,
the rootless psychiatrist, Palmer Anderson, is an American of
sorts, though we learn that his mother was Scottish, that he was
brought up in Europe, and that he has lived some years in Japan.
Out of the fog emerges (at Liverpool Station) the rugged,
earthy, rather ferocious figure of Honor Klein, whose role has
sometimes been found incongruous. But incongruity is her function. With her flashing samurai ritual, her incestuous relations
with her half-brother, and her tough, direct speech, she cuts out
cant, she shocks with truth, she reveals all and is ashamed of
nothing. No wonder the sophistications of this modern Restora-

tion comedy wither away under the onslaught of her formidable powers.

The sixth novel, *An Unofficial Rose* (1962), shifts its primary setting to a country house, with secondary scenes in a London flat. But London is not really a presence here. The real presence is Henry James: the style is in places deliberately Jamesian with, at times, something close to pointed parody. These touches are simply ways of signalling the mode, and we can and should go on to apprehend the brilliance of the way in which the author handles the delicate, slowly developing perceptions.

The Unicorn (1963) presents a violent contrast to the intricate nuances and slow discriminations of the Jamesian novel. Miss Murdoch here turns to create a Gothic novel based on the theme of the enchanted princess and set in a country that resembles parts of Ireland in its grim cliffs and deadly bogs. The first half of the book has all the fascination of a horrifying folktale, but once the scene and the characters have been set up the novel seems to have nowhere to go. The symbolism comes to seem obvious and even pretentious, as the latter half of the novel gradually collapses in a cloud of inanities.

Perhaps sensing a failure here, Miss Murdoch next attempted a shorter, less ambitious version of a Gothic tale. *The Italian Girl* (1964) represents a gothicized version of a D. H. Lawrence novelette, explicitly set in Lawrence country. "Our house . . . was a big ugly Victorian rectory, its red brick darkened by the sour wind that blew from the nearby collieries, whose slag heaps were invisible behind the trees." It is filled with the sort of mother-domination, sexual frustration, and conversations about sex that readers of Lawrence will recognize. The stage version by Miss Murdoch and James Saunders turned out well because the dialogue of the novel is good and can be freed, on the stage, from the awkward interposition of the first-person narrator, a Prufrockian character of very little interest.

The Red and the Green (1965) marks another violent shift, both in setting and in technique: here the author turns to the mode of the historical novel, basing her book upon the 1916 Easter uprising in Dublin. The novel has some brilliant scenes, but it is clogged with detail and tends to describe, rather than present, its action. The plot seems excessively intricate, the family relations are too complex to remember, the characterizations slide and blur, and the form of the book remains for me obscure.

At last, in *The Time of the Angels* (1966), Miss Murdoch returns to a truly London setting, in a grimly paradoxical way. This is the setting of a London annihilated: first by bombing, which has left only the Wren tower of Carel's church in the City; second by further demolition for a building site, with the construction postponed by legal complications, leaving a frozen wasteland; third by a thick, oppressive fog that makes vision of the scene impossible for most of the book. This obliteration of the scene is symbolic of the nihilistic state of mind in its central character, Carel, the faithless priest whose powerful abilities have turned toward the annihilation of will in all those closest to him: his daughters, his servant-mistress, and his brother. It is a fearful tale, successful and terrifying in its glimpse of the abyss beyond existentialism. It is Miss Murdoch's only truly "philosophical novel"; the allusions to Heidegger provide an accurate clue to her theme and design. It constitutes a ruthless criticism of what she has called "the neurotic modern novel" as distinguished from what she calls "the true novel (Balzac, George Eliot, Dickens)." [4] It is the kind of novel that she has elsewhere called "a tight metaphysical object, which wishes it were a poem, and which attempts to convey, often in mythical form, some central truth about the human condition." That is to say, it is "a novel like *The Stranger* of Camus, which is a small, compact, crystalline, self-contained myth about the human condition." She prefers, she says, this sort of novel to the other kind that rivals it in modern literature: the "loose journalistic epic, documentary or possibly even didactic in inspiration, offering a commentary on current institutions or on some matter out of history." [5] It may well have seemed that Miss Murdoch had reached the end of her career at this point: for she had, in *The Red and the Green,* shown how one might fail in this kind of documentary or historical novel; and she had now provided, with

4. Iris Murdoch, "The Sublime and the Good," *Chicago Review,* vol. 13, no. 3 (1959), p. 53.
5. Iris Murdoch, "The Sublime and the Beautiful Revisited," *Yale Review,* 49 (1960), 264–265.

horrifying success, an extreme example of "solipsistic form" in the "metaphysical novel" of modern neurosis.

But the result of these many years of experimentation has been quite the opposite. In her last three novels, all firmly set in whole or part in the London scene, she has emerged in serene command of her own individual mode, working toward the "true novel" in the ample dimensions of a Dickens or a George Eliot, while dealing with all the neurotic issues of a society which appears "menacing, puzzling, uncontrollable, or else confining, and boring." Within this ample form she pursues her grand conviction that "incomparably the most important thing" to be revealed by a novel is "that other people exist." These three novels move toward the goal she had set for herself in a lecture of 1959: "It is indeed the realization of a vast and varied reality outside ourselves which brings about a sense initially of terror, and when properly understood of exhilaration and spiritual power. But what brings this experience to us, in its most important form, is the sight, not of physical nature, but of our surroundings as consisting of other individual men." [6] Or, we might say, individual men and women deeply involved with the surroundings that men and women have made — and best of all, in London.

The Nice and the Good (1968) develops its vast range of characters by means of skillful oscillation between a seaside house in Dorset, where unhappy exiles gather with their problems, and London, where in Earls Court, in Chelsea, or before the great Bronzino in the National Gallery these dilemmas are resolved. This novel does not have the density of Dickensian detail that we find in the London settings of the last two; but the book, with its basically London characters, is clearly moving in this direction:

Ducane's Bentley moved slowly along with the rush-hour traffic over the curved terracotta-coloured surface of the Mall. Clouds of thick heat eddied across the crawling noise of the cars and cast a distorting haze upon the immobile trees of St. James's Park, their midsummer fullness already drooping. It was the sort of moment when, on a hot evening, London gives an indolent sigh of despair.

6. *Ibid.,* 265, 267, 268.

There is a pointlessness of summer London more awful than anything which fogs or early-afternoon twilights are able to evoke, a summer mood of yawning and glazing eyes and little nightmare-ridden sleeps in bored and desperate rooms (chap. xvi).

A Fairly Honourable Defeat is, like *Bruno's Dream,* almost wholly set in "Iris Murdoch's London." But this time the major setting, in the area of The Boltons, is one of greater elegance and sophistication: "Feathery bushes and plump trees posed motionless with evening against white walls yellowed by a powdery sun. Pink roses clambered upon stucco balustrades and multi-coloured irises peered through painted lattices" (chap. ii). Against the atmosphere of The Boltons is placed the decaying (and Dickensian) atmosphere of Tallis' house in Notting Hill, a step down from Danby's moldy house on Stadium Street:

The window, which gave onto a brick wall, was spotty with grime, admitting light but concealing the weather and the time of day. The sink was piled with leaning towers of dirty dishes. The draining board was littered with empty tins and open pots of jam full of dead or dying wasps. A bin, crammed to overflowing, stood open to reveal a rotting coagulated mass of organic material crawling with flies. The dresser was covered in a layer, about a foot high, of miscellaneous oddments: books, papers, string, letters, knives, scissors, elastic bands, blunt pencils, broken Biros, empty ink bottles, empty cigarette packets, and lumps of old hard stale cheese. The floor was not only filthy but greasy and sticky and made a sucking sound as Hilda lifted her feet (chap. v).

These settings are admirably functional. Rupert, prosperous civil servant and would-be philosopher, lives in Priory Grove (Priory Walk),[7] just off The Boltons, and his pretensions are well indicated on the opening page by the emphasis on his latest luxury — "a diminutive swimming pool which made a square of

7. The true location is indicated by details at the opening of chap. viii: "When Morgan reached the gate she knew Julius must have turned to the right, otherwise he would still be in view. She ran to the corner of Gilston Road and looked both ways but could see no sign of him . . . The Boltons was nearer than the Fulham Road. She turned right again . . . She reached Tregunter Road and looked along it, crossed to the other side and looked again . . . Gasping already with breathlessness and fear she began to run along the left hand curve of the Boltons."

flashing shimmering blue in the middle of the courtyarded garden" — the pool, frequently mentioned throughout, in which
he appropriately drowns at the close. In spite of his pretensions,
Rupert is likable and well-intentioned. But he understands very
little, least of all himself, his son, and his sister-in-law Morgan.
His lack of self-knowledge exposes him to the machinations of
the wandering cynic Julius, whose belief in humanity has been
almost entirely lost, apparently through his experience in a Nazi
concentration camp. Julius takes a malevolent joy in manipulating people, but at bottom his destructive plots arise from his
disgust with human follies and vanities. Here he means no more
than to shake Rupert's self-satisfaction and explode his pretensions to be a philosopher.

The real villain in the piece is Julius' ex-mistress, Morgan:
she is indeed Fata Morgana, Morgan-le-fay, the treacherous
sister who destroys, in this case, her brother-in-law. (The hint
in her name is borne out at the opening of part two, when Rupert
remembers "what Hilda called 'the Tallis fantasy.' 'Morgan's
living in Malory or something.' Rupert could not quite envisage
Tallis as an Arthurian knight.") She is hardly human; her state
of mind throughout the book is accurately predicted in her own
description as she first enters: " 'I don't know what I'm doing,'
said Morgan. 'I don't know where I'm going. I have no plans. I
have no intentions. I have no thoughts. I have just got off a jet
plane and I feel crazy' " (chap. iii). But the jet plane, except as
an indication of her rootlessness, has little to do with her state of
mind, which she again describes accurately in a conversation
with Rupert after she has rested: " 'How very peculiar one's
mind is. There's no foothold in it, no leverage, no way of changing oneself into a responsible just being. One's lost in one's own
psyche. It stretches away and away to the ends of the world and
it's soft and sticky and warm. There's nothing real, no hard
parts, no centre' " (chap. vii). Morgan is utterly without principle, yet she is not consciously vicious. Her trouble is that, for
all her university degrees, she is not really conscious of anything
except her own physical twitches and touches. There is much
that she could have done, with even a small measure of humanity. If she had had a slight perception into the true nature of
Julius' needs — if she had been able to perceive him at all as a

separate person, outside the fantasy of her own sexual delights — she might have found a way of telling him about her pregnancy, perhaps helping both him and herself. Julius is shocked when she tells him about her abortion, and there are strong implications that he would much have liked to have a son. Or she could have helped her deserted husband Tallis, the Good Samaritan of Notting Hill, to clean up his hovel and do his good works. Despite his wretchedly poor and disorganized way of life, he is a man of character, stubborn in his belief that humanity, in all its guises, is worth helping. He is, significantly, the only person whose advice Julius will heed, the only person whom Julius comes, though reluctantly, to respect.

There is one other man of character in the book: the quiet, austere, middle-aged homosexual, Axel. From the beginning of the book he feels deep hostility toward Morgan, partly motivated by her friendship with his younger friend Simon. But his dislike is based upon a fairly accurate view of Morgan. He sees her, at first, as "fundamentally a very silly person" and predicts that she "will make — some ghastly muddle" (chap. ii). Later, in an angry mood, he cries out to Simon: "Can't you see that she's completely malevolent, that she enjoys destroying things?" (chap. xvi). As a man of principle, Axel realizes that Morgan's emptiness is dangerous. Meanwhile, Miss Murdoch's bold attempt to display in Axel and Simon a pair of male lovers is a success unprecedented in English fiction. This success is, in fact, essential in developing the novel's basic issues.

These issues emerge exactly in the middle of the book, after the author has devoted two hundred closely-packed pages to the establishment of all her characters. This is her longest and most ambitious book: she needs not only a long space to build up the complexity of her characters, she needs an equally long space in which to explore the problem that Julius now poses, near the close of the novel's part one (chap. xix).

Human beings are roughly constructed entities full of indeterminacies and vaguenesses and empty spaces. Driven along by their own private needs they latch blindly onto each other, then pull away, then clutch again. Their little sadisms and their little masochisms are surface phenomena. Anyone will do to play the roles.

They never really see each other at all. There is no relationship, dear Morgan, which cannot quite easily be broken and there is none the breaking of which is a matter of any genuine seriousness. Human beings are essentially finders of substitutes.

Part two is devoted to revealing the degree of truth in Julius' cynical manifesto. He is partly right about Rupert and his wife Hilda: they are easily broken apart — but the results are disastrous. And he might have been partly right about Axel and Simon; theirs is a precarious relation, and one feels that Julius could have shattered it if he had chosen to try. And he is right about the boasted "love" between the two sisters, Morgan and Hilda: it proves empty. Far from helping Morgan as she promises so strongly in the opening of the book, Hilda ends up being "helped" by Morgan and allowing Morgan to take on the superior role. Hilda's will has been destroyed.

But other relations are not so easily broken. Tallis remains faithful to his love for Morgan; he is unshakable in his deep devotion to his miserable father; and he remains devoted, rather neurotically, to the memory of his dead young sister. And at the close (chap. xxi), Julius rather pathetically reveals his own inner needs when he tries to justify himself and to establish some kind of relation with Tallis:

> Tallis rose and Julius fingered the door. They looked at each other and then looked away.
> "I'm sorry," said Tallis. "But there it is."
> "I quite understand. Well, what am I to do?"
> "What do you mean?"
> "You know what I mean."
> "Oh, just go away," said Tallis. "I don't think you should live in the Boltons or Priory Grove. Go right away."
> "Yes, yes, of course. I didn't really intend to settle here. I was only playing with the idea. I'll go abroad. I may take on another big assignment quite soon. This was just an interim."

Then, after Tallis has agreed to let Julius repay Morgan's debt, Julius lingers on: " 'Yes, well, I must be going,' said Julius. 'Goodbye. I suppose in the nature of things we shall meet again.' He still lingered. 'You concede that I am an instrument of jus-

tice?' Tallis smiled." He, and we, cannot agree with this estimate
of Julius' activities. For the whole sorry tale of the disruption
caused by Julius and Morgan cannot be called "justice." And
the results are sorry beyond Julius' expectation: he never meant
to lead Rupert to death. The breaking of a human relationship is
indeed a matter of "genuine seriousness." And Julius' embar-
rassed efforts to justify himself before Tallis show how Julius too
has been defeated, in a sense, for his cynical manifesto is less
than a half-truth. The title of the novel is double-edged. Human
nature has suffered a defeat in the book: Tallis is unhappy and
deserted; Rupert is dead; Hilda is uprooted from Priory Grove
and made to live in California, in submission to the execrable
Morgan. But the defeat is fairly honorable, for the heart of
Julius' cynical manifesto has been disproved. Human beings do
not easily find substitutes for a broken relation; Julius himself,
as he leaves Tallis, shows the deep and genuine seriousness inherent in all human relationships.

That other people exist, that any sense we have of "spiritual
power" must arise from a recognition that our surroundings consist primarily "of other individual men" — this is the great and
basic theme of this recent "trilogy" of true novels. They display
individual men and women in all their vulnerable and frequently
pitiful weaknesses. And yet, through the quality of human affection revealed in its relation to one "beloved city," human nature
finds a way of vindication and possible redemption. In her subtle
exploration of man's present need to preserve the integrity of
each individual being, Miss Murdoch has established herself as
the most significant novelist now living in England.

RICHARD POIRIER

The Performing Self

In illustrating what I mean by "the performing self" I will be concerned mostly with Robert Frost, Norman Mailer, and Henry James. Since I could almost as profitably consider the self as performance in Byron, in Yeats, or in Lawrence, and since I will have something to say about Andrew Marvell as well as Thoreau, I am less sure of the significance that all three of my principal illustrations are American than that each of them is of an extreme if different kind of arrogance. Whether it be confronting a page of his own writing or an historical phenomenon like the assassination of Robert Kennedy or a meeting with Khrushchev or the massive power of New York City — each one treats any occasion as a "scene" or a stage for dramatizing the self as a performer. I can't imagine a scene of whatever terror or pathos in which any one of them would not at every step in his account be watching and measuring his moment-by-moment participation. And this participation would be measured by powers of rendition rather than by efforts of understanding: since the event

This article first appeared in Richard Poirier, *The Performing Self* (Oxford, April 1971), pp. 86–111, copyright © Oxford University Press, and is reprinted here by permission of the author and publisher.

doesn't exist except in the shape he gives it, what else should he
be anxious about? It is performance that matters — pacing,
economies, juxtapositions, aggregations of tone, the whole conduct of the shaping presence. If this sounds rather more brutal
than we imagine writers or artists to be, then that is because performance is a brutal business. As Edwin Denby argues, dancing
on points is an extraordinarily brutal — he uses the word savage
— business, regardless of the communicated effect of grace and
beauty. We can learn a great deal about art by telling the dancer
from the dance. Dancers themselves do; and writers are always
more anxious than are their critics to distinguish between writing
as an act, *écriture,* and the book or poem.

Indeed, each of the three writers I will mostly discuss admits
with unusual candor that what excites him most in a work is
finally himself as a performer. Performance is an exercise of
power, a very curious one. Curious because it is at first so furi-
ously self-consultive, so even narcissistic, and later so eager for
publicity, love, and historical dimension. Out of an accumulation
of secretive acts emerges at last a form that presumes to compete with reality itself for control of the minds exposed to it.
Performance in writing, in painting, in dance is made up of thousands of tiny movements, each made with a calculation that is
also its innocence. By innocence I mean that the movements
have an utterly moral neutrality — they are designed to serve
one another and nothing, no one else; and they are innocent, too,
because contrived with only a vague general notion of what they
might ultimately be responsible for — the final thing, the accumulation called "the work." "The bridge spans the stream," as
Henry James puts it, "after the fact, in apparently complete independence of these properties, the principal grace of the original design. *They* were an illusion, for the necessary hour; but
the span itself, whether of a single arch or of many, seems by the
oddest chance in the world to be a reality; since actually the
rueful builder, passing under it, sees figures and hears sounds
above: he makes out, with his heart in his throat, that it bears
and is positively being 'used.' "

If James wants to believe that "they" — the original design
and the acts of the builder prompted by it — prove in the end to
have been an "illusion" when measured against the reality of

the finished structure, then it has to be said that his Prefaces are given almost wholly to an account of such "illusions." Perhaps it would be better to say that their relationship is a dialectical one; that there exists a perpetually tensed antagonism between acts of local performance, carried out in private delight and secretive plotting, and those acts of presentation when the author, spruce, smiling, now a public man, gives the finished work to the world. The gap between the completed work, which is supposed to constitute the writer's vision, and the multiple acts of performance that went into it is an image of the gap between the artist's self as he discovered it in performance and the self, altogether less grimy, that he discovers afterward in the final shape and the world's reception of it. The question, responded to quite differently by the writers I will look at, is simply this: which kind of power — of performance or of the contemplatable visions that can be deduced from their end results — is the more illusory when it comes to understanding a literary work? There is no answer to this question. Rather, it posits a condition within which any writer, and any critic, finds himself working. It is a question not of belief in meanings but of belief in one kind of power and energy or another — one kind in the supposed act of doing, the other in the supposed result.

Frost was as obsessed with power in its public and in its private forms as any writer in this century, which is why he kept pretending he wasn't. It made him resist, to the point of meanness, the weakening pulls of liberal humanitarianism. In a letter written three weeks after Roosevelt defeated Landon in 1936 Frost feels compelled, by the nature of a personal confession, to assure Louis Untermeyer, that "I don't mean it is humanity not to feel the suffering of others"; he then proceeds to talk about the election and the metaphors that governed it.

I judge half the people that voted for his Rosiness were those glad to be on the receiving end of his benevolence and half were those glad to be on the giving end. The national mood is humanitarianism. Nobly so — I wouldn't take it away from them. I am content to let it go at one philosophical observation: isn't it a poetical strangeness that while the world was going full blast for the Darwinian metaphors of evolution, survival values and the Devil take the hindmost, a polemical Jew in exile was working up the metaphor of

the State's being like a family to displace them [Darwinian meta-
phors] from the mind and give us a new figure to live by? Marx had
the strength not to be overawed by the metaphor in vogue . . . We
are all toadies to the fashionable metaphor of the hour. Great is he
who imposes the metaphor.

Over against such convictions about the historical reverbera-
tions of "working up the metaphor" has to be placed Frost's
own disavowals of any desire to be thought a poet of Western
civilization. "Eliot and I have our similarities and our differences," he once wrote. "We are both poets and we both like to
play. That's the similarity. The difference is this: I like to play
euchre. He likes to play Eucharist." When he talks about "working up the metaphor" in his own poetry, he seldom betrays any
fantasies about the effects of such work upon the direction of
civilization or even upon the consciousness of his own times. If
poetry is an act of power for him, then it's of a power that claims
a smaller sphere of influence than that assumed by Yeats or
Lawrence or James, the manipulator of continents, or Mailer,
whose body, one gathers, is the body politic of America. "I look
upon a poem as a performance," Frost avows in the *Paris
Review* interview. "I look on the poet as a man of prowess" —
but he then adds a clarification which is also a brake on self-
aggrandizement — "just like an athlete."
    Not surprisingly, and with consequences for his poetry that I
will return to, Frost speaks of this prowess in ways as nearly
sexual as athletic and that insist, in their freedom from metaphysical cant, on a difference crucial to my argument: a difference between the mood or meaning that may be generated by
the theme of a poem on the one hand and, on the other, the
effect of the energies expended by the writer in his acts of performance. In the same interview, he talks about the first poem
he ever wrote and then, more generally, about writing poetry:

I was walking home from school and I began to make it — a March
day — and I was making it all afternoon and making it so I was
late at my grandmother's for dinner. I finished it, but it burned
right up, just burned right up, you know. And what started that?
What burned it? So many talk, I wonder how falsely, about what it
costs them, what agony it is to write. I've often been quoted "No

tears in the writer, no tears in the reader. No surprise for the writer, no surprise for the reader." But another distinction I make is: However sad, no grievance, grief without grievance. How could I, how could anyone have a good time with what it cost me too much agony, how could they? What do I want to communicate but what a *hell* of a good time I had writing it? The whole thing is performance and prowess and feats of association. Why don't critics talk about those things — what a feat it was to turn that that way, and what a feat it was to remember that, to be reminded of that by this? Why don't they talk about that? Scoring. You've got to *score*. They say not but you've got to score, in all the realms — theology, politics, astronomy, history and the country life around you.

In his list of "realms" wherein poetic "prowess" or "scoring" is exercised, there is conspicuously a division rather than any confusion among them; and this self-restraining kind of discrimination extends even to a division between the effect of the poem and the effect of writing it. If the poem expresses grief, it also expresses — as an *act,* as a composition, a performance, a "making," — the opposite of grief; it shows or expresses "what a *hell* of a good time I had writing it." This is a difficult distinction for most critics to grasp, apparently. It is what Yeats means when he says that "Hamlet and Lear are gay" — "If worthy their prominent part in the play" Hamlet and Lear, either on the theatrical stage or the historical one, "do not break up their lines to weep." Frost would not have needed Yeats because he had Emerson, who could write in "The Poet" that "an imaginative book renders us much more service at first, by stimulating us through its tropes, than afterwards when we arrive at the precise sense of the author." This is the same Emerson whose comments on human suffering were sometimes tougher than anything even Frost could say. Emersonian idealizations of human power and energy in action, like any fascination for the purity of human performance, tends to toughen artists far more, I suspect, than we'd like to believe. In "Experience" he writes: "People grieve and bemoan themselves, but it is not half so bad with them as they say. There are moods in which we court suffering, in the hope that here at least we shall find reality, sharp peaks and edges of truth, but it turns out to be scene-painting and counterfeit. The only thing grief has taught me is to know how shallow it is. That, like all the rest, plays about the surface, and never introduces me into the reality, for contact with which we would even pay the costly price of sons and lovers."

An equivalent toughness, along with some of Emerson's faith in human enterprise, informs a letter from Frost to an obscure American poet named Kimball Flaccus. An indifference, even a disdain for any preoccupation with social conditions coexists in the letter with a concern for the primacy of personal performance. It is significant that Frost at the same time recognizes that nothing he can do as a "performer" can have much relevance to the shape of society. His seeming callousness, like James's persistent relish in the "picturesque" (often meaning human misery under glass), is in part at least derived from a feeling about the essential irrelevance of literature to the movements of daily life, much less those of large social organisms. Which takes me for a moment to a more general point: namely, that literary teachers and critics should stop flattering the importance of their occupations by breast-beating about the fact that literature and the humanities did not somehow prevent, say, the gas chambers. They had nothing to do with the gas chambers, shouldn't have, couldn't have, and the notion that they did has been prompted only by self-serving dreams of the power of literature or of being a literary critic: George Steiner's dream or the dream of the teacher who gradually confuses his trapped audience of students with the general public. The value of a letter like Frost's is that it helps cleanse us of pretensions and vulgarities about the political power of literature, even while affirming the personal power that can be locked into it.

My dear Flaccus:

The book has come and I have read your poems first. They are good. They have loveliness — they surely have that. They are carried high. What you long for is in them. You wish the world better than it is, more poetical. You are that kind of poet. I would rate as the other kind. I wouldn't give a cent to see the world, the United States or even New York much better. I want them left just as they are for me to make poetical on paper. I don't ask anything done to them that I don't do to them myself. I'm a mere selfish artist most of the time. I have no quarrel with the material. The grief will be simply if I can't transmute it into poems. I don't want the world

made safer for poetry or easier. To hell with it. That is its own look-
out. Let it stew in its own materialism. No, not to hell with it. Let
it hold its position while I do it in art. My whole anxiety is for myself as a performer. Am I any good? That's what I'd like to know
and all I need to know.

Frost's distinction between those poets who want to make the
world poetical and those like himself who are content to reform
it only on paper suggests why he calls Marx a "polemical" and
not a "poetical" Jew for "working up the metaphor" that transformed the political life of the twentieth century. As a poet Frost
comments on the "poetical strangeness" of Marx not having been
"overawed by the metaphor in vogue," and this is, not acciden-
tally, what Frost often felt about his own career. But the analogy
between Frost and Marx would hold in Frost's mind only for
comparative performances, not at all for comparative results.
You do not "score" in one realm by scoring in another, and the
presumption that you do may mean that you truly score in none
at all, as some of our currently distinguished topical novelists
will eventually discover. It is this tough self-knowledge that
makes Frost so watchful of himself as a performer in his poetry,
and so wry about himself as a sage for the world — as someone
who can rest on the results of performance. Leaving the world
to stew in its own materialism doesn't mean that he won't use the
world; it means that he sees no way it might use him. Hence his
reticence and contempt, his playfulness about worldly wisdom
or even otherworldly wisdom.
    In his skepticism about the power of literature and his delight
in his prowess as a writer, Frost represents a complication of
the metaphor of self as performer which can be further eluci-
dated by comparing him with Thoreau and Andrew Marvell and
then contrasting all three to Norman Mailer and Henry James.
(I take it as understood that I am trying to describe instances of
a problem rather than to produce any kind of as yet recognizable
literary history.) Frost, Thoreau, Marvell, Mailer, James — all
are preoccupied with the possible conjunctions of acts of poetic
with acts of public, or sometimes even political, power. But
Mailer's case is that of a writer who really believes that when he
is "working up the metaphor" he is involved in an act of histori-

cal as well as self transformation. "I am imprisoned with a perception," he has said, "which will settle for nothing less than making a revolution in the consciousness of our time"; and it is indicative of what I'm saying about him here that he is not "imprisoned *in* a perception," for so a mere mortal would ordinarily put it, but *"with"* one, both lodged in a prison that must be as large as it is mysterious in its location. In his desire to literalize his own hyperboles, Mailer is less a twentieth-century than a Renaissance character, a Tamburlaine, a Coriolanus, even Milton's Satan. All of these, as Thomas Edwards has shown me, have some difficulty distinguishing the energy of their personal performance as shapers of a world in words from that energy we might call God, the difference being that God got there first and is stabilized in forms called reality, nature, the world. To help distinguish between satanic performers on the one hand and performers like Frost on the other, think of the matter of staging. For the one, all the world is literally a stage and all the men and women merely players or, if you're a writer of this disposition, directors. Some critics are of this disposition, too, speaking of all things as fictions and thereby questioning the legitimacy of distinguishing novels from history as if history were *equally* fictive. For the other, the type of Frost, Thoreau, or Marvell, the world and its people do not as often seem a species of fiction. They seem, to use an old-fashioned word, "real"; and even when they do seem no more than fictions, then the fictions are of a different status than those endowed by literature or by writers. At the very least Frost's kind of writer wants to make a distinction between the stage that is the world and those other stages that take up some space on it, with curtains and covers, under the names of plays and poems and novels.

Marvell is especially sophisticated about these matters. He announces himself as an actor and scene-maker within poems designed also to excite the envy of those actors trying to "make it," in quite another sense of the term, on the stage of the world. He seems to say to them: since you are looking for "the palm, the oak, or bays," unless of course I take you too literally (or you take yourself too literally), come to the garden, where you can find all these and more, "all flowers and all trees." For an analogous performance there is Thoreau in his American garden, the beanfield, where, "determined to know beans," and making a profit which he can itemize out to $8.71½, he tells us that it was "not that I wanted beans to eat, for I am by nature a Pythagorean, so far as beans are concerned, but perchance, as some must work in fields if only for the sake of tropes and expression to serve a parable-maker one day." When he says a bit later that "I sometimes make a day of it," he is characteristically punning in favor of his role as poet and maker and punning against ordinary idiom, familiarity with which can threaten the vitalities he finds in language.

The punning of Thoreau and Marvell, who are perhaps the most seriously intentioned punsters in English before Joyce, is a way of showing that the words by which the world carries on its sensible business are loaded with a radical content. It is within the subversive power of the poet to release that radical content. This is power of a sort, but it is not great, not the best kind perhaps even for a poet. It wasn't his puns but his refusal to pay taxes that put Thoreau in jail, and it wasn't Marvell's poetry, most of it published only after his death, that gave him his position so much as his being for twenty years the Member of Parliament for Hull, and a rather violent politician. If Thoreau and Marvell satirize worldly power because it cannot control even the words by which it tries to make sense of itself, both writers can be equally satirical about literary performances, including their own, which pretend to give a controlling shape to that world. They are wary of the expansive "I" who performs in their works, just as Frost is of the "he" who in "The Most of It" asks the world to give him back a poem: "He would cry out on life, that what it wants / Is not its own love back in copy speech / But counter-love, original response." What it gives back looks indifferent enough and sounds, as Frost describes it, like a retaliation: "As a great buck it powerfully appeared, / Pushing the crumpled water up ahead, / And landed pouring like a waterfall, / And stumbled through the rocks with horny tread, / And forced the underbrush — and that was all."

The world performs itself in its own terms and metaphors. Marvell discovers this in one of the most remarkable passages of literary criticism in English literature from one of its most remarkably neglected masterpieces, "Upon Appleton House." The

poem is only incidentally a country-house poem, celebrating but
as often making fun of the efforts of Lord Fairfax to build a
model "civilization" in retirement rather than, as he possibly
might have done, in the government of Cromwell. The poem as-
sertively refers to "scenes" as the places where men perform the
acts that make civilization. These include the poem itself as a
"scene," with Marvell as poet and burlesqued figure of "easie
philosopher." His most self-exhilarating performance is as pastoral poet, a dangerously smug role to take given the other historical "scenery" of the poem. Marvell moves from the garden,
described as if it were a military bastion, and from lamentations
about the devastations of civil war, to the great mowing scene.
A "scene" is what he insists it is, a "scene" where he performs as
a poet and is exposed for doing so by those other elements of the
"scene" which can be called life:

> No scene that turns with engines strange
> Does oft'ner than these meadows change:
> For when the sun the grass hath vexed,
> The tawny mowers enter next;
> Who seem like Israelites to be
> Walking on foot through a green sea.
> To them the grassy deeps divide,
> And crowd a lane to either side.
>
> With whistling scythe and elbow strong,
> These massacre the grass along;
> While one, unknowing, carves the rail,
> Whose yet unfeathered quills her fail.
> The edge all bloody from its breast
> He draws, and does his stroke detest;
> Fearing the flesh untimely mowed
> To him a fate as black forbode.
>
> But bloody Thestylis, that waits
> To bring the mowing camp their cates,
> Greedy as kites has trussed it up,
> And forthwith means on it to sup;
> When on another quick she lights,
> And cries, "He called us Israelites";
> But now to make his saying true,
> Rails rain for quails, for manna dew.

The metaphor-making of the poet here is equivalent to the machinery for a Renaissance masque referred to in the first line. The poet's language "changes" the meadow into some equivalent of the real sea that really did part, so we've been told, at the behest of a real (and active) political leader, Moses; and the poet's metaphor-making tries also to change the mowers into "Israelites," after which he will talk of this "scene withdrawing" to reveal the "table Rase" for what he calls other "pleasant Acts." The effect is of cocky playacting, something Chaplinesque in the sad and zany way the poet becomes so zealous in his "working up the metaphor" that he burlesques his own stylishness, just as he has before burlesqued Fairfax's. But his overextension doesn't go unreprimanded. In a moment unique in the history of poetry, the girl he has invented as something better than she is turns on him, looks out of the "scene," out of the poem, one might say. She casts off her role as a pastoral figure in an historical-biblical masque and rejects his performance — "He called us Israelites," she remarks. Her repudiation is implicit whether one takes her tone as angry or merely shrugging. Apparently one result of the civil war is that the lower classes won't easily take directions from pastoralists or mythologizers who write poetry in retirement. But neither the poem nor the performance are thereby deflected from the theatrical path on which they've been moving. Indeed, both have been all along satirical of their own procedures, even while these have managed to satirize some of the transitional aspects of contemporary English life and politics. Loss of poise is the least of the poet's worries as he surveys the many other kinds of losses to England and to civilization in the poem; and besides, he has already hedged his bets on Thestylis by suggesting that she was a "bloody" camp follower even before she turned on him. With aristocratic good will he knows how to make the most of a diminished thing.

Such a poet as Marvell or Frost can be proud of his power as a performer, because the "scene" of the poem is in fact far more precarious and unstabilized than is the "scene" which is the world. One can't depend, as Marvell discovers, even on literary convention to keep fieldhands in their pastoral places. In a way, performances in poetry can prove not that the world is too tough for the performer but that he is too tough for the world. The

scene of the poem is more expanded and expansive than the
scene which is the world, and the poet's relationship to the scene
of the poem is necessarily dynamic, exploratory, coolly executed
to a degree that no comparable "scene" in life could very well
bear. Frost's sonnets offer a convenient illustration. Take "Putting in the Seed":

> You come to fetch me from my work to-night
> When supper's on the table, and we'll see
> If I can leave off burying the white
> Soft petals fallen from the apple tree
> (Soft petals, yes, but not so barren quite,
> Mingled with these, smooth bean and wrinkled pea;)
> And go along with you ere you lose sight
> Of what you came for and become like me,
> Slave to a springtime passion for the earth.
> How Love burns through the Putting in the Seed
> On through the watching for that early birth
> When, just as the soil tarnishes with weed,
> The sturdy seedling with arched body comes
> Shouldering its way and shedding the earth crumbs.

The excitement here is in the voice finding its way from the
homey jocular affections of the first lines to the high ceremonious
tone of the last five. That change and the way it registers as a
performance of self-discovery is what the poem is about. As the
man putting in seed discovers that the literal description, if it
can be called that, of his daytime occupation is a metaphoric description of his nighttime lovemaking and that both bring life out
of the earth, he is suddenly transformed into something other
than the man we knew at the outset. His voice becomes of no
age or place or time celebrating its liberation into myth, even
as the man, the farmer and husband, continues expertly to wrap
and plant the seed. Or take the final question in "The Oven
Bird" — of "what to make of a diminished thing." Only the poet
as maker can answer the question and not the bird, a "most ex-
planatory bird," as Reuben Brower points out, "who *makes* the
solid tree trunks sound again." The answer is implicit in the performance of the poem, as in the steady iambic push against the

trochaic falling: "He says the early petal-fall is past, / When pear and cherry bloom went down in showers." The metrical performance shows what it is like to meet and answer the "fall" — both the season and the condition. Birds are always a kind of wonder to Frost because like poets they sing but are not, as are poets, in the same need of being noticed. They sing, but they do not in Frost's sense "perform": remember that "one had to be *versed* in country things / Not to believe the phoebes wept" for the human desolation around them. One would be a bad poet of nature if he thought that birds were poets at all. Wanting to be noticed is wanting to be loved, and finally Frost's emphasis on the poet as a man of prowess refers us to "realms" of enactment more elementary than the world of public affairs which he would "let stew in its own materialism." It refers to the creative thrust of love. Poetically, this means a thrust of the voice against the "fall" in all conceivable senses of that word. We know about the fall partly because, in the beautiful sonnet "Never Again Would Birds' Song Be the Same," we learn that "the daylong voice of Eve / had added to their own an oversound."

Frost's dread is that there will only be silence, no sound at all, in response to his voice as it tries to perform with Eve in nature ("As vain to raise a voice as a sigh / In the tumult of free leaves on high," he writes in "On Going Unnoticed") or with Eve in love (as in "Bereft," or "Acquainted with the Night," where "an interrupted cry / Came over houses from another street, / But not to call me back or say goodby") or in "The Subverted Flower" where, faced by a woman's frigidity that is turning him into a beast ". . . with every word he spoke / His lips were sucked and blown / And the effort made him choke / Like a tiger at a bone." When Frost uses so strong a word as "anxiety" in saying that "my whole anxiety is for myself as a performer" I suspect that he is talking about himself as he exists in sound, and that not being listened to and not being answered in sound is equivalent, for him, to the horror of loss of creative power. In this light we might best understand both the embarrassment and strangeness of his once writing to William Stanley Braithwaite, the Black poet-critic-anthologist, that "it would seem absurd to say it (and you mustn't quote me as saying it) but I suppose the fact is that my conscious interest in people was at first no more than an almost technical interest in their speech — in what I used to call their sentence sounds."

The connection between the making of sound and the discovery of human relatedness — between, eventually, poetic prowess and sexual prowess — is implicit in more poems by Frost than I can mention here and is exemplified with particular force and wit in "All Revelation," where the sexual, phallic, orgasmic punning is the most notable aspect of his performance. Responses to the thrusts of love are even more mysterious in this poem than are answers to mental thrusts, but it is clear that the "revelations" he seeks come from performances for which sex is a wholly proper metaphor. And this sexual performance, like poetic performance, is very much the thing in itself (". . . what can of its coming come") without the attendant metaphysics of other poets who also think of themselves as men of "prowess" like Lawrence, Hemingway, and Mailer.

Which takes me now, more briefly, first to Mailer and then to Henry James. I choose these two because they are notorious self-advertisers when it comes to literary performances: Mailer in nearly everything he's written since *Deer Park,* the third of fourteen books; James in his literary criticism, his *Notebooks,* some of his travel writing (especially his standoff confrontation with New York City), and the Prefaces, those unabashed reconstructions and contemplations of a performing self. It is worth noting parenthetically that self-conscious performers, writers who like to find themselves in acts of composition, are often more than ordinarily prolific. Think, for another example, of Dickens. Dickens is best identified for me in Robert Garis' indispensably original study *The Dickens Theater,* and some of the criticisms I shall make of James and Mailer are encouraged by Garis' brilliant discussions of the aesthetics of performance. My criticisms depend, as well, on the hope that having written at length on James and having been one of the few who honored the very large claims made by *An American Dream* and *Why Are We in Vietnam?* I needn't be unduly cautious about using either of these writers in an illustratively negative way — as examples of some of the dangers inherent in literary self-performance. In any case, the failures I will be discussing occur at

an extremity of heroic effort in verbal dexterity: the confrontation of the writer's performing self with the irreducible power of
death.

Those with a relatively greater confidence in their powers of
self-performance as against the resistant or indifferent powers
of history show a correspondingly greater theatricality in the face
of death than would writers of the type of Frost or Marvell or
Thoreau. Thus, in the "Horatian Ode," as Thomas Edwards
shows in his forthcoming book *Imagination and Power*, Charles
is a successful performer because he is so fine an actor while
being so entirely unhistrionic: "He nothing common did or mean
/ Upon that memorable scene, / But with his keener eye / The
ax's edge did try." Appropriate to his magnificent balance at the
juncture of life and death is a pun that balances both conditions
in one word: the keenness of the eye and of the ax are fused in
the Latin derivative of axe, *acies,* which can mean both eyesight
and blade. Eye and blade will indeed soon meet and share inani-
mateness; but, before that, the keenness of the axe in no way
lessens and is indeed excelled by the answering life of the King's
eye.

As against this kind of performance I want to consider a passage from Mailer and one from James where there is something
like enviousness at work in the face of the magnitude of death,
a violent and unsuccessful magnification of the self through
language in the effort to meet and overwhelm the phenomenon
of death. Mailer, who is surely one of our most astute literary
critics, shows his awareness of these issues whenever he talks of
Hemingway. In an interview printed in *Presidential Papers* he
makes a remark to which I will return later — that "the first art
work in an artist is the shaping of his own personality." And then
he goes on directly to talk about Hemingway and death.

Hemingway was on the one hand a man of magnificent senses.
There was a quick lithe animal in him. He was also shackled to a
stunted ape, a cripple, a particularly wild dirty little dwarf within
himself who wanted only to kill Hemingway. Life as a compromise
was impossible. So long as Hemingway did not test himself, push
himself beyond his own dares, flirt with, engage, and finally embrace
death, in other words so long as he did not propitiate the dwarf, give
the dwarf its chance to live and feel emotion, an emotion which

could come to life only when one was close to death, Hemingway and the dwarf were doomed to dull and deaden one another in the dungeon of the psyche. Everyday life in such circumstances is a plague. The proper comment on Hemingway's style of life may be not that he dared death too much, but too little, that brave as he was, he was not brave enough, and the dwarf finally won. One does not judge Hemingway, but one can say that the sickness in him was not his love of violence but his inability to live as close to it as he had to. His proportions were tragic, he was all-but-doomed, it is possible he would have had to have been the bravest man who ever lived in order to propitiate the dwarf.

For those who persist in being mean-spirited about Mailer's self-advertisements and promotions his fascination with Hemingway, even in so splendidly written a passage as this, will seem little more than competitive vulgarity, part of a little-boy obsession with physical bravery and with being the biggest man in town. If Mailer is guilty of any kind of vulgarity it is only the kind essential to any work of art — works of art do, after all, aspire to popularity. When Mailer says that the "first art work in an artist is the shaping of his own personality" he is saying something the reverse of what is normally considered vulgar. He is saying that he cannot take the self in him for granted and that he cannot look outside himself for an acceptable self-image. The self is shaped he says "in" the artist, and this shaping he calls "work" — no easy job, nothing anyone can do for you and, indeed, made more difficult by the fact that some of the material "in" you has insinuated itself from outside. Hemingway is a writer who has done this shaping with such authority, has given such accent and prominence to the "first art work" which is himself, that he can count on getting the kind of attention for subsequent art works — for his books, that is — that Mailer would like for his own.

From all this enterprise Mailer is looking for a rather simple and decent reward: he wants to assure us that he will be read with care bordering on fear, with expectation bordering on shame. Describing his efforts, as he worked on *Deer Park,* to twist his phrases so that they could be read well only when read slowly, he has to admit the cost: "Once you write that way, the quick reader (who is nearly all your audience) will stumble and

fall against the vocal shifts of your prose. Then you had best
have the cartel of a Hemingway, because in such a case it is
critical whether the reader thinks it is your fault, or is so in awe
of your reputation that he returns to the words, throttles his
pace, and tries to discover why he is so stupid as not to swing on
the off-bop of your style." Faced with writing about the moon-
shot — how will Mailer make himself the central character of
that, one wondered, until he emerged as the star Aquarius, the
sign under which he was born — Mailer begins with a quotation
from Hemingway about death and then evokes his loss as if it
removed the one shield between himself and the overpowering
force of technology: "now the greatest living romantic was dead.
Dread was loose. The giant had not paid his dues, and dread
was in the air. Technology would fill the pause. Into the silences
static would enter." Static, that is, were it not for the performing
voice of you-know-who, making it still conceivable that man is
"ready to share the dread of the Lord," to visit the craters of
the moon, which is death, and still to exert the imagination however much it seems overmatched in power by technology.

There's something lovably, even idealistically youthful in
Mailer's aspiration for fame. He wants to make himself an "art
work" which will provide the protective and illuminating context for all the other works he will produce. But the habits thus
engendered can and do lead to something like over-self-produc-
tion. Mailer's way of letting everything come to life within that
work of art which is himself means that he must be extraordinarily ruthless in appropriating through metaphors any experience that threatens to remain independent of him. Whenever he
feels even possibly "overawed by the metaphor(s) in vogue" for
a given situation, he doesn't replace them so much as he tries to
appropriate them to himself by a rare blend of emulation and
mimicry. The consequence, as in his writing about the assassination of Robert Kennedy in *Miami and the Siege of Chicago,* can
be at times a bit terrified, extemporized in a frantic way, tasteless.

Yet he is such a totally serious writer that some discriminations are in order. *Armies of the Night* is full of beautifully accomplished accounts of Mailer's efforts to seize control of public
occasions — efforts that are made by Mailer as a public act on

the spot and later described by that other acting self who is
Mailer the writer. Very often the writer succeeds in the writing
by admitting that he failed as a participant. History and the
writing of history are not confused as actions. *Miami and the
Siege of Chicago* is quite a different book. To do the writing at
all, on a deadline from *Harper's Magazine,* he had to stay away
from the real action, away from the cops and out of jail. The
burden on the writing, the burden of a self determined to force
its claims upon history, became as a result too much for the style
to bear. Especially so when Mailer inserts himself as a bargainer
between Kennedy and God, and does so in terms that protect
him from Faustian absurdity only by his becoming a version of
Hugh Heffner, even if a somewhat Hawthornian version:

A few nights after this debate, the reporter was awakened from a
particularly oppressive nightmare by the ringing of a bell. He heard
the voice of an old drinking friend he had not seen in two years.
"Cox," he shouted into the phone, "are you out of your skull?"
[Note that image, as if it came to him before he heard that Kennedy
had been shot in the head, and note also that the nightmare itself
is a sign of premonitory powers we are not meant to think acci-
dental.]
   "What do you mean by calling at three A.M.?"
   "Look," said the friend, "get the television on. I think you ought
to see it. Bobby Kennedy has just been shot."
   "No," he bellowed. "No! No! No!" his voice railing with an ugliness and pain reminiscent to his ear [and here the self-watchfulness
begins, as he moves to the center of the occasion] of the wild grunts
of a wounded pig. (Where he had heard that cry he did not at the
moment remember.) He felt as if he were being despoiled of a vital
part of himself [perhaps his brain? — his own skull as a match for
Robert Kennedy's?] and in the middle of this horror [a vague reference, and not to the assassination] noted that he screamed like a pig,
not a lion, nor a bear. The reporter had gone for years on the prem-
ise that one must balance every moment between the angle in oneself and the swine — the sound of his own voice shocked him therefore profoundly. The balance was not what he thought it to be. He
watched television for the next hours in a state which drifted rudder-
less between two horrors. Then, knowing no good answer could
come for days, if at all, on the possible recovery of Bobby Kennedy,
he went back to bed and lay in a sweat of complicity [from dupli-

cating the "horror" of the assassination with one of his own he now moves into position to share part of Kennedy's], as if his own lack of moral *witness* (to the subtle heroism of Bobby Kennedy's attempt to run for President) could be found in the dance of evasions his taste for a merry life and a married one had become, as if this precise lack had contributed (in the vast architectronics of the cathedral of history) to one less piton of mooring for Senator Kennedy in his lonely ascent to those vaulted walls, as if finally the efforts of brave men depended in part on the protection of other men who saw themselves as at least provisionally brave, or sometimes brave, or at least — if not brave — balanced at least on a stability between selfishness and appetite and therefore — by practical purposes — decent. But he was close to having become too much of appetite — he had spent the afternoon preceding this night of the assassination in enjoying a dalliance — let us leave it at that — a not uncharacteristic way to have spent his time [the talk of "architechtronics of the cathedral of history," of "the lonely ascent" to power with respect to Kennedy is matched here by the tone and vocabulary not of a sport but of a sport of royal blood — "enjoying a dalliance" — and privilege — "let us leave it at that." How else can he imagine that his subsequent offer to the Lord would weigh sufficiently in the balance?] . . . he prayed the Lord to take the price on his own poor mortal self (since he had flesh in surfeit to offer) he begged that God spare Senator Kennedy's life, and he would give up something, give up what? — give up some of the magic he could bring to bear on some one or another of the women, yes, give up that if the life would be saved, and fell back into the horror of trying to rest with the sense that his offer might have been given too late and by the wrong vein [the pun is too tasteless to need explanation] — confession to his wife was what the moral pressure had first demanded — and so fell asleep with some gnawing sense of the Devil there to snatch his offering after the angel had moved on in disgust.

The energy that goes astray in this passage is the same energy that elsewhere manifests itself as genius. And one wishes for Mailer's sake, as one has so often for Lawrence's, that there existed the kind of criticism James called for at the beginnings of the century. In his Preface to *Wings of the Dove* he expressed the still vain hope that "surely some acute mind ought to have worked out by this time the 'law' of the degree to which the artist's energy fairly depends on his fallibility. How much and how often, and in what connections and with what almost in-

finite variety, must he be a dupe, that of his prime object, to be
at all measurably a master, that of his actual substitute for it —
or in other words at all appreciably to exist?" James is the great
theorist and exponent of "composition," as both a form of art
and a mode of existence. He speaks of the "thrilling ups and
downs, the intricate ins and outs of the compositional problem
. . . becoming the question at issue and keeping the author's
heart in his mouth," and claims that "one's work should have
composition, because composition alone is positive beauty."
However familiar this insistence, only three critics have taken
James strenuously at his word: Quentin Anderson, Lawrence
Holland and Leo Bersani. To do so raises, as these critics have
shown, quite disturbing problems about the nature of the human
meanings that can legitimately be extracted from what might be,
on James's part, a prior and more intense commitment to the
shapeliness of human actions. The final scene of *The Ambassa-
dors* has evoked a vast effort of interpretation that almost wholly
ignores James's to me astonishing admission that he faced the
problem of "how and where and why to make Miss Gostrey's
false connection carry itself, under a due high polish, as a real
one. Nowhere is it more of an artful expedient for mere consistency of form, to mention a case, than in the last 'scene' of
the book."

   "Composition" in James is never a matter of merely mechanical consistency of form. But despite his talk about "freedom,"
and his dramatizations in *The Turn of the Screw* of the horrors
that result from violations of it, James's announced preoccupation with form constitutes a kind of fearsomely benign exercise
of management and command. So much so that the "germ" of
a novel like *The Spoils of Poynton* exists pleasingly for him only
when it is most minuscule — a mere ten words — and the rest
of what his informant insists on telling him represents only
"clumsy Life again at her stupid work." The less given by Life
the greater will be his authority over what he takes, and for the
"master builder" this sense of authority is "the treasure of treas-
ures, or at least the joy of joys." It "renews in the modern
alchemist something like the old dreams of the secret of life."

   It is not surprising that James's efforts to deal with the death
of those nearest to him in his family — his efforts to do so as a

writer, that is, the only efforts I am concerned with here — constitute an extreme challenge to his authority as a shaper of life.
Death is "Life again at her stupid work," especially for a writer
to whom "the sense of the state of the dead is but part of the
sense of the state of the living." It is, however, "stupid work"
of a notoriously irresistible kind; it can't be disposed of even by
art as the merely wasteful part of a "germ" that was, clearly,
more than a germ of suggestion. No wonder that for all his
marvelous suppleness in the management of fictional death —
think of the timing of the final conversation between Ralph and
Isabel in *The Portrait of a Lady* — James should be so severely
challenged by the real deaths in his life; no wonder his tone when
meeting the graves of his mother, father, sister, and most cherished brother should lurch into a discomforting theatricality. He
describes a visit to the family grave in the Cambridge cemetery,
and the fact that the writing occurs in the *Notebooks,* not intended for publication, makes the self-consciousness about performance all the more remarkable.

The self-consciousness isn't merely implicit in verbal man-
nerisms; it is also a matter of James's actually referring to writing as an act barely possible against the pressures he encounters
as he proceeds, the problem, literally, of holding the pen:

Isn't the highest deepest note of the whole thing the never-to-be-
lost memory of that evening hour at Mount Auburn—at the Cambridge Cemetery when I took my way alone — after much waiting
for the favouring hour — to that unspeakable group of graves. It
was late, in November; the trees all bare, the dusk to fall early, the
air all still (at Cambridge, in general, *so* still), with the western sky
more and more turning to that terrible, deadly, pure polar pink that
shows behind American winter woods. But I can't go over this — I
can only, oh, so gently, so tenderly, brush it and breathe upon it —
breathe upon it and brush it. It was the moment; it was the hour; it
was the blessed flood of emotion that broke out at the touch of one's
sudden *vision* and carried me away. I seemed then to know why I
had done this; I seemed then to know why I had *come* — and to
feel how not to have come would have been miserably, horribly to
miss it. [The "it" is the apparent conjunction of circumstances that
make a "scene" and allow the increasing theatrical momentum of
the account.] The moon was there early, white and young, and

seemed reflected in the white face of the great empty Stadium, forming one of the boundaries of Soldiers' Field, that looked over at me, stared over at me, through the clear twilight, from across the Charles. Everything was there, everything *came;* the recognition, stillness, the strangeness, the pity and the sanctity and the terror, the breath-catching passion and the divine relief of tears. William's inspired transcript, on the exquisite little Florentine urn of Alice's ashes, William's divine gift to us, and to her, of the Dantean lines — "Dopo lungo exilio e martirio /Viene a questa pace" — took me so at the throat by its penetrating *rightness,* that it was as if one sank down on one's knees in a kind of anguish of gratitude before something for which one had waited with a long, deep *ache.* But why do I write of the all unutterable and the all abysmal? Why does my pen not drop from my hand on approaching the infinite pity and tragedy of all the past? It does, poor helpless pen, with what it meets of the ineffable, what it meets of the cold Medusa-face of life, of all the life *lived,* on every side. Basta, basta!

Everywhere in this enactment, in this recollection of what it was like to arrange the scene theatrically, in this report of what it feels like to write what is being written — at every italic, every allusion, every patterned repetition there is what Frederick Dupee notes as James's "characteristic passion and idiom." But there is disturbingly more than that. For one thing there is what James once described when feeling a physical chill at the recollection of a dead friend: "the power of prized survival in personal signs." He is using language designed to remind himself of how fully alive he is. For another, there is an imperialism with respect not only to the family but to the ambience, to the weather itself as a contributory theatrical factor. Without blinking, the imperialism looks forward to its hallucinated form in those terribly pathetic last days of James himself. Then, in delirium, his dictations to Theodora Bosanquet exposed his deep identification with Napoleon Bonaparte — including a letter he had signed in that name about the redecoration of the Louvre and the Tuileries and another, this one also addressed to "my dear brother and sister" but signed in his own name, in which he apportions them "your young but so highly considered Republic" as an opportunity for "brilliant fortune." Such was a way of facing, "at last, the distinguished thing."

Lest we be carried away by the poignancy of all this, let me insist that James, like Frost, probably had, at the terrible depths of creative power, "a *hell* of a good time doing it" — there at his desk, there at the cemetery arranging the scene for the desk, there even in his room dying when he dictated his last ruminations. What is literary criticism to do with something so wonderful, with literature as an act of keeping alive rather than an image of life or of living? Or let us forget literary criticism and ask what in the teaching of literature one can do with the phenomenon of performance. It seems to me that one way literature can and should be taught is in conjunction with other kinds of performance — with dance, music, film, sports — and that a comparative analysis of modes of performance can indeed keep literary study alive in the face of the competition now before it. We must begin to begin again with the most elementary and therefore the toughest questions: what must it have felt like to do this — not to mean anything, but to do it? I think anyway that that is where the glory lies: not in the tragedy but in the gaiety of Hamlet and Lear and of dry-eyed Shakespeare. Indeed, who knows if for Shakespeare there was even any dread to be transfigured? Maybe he took a beginning and it took him, as "germs" will do, and off they went.

WILLIAM H. PRITCHARD

The Uses of Yeats's Poetry

Describing Robert Frost's creation of an official role for himself, Randall Jarrell imagines Yeats saying about him, as Sarah
Bernhardt said of Nijinsky, "I fear, I greatly fear, that I have
just seen the greatest actor in the world." With equal justice the
remark could be made about Yeats — and no doubt was by
Frost at some time or other.

> Heart-smitten with emotion I sink down,
> My heart recovering with covered eyes;
> Wherever I had looked I had looked upon
> My permanent or impermanent images:[1]

Lines like these from "The Municipal Gallery Revisited" were
what first attracted me and I presume other readers to W. B.
Yeats. What we heard, we were convinced, was the accent of
passionate sincerity — extreme speech from the poet's heart of
hearts. Yet it could not be simply the heart speaking because
critics agreed that Yeats's poetry was subtle, complex, allusive

1. All quotations of Yeats's verse are from *The Collected Poems of
W. B. Yeats,* copyright The Macmillan Company (New York, 1956), by
permission of the publisher.

and thought through its images; was dramatic, ambiguous, and possessed the requisite amount of lyric tension. In other words, poetry as it used to be in the days of the Metaphysicals before things fell apart, Dryden and Milton were magniloquent, Tennyson and Browning ruminated. I may have owned a copy of *The Permanence of Yeats* (featuring essays by Brooks, Tate, Ransom, and others) before I did the *Collected Poems*; at any rate I had most certainly read the standard critical texts on Yeats's poetry before I was in any sense "inwards" with it. I knew that the most important poems were "Sailing to Byzantium," "The Second Coming," "Among School Children," and "Byzantium"; knew that there was a lot of magic around you didn't really have to believe in but which was at least preferable to modern science and a materialistic view of things; knew that mainly it was metaphor that counted.

An overall view of the poet's career was also provided: Yeats began by writing dream poetry characterized by lulling rhythms and Irish names (soon spiced with theosophical ones) whose message was that we should leave the unhappy world if possible and go away somewhere apart. These early poems could be condescended to, though a few of them possessed minor virtues and there was the popular "Innisfree" with something of the status of Paderewski's "Minuet." Then by a miracle Yeats broke free of these bad habits (though his example constitutes a warning: "No serious poet could propose to begin again where Mr. Yeats began" — F. R. Leavis) and proceeded to write harsher, sparer lyrics which confronted the real world, usually in scorn or bitterness. He went on to create a system out of which came the metaphors for some of his greatest poems, published in *The Tower*. The system was a bit maddening but didn't get in your way much once you looked up "perne in a gyre" and made the decision to pronounce it with a hard "g". He wrote some poems about Crazy Jane which were astonishingly sexual; and his *Last Poems* were simple, sensual, passionate, and bitter, though there was disagreement on whether they constituted a step forward or back from the *Tower* Yeats. On the whole his example was very much an inspiring one: along with T. S. Eliot he invented Modern Poetry, but he was a more human figure than Eliot, and certainly a better guide in relation to passionate love since he never did dirt on life. If he couldn't always be trusted on politics we could still forgive him: "You were silly, like us. / Your gift survived it all . . ."

This version of Yeats is not a pack of lies; if anything more than a private fantasy — and I assume it is familiar to other readers — then doubtless there is truth in it. But a fairly low-grade truth: an easy way of categorizing and understanding a strange writer that for all its good intentions manages to explain away the strangeness and tame a wild, a "fanatic" heart into the orderly subject of literary essays. And though the library is now filled with sound books on Yeats they will be of little help to a reader trying to feel the life of a particular poem, or asking whether it has any life, rather than studying up on Yeats's aesthetic, or his use of the Hero, or of History, or Tragedy. Scholars are notoriously adept at writing *around* poems by considering them as illustrations of something else; what that something else has to do with anybody sitting down and merely reading a poem is problematic. My concern here is for this mere reader of Yeats: I would like to imagine a more active one who is sometimes puzzled or uncertain, often moved but not always sure what he was moved by. My aim is to create a few difficulties where, well-wadded with stupidity, we walk about with a headful of critical essays that tell us what each line of every poem is supposed to mean or illustrate or import.[2]

2. I am not arrogant enough to suppose myself the first critic to be concerned with how the reader of Yeats behaves. From the great body of critical writing about Yeats after 1940, much of it concentrated on the analysis of individual poems, I would single out essays by Arthur Mizener, L. C. Knights, and Randall Jarrell (all from the *Southern Review,* Winter 1942), as "overviews" of the poet's career which spring from and always remain in touch with a common reader's responses to the poems. More recently, essays by John Holloway and Donald Davie (in *An Honoured Guest,* London, 1965) are similarly oriented and enlightening, as are the chapters on Yeats in C. K. Stead's excellent book *The New Poetic* (London, 1964).

Two recent books, in whole or in part about Yeats, present the most passionately opinionated readings of the poetry I have encountered and probably constitute the most adverse criticism, though much seasoned with admiration, his poems have received. Though in this essay I will not deal with F. R. Leavis' chapter on Yeats in his *Lectures in America,* nor Harold Bloom's recent *Yeats,* my reviews of them can be consulted: see "Discourses in America," *Essays in Criticism,* July 1969; and "Mr. Bloom in Yeatsville," *Partisan Review* (Spring 1971).

Suppose, that is, instead of glossing the "Heart-smitten with emotion" lines quoted earlier by saying that at this point in the poem Yeats feels overcome, conveys an attitude to us in such and such a tone, reveals his momentary speechlessness in the face of his old friends for whom he finds words later on — suppose instead of saying any of these things we tried to locate the reader by asking how he responds to "Heart-smitten with emotion . . ." What does he say? Does he say anything? Does he think yes, there I could be too, sinking down on my knees — I am like the speaker? Does he judge the speaker in any tentative way? Does he sympathize with him, admire him, or hold back and wait to see what happens next? Does he hesitatingly whisper a question about the sincerity of the gesture? Is it sincere or stagy, and how is it different from similar gestures in other poems? The moment in my own reading of Yeats when for the first time someone asked a question of this sort occurred in an undergraduate course of Lionel Trilling's which ended with Yeats. During a discussion of "To a Friend Whose Work Has Come to Nothing" Trilling quoted the final lines, "Be secret and exult, / Because of all things known / That is most difficult," then commented: "Of course that's not true, is it?" What happened next is lost to me, but I remember being annoyed at the liberty I thought Trilling had taken: *imagine* questioning the terms of a poem in this way and setting yourself up as judge of how much truth it speaks! Though I still feel that Trilling's remark was a (probably deliberate) simplification of Yeats's attitude, it loosened me up to the extent that I must have then determined not to spend the rest of my days explicating "Byzantium" in sound, objective ways, but to throw in my lot with Yeatsian subjectivity. If death and life were not till man made up the whole, "made lock stock and barrel / Out of his bitter soul," then neither are poems until they elicit the subjective voice of a reader, a voice with enough responsiveness in it to interest at least one other reader in the world.

This essay proposes to be exemplary of such an approach, insofar as it tries to connect statements about "Yeats" or "Yeats's poetry" with what a particular reader (me, or rather my best self) does on a specific poetic occasion. It also assumes that the subjective voice is most likely to be brought into play when one's response is ambiguous in the Empsonian sense — when hitherto uncharted possibilities are discovered in the poems and in oneself. And if talk about the uses of poetry sounds as though it is to be considered as equipment for living, I believe that we do so use it, but in strange ways. Poetry is a criticism of life; the difficulty is, as Paul Goodman says somewhere, in finding out what it's saying.

Some chronological distinctions may be of use at this point: "Early Yeats" designates the poems up through *The Wind Among the Reeds* and those from *The Green Helmet* and *In the Seven Woods* in which a similar manner predominates. "Middle Yeats" refers mainly to *Responsibilities* and *The Wild Swans at Coole* but reaches back to poems in the two previous volumes and forward to *Michael Robartes and the Dancer*; the term as used in this essay is little more than a convenient catch-all for attitudes and experiments tried in those poems from the second decade of this century. "Great Yeats" is *The Tower* and *The Winding Stair;* although I do believe those volumes contain some "great" poems, the term is employed to designate that period of maximum creativity which most critics agree can be located in the 1920's. And then there is "Late Yeats" — the *Last Poems.*

Early Yeats is the right place to begin asking questions about the uses of this poetry. Reading through the collected volume the eyes soon glaze over, as too often The Poet Pleads with the Elemental Powers; and the mind is not fully occupied with things like the ballad of Moll Magee, or the Foxhunter. But even apart from the often intrinsically lulling and deadening character of their rhythms — exactly what Yeats said he was trying to achieve in his early verse — it is more than usually hard to focus: what is there to focus *on* if one isn't specially interested in Yeats's use of the occult, or of Irish themes, or Pre-Raphaelite colors and odors? Pure sound and rhythm? A retreat to aesthetic purity might be in order if the rhymer were less of a histrionic and theatrical personality and more like the speaker of, say, Lionel Johnson's poems; with Yeats the presence of a personality, of an attractive and compelling poetic voice, makes impossible a retreat into admiration of "pure" anything. Years

ago Leavis referred to the "paradoxical energy" informing many
of these early dream-poems and first met in the introductory
"Song of the Happy Shepherd":

> The woods of Arcady are dead,
> And over is their antique joy;
> Of old the world on dreaming fed;
> Grey Truth is now her painted toy;
> Yet still she turns her restless head:
> But O, sick children of the world,
> Of all the many changing things
> In dreary dancing past us whirled,
> To the cracked tune that Chronos sings,
> Words alone are certain good.

On it runs, telling us the same thing over and over again: to
dream, to scorn action and deeds, to look over history and see
how nothing has survived but stories made of words, to gather
some "echo-harbouring" shell and speak fretful words to it so
that they may be reworded melodiously and thereby somehow
comfort us — as this very poem seeks to, by rewording melodiously sad truths. If not so calculatingly arresting in its movement, nor hushedly portentous in its sentiment as the familiar
"Innisfree," the poem still sounds unabashedly theatrical when
put next to a comparable "escapist" lyric by Robert Frost like
"Into My Own," the opening poem in his first volume: "I should
not be witheld but that some day / Into their vastness I should
steal away . . ." Unlike Frost's quiet confession, the histrionic
lecturer who announces that "I will arise and go now" or tells
us not to hunger fiercely after truth is continuous with the grand,
to some readers shrill, Yeatsian voice of "The Tower" or "Under
Ben Bulben" that pontificates about Man, the Soul, Ireland.

The finest moments in Early Yeats occur when this voice calls
out arrestingly and tells us to leave what we're doing and listen
to the news of a place where things go in more heart-stirring
ways than in the fretful ordinary world. Our acceptance of this
voice must be deliberately whole-hearted, naively unqualified by
our burden of knowledge. The "paradoxical energy" of these
languid poems is such that in the best of them Yeats never
simply says how sad or how weary all things are, but puts an

adverb before the adjective: how marvelously weary, how perfectly sad all things are, they exclaim. "Who will go drive with Fergus now / And pierce the deep wood's woven shade" — the poem is alive only when the reader experiences a simple thrill, abandons qualifications, and swings along with the advice "And no more turn aside and brood / Upon love's bitter mystery." Whatever the glories or sorrows of driving with Fergus, you will never be the same afterward; the game is, like that of the Happy Shepherd in the poem quoted earlier, to reword in melodious guile "Love's bitter mystery" so as to make the world of troubles *marvelous* troubles. If the willing reader is touched it is because certain inexpressible yearnings of which he may be either proud or ashamed or both have been touched. He has allowed himself to be taken in but feels rather exhilarated by the whole business.

By contrast, the typical Middle Yeats poem replaces the imperative mode ("dream thou / For fair are poppies on the brow / Dream dream . . .") with a rhetorical interrogative. This change of address is usually described by critics as coincident with Yeats's turning away from the enchantments of unreal dream and settling on the imperfect real world; his playwriting for the Abbey theater helped him achieve a new spare line, less indulgent diction, and the conversational, sometimes colloquial tone in which the poems are conducted. In other words, Yeats is praised for "withering into the truth," for "walking naked" the very way he liked to think of himself as having done.

But it is perhaps a doubtful compliment to accept a poet at no more than his own valuation of himself — as having turned from Dream to Truth — especially since we have the advantage of hindsight. Undeniably the poems have become craftier; the rhetorical interrogative is exploited with great suppleness.

> Why should I blame her that she filled my days
> With misery, or that she would of late
> Have taught to ignorant men most violent ways,
> Or hurled the little streets upon the great,
> Had they but courage equal to desire?
> What could have made her peaceful with a mind
> That nobleness made simple as a fire,

> With beauty like a tightened bow, a kind
> That is not natural in an age like this,
> Being high and solitary and most stern?
> Why, what could she have done, being what she is?
> Was there another Troy for her to burn?

The title, "No Second Troy," assures us that there wasn't — an unnecessary assurance, since it is the poem's essence to leave no room for doubt of any sort. Describing the style as colloquial or conversational is just about as useful or accurate as calling one of Hamlet's soliloquies impassioned. Surely these lines are no closer to language as it is "really used" by men than are the lines of "Who Goes with Fergus" or "Song of the Happy Shepherd." But a useful comment of Edward Thomas' on Frost's "colloquial" style may help with Yeats. Thomas is defending Frost against the strictures of Sturge Moore:

> All he [Frost] insists on is what he believes he finds in all poets — absolute fidelity to the postures which the voice assumes in the most expressive intimate speech. So long as these tones and postures are there he has not the least objection to any vocabulary whatever or any inversion or variation from the customary grammatical forms of talk. In fact I think he would agree that if these tones and postures survive in a complicated and learned and subtle vocabulary and structure the result is likely to be better than if they survive in the easiest form that is in the very words and structures of common speech.[3]

As opposed to the weakly connected flow of "ands" (surely the most significant word in Early Yeats) in the Fergus or Innisfree or Shepherd poems, the complicated and subtle structure of "No Second Troy" is strongly syntactical. Its strength will brook no oppositions, no qualifications, no perhapses.

All energies stand in the service of a style of triumph. Whoever or whatever the poem seems to be about (in this one it is Maud Gonne, a heroic Helen mocked by clown and knave) the ultimate hero is the "I," supreme in his capacities for bringing

3. *Letters from Edward Thomas to Gordon Bottomley* (Oxford: Oxford University Press, 1968), p. 251.

all to mind and disposing of it in a striking way — "Why, what could she have done, being what she is?" The beauty of this poem, and of the best Middle Yeats, is indeed like a tightened bow, on the surface for all to inspect; it doesn't yield any more than does one of Ben Jonson's epigrams (Yeats was reading him at the time) to critical probings after complex feelings and significances. The style of triumph cannot afford such complexities; or rather, they must be wholly contained by the lyric voice which impressively details them ("Why should I blame her . . . What could have made her peaceful . . . Why, what could she have done") only to place them firmly in the last line. For all "her" nobleness, the "I" is finally superior to her, as he is in more obvious ways to the citizens of "an age like this" who cannot appreciate her.

So where does this take us? To the conclusion, I think, that the celebrated turn toward reality in Yeats's poetry from roughly 1903 to 1915 is rather the substitution of one dream for another. Instead of imagining an isle to which he and a beloved would fly when or if things become other than they are, the poet creates tightened structures of rhetoric which protect and exalt him (or, in the case of "To a Friend . . ." appropriate a worthy other like Lady Gregory to Yeatsian lonely rectitude) even as they frequently say that he has been vanquished, is harassed and worn out: "No Second Troy," "The Fascination of What's Difficult," the prologue to *Responsibilities,* "To a Wealthy Man . . ." "To a Friend Whose Work . . ." "To a Shade" — these are some familiar examples. Put another way: if in these middle poems Yeats often achieves the "passionate syntax" he once spoke of, it is to the exclusion of the subjective exploration he later undertook. His very difficult and pregnant motto "In Dreams Begins Responsibility," when read in the light of *Responsibilities* and those poems beginning with "The Fisherman" and "Ego Dominus Tuus" which soon followed it, suggests less a rejection of dream in favor of reality than a felt necessity to ask harder and less rhetorical questions about the self which spins out the dream. How is responsibility incurred? What does it have to do with the kind of poem most worth writing, most subjectively (even more than syntactically) passionate, most sincere? These

questions, and the search for answering qualities of truth, passion, sincerity, kept Yeats productively busy in the remaining
twenty-five years of his life.

    "Ego Dominus Tuus," written in 1915 and published as part
of *Per Amica Silentia Lunae* — Yeats's first full formulation of
the anti-self theory — is usually condescended to as a poem,
then plundered for utterances that demonstrate what the poet
was thinking in 1915. Admittedly, the dialogue form looks precious and the dice are loaded (remember Pound's reference to
the one speaker, *Ille,* as really Willie) but it is an extraordinarily
engaging poem nonetheless, and its bold, extravagant formulations — like those which later mark *A Vision* at its best —
signal an audacious widening of Yeats's horizons. Because it is
longer and more unwieldy and leisurely in its development than
the tensely compressed lyric verse of Middle Yeats, it manages
to stay changing and fresh, not quite assimilated into our ears
even after many readings. Its point of maximum depth comes
after *Ille* has demonstrated, brilliantly and movingly, that the
chief imagination of Christendom, Dante Alighieri, did not "find
himself," but rather an image that was most unlike his own poor
self; *Hic* replies in a sensible you-go-too-far-old-fellow tone:

> Yet surely there are men who have made their art
> Out of no tragic war, lovers of life,
> Impulsive men that look for happiness
> And sing when they have found it.

Robert Browning perhaps? But *Ille* will allow no exceptions:

>   No, not sing,
> For those that love the world serve it in action,
> Grow rich, popular and full of influence,
> And should they paint or write, still it is action:
> The struggle of the fly in marmalade.
> The rhetorician would deceive his neighbours,
> The sentimentalist himself; while art
> Is but a vision of reality.
> What portion in the world can the artist have
> Who has awakened from the common dream
> But dissipation and despair?

Ille uses the same words — dream, reality, the world, singing — made familiar by Yeats's poetry since it announced that the woods of Arcady were dead; but if still exclusive, the analysis is now more interesting. When glossed, the lines say that an artist, a true singer, can have no truck with the world, no "portion . . . But dissipation and despair" since "art / Is but a vision of reality." This is a very sad or very promising situation, depending on how you look at it, so the poem looks at it in both ways: dissipation and despair are not just what morbid aesthetes from the Rhymers' club specialized in but what any man in his necessary dealings with life suffers — "while art / Is but a vision of reality." The phrase can be read with many different stresses, on art or vision or reality or even "Is but," or on all of them alike. A vision of reality, then, both less and more than reality — "Is but." Yeats went on in his autobiography to name this awakening from the common dream with terms like "ecstasy" or "tragedy" or "the quarrel with ourselves." The terms are less important than is the challenge laid down by these lines: namely, how to embody a vision of reality in poetry that is also humanly interesting — in fact, since his terms are so extreme, of supreme human interest — without succumbing to the world, the "common dream" from which bad poets never awaken and by which merely sensitive poets are ruined. Yeats refuses to be, in the words of a famous *New Yorker* cartoon, a very sick little poet.

Taking "Ego Dominus Tuus" as a prolegomenon to any future healthy poetry makes sense in the context of four gravely impressive poems which followed it in the next few years: "Easter 1916," "In Memory of Major Robert Gregory," "A Prayer for My Daughter," and "The Second Coming." Each presents an awakening from a dream, common or otherwise, in the interests of a vision of reality; each focuses intently on some person or event outside the lyric speaker; each presumes to speak in public, though not propagandistic, ways. They have in common the central presence of an unhappy mind — dried up, distracted, unfeeling or in despair — which is touched by something outside itself and changed thereby. An argument could be made that these poems represent the peak of Yeats's achievement, especially for readers dissatisfied with what they see as the self-absorption, aestheticism, or inhumanity of Great and Late Yeats.

The first three ("The Second Coming" less so) require that human feelings and responses be brought into play as Yeats's previous verse has seldom demanded; there is nothing esoteric in their concerns and little in the language that embodies them. They succeed in being intensely personal, subjective (in Yeats's phrase from the *Autobiography*) in that they recreate all that exterior fate snatches away. If in dreams begins responsibility, these are preeminently the poems where those dreams are given their most imaginative, balanced exploration and where their costs — to life — are most vividly set forth.

Frank Kermode's term "romantic image" is still the best for pointing at what is coherent, unified, powerful — at whatever the poet is not — which can only be approximated by the language of a particular poem. But of course merely applying the term to the "image" of a poem is no indicator of quality or value. Some images, as it were, are more "romantic" than others: a simpler-minded Yeats could have worked a good vein and written poem after poem exclaiming about a Fisherman or some comparable anti-self — how admirable, how unlike my own poor self! Instead he discovered that a romantic image need not be merely consolatory, a wistful gesture at something you are not (as if one should improve his shy personality by becoming talkative and outgoing), but something to be literally admired, wondered at, shocked by, not to be contemplated without a tinge of fear or dread. Take the elegy to Robert Gregory. If it consisted only of endless variations on what a splendid portmanteau fellow Gregory was ("Soldier, scholar, horseman, he, / And all he did done perfectly") the poem would, and to some extent does, have the limitations of conventional special pleading. It moves rather towards a conclusion where Gregory becomes an image, a pure spirit who understood "all" — "All lovely intricacies of a house," "All work in metal or in wood" — in his undivided, unified being "As though he had but that one trade alone." So it is with something like self-consummation — for reader and poet — that this spirit's apotheosis is evoked:

> Some burn damp faggots, others may consume
> The entire combustible world in one small room
> As though dried straw, and if we turn about

> The bare chimney is gone black out
> Because the work had finished in that flare.
> Soldier, scholar, horseman, he,
> As 'twere all life's epitome.
> What made us dream that he could comb grey hair?

What indeed! The question is not quite so loaded as "Was there another Troy for her to burn?" nor so simply inviting as "Who will go drive with Fergus now." The poet has been awakened from one of those "common dreams" — of the loved hero's living to comb grey hair — and the alternative is not dissipation or despair; rather, the sudden, glamorous, and passionate extinction of life. A passage from Yeats's autobiography tells us about violent energy, like a fire of straw, being useless in the arts. But we don't need it here to see that the poet, burning damp faggots like the rest of us, has nevertheless preserved himself, has made something out of experience maybe less glamorous but surely more enduring than any "flare" set off by Gregory. Yet this self-preservation isn't presented as a triumph, and more is asked of the reader here than in earlier poems: while he must give his admiration to Gregory — the image — he must also imagine experience through the complex, depressed, and extraordinarily *tonal* world of the man who remains behind: "I had thought, seeing how bitter is that wind / That shakes the shutter . . ." Nobody gets a cheer at the end of the poem. There is no convenient outlet for one's mixed feelings about heroic life, the art that celebrates it, and the artist who suffers, with whatever discretion, to create it.

It is "Easter 1916" that most movingly depicts how responsibility begins in dreams. After the flexible tone of the first two sections places the Irish revolutionaries, as well as the speaker's social — indeed tonal — judgments of them ("What voice more sweet than hers / When, young and beautiful / She rode to harriers?"), an anonymous voice sings out:

> Hearts with one purpose alone
> Through summer and winter seem
> Enchanted to a stone
> To trouble the living stream.
> The horse that comes from the road,

> The rider, the birds that range
> From cloud to tumbling cloud,
> Minute by minute they change . . .
> The stone's in the midst of all.

Efforts to paraphrase this moment are even less satisfactory than usual; we know by section four when Yeats points the moral ("Too long a sacrifice / Can make a stone of the heart") that the revolutionaries have been transformed utterly, beyond the language of social judgment; also that they have been enchanted to a stone, a fixed idea which turned their hearts to stone. But as, in the flux of section three, "the long-legged moor-hens dive, / And hens to moor-cocks call," it's not clear that we hold *any* distinct idea. Enchanted by events beyond our discourse we wake only to confront the painful questions which end the poem, finally and most unbearably — "And what if excess of love / Bewildered them till they died?"

After these questions the salute to MacDonagh and Mac-Bride and the repetition of "A terrible beauty is born" are ways of using words that recognize their formulaic character, thus their limitations. Even in using them one has looked beyond them. To write, in the language of "The Fisherman," a poem cold and passionate as the dawn, which is what Yeats did in "Easter 1916," demands a full exploitation of the tone and syntax through which ordinary life — "the casual comedy" — is set forth. Then beyond that, springing out from it and against it, is the momentary presence of a toneless voice singing of a realm beyond comedy or bitterness or society, where horses plash and moor-cocks call and where things do not yield up their meanings to the words that would summarize them. The result is a muted and impersonal poem which remains with us and is not easy to live with; its "responsibility" involves no clear course of action but rather a fitful seeing-around of all action.

Compared to this truly ambiguous poem, "The Second Coming" is single-minded, visionary, even optimistic in its bearing as it uses and transforms the public situation of "Easter 1916" — "The best lack all conviction, while the worst / Are full of passionate intensity" — into striking private capital. The visionary motive hints of things to come: of "Sailing to Byzantium," "Two

Songs from a Play," "Leda and the Swan"; of "Byzantium," "The Gyres," and "Lapis Lazuli." Such poems are informed with a voice by turns hushed and exultant: neglecting the middle range of speech, relatively uninterested in cultivating nuance and shade of tone, it is at home only in extremes of pitch, it brooks no obstacles nor is it concerned with posing unanswerable questions to itself. Leavis called Shakespeare's verse "exploratory-creative" of experience; though some of Yeats's poems could be so termed, they are not the ones in the list above, whose prevailing gesture towards experience is imperious or dismissive or brilliantly exploitive of it. As with Early Yeats the favored mood is imperative; as with Middle Yeats the style of triumph is in vogue, though bolstered now by systematic mythical-historical "truths" of character and epoch.

For all their invocations of gyres, the Magnus Annus, a vast image out of Spiritus Mundi — the difficulties of these poems are superficial, mainly disappearing once one finds the way around their surfaces; they change and deepen less upon re-reading than do the poems I term ambiguous. One recites, declaims, gestures his way through "The Second Coming" or "Byzantium" (what pleasure there is, say, in intoning "At midnight on the emperor's pavement flit / Flames no faggot feeds nor steel has lit") and finds himself close to an experience in pure declamatory rhythms. So too the outcome of these poems seems predestined, somehow made up in the poet's mind before he wrote the first line — though of course the revisions tell us this was not in fact the case. As for their personal reference, the presence of an "I" in "The Second Coming" ("The darkness drops again; but now I know . . .") or in "Byzantium" ("I hail the superhuman / I call it birth in life . . .") is but a convenience, a register for visionary supersensations from which knowledge is ecstatically gained.

In other words, little or no complex penetration of a mind occurs in these poems, with the result that the reader, too, escapes unscathed, changed not utterly but only theatrically, very much for the nonce. Yeats's famous remark about beginning to live when we conceive life as tragedy is anterior to these poems, which, though they can be *about* tragedy — as in "Lapis Lazuli" — about the "fury and the mire of human veins" ("Byzantium"), are by that token outside of it, detached from it. And the reader is occupied with watching a performance by a magnificently skilled conjurer (what will he think of next? where will he move?) rather than with bearing witness to tragic experience undergone through the sequence of the poem.

But Yeats knew very well that if conceiving life as tragedy is the beginning of living, then poems would transcend the fury and mire of human veins only at their peril. Not uncritical of his own romantic image, he attempted, increasingly in the poems from *The Tower* and beyond, to put difficulties in the way of the would-be transcender. So in a poem like "Dialogue of Self and Soul" the enraptured Soul affirms the virtues of silence to the degree that he fades right out of the poem, conveniently leaving Self three stanzas in which to proclaim his commitment to the "frog-spawn of a blind man's ditch," then, having converted life to its lowest terms, to forgive himself and affirm the lot:

> We must laugh and we must sing,
> We are blest by everything.
> Everything we look upon is blest.

Very well, and undeniably thrilling, but as much of a brag as the corresponding movement upward towards becoming a golden bird set on a bow, and no more the occasion for complex feelings on the reader's part. For all its stylistic nobility this sudden casting out of remorse is a bit glib.

I want now to argue that the deepest poetic alternative to the arrogant single-mindedness with which a romantic image disdains and rejects the world is not a corresponding single-mindedness in the other direction, saying Yes rather than No to life. Yeats's problem, which he came to grips with superbly in a number of poems, was to get the rival claims of the image and of life — as he often called it, the Heart — stated in all their fulness and exclusiveness; then to end the poem in such a way that neither he nor the reader could say exactly where triumph was, or if it were properly a triumph at all. Not to give in to misery, to the passive suffering of which he accused Wilfred Owen's poetry, nor loudly to affirm "What matter"; but, in Jar-

rell's marvelous phrase about Frost's best work, to write poems
which make either optimism or pessimism a hopeful evasion.

> Heart-mysteries there, and yet when all is said
> It was the dream itself enchanted me:

The poems to be considered from Great and Late Yeats I first
selected by impulse as particularly compelling, only to see on
reflection their common concern with those matters of the heart
experienced before "all is said." "What shall I do with this absurdity — O heart, O troubled heart" begins "The Tower"; and
though the question refers to the "caricature" of "decrepit age,"
the poem proceeds to locate the heart's trouble in a less facile
way. "The Tower," along with "Meditations in Time of Civil
War," "Among School Children," "Her Vision in the Wood,"
"Parnell's Funeral," "The Circus Animals' Desertion," and
others, are evidence of a human fineness of response that has
been ignored by those who accuse Yeats of ending where he
began, in but a fancier version of aestheticism. Their pleasures
and difficulties are many; I shall select from them only a few
crucial moments where the engaged reader's life is fullest.

Part I of "The Tower" asks what to do with decrepit age, then
II takes thirteen winding stanzas to prepare for the closing affirmation of III. The final stanza of II is my interest, coming as
it does after the poet has sent imagination forth to call up all
sorts of people from history, legend, his own writings as aids and
witnesses to his dilemma. This calling up is often broken in
upon by the caller's impatience with his own game ("And followed up those baying creatures towards — / O towards I have
forgotten what — enough!"); only Hanrahan is finally allowed
to remain, on the purely fictional grounds that he has "reckoned
up every unforeknown, unseeing / Plunge . . . into the labyrinth of another's being." At this point Yeats poses the question
all this rambling has led up to:

> Does the imagination dwell the most
> Upon a woman won or a woman lost?
> If on the lost, admit you turned aside
> From a great labyrinth out of pride,

> Cowardice, some silly over-subtle thought
> Or anything called conscience once;
> And that if memory recur, the sun's
> Under eclipse and the day blotted out.

At which point the day is blotted out and the "I" proceeds to write his will, choosing "upstanding men" who, like the Fisherman of an earlier poem, do not exist, are but a dream. Yet this resolution, grand as it is, is also somewhat diversionary: the poignancy brought into the poem by asking shrewdly whether the imagination dwells the most on a woman lost (and clearly suggesting that it does) cannot be blotted out. "Too long a sacrifice can make a stone of the heart" ran the line from "Easter 1916." In terms of "The Tower" one should read: too long a dwelling on the romantic image of what you don't have, be it Maud Gonne or another, has its own costs to the heart. And though the third section of the poem boldly sets out to make these human costs "Seem but the clouds of the sky / When the horizon fades," the very beautiful "bird's sleepy cry" which ends the poem only too hauntingly reminds us of them.

The costs of homage to the romantic image are resonantly generalized in the penultimate stanza of "Among School Children":

> Both nuns and mothers worship images,
> But those the candles light are not as those
> That animate a mother's reveries,
> But keep a marble or a bronze repose.
> And yet they too break hearts — O Presences
> That passion, piety or affection knows,
> And that all heavenly glory symbolise —
> O self-born mockers of man's enterprise;

These heartbreakers and mockers of man's enterprise live in the "where" of the final stanza, that mythical realm where art is not a vision of reality but indistinguishable from it: an unironic paradise where leaf, blossom, or bole, dancer and dance, are one. Yeats's paradise is not treated with the condescending wit Wallace Stevens employs in "Sunday Morning" to set forth his boringly perfect realm, because it is evoked out of a less firm acceptance of our mortal lot than is felt when Stevens intones "Death is the mother of beauty." To call, as Yeats does, the images "self-born mockers of man's enterprise" is to speak painfully from *here,* where sons give mothers pains and nuns can't live up to their aspirations, where the extravagance of lyric invention and its grandeur of apostrophe ("O chestnut-tree, great-rooted blossomer") is a measure of how much deprivation a man can feel because he is what he is, alas, and not another thing.

"Among School Children" seems to me Yeats's finest poem because it is inclusive, ultimately impersonal but also modest, as the old scarecrow fades out into the guise of any and all of us. I can't imagine, that is, a reader who would not want to be spoken for by the last two stanzas of the poem, stanzas which elevate and ennoble life rather than transcend it or puff it up or sweep it out of the way. They are in addition an antidote to over-zealous iconographers who would focus excitedly only on the meanings of chestnut-tree or dancer, forgetting that "And yet they too break hearts." Yeats went on to write a wonderful poem about an old woman, bitter in her bodily misery, who thought she was watching a ritual grieving for the fatal wounding of Adonis ("It seemed a Quattrocento painter's throng, / A thoughtless image of Mantegna's thought") when all the time it was her own suffering lover, who suddenly — a "beast-torn wreck" — fixes an eye on the woman, and she proceeds to fall senseless among the crowd, unaware "That they had brought no fabulous symbol there / But my heart's victim and its torturer." The imagination does dwell the most upon a woman (or a man) lost; no fabulous symbol there, but a heart's victim and torturer. If a reader doesn't feel the tug at his own heart no critic should try to argue him into it. But "Her Vision in the Wood" is, like "Among School Children," both humanizing and tragic in the peculiarly ecstatic way Yeats conceived of tragedy; all arrogant self-congratulation has been purged, leaving only the best poetic self.

These late poems speak most movingly about the paradox of being a poet: how a heightened capacity for the imaginative entertaining of images, dreams, "presences" seems to involve waverings, dissatisfactions, guilt about matters of the heart —

the human condition — and attendant self-lacerations ("Admit
that you turned aside from a great labyrinth"). Wordsworth's
fine lines from "Resolution and Independence" are about all
men — "As high as we have mounted in delight / In our dejection do we sink as low." But since the poet mounts highest in
delight and it is his obligation to share this delight with other
men, then it seems hard that "We poets in our youth begin in
gladness / But thereof come in the end despondency and madness." Out of this discovery, and out of his own poems about
the heart as victim and torturer, came the heroic stock-taking of
what has good imaginative reason to be thought of as Yeats's
final poem, "The Circus Animals' Desertion." It is a bona fide
modernist poem in that, like so much of Eliot or Stevens or
Williams, it is about itself and about Poetry, extraordinarily self-
absorbed even as it mounts a criticism of certain aggrandizing
and inhuman tendencies in the poet's omnivorous self. It also
manages to be — and this in distinction to many modernist
poems — boldly though not crassly unrepentant, and it ends in
exultation, not prayer. In the first of its three parts (a single
stanza) the "broken man" says he may have to be satisfied with
his heart now in dried-up age, though he remembers how his circus animals, winter and summer, have been on show. He then
goes on, in II, to name some of them — old performers and
figures like Oisin or the protagonist of *The Countess Cathleen* —
and tells how these dreams and images usurped the thought and
love usually devoted to human affairs. The final stanza of II:

> And when the Fool and Blind Man stole the bread
> Cuchulain fought the ungovernable sea;
> Heart-mysteries there, and yet when all is said
> It was the dream itself enchanted me;
> Character isolated by a deed
> To engross the present and dominate memory.
> Players and painted stage took all my love,
> And not those things that they were emblems of.

The beautifully pointed economy and accuracy of these lines,
lordly in their cool analysis of how it was, won't stand to be
contradicted; and it has seemed to some readers that the famous

single stanza which ends the poem in III comes down unequivo-
cally, and at long last, on the side of the heart and opposed to
the "masterful images" that grew in pure mind. Those who want
Yeats to emerge as a last-minute humanist, saved in the knick
of time from his own players and painted stage, tend to salute
this final stanza as a very good thing to have said. But what in
fact *is* said? How is the heart affirmed and accepted?

> These masterful images because complete
> Grew in pure mind, but out of what began?
> A mound of refuse or the sweepings of a street,
> Old kettles, old bottles, and a broken can,
> Old iron, old bones, old rags, that raving slut
> Who keeps the till. Now that my ladder's gone,
> I must lie down where all the ladders start,
> In the foul rag-and-bone shop of the heart.

This poetry says, when all the poetry is taken away from it, that
with the circus animals, the ladder gone, the poet will settle at
last for his heart in all its sordidness and poverty. Yet with the
poetry left in, as it were, the effect is to substitute a whole new
array of circus animals for the old departed ones, the difference
being that the new ones are called by sensationally low names
like "that raving slut / Who keeps the till." Who will go drive
with Fergus now? Yeats never ceases to issue invitations to himself; if the place of lying down is to be the heart rather than the
dream he will make sure it's no ordinary heart, but one never
seen before on sea or land — a foul rag-and-bone shop of a
heart. When all is said it was the dream itself that enchanted
him: but this final poem says that "all" most fully and elo-
quently.

Triumph or defeat, then? Optimistic or pessimistic? A reader
confronted with this poem can't use it to improve his own life as
a shot in the arm to further endeavours of a particular sort. If
he accepts it he must live with a strange imagination whose intransigence is supreme, whose reference to human life is as
ambiguous as the acceptance of the heart in "The Circus Animals' Desertion." And perhaps the main or only use of Yeats's
poetry is that it teaches us to extend our notions of what it is

to accept the heart, to be enchanted by a dream; that — as "Character" is "isolated by a deed / To engross the present and dominate memory" — his poetry so engrosses and dominates us as to make it unclear and unimportant whether we use it or are used by it.

JOHN PAUL RUSSO

Richards and the Search for Critical Instruments

From his very first books down to *So Much Nearer* (1968) and
Poetries and Sciences (1970), I. A. Richards has exposed the
dangers that arise from being overly committed to one critical
metaphor or model or to what Coleridge calls a "speculative instrument" for the mind. Shakespeare found this "glassy essence"
resistant to definition, though he never stopped seeking metaphors:

> nor doth the eye itself,
> That most pure spirit of sense, behold itself,
> Not going from itself . . .
> For speculation turns not to itself
> Till it hath travelled and is married there
> Where it may view itself.
> *Troilus and Cressida,* III.iii.105

The eye serves as the model, but the mind is — the "itself,"
which Shakespeare almost crystallizes by repeating the word
"itself." Matter has no *Inward,* Coleridge argues in the *Biographia Literaria;* planes give way to successive planes of matter.

133

But the mind he names the *"something-nothing-every-thing."*
The critical models we construct for the mind (and *in* the mind)
have ways of taking over completely. Yet as most thinkers have
agreed, in no way other than by metaphor can one consider what
the mind really is. Locke, one recalls, compared the mind to a
dark cabinet, or a room, empty at birth but gradually furnished
with the gaudy decor of experience. Hume likened it to a theatre; Coleridge again to a fair luminous cloud, Wordsworth to a
dark yew tree. I. A. Richards likens the mind to "synaesthetic
equilibrium" or the balance and coordination of opposed impulses or, quoting Eliot's comment on it, "a perfectly-working
mental Roneo Steel Cabinet System." Richards admits of Eliot,
"a few decades later he would have called it a Computer." [1]

"Computer," "feedback," and "feedforward" have in fact
made their way into the Richardsian vocabulary, but Richards
has always maintained what he calls a hearty skepticism about
his models that is the heritage of a cultural and scientific relativism. From one field of learning to the other, thinkers emphasize the profound difference between employing the metaphor
or model and treating it as the literal thing. By his principle of
complementarity Niels Bohr laid down that it was impossible to
describe a system in abstraction from the very apparatus used for
its investigation; "rather, a variety of models, each corresponding
to a possible experimental arrangement and all required for a
complete description of possible physical experience, stand in a
complementary relation to one another . . . each is a necessary
part of the complete description." And Gilbert Ryle defines
metaphor as the "presentation of facts belonging to one category
in the idioms appropriate to another." [2] Yet the "possible physical experience" and the "facts belonging to one category," when
dealing with the mind, are the *something-nothing-every-thing.*
Most people in our culture, Richards warns in *Design for Escape*

1. On two occasions I. A. Richards kindly offered to read and correct
my lectures on his work. He made numerous interlinear notes and lined
the margins as well. I have included a number of these notes in the
text and will indicate them hereafter simply as "R.n."
2. J. Robert Oppenheimer's phrasing of the principle of complementarity is quoted by Richards in *Speculative Instruments* (New York:
Harcourt Brace, 1955), pp. 114–115; Gilbert Ryle, *The Concept of Mind*
(London: Hutchinson, 1949), p. 8.

(1968), cannot differentiate between the model and the mind
— the model has taken over completely[3] — hence the ease with
which certain dials are twisted one way or another by the Establishment or the anti-Establishment. How can the mind use the
model — for poetry, for learning, for criticism — and not be
used by it? Richards has explored this question more continu-
ously than any other writer on language and literature in our
century. He remarked in *Practical Criticism* (1929) that "nine-
tenths, at the least, of the ideas and the annexed emotional responses that are passed on — by the cinema, the press, friends
and relatives, teachers, the clergy . . . to an average child of
this century are — judged by the standards of poetry — crude
and vague rather than subtle and appropriate." In 1968 he wrote
that "things are getting worse with the world, not better —
largely because of a decreasing supply of effectively capable people," and he proceeded to map out a strategy.[4]

How can we use "speculative instruments" as models to think
with "as well as about," Richards adds, "about only through
thinking wittingly with them?" (R.n.) Shall we put a Richards'
model to the test?

In the first decades of the century Cambridge University was
a center of philosophical controversy. "You had no apparent
awareness — quite contrary to the fact," Richards reminisces,
"no apparent awareness in lecturers that others had ever thought
about [philosophical thinking and language] before. Whitehead,
Russell, Moore, McTaggart and the rest were all prophets, as it
were, of various kinds. They would occasionally make a reference to someone — but it was in order to controvert." Their
very contrary attempts at proselytizing the young Richards left
him philosophically agnostic or, rather, persuaded him that philosophy was running aground on the problem of meaning, of

3. "Maybe it was Korzybski who most insisted on the point in modern
times. Forgetting that 'the map is NOT the region' is an error surely as
old as MIND" (R.n.). See Alfred Korzybski, *Science and Sanity: An
Introduction to Non-Aristotelian Systems and General Semantics* (1933),
4th ed. (Lakeville, Conn.: International Non-Aristotelian Library Publishing Co., 1958), p. 58.

4. *Practical Criticism: A Study of Literary Judgment* (New York:
Harcourt Brace, 1929), p. 248; *Design for Escape: World Education
through Modern Media* (New York: Harcourt Brace, 1968), p. 3.

semantics, of the central importance of language in the determination of thinking. Late on the night of 11 November 1918, in Cambridge a night of riots and rejoicing over the Armistice, Richards found himself in a long conversation with C. K. Ogden, from whom he had rented rooms next to the Cavendish Laboratory. "We went on and on, and the whole of our book, *The Meaning of Meaning,* was talked out clearly in two hours. One of the chapters was on the theory of definitions; we found we could agree. It's a most extraordinary experience, finding you can agree with someone . . . It doesn't perhaps look as though it was such fun, but it was much of it written in the spirit of 'Here's a nice half-brick, Whom shall we throw it at?' " [5]

Four years later Richards published his critique on art theory in *The Foundations of Aesthetics,* written in collaboration with C. K. Ogden and James Wood. His ideas are fully articulated in *The Meaning of Meaning* (1923), written with Ogden, and *Principles of Literary Criticism* (1924). Although his concern, then as now, was primarily language, he found it necessary to construct a theory of mind and value, or "intellectual priorities." With the underpinnings of a solid British empiricism he built a model on the best strictly neurological principles in postwar England. In his detour to science he appears more positive than the Cambridge positivists with whom he had parted company. Were they, as he ponders now, "a shade too abstract?" "I should have made it clear my model was to be found in Sherrington" (R.n.), writes Richards; for nowhere in his early works is Sherrington mentioned by name. This should not appear unusual, for the terms and scientific metaphors of Sherrington and his school were commonly known and applied by scientists and social scientists alike.[6]

5. "I. A. Richards: An Interview conducted by B. A. Boucher and J. P. Russo," *Harvard Advocate,* 103 (December 1969), 3.
6. For example, W. B. Pillsbury, *Attention* (London, 1908), pp. 75, 239, 259; H. R. Marshall, *Consciousness* (New York, 1909), p. 101; William McDougall, *Body and Mind* (New York, 1911), pp. 265–268 and esp. pp. 272–280; Edwin B. Holt, *The Concept of Consciousness* (London, 1914), pp. 320–321, 328; and Henri Piéron, *Le Cerveau et la pensée* (Paris, 1923), trans. C. K. Ogden as *Thought and the Brain* (New York and London, 1927), pp. 3–23. On occasion, metaphors are shared; the telephone exchange and the railroad junction were popular models for the mind, an early instance of nature's imitating technology.

Sir Charles Scott Sherrington (1857–1952) studied at Cambridge a generation before Richards. There he worked in the laboratory of Professor Michael Foster, a physiologist with Darwinian leanings, who had served as T. H. Huxley's demonstrator in the first course on practical physiology in London in 1870. Sherrington took a double first in the Natural Science Tripos, received his B.A. in 1884, and three years later was elected Fellow of Gonville and Caius College. Afterwards he became Holt Professor of Physiology at Liverpool (1895–1913) and Wayneflete Professor of Physiology at Oxford (1913–1935). He was awarded the Order of Merit in 1924 and the Nobel Prize in Medicine in 1932. An experimental genius of the first magnitude, Sherrington ranks among the most distinguished biologists of the century, and his *Integrative Action of the Nervous System* (1906) has become a classic in its field. His work, according to Judith P. Swazey, "gave unified meaning to a host of phenomena and processes previously discussed in isolation." Sir John Eccles, a leading scientist in this field today, writes that "in almost every respect Sherrington's experimental and conceptual developments from the 1880's to 1906 were on the direct path to current views of the nervous system's integrative action." [7]

"Impulse" is a neurophysiological term that has a long scientific history. It derives from the studies of Thomas Willis, who became Sedleian Professor of Natural Philosophy at Oxford in 1660. To Willis an impulse was simply the movement of animal spirits — an ancestor of the modern nerve "message" — along or through a fibre or in the brain, regarded as a kind of diffused nerve. In Sherrington's model the impulse signifies a "state of excitement," a physicochemical event occurring upon some stimulus from the environment. Such impulses travel through the nervous system in patterns known as reflex arcs, which are complexly integrated, as Sherrington writes, in order to "bind one part of the organism to another part in such a way that what the environment is doing to the organism at one place may appropriately call forth or restrain movement or secretion in the

7. Swazey, *Reflexes and Motor Integration: Sherrington's Concept of Integrative Action* (Cambridge, Mass.: Harvard University Press, 1969), pp. 169, 172.

muscles or glands wherever situated in the organism." [8] Reflex arcs interpenetrate unceasingly, since about three billion impulses are generated each second.

The unifying thesis of *Integrative Action,* the one from which Richards would draw his model, concerns the interplay of various impulses along their reflex arcs in the nervous system, including "all the resources of" the brain (R.n.). What happens when different impulses compete with one another for the activation or restraint of a given muscle? "The usual thing in nature is not for one exciting stimulus to begin immediately after another ceases, but for an array of environmental agents acting concurrently on the animal at any moment to exhibit correlative change in regard to it, so that one or other group of them becomes — generally by increase in intensity — temporarily prepotent. Thus there dominates now this group, now that group in turn." [9] To describe how impulses are coordinated and how some eventually become dominant, Sherrington postulated the "principle of the common path." Impulses are either "allied" or "antagonistic" to one another as they stand in competition for the various pathways of the nervous system; a common path is the one upon which the allied impulses must travel to perform (or restrain) a given action. The *final common path,* the one that leads out of the nervous system into the effecting muscle, must both canalize all essential impulses and avert all unnecessary ones, according to their relative merit (that is, intensity, frequency) in performing the action. The final common path is teleologically oriented toward serving but one purpose at a time. The nervous system coordinates the entire process, if not at the discretion of the individual will, then in response to outside forces acting upon the individual.

For his own model Richards borrowed the concept of the final common path and, as he notes, "generalized the term to make it cover all 'final common paths,' however complex, and their competitions as to outcomes" (R.n.). In effect, he generalized the term to refer to all the activities of the mind; later he extended

8. Quoted by Lord Cohen of Birkenhead in *Sherrington: Physiologist, Philosopher and Poet,* The Sherrington Lectures IV (Liverpool: Liverpool University Press, 1958), p. 34.
9. Charles S. Sherrington, *The Integrative Action of the Nervous System* (New York: Charles Scribner's Sons, 1906), p. 118.

his model to refer to all the "activities" of a poem. Richards, too, begins with the stimulus — which could be an image or metaphor in a poem — that elicits or triggers the impulse. Like Sherrington's "allied" and "antagonistic" impulses, Richards' impulses may be either "appetencies" ("strivings towards") or "aversions" ("turnings from"). Whether appetencies or aversions are desirable or not depends upon their compatibilities with other impulses.[10]

Sometimes the consequence of a mental event is simply action:

$$\textit{stimulus to impulse to action.}$$

However, where a great number of different impulses (both appetencies and aversions) converge about the final common path, and when they tend to balance one another, impulses resolve into attitudes, "imaginal and incipient activities or tendencies to action," *but not actions themselves.* In a saint or a debauchee, one attitude or set of impulses tyrannizes the rest — to the individual's detriment and paralysis. For Richards, "fortunate people" are those who are able to entertain many different attitudes and to achieve thereby a "well-balanced life," a "fine ordering of responses" with impulses "mutually modified," an "energy system of prodigious complexity and extreme delicacy of organisation which has an indefinitely large number of stable poises" and, as one might expect after Sherrington but with a Richardsian twist, "integrity" defined as "the wholeness . . . of the experience." [11]

At this point one should stress that Richards manufactures intellectual categories out of physical ones. He readily admits that his definition of impulses is "vague . . . but therefore suit-

10. "Glad you stress the *Integrative Action.* Sherrington, after retirement, wrote what may be an important philosophical book. But though I often tried, I never managed to read much of it with any profit. The *Integrative Action* book I did read. It became for me an instrument I could think *with*" (R.n.).

11. *Principles of Literary Criticism* (London: Kegan Paul, 1925), pp. 112, 53, 62, 243, 104, 276; see also *Science and Poetry* for a discussion of the mind "as a system of very delicately poised balances, a system which so long as we are in health is constantly *growing*," reprinted in *Poetries and Sciences* (New York: W. W. Norton, 1970), p. 25.

able to our at present incomplete and hazy knowledge of how
impulses are related." While he values the scientific basis of his
model — "it will be observed that no special ethical idea is introduced" — he is at pains to underscore its hypothetical nature.
Furthermore, in acknowledging his debt to Bentham's *Principles
of Morals and Legislation,* Richards cautiously defends his concept of value against charges of hedonism, of making the arts a
"box where sweets compacted lie." Following Mill and G. E.
Moore in their revision of utilitarianism, he argues that "no
hedonic theory of value will fit the facts over even a small part of
the field, since it must take what is a concomitant merely of a
phase in the process of satisfaction as the mainspring of the
whole." [12] Thus if stimuli trigger impulses, nevertheless "triggering does not work without the explosives in the cartridge,"
writes Richards in a marginal note, "and it is they who really
?create? — in connection with the barrel — the shot" (R.n.).

Several passages help reveal how Richards developed his
model out of Sherrington. The basic unit in Sherrington's theory
is the reflex:

A simple reflex is probably a purely abstract conception, because all
parts of the nervous system are connected together and no part of it
is probably ever capable of reaction without affecting and being
affected by various other parts, and it is a system certainly never
absolutely at rest. But the simple reflex is a convenient, if not a
probable fiction. Reflexes are of various degrees of complexity, and
it is helpful in analyzing complex reflexes to separate from them
reflex components which we may consider apart and therefore treat
as though they were simple reflexes.
                    Integrative Action of the Nervous System, pp. 7–8

Richards' description of *his* basic unit, the impulse, parallels
Sherrington's closely:

In actual experience single impulses of course never occur. Even the
simplest human reflexes are very intricate bundles of mutually de-

12. *Principles of Literary Criticism,* pp. 51, 70. See also pp. 59–60. For
a recent reformulation and a new genetic model, see *So Much Nearer:
Essays Toward a World English* (New York: Harcourt Brace, 1968),
p. 4.

pendent impulses, and in any actual human behavior the number of simultaneous and connected impulses occurring is beyond estimation. The simple impulse in fact is a limit, and the only impulses psychology is concerned with are the complex. It is often convenient to speak as though simple impulses were in question, as when we speak of an impulse of hunger, or an impulse to laugh, but we must not forget how intricate all our activities are.

Principles of Literary Criticism, p. 86

On a higher plane the integration of "reflexes" or "impulses" results in behavioral patterns:

With the nervous system intact the reactions of the various parts of that system, the "simple reflexes," are ever combined into great unitary harmonies, actions which in their sequence one upon another constitute . . . "behaviour . . ."   *Integrative Action,* p. 237

Most behaviour is a reconciliation between the various acts which would satisfy the different impulses which combine to produce it; and the richness and interest of the feel of it in consciousness depends upon the variety of the impulses engaged.   *Principles,* p. 109

What for Sherrington are "great unitary harmonies" on a physical level become for Richards the full interplay and "reconciliation" of a wide variety of attitudes. Elsewhere Sherrington defines a higher organism on the evolutionary scale as one capable of dominating its environment "more variously and extensively." The highest forms on the scale will therefore be among the latest.

This grading of rank in the animal scale will be nowhere more apparent than in the nervous system . . . The more numerous and extensive the responses made by a creature to the actions of the world around upon its receptors, the more completely will the bundle of reflexes, which from this standpoint the creature is, figure the complexity of the world around, mirroring it more completely than do the bundles of reflexes composing "lower" creatures.

Integrative Action, p. 237

According to Richards' theory, Sherrington's phylogenic model has its counterpart within the individual mind; and the model is employed to differentiate between cruder and more sophisticated responses and, later, between cruder and more sophisticated people:

> The primitive and in a sense natural outcome of stimulus is action; the more simple the situation with which the mind is engaged, the closer is the connection between the stimulus and some overt response in action, and in general the less rich and full is the consciousness attendant . . . The increased complexity of the situation and the greater delicacy and appropriateness of the movements required for convenience and safety, call forth far more complicated goings on in the mind . . . Indeed, the difference between the intelligent or refined, and the stupid or crass person is a difference in the extent to which overt action can be replaced by incipient and imaginal action.   *Principles*, pp. 109, 111

All experience, then, whether aesthetic or otherwise, differs only in degree and not fundamentally in kind — only to the degree to which it stimulates impulses and the manner in which they interplay. "When we say that anything is good we mean that it satisfies, and by a good experience we mean one in which the impulses which make it are fulfilled and successful." [13] For the mind as a whole consists of "bundles of mutually dependent impulses" — the metaphor is borrowed directly from Sherrington — each in its self-seeking quasi-Darwinian way desiring satisfaction, either in being spent in action to adjust to or dominate the environment, or in becoming the dominant attitude. Since our own object in life is to keep as little frustrated as possible, certain kinds of experience, of which poetic experience is the highest to Richards, will be more highly organized and hence more valuable than others. Experiences are valuable when they satisfy impulses without involving the frustration of equal or more important impulses. To quote Hesiod on the birth of the Muses, "They bring forgetfulness of sorrows / and rest from anxieties" (Lattimore trans.).

Because it would be impossible here to do little more than suggest the complexity and development of Richards' theory of

13. *Ibid.*, p. 58. "The kind / degree opposition is usually a prompter to reflection; you can always GENERALIZE so that what has been kind-difference becomes DEGREE only. See on this my *Basic Rules of Reason* [London, 1933], pp. 122–124" (R.n.).

language over the past fifty years, I shall confine attention to the relation between the Sherringtonian model and the "activities" of a poem. In this way the early works — *The Meaning of Meaning* through *Coleridge on Imagination* (1935) — can be treated together conveniently without doing serious injustice to the integrity of each volume. The concept of the final common path is taken to cover all the elements of the poem as well as the mind. But the poem proves to be a very different entity from either the poet's or the reader's organization of impulses, because the poem is an organism all to itself. Like the mind, it is an "energy system" full of opposing attitudes that continually formulate stable, if temporary, poises — poises that tumble only to allow a new equilibrium to establish itself. At times these poises subtly interpenetrate their respective contexts. The poem comes equipped with its own positive and negative poles, balancing a yes with a no: in tragedy, for example, pity with fear. Some of Richards' more recent essays and addresses, "How does a poem know when it is finished?" (1963) and "How a poem protects itself" (1969), point to the living essence and tension of the aesthetic object.

Two basic uses of language were formulated in *The Meaning of Meaning* and *Principles;* both uses involve the intentions or the meanings "which words, as we use them, carry, owing to the contexts (settings) within which and through which . . . they work" (R.n.).

1. Referential language leads people to think about this rather than that. It may be detected by asking whether a given statement is true in the strict scientific sense. If the question is meaningful, then the language is referential. Such language enables people to think in one way or another (in one way *rather* than another). In a marginal note Richards writes that referential language has the purpose of "pointing to whatever; it leaves it to the whatevers to do any ʔconvincingʔ that occurs."

2. Emotive language stimulates impulses that form emotional attitudes. This type of language may use reference, but its effects are measured in terms of its capacity for organizing attitudes on as broad a basis as possible. "Reference is frequently the means of releasing (triggering) components of the poem" (R.n.). In *Science and Poetry* (1926) the term "pseudo-statement" is in-

troduced to label a type of statement justified entirely by its
effect in realizing or organizing impulses into attitudes. It is
something which may seem to give information about the world
through plot, image, and sound. But "whether it does so or not
isn't poetically important. (Medically it might be)" (R.n.). In a
way pseudo-statements resemble Eliot's burglar's meat, what the
poet throws to the dog to keep him busy and quiet while he goes
about the really important business.

According to the Sherringtonian model, referential language
forms a convenient parallel for

$$stimulus \text{ to } impulse \text{ to } action,$$

and emotive language for

$$stimulus \text{ to } impulse \text{ to } attitude.$$

The poem itself can be analyzed in terms of the organization into
balancing or opposed attitudes that tend to interpenetrate con-
textually, though one attitude may eventually predominate. Allusion, ambiguity, irony each in its fashion is invaluable in bringing in sets of attitudes and opposing or complementary ones.
Irony, typically considered to be a device whereby a writer implies the opposite of his verbal statement, is taken here in the
sense given it by the German Romantics. A poem may express
one view but at the same time ambiguously contain the opposing
view (in Rilke's poetry or Mahler's music, for example).
"Irony," wrote Friedrich Schlegel among his literary aphorisms,
"is a clear consciousness of an eternal agility, in an infinitely
abundant chaos." In *Coleridge on Imagination* Richards praises
Eliot's *Ash Wednesday* for its "movements of thought and resultant ponderings . . . In these searchings for meanings of a
certain sort its being consists."

In his later poems Richards' metaphors carry out their once
critical functions. He may compare himself to a ball tossed back
and forth, as it "shares" in the hope and despair of the players
("Ball Court"); in "Complementary Complementarities" he
dwells on Bohr's principle regarding the variety of models necessary for investigating any particular reality. He several times
borrows the image of an eddy from Coleridge's "Dejection: An
Ode"; "an eddy is a type or example of that 'balance or recon-

ciliation of opposite or discordant qualities' which *Biographia Literaria* (chap. xiv) is to point to as the work of 'the poet in ideal perfection.' " [14] In "The Eddying Ford" Jacob wrestles with an angel (Genesis 32), and the eddy in the ford of Jabbok symbolizes the temporary ponderings, movements of conscience in themselves but within the larger living stream of life. In "Theodicy" Faustus and Lucifer even declare a temporary truce. These last two poems are from a forthcoming volume to be entitled appropriately *Internal Colloquies;* two sections are titled "Conjectures" and "Moods and Tenses." Finally, in an unpublished lecture on the Book of Job delivered at Yale University in winter 1969–70, Richards explained that the various parts of Job, written by different hands, actually contradict one another — to the advantage of the entire book. In Job there is an archetype of the world of literature itself, for the greatest questions are being debated and all sides are brought into play. "The more one feels that one has in some measure entered into it, the more there seems to be waiting to be explored. The reaching never reaches. It would be incredible if it did since the question we are invited by the Poem of Job to explore is nothing less than: What is man that thou are mindful of him? Or, What for a human being is human justice?"

The binomial opposition of referential and emotive language as set forth in *The Meaning of Meaning, Principles,* and *Science and Poetry* underwent revision in *Practical Criticism* (1929). Instead of two kinds of meaning, four types were postulated: sense (directing attention to items), feeling (attitude toward the items or state of affairs), tone (attitude toward listener), and intention (purpose, the speaker's aim). In scientific writing sense, corresponding to referential elements earlier, will predominate over feeling and tone. In poetry tone and feeling play much larger roles. In all its essentials, the Richardsian system

14. "Coleridge's Minor Poems," an unpublished lecture in honor of Edmund L. Freeman, University of Montana, Missoula, ca. 1960.

In *Principles* (p. 248), Richards concentrates on the *response* of the individual and does not locate the balance of opposed attitudes within the work. Later analyses of poems (in Richards or in the criticism of Cleanth Brooks) reveals that a useful way of locating the response is to observe its being triggered by "oppositions," tensions, and so on, within the poetic structure itself.

was still intact. The additions served to define more clearly the relation of the speaker to his audience.[15]

Darwin has been mentioned, not capriciously, for he lurks in the background of Sherrington's presentation of the conduct of the nerve impulse and sometimes steps to the fore: "In general terms we may say that the effect of any reflex is to enable the organism in some particular respect to better dominate the environment." Or, the relation between nerve and muscle "can only be such as to lead to 'purposive' movement." [16] But to what purpose? Reviewing for *Scrutiny* in 1933, D. W. Harding claimed that Richards' central attitude toward art "is clear: he pins his faith to the possibility of its being shown to be a means of further progress along the lines of what we regard as biological advance." [17] I am not sure what Harding intends here, but it is not at all clear. Richard shuns the purely Darwinian alternative and speaks not of mastering one's environment so much as mastering oneself. His exemplars are "those fortunate people who have achieved an ordered life, whose systems have developed clearinghouses by which the varying claims of different impulses are adjusted. Their free, untrammelled activity gains for them a maximum of varied satisfactions and involves a minimum of suppression and sacrifice." [18]

Richards' adoption of the final common path as a speculative instrument is highly selective. He is far more interested in a lecture of Sherrington's just previous to the one from which I

15. Borrowing a new "speculative instrument" from Claude E. Shannon and Warren Weaver in *The Mathematical Theory of Communication* (Urbana: University of Illinois Press, 1949), Richards later constructed a model that generates *seven* components (indicating, characterizing, realizing, valuing, influencing, controlling, purposing) capable of dealing with a wide area of semantic situations. See *Speculative Instruments,* chap. ii, "Toward a Theory of Comprehending." From originally two uses of language to four aspects of meaning (in *Practical Criticism*) then to seven categories, Richards has proceeded cautiously, arguing along the way that each analysis "is supplementary to and not in conflict with" previous discussion (*Poetries and Sciences,* p. 111).

16. *Integrative Action,* p. 236; *Medical-Chirugical Transactions,* 82 (1900), 469.

17. "I. A. Richards," in *The Importance of Scrutiny: Selections from Scrutiny: A Quarterly Review* (1932–1948), ed. G. E. Bentley (New York: G. W. Stewart, 1948), p. 352.

18. *Principles of Literary Criticism,* p. 53. See n. 22 below.

extracted the Darwinian passage above. One paragraph in particular seems to have struck Richards, the close of the Sixth Lecture in *Integrative Action*:

Releasing forces acting on the brain from moment to moment shut out from activity whole regions of the nervous system, as they conversely call vast other regions into play. *The resultant singleness of action from moment to moment is a key-stone in the construction of the individual whose unity it is the specific office of the nervous system to perfect.* The interference of unlike reflexes and the alliance of like reflexes in their action upon their common paths seem to lie at the very root of the great psychical process of "attention." [19]

Attention! There is hardly a word in the whole of Sherrington's massive volume with more unexplored ramifications. With his own Cartesian formulae Sherrington himself would explore these issues in his Rede Lecture in 1933, *The Brain and Its Mechanism,* and more fully, after retirement, in the Gifford Lectures published as *Man on His Nature* (1940). But Richards had already taken up the issues in 1922 in his first book (with Ogden and Wood), *The Foundations of Aesthetics.* Again, the Richardsian language moves in a direction similar to Sherrington's: "As we realise beauty we become more fully ourselves the more our impulses are engaged. If, as is sometimes alleged, we are the whole complex of our impulses, this fact would explain itself. Our interest is not canalised in one direction rather than another. It becomes ready instead to take any direction we choose. This is the explanation of that detachment so often mentioned in artistic experience. We become impersonal or disinterested." [20] Just as in Sherrington the "alliance of like" and the

19. *Integrative Action,* p. 234.
20. C. K. Ogden, I. A. Richards, and James Wood, *The Foundations of Aesthetics* (London: George Allen and Unwin, 1922), p. 78. An interesting parallel can be drawn between this passage and one from Coleridge's *Biographia Literaria* on the nature of the poet: "The poet, described in *ideal* perfection, brings the whole soul of man into activity, with the subordination of its faculties to each other, according to their relative worth and dignity. He diffuses a tone and spirit of unity, that blends, and (as it were) fuses, each into each, by that synthetic and magical power, to which we have exclusively appropriated the name of imagination. This power . . . reveals itself in the balance and reconciliation

"interference of unlike" reflexes result in attention, so in Richards balance and coordination of impulses "experienced together" lead to attitudes, to equilibrium and harmony, to disinterested and impersonal behavior. "Expectation, usually described as a cognitive attitude," he further advances in *Principles,* "becomes a peculiar form of action, getting ready, namely, to receive certain kinds of stimuli rather than others." [21]

A peculiar form of action, yes, but not action itself. "Indeed the difference between the intelligent or refined, and the stupid or crass person is a difference in the extent to which overt action can be replaced by incipient and imaginal action." [22] Though Richards nowhere disparages social or political action in his early writings, the general thinking hovers over "imaginal and incipient activities," attitudes, and Paterian states of feeling. He values mental awareness and fulness of intellectual and emotional life. His ideal person is unworldly and antimaterialistic, tolerant, skeptical of inherited codes. And here Richards discloses another debt, I am tempted to add, another speculative instrument: Cambridge humanism at the turn of the century, exemplified by the kindly Goldsworthy Lowes Dickinson,[23]

---

of opposite or discordant qualities . . ." (chap. xiv). Like Coleridge and J. S. Mill (particularly in the essays on Bentham and Coleridge), Richards attempts to bring together elements of the idealist and empiricist traditions, describing areas of common agreement and objective and developing a position that builds on the achievements of both.

21. *Principles of Literary Criticism,* p. 88.

22. *Ibid.,* p. 111. It is significant that Richards' preoccupation with attitude over action cuts athwart Sherrington's form of social Darwinism; there is no better instance of Richards' independent stance, his freedom *from* his models, and his selectivity regarding their implications.

23. As G. L. Dickinson writes on the Cantabrigian ideal: "It does not become a Cambridge man to claim too much for his university, nor am I much tempted to do so. But there is, I think, a certain type, rare, like all good things, which seems to be associated in some peculiar way with my alma mater. I am thinking of men like Leslie Stephen . . . like Henry Sidgwick, like Maitland, like one [Frank Ramsey] who died but the other day with all his promise unfulfilled. It is a type unworldly without being saintly, unambitious without being inactive, warm-hearted without being sentimental. Through good report and ill such men work on, following the light of truth as they see it; able to be sceptical without being paralysed; content to know what is knowable and to reserve judgment on what is not. The world could never be driven by such men, for the springs of action lie deep in ignorance and madness. But it is they who are the beacon in the tempest, and they are more, not less, needed now than ever

J. M. E. McTaggart (whom Richards studied "very deeply"), Leslie Stephen (who had long since left Trinity Hall), and particularly the philosopher behind Bloomsbury, G. E. Moore. What was the extent of Moore's influence over Richards? "Enormous, and it shaped me in a thousand ways — *negatively*. I spent seven years studying under him and have ever since been reacting to his influence," Richards said in 1968. "Where there's a hole in him, there's a bulge in me . . . He could hardly ever believe that people could mean what they said; I've come to think they hardly ever can say what they mean." [24] Moore follows in the utilitarian ethical tradition; but he rejected hedonism and, further than Mill, analyzed the qualities of other experiences, not in themselves pleasurable, which might deepen one's spiritual well-being. To this side of Moore's thought Richards is allied when he speaks not of the Darwinian robot, by necessity bent on activity and domination, but the fully developed and well integrated human being. Here is Moore in the famous chapter "The Ideal" from *Principia Ethica* (1903): "By far the most valuable things, which we know or can imagine, are certain states of consciousness, which may be roughly described as the pleasures of human intercourse and the enjoyment of beautiful objects." Richards' ideal of "those fortunate people" follows Moore: "Their free untrammelled activity gains for them a maximum of varied satisfaction . . . Particularly is this so with regard to those satisfactions which require humane, sympathetic, and friendly relations between individuals.[25]

before. May their succession never fail!" Quoted by J. M. Keynes, *Essays in Biography* (New York: Harcourt Brace, 1933), pp. 302–303.

See also Leslie Stephen, *The Science of Ethics,* 2nd ed. (New York: G. P. Putnam's Sons, 1907), pp. 345–369. Stephen attempts to protect utilitarian ethical theory from the ravages of extreme social Darwinism by assimilating some evolutionary doctrine. His model of the social system is a human being that internalizes human conflict. Health is attained by "equilibrium" within the "internal organism": "The moral instincts of the society correspond in the same way to the social development, and express at every instant the judgment formed of the happiness and misery caused by corresponding modes of conduct. As they become organised the whole society becomes more efficiently constituted . . ." (pp. 355–356: see also pp. 352–353).

24. "I. A. Richards: An Interview," p. 4. See also *Principles of Literary Criticism,* pp. 38–39.

25. *Principia Ethica,* 1903 (Cambridge, Eng.: Cambridge University Press, 1929), p. 188; *Principles of Literary Criticism,* p. 53.

Implicit in Richards' early books, though not as clearly in his later books and projects, is Moore's spiritual and unworldly, even antiworldly, blend of humanism and aestheticism. "Imaginal and incipient action which does not go so far as actual muscular movement," he remarks in *Principles,* "are more important than overt action in the well-developed human being." It is true that Richards qualifies the exclusive value of those highly charged "moments" or "states of mind" (the psychical category for Sherrington's "states of excitement"). Many ecstatic instants prove to be without value: "the character of consciousness at any moment is no certain sign of the excellence of the impulses from which it arises." In fact, "too great an insistence upon the quality of the momentary consciousness which the arts occasion has in recent times been a prevalent critical blunder." Here Richards faults the extreme tendencies of the Aesthetic Movement; yet Moore and the Bloomsbury circle had likewise qualified their aestheticism without disowning it, and Moore even made it philosophically respectable in its intellectual and social, if not its sensational, aspects. But Richards stresses that "the after-effects [of the charged moment of consciousness], the permanent modifications in the structure of the mind, which works of art can produce, have been overlooked. No one is ever quite the same again after any experience; his possibilities have altered in some degree." [26] Yet in what ways we are different, for what new action we are ready, or what new possibilities have arisen are all left open questions.

Aftereffects, like motives, are of course what Moore found so ambiguous. For our motives are densely shrouded in their origins and may reach back generations; the effects of our behavior upon others are equally unknowable. On page after page of the *Principia* the dolorous theme is pursued. "We can certainly only pretend to calculate the effect of actions within what may be called the 'immediate future,' " but no rational consideration places that future "beyond a few centuries at most; and, in general, we consider that we have acted rationally, if we think we have secured a balance of good within a few years or months or days." And, quite possibly, seconds. In *To the Lighthouse* Lily

26. *Principles of Literary Criticism,* pp. 111, 132.

Briscoe is only certain that she *had* her vision. Happily we do possess reflective judgment, continues Moore, but for what use in the end when any moral law is "capable of being confirmed or refuted by an investigation of cause and effect? . . . The extreme improbability that any general rule with regard to the utility of an action will be correct seems, in fact, to be the chief principle which should be taken into account in discussing how the individual should guide his action." [27] And so, despite Moore's protestations that we must persistently study the results of our actions, morality was parted from action even while the special theory of relativity was being formulated. Noel Annan has described the aftereffects on Moore's Cambridge students: "If you are convinced that it is your duty to follow the inner light and to purify your state of mind without reference to any worldly standard, you begin to despise the world so strongly that you ignore your relation to it . . . Moore's morality was jettisoned from his religion and the undergraduates who were to form the Bloomsbury circle went on to deny that there was any close connection between *being* good and *doing* good." [28]

In laying down his principles, then, Richards would readily have acknowledged that art could and must alter our behavior. Yet within his system there was no really respectable place for action. This is perhaps the largest lacuna in his early work and in the work of the various schools descended from him. Action, social and political, must play a role in ethics and we have learned, belatedly, that we can neither live nor survive by any simple cultural relativism. Richards himself claims that the great theories of art have in fact been the moral theories. For although human intercourse with one's friends and the enjoyment of beautiful objects are, as Moore would say, good by themselves, they are simply not enough.

Richards has been criticized considerably for his attitude / action opposition.[29] Such criticism will increase before it wanes,

27. *Principia Ethica*, p. 165.
28. *Leslie Stephen* (Cambridge, Mass.: Harvard University Press, 1952), p. 125.
29. See W. H. N. Hotoph, *Language, Thought and Communication: A Case Study of the Writings of I. A. Richards* (London: Routledge, 1965), pp. 235–244.

since our culture is currently reassessing itself almost entirely in
terms of *action*. But again, it is wiser to regard Richards' use of
Moore, as of Sherrington, in terms of a speculative instrument.
Although he does not develop what he means by the "after-
effects" of those states of mind, he is cognizant of them; and at
the outset of chap. xxxi of *Principles,* "Art, Play, and Civilisation," he states plainly: "The value of the experiences which we
seek from the arts does not lie, so we have insisted, in the exqui-
siteness of the moment of consciousness; a set of isolated ecsta-
sies is not a sufficient explanation. Its inadequacy is additional
evidence that the theories of value and of the mind upon which
it rests are defective." What clearer indication of his dissatisfaction with treating models as complete systems or ends? "Everybody knows the feeling of freedom, of relief, of increased competence and sanity, that follows any reading in which more than
usual order and coherence has been given to our responses. We
seem to feel that our command of life, our insight into it and our
discrimination of its possibilities, is enhanced, even for situations
having little or nothing to do with the subject of the reading."
The language recalls Coleridge on the imagination, but actually
Richards points to the major theme of his later work: the education and development of the planet in language and art.

Had Richards been an undergraduate at Cambridge ten or
fifteen years earlier, he might have easily fitted in with the char-
ter members of the Bloomsbury circle, with such young men as
Leonard Woolf and J. M. Keynes. Perhaps a greater parallel,
however, exists between Richards and their direct intellectual,
in some cases genealogical, ancestors at the turn of the nineteenth century — members of that earnest religious affiliation
that met at the home of John Thornton, on Clapham Common,
known afterwards as the Clapham Sect. The confident William
Wilberforce, Hannah More, Zacharay Macaulay, and James
Stephen (grandfather of Sir Leslie) espoused a host of causes,
some practical and others less so, from the abolition of slavery
and the relief of chimney sweeps to spreading primary education
— and the Holy Bible — through England, India, Africa, and
Australia. Their broad evangelical morality seemed capable of
sweeping every obstacle before them. They had no set program

for action. "What shall we abolish next?" Wilberforce is said to have asked on the night of the abolition triumph. Yet by following an inner light they possessed almost instinctive knowledge of what needed to be done to make a better world.

Principles of Literary Criticism and *Practical Criticism,* though they did not advance a theory of moral action, went far towards clearing the mind of false lights. Richards recognizes that his cherished ideal — awareness, freedom from social and political anxiety, full intellectual development — is impossible of attainment in the modern world, one that for improvement now demands so much of its teachers, planners, and researchers. In many ways Richards' own life illustrates the point, and any consideration or criticism of one or another of his "speculative instruments" must take into account the development and activity of the entire life. The same would hold equally true for Coleridge. For Richards possesses an almost missionary zeal for education and world literacy: he left his Fellowship at Magdalene, Cambridge, and spent several years teaching in China, hoping among other things to introduce Ogden's Basic English, a simplified version of English based on 850 key words. He wrote *Basic Rules of Reason* (1933), *Basic in Teaching: East and West* (1935), and *Basic English and Its Uses* (1943) to set forth the program. He has spent the past thirty-two years as an emissary to another country, our own. His innumerable projects — "Language through Pictures" in four languages; experimental teaching machines; the development of the Harvard School of Education; the development of television for teaching; filmstrips and tapes; translations of Plato's dialogues on the death of Socrates, the *Republic,* and Homer's *Iliad* all into Basic English (he had to go up to about 1,450 words for the *Iliad* "because swords and spears are just no longer basic"); volumes of poems and plays; and now his interest in the use of satellites and computers for increasing world literacy — all spring from a tonic personality and a force of mind that seems calculable only in thermonuclear terms. One of his latest books is subtitled *World Education through Modern Media* (1968). Nearing eighty, he is currently at work on a study of apocalyptic questions in Job, Homer, Dante, Cervantes, Coleridge, Shelley, and Tolstoy, tentatively entitled *Beyond.* As he said in a recent interview:

I've been only concerned to produce something really better than anyone else has . . . It's the old mousetrap story [build a better mousetrap and the world will beat a path to your door]. Only, the mice have to become insufferable first. Until then we all stick to our old ineffective mousetraps. I think we have a better way of teaching English, but while you're teaching beginning English, you might as well teach everything else. That is to say, a world position, what's needed for living, a philosophy of religion, how to find things out and the whole works — mental and moral seed for the planet. In this way the two-thirds of the planet that doesn't yet know how to read and write would learn in learning how to read and write English, the things that would help them in their answers to "Where should man go?"

DONALD WESLING

The Prosodies of Free Verse

"all the deformities take wing"
William Carlos Williams

"The music of verse merits more attention than it has been honoured with. It is a subject intimately connected with human nature." Thus Lord Kames in his *Elements of Criticism* (1762). That the music of verse still merits attention, that more than ever we need to relate prosody to our full humanity is urged in the first line of Charles Tomlinson's recent poem "The Chances of Rhyme":[1]

> The chances of rhyme are like the chances of meeting —
> In the finding fortuitous, but once found, binding . . .
> To take chances, as to make rhymes
> Is human, but between chance and impenitence
> (A half-rhyme) come dance, vigilance
> And circumstance (meaning all that is there
> Besides you, when you are there).

With his own poem as elaborate demonstration, Tomlinson proposes extending the category of rhyme to internal and impaired

1. *The Way of a World,* copyright 1969 (London), p. 59; reprinted by permission of the author and Oxford University Press.

155

homophonies. Taking rhyme in its broadest sense, he relates
modern prosody to the history of ideas by reaffirming the modern tendency to isolate the fortuitous or antiteleological in artistic creation:

> Yet why should we speak
> Of art, of life, as if the one were all form
>   And the other all Sturm-und-Drang? And I think
> Too, we should confine to Crewe or to Mow
>   Cop, all those who confuse the fortuitousness
> Of art with something to be met with only
>   At extremity's brink, reducing thus
> Rhyme to a kind of rope's end . . .

Such lines are one measure of how far traditional poetry has
modified itself to encompass the methods and prosodies of free
verse. But because I am not here directly concerned with the
phenomenon of rhyme, I need only gratefully accept Tomlinson's reformulation of Mallarmé's "Toute Pensée émet un
Coup de Dés." With Tomlinson, I shall attempt to confine to
Crewe or to Mow Cop those who speak as if poetic art were all
form, most particularly certain conservative prosodists who
(like J. V. Cunningham in the title of his book of poems) disdain the chances for *The Exclusions of a Rhyme* (1960). In
this enterprise I am not unaware of supportive definitions from
the field of cybernetics, where unpredictability, or chance, signifies information, meaningfulness in the message.

Most poets before the Romantics, and the majority since,
have required a body of exclusions or limitations which oper-
ated before the poem began. Coleridge called this "shape as
superinduced" and opposed it with a conception that prefigured
the nature of avant-garde writing — "form as proceeding." As
Jean Rousset has remarked, "the great victory of modern art,
or rather of the mode of concern this art has for the creative
process," is that "conception and execution are contemporane-
ous, the image of the work is not anterior to the work." [2]
Searching for a private voice within the public language, for

2. Quoted in Pierre Daix, *Nouvelle Critique et Art moderne* (Paris,
1968), p. 148 (my translation).

what D. H. Lawrence called "direct utterance from the instant,. whole man . . . instantaneous like plasm," [3] modern poetry becomes an art of invention, not of expression. For the classical writer, according to Roland Barthes, the poetic "never evokes any particular domain, any particular depth of feeling, any special coherence, or special universe"; but modern poetry "is a quality *sui generis* and without antecedents . . . opposed to classical poetry by a difference which involves the whole structure of language." [4] I shall return to the questions of voice and linguistic structure, but at this point it seems apt to note that, insofar as modern poetry is a French invention and Rimbaud's demand in the "Lettre du Voyant" — "Il faut être absolument moderne" — is prototypical, the discoverer of vers libre in France is also the founder of the literary avant-garde. The lucid violence of this credo, the logic of his abandonment of poetry, testify to an absolute questioning of the fact of literature. Believing with Rimbaud that "les inventions d'inconnu réclament des formes nouvelles," the finest free-verse poets liquidate technical form so as to emphasize randomness in their prosodies. As they abandon meter and rhyme and often metaphor, meanwhile inventing a variety of self-deflating rhetorical devices, a hatred of poetry — of the category of the aesthetic — comes into the poem itself. Thus the term "free verse": a poetry which defines itself by contradiction, an antipoetry.

Rimbaud's phrase "formes nouvelles" obliges us to work through another, more immediately rewarding contradiction. If discoveries of the unknown call for new forms, these will still be aesthetic structures and recognizable as such. If the poem is to be more than asyntactical gibberish, more than the rudimentary configuration of type which is contemporary concrete poetry, the freedom must be partial, conditional. This brings us to T. S. Eliot's famous claim that "no verse is *libre* for the man who wants to do a good job" and to his related remark in a little-known article of 1917: "The ghost of some simple metre should lurk behind the arras in even the 'freest'

3. "Poetry of the Present," *Complete Poems*, ed. V. de Sola Pinto and F. V. Roberts (New York, 1963), I, 184, 185.
4. *Writing Degree Zero*, trans. A. Lavers and C. Smith (London, 1967), pp. 48–49.

verse; to advance menacingly as we doze, and withdraw as we rouse. Or, freedom is only truly freedom when it appears against a background of an artificial limitation." [5] Of course. Barthes has written similarly that "writing as Freedom is . . . a mere moment" because, though today I can select a certain mode of writing, and in so doing assert my freedom, "it is impossible to develop it within duration without gradually becoming a prisoner of someone else's words and even of my own" (p. 23). It is in this context that "avant-garde," like "free verse," may seem a misnomer; for in the first instance the artist does not move towards the future or towards freedom, but rather takes a step away from the past by a complex process of rejecting and contributing best described by the stylistic concept of deformation. His distortions, we assume, are significant. John Thompson, in *The Founding of English Metre* (1961), describes a time in the late sixteenth century when meter and rhyme were themselves significant distortions in just this sense. If I am right, however, with Whitman and Rimbaud the dynamics of stylistic genesis required the obliteration of classical meter — a process continuing down to the present by which norms of meter and rhyme, having become increasingly binding during the three classicistic centuries, are gradually being themselves turned into deviants.

When the history of this transformation is written, I believe the late nineteenth century will be seen as a time of terrible quandary for traditional versification. To take the case of one representative figure: intensely dissatisfied with the received system, Thomas Hardy could not see his way to breaking the molds and had to content himself with writing virtually every poem in homemade metrical and stanzaic forms. By contrast, the explicit intention of free verse was to do as much violence as possible to meter and rhyme, the two most legislative conventions of traditional poetry. Dissonance, deformity become stylistic ideals: "Dissonance / (if you are interested) / leads to discovery" writes W. C. Williams in *Paterson* (IV.2), and Robert Duncan praises in "old poets" like Pindar and Whitman "their faltering, / their unaltering wrongness that has style" ("A

---

5. "Reflections on *Vers-Libre*," *New Statesman*, March 3, 1917, p. 519.

Poem Beginning with a Line by Pindar"). "Move yrself out
away from any declared base," Charles Olson wrote in a letter
to Cid Corman: "It is almost exclusively when you have hewn
to the pentameter that I have found fault." [6] The first flourish-
ing of free verse, just after 1910, was in the moment of cubism
and indeterminate music; but the medium of language proved
resistant to the more thoroughgoing forms of experimentalism
in the other arts, so that by and large, despite the massive deformation I have suggested, rhythm, sense, and structure as
such are not abandoned in the best free verse. For this I shall
adduce evidence, but first it is necessary to rule out of court one
of the leading arguments of the adversaries of free verse.[7] Conservative theorists wish to restrict the theory of expressive deviation to variants within the traditional system; they have not conceived there might be a broader variation, expressive in its
way, which attempted demolition of that system. The principle
of expressive variation from a metrical norm, according to Paul
Fussell, Jr., in *Poetic Meter and Poetic Form,* "is certainly the
primary source of metrical pleasure for the modern critical
reader." And thus, the argument runs, lacking any "counterpoint" between the fixed element of metrical regularity and the
variants got by the poet's bucking against this the actual
rhythms of language, free verse must offer inferior pleasures.
J. C. Ransom's assertion that the poet "is capable of writing
smooth meters and then roughening them on purpose . . . of
writing a clean argument, and then of roughening that too," [8]

6. *Letters for Origin, 1950–1956,* ed. A. Glover (London, 1969),
p. 85.
7. The following chronology lists a fair sampling of adversaries, nearly
all of whom argue the principle of expressive variation from a metrical
norm: H. Lanz, *The Physical Basis of Rhyme* (Stanford, 1931); Y. Winters, *In Defense of Reason* (Denver, 1947); G. Hough, "Free Verse,"
British Academy Warton Lecture, 1957, collected in his *Image and Idea*
(London, 1960); W. K. Wimsatt, Jr., and M. C. Beardsley, "The Concept
of Meter: An Exercise in Abstraction," *PMLA,* 74, 5 (December 1959);
John Hollander, "Experimental and Pseudo-Experimental Metrics in Recent American Poetry," in *Poetics,* I (Warsaw, 1961); J. V. Cunningham,
"The Problem of Form," in *The Journal of John Cardan* (Denver, 1964);
P. Fussell, Jr., *Poetic Meter and Poetic Form* (New York, 1965); Martin
Dodsworth, intro. to *The Survival of Poetry* (London, 1970).
8. "Wanted: An Ontological Critic," in S. Chatman and S. R. Levin,
eds., *Essays on the Language of Literature* (Boston, 1967), pp. 281–282.

cannot of course be disproved; but if it seems absurdly uneco-
nomical to think this of the traditional poet, it will seem even
less rewarding to condemn the experimental poet for not working within the metrical norms he is attempting to destroy.

The issue cannot be settled, as so much of extant literature
on it assumes, in wholesale and a priori fashion — especially as
the reader will, I submit, derive another, equally valid source of
pleasure from the perception in free verse of a far wider variety
of rhythmic patterns than that achieved by expressive variation
from the notional foot. Such *Gestalten,* of expectation, delay,
resolution, exercise his grasp of grammar and the delicacy of his
ear. So, to move towards a workable uncertainty principle, we
must survey the main types of unpredictability in the prosodies
of free verse. Then we shall be in a position to discriminate the
pleasures of this body of poetry, to suggest standards for judg-
ing its success or failure, and to specify the cultural ideals it
proposes to substitute for the authority, hierarchy, monumen-
tality, and vanquished difficulty which are associated with classical versification.

To begin, I must follow the poets themselves in their strategic abandonment of meter and rhyme. It is much to his credit
that Paul Valéry, a traditional poet highly conscious of the modern plurality of styles, admits that if he were to be "seized by
a desire to throw away rhyme and everything else . . . and to
abandon myself completely to the desires of my ear," he should
find "no truth essential to poetry" standing in his path.[9] Another poet who sets himself extra trammels and conditions,
Donald Davie, has written of the professional poet as translator
that he will "realize . . . in translating rhymed verse the
rhyme is the first thing to go, and metre the second; whereas
the amateur, wretched sceptic that he is, cannot be sure of having poetry at all unless he has these external features of it." [10]
Of course, nobody would wish the valuable criteria of meter
and rhyme abolished for the study of poems consciously written in the traditional patterns. But the argument that the willing

9. *The Art of Poetry,* trans. Denise Folliot with intro. by T. S. Eliot
(New York, 1961), p. 195.
10. *The Poems of Dr. Zhivago* (Manchester, 1965), p. 3.

limitations of formal bondage "evoke" creative activity in the poet, like the argument that meter as an absent norm has nothing to do with the real nature of poetry, is as yet unexplored. In the absence of convincing evidence from either side of the question, even this article's provisional demonstration that metrical form is not the sine qua non of poetic shapeliness may serve to enliven the study of prosody. Valéry never abandoned himself completely to the desires of his ear, but if as reader I do so — if I assume that "process and individuality require each other" (A. N. Whitehead), and that every poem creates its own convention, I think I will find it impossible to carry my strict empiricism very far. Affinities, limits, regularities begin to show up, and instead of doing absolute case law I find myself doing what Harvey Gross calls "prosody as rhythmic cognition." [11] And in so doing I discover that the ideal unit of poetic study is not the notional foot but the whole poem.

Taken with Gross's chapter, Benjamin Hrushovsky's constitutive article "On Free Rhythms in Modern Poetry" [12] affords the most intelligent and rewarding way into our discussion of the cooperative behavior, the convergence of forms in free verse. Hrushovsky takes the view that "a mere naming of the meter is as meaningless for the interpretation of an individual poem as the naming of its general idea; both are abstractions"; whereas rhythm, as an "organic" phenomenon, "can be appreciated fully by a phenomenological approach to the poem, that is, by going within it and moving in a hermeneutic circle from the whole to the parts, and vice versa." Working along these lines, the next step is to substitute a multi-unit prosody for a prosody comprised of one or two a priori units and thereby to understand the poem, as modern linguists understand language, as a system of relations rather than an addition of particles. In order to account both for the eventfulness of the detail and the continuity of the whole, such a prosody or set of prosodies would require at the very least the following rank scale of poetic

11. See Chapter I, *Sound and Form in Modern Poetry* (Ann Arbor, 1964).
12. In T. A. Sebeok, ed., *Style in Language* (Cambridge, Mass., 1960), p. 180.

elements, which I have adapted from M. A. K. Halliday's model
for English grammar:[13] poem, stanza, line, word, syllable. As
in the theory of grammar, as described by Halliday, one moves
down the rank scale from sentence to morpheme to study syntax, and up the rank scale to characterize the whole utterance,
so in the criticism of free verse one moves down the rank scale
of units to study local effects of movement or diction or sound,
up the rank scale to study line, stanza, poem. Here, no unit is
more unique than any other; "criteria of any given unit always
involve reference to others, and therefore indirectly to all the
others"; "each place and each element in the structure of a
given unit is defined with reference to the unit next below"; and
"the smallest unit has no structure." Finally, for the description
of particular effect, the best method is to shunt up and down
the rank scale as required. The rank scale's delicacy of description requires it to include an adequate treatment of meter and
rhyme at appropriate levels, should this be warranted in a given
text.

For my purpose the most interesting position on the scale
is at the vexed middle rank of the line, which is equally liable
to be taken downwards to syntax and accent or upwards in the
direction of the whole poem. One suspects that this very instability will make study of the line rewarding. It affords a larger
unit for analysis than the foot in traditional scansion, which
I have in any case rejected, yet one not so large as the whole-
poem unit, which considerations of space make impractical.
Again, as Hrushovsky points out, the differentia of poetry from
prose and the mark of poetry's "ontologically different frame-
work" is the verse line: "it is hard to overestimate its importance in creating the poetic rhythm and very being of the poem"
(p. 186). Conservative prosodists have naturally argued to the
contrary that free verse blurs the distinction between prose and
poetry, showing grudging interest only when it makes its intermittent approaches to a "normal verse rhythm." Thus Yvor
Winters claims little hope that many readers will understand the
"scansion" he proposes for his own free verse in "The Bitter

13. "Categories of the Theory of Grammar," *Word* (December 1961).
The remainder of this paragraph relies on Halliday; see esp. pp. 253, 254,
256, 262, 286.

Moon," where a "free verse meter" and an iambic meter are said
to be "running concurrently" and in counterpoint, and where
several lines are "broken in two for the sake of emphasis." "The
free verse foot," he says, "is very long, or is likely to be." [14]
And Graham Hough, in his analysis of D. H. Lawrence's
"Snake," cannot lay the ghost of meter: "Alter the typography
and break the line after 'mused,' and again we have two perfectly straightforward blank-verse lines." [15] Conservative prosodists often share Hough's "vulgar suspicion that much free verse
is really prose" because traditional scansion permits them to see
the line only as a distribution of relative stress-values. In this
way free verse may be reduced to the reflex of traditional poetry, a mere *vers libéré*. Since, however, there is no free verse
foot, and since it is strictly impermissible to alter typography in
a genuine confrontation of all the linguistic features of the line,
we must accept Zygmunt Czerny's axiom that each line in free
verse is "quantitatively independent of the previous one" and
Barbara Herrnstein Smith's that the line is "not a constant unit
but the acknowledgement of a limit of variability." [16] In fact,
the line is the notation of how the poem is to be read.

   Examples are timely. As I read the citations from English
and American poets that follow, I attempt to stay close to what
Charles Olson has called

> The contingent motion of
>   each line as it
>   moves with — or against —
>   the whole — working
> particularly out of its immediacy.[17]

It is something of a scandal that we have not, in English at any
rate, anything like a detailed defense of the postulate that prosody is meaning. Attempting to remedy this by looking at the

   14. See "The Influence of Meter on Poetic Convention," *In Defense
of Reason*, pp. 103ff.
   15. *Image and Idea*, esp. pp. 95ff.
   16. Zygmunt Czerny, "Le Vers libre français et son art structural,"
Poetics, I (Warsaw, 1961), p. 249 (my translation); Barbara Herrnstein
Smith, *Poetic Closure* (Chicago, 1968), p. 95.
   17. *Letters for Origin*, p. 85.

relation between the line and the larger units of grammar —
specifically, at the coincidence or noncoincidence of line and
sentence — I am sensible that the account offered here is tentative, exploratory, and will only reach a workable level of gen-
erality if it can be applied by others to free verse in languages
other than English. For hints as to method, I draw upon P. J.
Wexler's notion of the grammetrical, a hybridization of grammar and metrics "whose key hypothesis is that the interplay
of sentence-structure and line-structure can be accounted for
more economically by simultaneous than by successive analysis." [18] Wexler's notions have been developed for intensive analysis of the French classical alexandrine, where "sentences and
lines generally have coincident boundaries," and I must hope
I do not extend the hypothesis unduly by applying it to a poetry
which most often glorifies the device of enjambment and which
is metrical only in the simple etymological sense of "measured."
That Wexler must rely for his analysis "on categories which it
is one object of the analysis to change" is an equal challenge for
the critic of free verse. But there is no need to apologize for
edging towards the linguist's province of prose rhythms and
grammar — no need to fear a blurring of the distinction between prose and verse, and this for a reason already suggested
by Barthes' phrase on modern poetry as "a quality *sui generis*."
Where classical poetry is "a Prose either ornamental or shorn of
liberties," modern poetry is a different language, "no longer an
attribute but a substance, and therefore it can very well re-
nounce signs, since it carries its own nature within itself, and
does not need to signal its identity outwardly: poetic language
and prosaic language are sufficiently separate to be able to dis-
pense with the very signs of their difference." [19] Plainly, on this
level the poetics of free verse may stand for modern poetry as a
whole, affirming as they both do in the most radical way that it
is poetry which makes language possible, not the other way
round.

18. See "On the Grammetrics of the Classical Alexandrine," *Cahiers
de lexicologie*, 4 (1964), 61–72; and "Distich and Sentence in Corneille
and Racine," in R. Fowler, ed., *Essays on Style and Language* (London,
1966), pp. 100–117.
19. *Writing Degree Zero*, p. 49.

Ezra Pound ends Canto II:

> And So-shu churned in the sea, So-shu also,
>> using the long moon for a churn-stick . . .
> Lithe turning of water,
>> sinews of Poseidon,
> Black azure and hyaline,
>> glass wave over Tyro,
> Close cover, unstillness,
>> bright welter of wave-cords,
>
> Then quiet water,
>> quiet in the buff sands,
> Sea-fowl stretching wing-joints,
>> splashing in rock-hollows and sand-hollows
> In the wave-runs by the half-dune;
> Glass-glint of wave in the tide-rips against sunlight,
>> pallor of Hesperus,
> Grey peak of the wave,
>> wave, colour of grape's pulp,
>
> Olive gray in the near,
>> far, smoke grey of the rock-slide,
> Salmon-pink wings of the fish-hawk
>> cast grey shadows in water,
> The tower like a one-eyed great goose
>> cranes up out of the olive-grove,
>
> And we have heard the fauns chiding Proteus
>> in the smell of hay under the olive-trees,
> And the frogs singing against the fauns
>> in the half-light.
> And . . .[20]

As metrist I can scan this. As linguist I can describe how the long, loose-jointed sentence is generated. Yet will these enquiries, taken singly, suggest what sort of fictional duration is portioned out for the mind's ear? Let us instead, neither scanning nor parsing, honor Pound's own determination of 1912

20. *The Cantos,* copyright 1934 (New York), pp. 9–10; reprinted by permission of New Directions Publishing Corporation.

"as regarding rhythm: to compose in the sequence of the musical phrase, not in sequence of a metronome." [21] The grammetrical hypothesis offers a more appropriate accuracy for those
prosodies which measure human time by sounding in the ear.
One of the most sensitive grammetrical readers, Josephine
Miles, rightly says that phrasal poetry such as this emphasizes
"line-by-line progression, and cumulative participial modifica-
tion in description and invocation without stress on external
rhyming or grouping." [22] The passage is phrasal in its metric as
in its grammar: cumulative, processional, Whitmanic, with its
verbs turned to participles and with an abundance of adjectives
and nouns in heavy modifications and compounding of subjects.
Like much free verse it aims for vigor, not marmoreal solidity;
for local detail and continuous transition, not (within reason)
firmness of outline. A conscious preference for weakened shape
accounts for the co-presence here of an extended sentence of
dubious cohesion, and the concluding sentence fragment "And
. . ." which conflates line-rank with word-rank. The disposition of shorter and longer lines, too, and of shorter and longer
accents (for example, in "of the rock-slide," two very weak
stresses followed by two forcible stresses), confirms one's sense
that free verse veers towards extremes, testing the limits of variability in meter as in grammar. Yet Pound's lines, with their
elaborate, carrying repetition of sound and theme, their word-
jamming, are anything but slack.

I have used the term Whitmanic, a short reference to a
group of attitudes at once moral and technical. In Whitman,
as Leo Spitzer points out, ancient grammatical devices of
anaphora and asyndeton are employed in a new prosody, a "chaotic enumeration" whose very eclecticism and inclusion of in-
comparables is the mark of its modernity. At best, expressing
separation as well as unity, "the stylistically heterogeneous series
becomes the expression of metaphysical coherence"; and since
to catalogue this democracy of things requires a human, demo-
cratic style, "Whitman has adapted the biblical verset and syn-

21. *Literary Essays of Ezra Pound,* ed. T. S. Eliot (New York, 1954),
p. 3.
22. *Eras and Modes in English Poetry* (Berkeley and Los Angeles,
1964), p. 11.

tax for his bible of the flesh." [23] If in Pound the additive procedures are more various and complex, this is unquestionably
the legacy of Whitman's powerful use of the coincident line and
sentence. Whitman's explosion of syllable-stress metric, disyl-
labic foot, pentameter line — of that tradition of English regularity antagonism to which made an American free verse "as
inevitable as the Declaration of Independence" [24] — is the occasion for Pound's 1916 tribute: "It was you that broke the
new wood. / Now it is a time for carving" ("A Pact"). Thus,
as he begins his Cantos, Pound has consciously decided to mark
out more craftsmanly cadences upon or within Whitman's
verset. More recently William Carlos Williams has spoken of
a "tremendous change in measure, a relative measure, which
[Whitman] was the first to feel and embody in his works"
though he hadn't enough power over his verses to turn them
"this way, then that, at will." [25] On the strength of such testimony I assume that Whitman's end-stopped lines, rising to
heavy accent as they close, with boundaries so often equivalent
to those of the larger units of grammar, constitute the precom-
position or matrix of free verse in English. However, though
the verset has logical and chronological priority, I shall not
here discuss any of the admirable poets who have used it (among
them Claudel, Perse, Char, Jeffers, McClure, Dickey), but instead press on to a selection of those who have been slowing
and dismembering the extended line from within.

A culminating moment for grammar and metrics is Pound's
Cathay (1915), where Ernest Fenollosa's literal translations,
along with his theories about the rapidity of English sentence
order, are taken up and surpassed by an inventive metrist. The
grammatical theories, summarized in Donald Davie's phrase "the
impetus with which a sentence drives through its verb from sub-

23. *La enumeración caótica en la poesía moderna* (Buenos Aires,
1945), pp. 9, 35 (my translation).
24. The phrase is Edwin Fussell's: "Given the nature of poetry, and
the facts of American history, free verse was as inevitable as the Declaration of Independence"; see Fussell's "Meter-Making Argument," in R. M.
Ludwig, ed., *Aspects of American Poetry* (Columbus, Ohio, 1962), an
admirable study to which the present essay owes much.
25. See Williams' contribution to Milton Hindus, ed., *Leaves of Grass
100 Years After* (Stanford, 1955), pp. 28, 22.

ject to object," [26] are enacted in the one-line sentences of
Cathay's "South Folk in Cold Country" and in the superb line
about the paired butterfles in "The River Merchant's Wife":
"They hurt me. I grow older." But other lines in the "Wife"
poem show Pound attempting to delay or withstand the impetus
of the sentence while keeping to his habit, virtually a norm, of
the line equivalent to the sentence:

> At fourteen I married My Lord you.
> I never laughed, being bashful.
> Lowering my head, I looked at the wall.
> Called to, a thousand times, I never looked back.[27]

None of these sentences is ordinary: only the second begins
with the subject, and even there the right-branching participial
construction is rare; the other lines even more unusually branch
to the left by placing modifying clauses before the subject. Betraying Fenollosa's rather limited grammatical principle, Pound
captures the delicate reticence of the Chinese woman who is the
nominal speaker of the poem.

The numbered lines of Louis Zukofsky's "Poem beginning
'The'" — all but the very first ("The") plundered from books
and tags of speech and carefully noted in the epigraph —
achieve another effect with the same device of horizontal strati-
fication, one line below another rather than following it: the
effect of clutter, of a mind which can barely begin to take stock
of its contents. And Ted Hughes's mock-metaphysics in his
recent series of Crow poems finds the appropriate tone with a
progression of unattached, staccato line-sentences, as in "Crow
Communes":

> "Well," said Crow, "What first?"
> God, exhausted with Creation, snored.
> "Which way?" said Crow, "Which way first?"
> God's shoulder was the mountain on which Crow sat.
> "Come," said Crow, "Let's discuss the situation."
> God lay, agape, a great carcase.

26. *Ezra Pound: Poet as Sculptor* (London, 1965), p. 250.
27. *Personae: The Collected Poems of Ezra Pound,* copyright 1926
(New York), p. 130; reprinted by permission of New Directions Publishing Corporation.

'Crow tore off a mouthful and swallowed.

"Will this cypher divulge itself to digestion
Under hearing beyond understanding?"

(That was the first jest.)

Yet, it's true, he suddenly felt much stronger.

Crow, the hierophant, humped, impenetrable.

Half-illumined. Speechless.

(Appalled.) [28]

By contrast with the laconic inevitability of Hughes's lines, the end of David Gascoyne's "Salvador Dali" is an example chosen from the multitude of inferior free-verse poems which employ the technique of catalogue:

Heraldic animals wade through the asphyxia of planets,
Butterflies burst from their skins and grow long tongues like plants,
The plants play games with a suit of mail like a cloud.
While the children are killed in the smoke of the catacombs
And loves float down from the cliffs like rain.[29]

The lines, like their grammar, are loose, flaccid; for in his haste to yoke together surrealist images Gascoyne has not seen fit to turn his verses this way, then that, at will.
    In Hughes's line

Crow, the hierophant, humped, impenetrable,

the bold segmentation of rhythm into two halves halved creates a pouncing from word to word, a metrical exaggeration which reinforces the irony levelled against the presumptuous, quasi-

28. *The Listener,* July 30, 1970, copyright 1970 (London), p. 156; reprinted by permission of the author and the editor of *The Listener.*
29. *Collected Poems,* ed. with intro. by Robin Skelton, copyright 1965 (London), pp. 21–22; reprinted by permission of Oxford University Press.

human crow. It is a metric, moreover, which derives from the naked symmetry of grammar, subject + apposition balanced against predicate + predicate adjective. As Donald Davie brilliantly shows, it was Pound who originated this method of disrupting the line from within:

It was only when the line was considered as the unit of composition, as it was by Pound in *Cathay,* that there emerged the possibility of "breaking" the line, of disrupting it from within, by throwing weight upon smaller units within the line. . . . It . . . has to do with the reconstituting of the verse-line as the poetic unit, slowing down the surge from one line into the next in such a way that smaller components within the line (down to the very syllables) can recover weight and value.[30]

Once the line had been thus reconstituted and its smaller units dignified, Imagist prosodies could be enriched by a more meditative, discursive voice. This is precisely what occurs in *The Waste Land,* in *A Draft of XXX Cantos,* and in other poems since, which isolate and dismember the verse line — very often, I believe, intending to give meter a symbolic form to express the thematic contrast between the historical moment and an imagined or lost moment of innocence or wholeness. The political section of Robert Duncan's "Poem Beginning with a Line by Pindar" is one instance:

A stroke.   These little strokes.   A chill.
    The old man, feeble, does not recoil.
Recall.   A phase so minute,
    only a part of the word in-jerrd.

    The Thundermakers descend,

damerging a nuv.   A nerb.
    The present dented of the U
nighted stayd.   States.   The heavy clod?
    cloud.   Invades the brain.   What
    if lilacs last in *this* dooryard bloomd?

30. *Ezra Pound: Poet as Sculptor,* pp. 45, 246.

Hoover, Roosevelt, Truman, Eisenhower —
Where among these did the power reside
That moves the heart? What flower of the nation
bride-sweet broke to the whole rapture?
Hoover, Coolidge, Harding, Wilson,
hear the factories of human misery turning out commodities.[31]

The contrast between the time of President Eisenhower's stroke in the 1950's and the "whole rapture" of Whitman's time of promise is largely conveyed, here, by dismembered lines and deformed words and quotations. In the opening of Edward Dorn's "Hemlocks," lines and syllables are retarded to an entirely different rhythmic purpose, yet still the theme is loss:

> Red house. Green tree in mist.
> How many fir long hours.
> How that split wood
> warmed us. How continuous.
> Red house. Green tree I miss.
> The first snow came in October.
> Always. For three years.
> And sat on our shoulders.
> That clean grey sky.
> That fine curtain of rain
> like nice lace held our faces
> up, in it, a kerchief for the nose
> of softest rain. Red house.[32]

Repeating with slight change a few simple elements, Dorn achieves an elegiac drone in which minute rhythmic and grammatical and lexical deflections — like "mist" that is missed — need to be registered, and in which statements like "How continuous" and "Always" are sadly controverted by the fragmented form of the utterance.

Another, more emphatic dismemberment puts space between the lobes of the line, sending it across and down the page in clots of phrase. In the Canto II passage, Pound's indentation

31. *The Opening of the Field,* copyright 1960 (New York); reprinted by permission of Grove Press.
32. *Hands Up,* copyright 1964 (New York); reprinted by permission of the author.

creates a doubling of lines which is only apparent; for where
visually there are two distinct lines in

> Grey peak of the wave,
> -   wave, colour of grape's pulp,

metrically there is one. Or, more precisely, since they are conceived and apprehended at once, the visual dismemberment is
the rhythmical one, producing a poetry which as Davie says
"moves forward only hesitantly, gropingly, and slowly; which
often seems to float across the page as much as it moves down
it" (p. 119). There are antecedents in Mallarmé's "Un Coup
de Dés"; Mayakovsky arrived at the form independently in the
1920's; Pound has on occasion employed it masterfully. But
the method is best justified in the achieved "relative measure"
of the later work of W. C. Williams, for instance in the poem
"To Daphne and Virginia":

> There is, in the hard
>   give and take
>   of a man's life with
>   a woman
> a thing which is not the stress itself
>   but beyond
>   and above
> that,
>   something that wants to rise
>   and shake itself
> free.[33]

Grammetrically one must respond to the stress and its transcendence, to the cluster of accents in "the hard / give and

33. *Pictures from Brueghel: Collected Poems, 1950–1962,* copyright
1954 (New York); reprinted by permission of New Directions Publishing
Corporation. See also the preface to "Un Coup de dés" (in *Poems,*
trans. R. Fry [New York, 1951], pp. 156–158), where Mallarmé says his
"subdivisions prismatiques de l'Idée" are spaced so as to speed or retard
his lines, a method which does not "transgress" the older French versification, "seulement la disperse." For an instance of the three-tier line in
Mayakovsky, see his "Brooklyn Bridge" (1925), in *The Bedbug and Selected Poetry,* facing-text trans. by M. Hayward and G. Reavey (Cleveland and New York, 1960), pp. 173ff.

take," and to the lift of the final enjambment onto "free." The passage, though brief, is evidence for the contention that free verse recovers intensity at the rank of word and syllable.

That this method incites to considerable delicacy of rhythm and tone can be illustrated by the affectionate formality of Williams' lines to his wife, which begin "Asphodel, That Greeny Flower":

> Of asphodel, that greeny flower,
>   like a buttercup
>   upon its branching stem —
>   save that it's green and wooden —
>   I come, my sweet,
>   to sing to you.[34]

Delaying its subject, the sentence syncopates its left-branching grammar against a typography which floats to the right; the pastoral decorum of the inverted phrasing and of "I come . . . / to sing" is playfully, impatiently, modified by details packed into midsentence by apposition, simile, dash. It seems that where the end and, less significantly, the beginning of the conventional verse lines are points of greatest interest, in free verse of this sort — with more ends, more beginnings — each of the phrasal members of the line gains identity and weight, producing climaxes of rhythm smaller but more continuous.

In an article published after his death, Williams said that when "the bracket of the customary foot has been expanded so that more syllables, words, or phrases can be admitted into its confines" the poetic measure will vary "with the idiom by which it is employed and the tonality of the individual poem." [35] Davie has shown that in Pound's *Cathay* and *Homage to Propertius* "the ear allows itself to be persuaded by the mind into regarding the lines as metrically equal because they are equal syntactically" (p. 89). In somewhat the same way, Williams would presumably argue, ear and eye persuade the mind to regard the portions of the line as metrically equal because they are equal

34. *Pictures from Brueghel*, p. 153; reprinted by permission of New Directions Publishing Corporation.
35. "Free Verse," in *Encyclopedia of Poetry and Poetics*, ed. A. Preminger (Princeton, 1965), p. 289.

syntactically, thematically, or visually. Of course, such a relative measure once achieved can quickly become a stylistic trick, and the dismemberment and retardation of the line puts into harsh focus the inadequacies of a poet whose rhythms are derivative:

> You can stay
>   but you know
>   there's no place
>   for affection,
>   no occasion
>   for comfort
>   in the crossing
>   of ways.
>   You can speak
>   but you know there's no place
>   for affection
>   making other
>   in special,
>   the one,
>   the woman
>   or the son
>   at best a moment,
>   isolate and circled
>   with the stench
>   of despair.
>   If you stay
>   then you know
>   there's no place
>   for affection.[36]

Sidney Goldfarb's "Border Song" has reduced Williams' form to a formula with no rhythmic impulse beyond indentation and crude repetition. Clearly, typographical manipulation will not redeem the woodenness of a poet's ear or the poverty of his lexicon.

Consideration of the Williams passages, where lines though dismembered are not coincident with sentences, brings home the need of a theory of dismemberment for a complementary

36. *Speech, For Instance,* copyright 1969 (New York), p. 23; reprinted by permission of Farrar, Straus & Giroux.

theory of continuity. Because the distinguished poem usually contains lines which are coincident with sentences and lines which are not, and because there must be a way to move in theory up the rank scale from lower to higher units, we must question Davie's statement that "any submergence of the line by enjambment into larger units inevitably produced the blurring of edges that Pound and all the imagists, no less than Williams, would castigate as 'muzzy.' " Even in the most disjunctive Imagist poems, revaluation of the syllable, word, and line are matched by shifts at the top of the rank scale — inevitably. Indeed, Pound and especially Williams, feeling the special position of the line in the middle of the scale, are disposed equally to dismember it or to submerge it in stanza or in whole poem — often, as I have just shown, dismembering and submerging one and the same line. And, in Williams especially, the abandonment of sentence boundaries — that is, of punctuation — is the exact reflex of the abandonment of line boundaries in his metric. Charles Olson, too, in the note to his poems written expressly for *Selected Writings,* implicitly acknowledges the volatile position of the line by declaring that his poems give the effect of enjambment with no enjambment: "The lines which hook-over should be read as though they lay out right and flat to the horizon or to Eternity." [37] This perception of the contradictory isolation and submergence, retardation and speed of the verse line brings us to the very center of our subject.

Only a lunatic would attempt to surmount the contradictions: that is why Robert Creeley, in a poem dedicated to Olson, calls the poet "Le Fou."

> who plots, then, the lines
> talking, taking, always the beat from
> the breath
>   (moving slowly at first
> the breath
>   which is slow —
>
> I mean, graces come slowly,
> it is that way.

37. *Selected Writings,* ed. R. Creeley (New York, 1966).

> So slowly (they are waving
> we are moving
>   away from   (the trees
>   the usual   (go by
> which is slower than this, is
>   (we are moving!
>   goodbye[38]

This accords perfectly with Donald Davie's description of a Poundian poetry "in which, if the perceptions are cast in the form of sentences, the sentence is bracketed off and, as it were, folded in on itself so as to seem equal with the disjointed phrase" (p. 119); but when Davie presses further to call this "a poetry (we might almost say) of the noun rather than the verb" (p. 119), Creeley's poem no longer seems to fit, so stubbornly does it celebrate both the aesthetic of meditative retardation ("graces come slowly") and the aesthetic of continuity or speed ("we are moving!"). What at first appears a random juxtaposition of theme and language, in Creeley's bracketed and unbracketed sentence fragments, soon begins to look purposeful: differing syntaxes are understood separately yet together as they converge on another towards agreement in the gesture of "goodbye." One would prefer to describe this as a poetry where extremes of dismemberment coexist with extremes of continuity, a poetry of process where at best the noun is teased into motion. Its main stylistic signature is the cataloguing of things by apposition, and of actions by accumulating present participles. "Graces come slowly" and yet we are, Creeley hopes, "moving / away from" the usual versification — "which is slower than this," one assumes, because here one grammetrical perception is made to follow instantly on another by the exercise of that "progressive transition" Coleridge defined as "method" in poetry and in human intelligence. Since "method" in this sense means the ability to grasp wholes in imagination, the next step is to take the line up the rank scale towards the whole poem. I therefore turn to cases where line and sentence are not coincident.

38. *For Love: Poems 1950–1960,* copyright 1962 (New York), p. 17; reprinted by permission of Charles Scribner's Sons.

It was not the end of the matter when, after 1910 and the trochee's heave, the line was isolated and dismembered to break the pentameter. Enjambment, avoided by the Imagists, was to return in the absence of meter; indeed, so powerfully that the free-verse poet's primary skill may be to prevent his continuities from becoming torrents of language like these final lines of Robert Mezey's "How Much Longer":

> Bridges kneel down, the cities billow and plunge
> like horses in their smoke, the tall buildings
> open their hysterical eyes at night,
> the leafy suburbs look up at the clouds and tremble —
>
> and my wife leaves her bed before dawn, walking
> the icy pasture, shrieking her grief to the cows,
> praying in tears to the softening blackness. I hear her
> outside the window, crazed, inconsolable,
> and go out to fetch her. Yesterday she saw
> a photograph, Naomi our little girl
> in a ditch in Viet Nam, half in the water,
> the rest of her, beached on the mud, was horribly burned.[39]

At least as much as traditional versification, the relative measures lend themselves to triviality, imprecision, rant. Mezey's purposeless enjambments and adjectives do not show him indulging the "fallacy of expressive form," that prosodic indiscretion unknown until it was invented by the adversaries of free verse. The danger is not that such poems should be shapeless because too personal: intensely personal poets like Whitman and Lawrence most often justify their measures by configurations of grammar, while even here the falling torrent of language does find shape of a sort. However, unless the poet breaks his sentences over his lines with care, his patterns of flow will be wearyingly similar and prosodically as uninteresting as the second-order metered poetry he wants to avoid. Yvor Winters' poems in free verse, so often do they end lines on the unkinetic particles of grammar, are textbook examples of spuri-

39. *Kayak 16,* copyright 1969 (San Francisco), p. 4; reprinted by permission of the editor of *Kayak.*

ous continuity. "The Rows of Cold Trees" is a rather extreme example:

> To be my own Messiah to the
> burning end. Can one endure the
> acrid, steeping darkness of
> the brain, which glitters and is
> dissipated? Night. The night is
> winter and a dull man bending,
> muttering above a freezing pipe;
> and I, bent heavily on books; the
> mountain iron in my sleep and
> ringing; but the pipe has frozen, haired with
> unseen veins, and cold is on the eyelids: who can
> remedy this vision? [40]

This is truncated iambic pentameter. Rewritten as rough blank verse, or as a plausible free verse with perhaps one or more words from each line shifted right and down to begin the next line, this might gain the minimum of prosodic excitement. But because Winters has not decided between a metrical and a nonmetrical prosody, the poem remains slack as it stands.

Continuation in prosody is motion towards a goal, of course, but neither the motion nor its completion are sufficient to give the shape of the poem a symbolic form which reinforces, indeed, is, the meaning. To be fully significant the grammetrical motion must also be resisted, must make some show of encompassing and resolving discontinuities. Only then is displayed the mutual influence of one part on another within the whole. Kurt Koffka defines the Gestaltist law of "good continuation" as the mind's craving for stable shapes, its tendency to perpetuate a motion and follow the line of least resistance: "Psychological organization will always be as 'good' as the prevailing conditions allow. In this definition the term 'good' is undefined. It embraces such properties as regularity, symmetry, simplicity." [41] If we adapt this to the arts, "good" does not and cannot mean "aesthetic"; for the better the psychological organization, the

40. *Collected Poems,* copyright 1960 (Denver), p. 33; reprinted by permission of the Swallow Press, Chicago.
41. *Principles of Gestalt Psychology* (New York, 1935), p. 110.

less likely is it that expectation will be aroused by discontinuity or by deviation from a norm. When Winters ends so many free-verse lines on very weak syllables, as above, isolating the lines rhythmically while submerging their grammar, he shows a residual need for the "good" psychological organization of stable shapes and small units. Since this is inappropriate to the prevailing conditions of maximal unpredictability in nonmetrical prosodies, he botches his experiment.

In successful free verse, where expectation is aroused by the inhibition of a tendency to respond, it should be possible to imagine a poem which tests the grammetrical limits of continuity and its resistance. Such a poem might consist of a single, relentless sentence whose main clauses are split again and again by the accumulation of detail: a sentence whose divergent members are seen to cooperate only when it is complete and whose division into lines the reader finds a welcome impediment. Tony Harrison's "Isla de la Juventud" is just such a poem:

> The fireflies that women
> once fattened on sugar
> and wore in their hair
> or under the see-through
> parts of their blouses
> in Cuba's *Oriente,*
> here seem to carry
> through the beam where they cluster
> a brief phosphorescence
> from each stiff corpse
> on the battlefield that looks
> like the blown-up towel
> of a careless barber,
> its nap and its bloodflecks,
> and if you were to follow,
> at Santa Fe's open-air
> cinema's Russian
> version *War & Peace,*
> the line of the dead
> to the end, corpses,
> **cannons and fetlocks,**
> scuffing the red crust
> with your snowboots

> or butt-end of your rifle,
> you would enter an air
> as warm as the blankets
> just left by a lover,
> yours, if you have one,
> an air full of fireflies,
> bright after-images,
> and scuffed Krásnoe snow
> like unmeltable stars.[42]

Harrison reveals hidden analogies between geographical places, war and love, art and experience. Enabling these thematic connections is a prosodic continuity which takes the reader's span of attention beyond even the embedded constituent sentence to its matrix, finally to resolve apparently unrelated lines and phrases within a frame where sentence, stanza, and poem come to rest. Enjambed lines and highly self-embedded sentences are common in free verse, whose unstable structures often, as here, force the reader to the temporal limits of his response to larger groupings. Or the same elements, employed as in W. S. Merwin's "In the Time of the Blossoms," may force the reader into a sudden restructuring of the whole verbal situation.

> Ash tree
> sacred to her who sails in
> from the one sea
> all over you leaf skeletons
> fine as sparrow bones
> stream out motionless
> on white heaven
> staves of one
> unbreathed music
> Sing to me[43]

As from figure to ground, with no piecemeal fumbling, Merwin's last line shifts the reader from the grammatical pattern of description to the pattern of invocation, from catalogue to

42. *The Loiners,* copyright 1970 (London); reprinted by permission of the author and London Magazine Editions.
43. *The Carrier of Ladders,* copyright © 1970 (New York); originally appeared in *Poetry;* reprinted by permission of Atheneum Publishers.

plea. Here and in Harrison's poem, lines do not end in weak particles and are occasionally given a minimal integrity by unobtrusive end or internal rhyme. The lines remain, however, systematically enjambed and as such are figures on the ground of the larger unit, the stanza which is the poem. By contrast, the dismembered line is ground to the figures of its smaller units. Thus, to express in the language of Gestaltist psychology[44] what I have above described as the volatility of the line: when a poem contains lines both isolated and submerged, the middle units on the rank scale engage in a protean series of identity shifts as between figure and ground.

The free verse poet who abolishes punctuation emphasizes such shifts in identity, but at the risk of incoherence. The finest of those who have attempted the unpunctuated poem — Apollinaire, Williams, Dickey, Merwin — have realized the degree to which it puts pressure on grammar, and accordingly restrict their sentences to a single, clear meaning. A minor lyric from Stuart Montgomery's *Circe* derives its success from the cohesion of its grammar, as well as from its happily random enjambment, assonance, and rhyme.

> clear amber
> they say in Italy
> are tears of Circe but
>
> men in the act she wept over
> turned to insects and slept
> arms aching in amber for more
>
> than three thousand years
> now dangle mounted in silver
> as charms over their breasts or
>
> worn by women on the
> fourth or heart finger
> for love and against age[45]

44. See *Principles of Gestalt Psychology,* p. 191: "If conditions are such as to produce segregation of larger and smaller units, the smaller will, *ceteris paribus,* become figure, the larger ground."

45. *Circe,* copyright © 1969 (London), p. 37; reprinted by permission of the author and Fulcrum Press.

Merwin's sentences in "The Room" are far more dubious than this, but arguably possess a functional ambiguity that will permit more than one legitimate meaning.

> I think all this is somewhere in myself
> The cold room unlit before dawn
> Containing a stillness such as attends death
> And from a corner the sounds of a small bird trying
> From time to time to fly a few beats in the dark
> You would say it was dying it is immortal[46]

Another person, perhaps the reader, might say the bird is dying and the opposing poet might respond "it is immortal"; or again, "you" might utter both sentences, contradictorily; or "You would say" is the conventional phrase whereby a speaker extorts agreement from his listener, in which case the poet utters the contradictions. There may be other possibilities; but however the last line is taken, the powerful, unexpected assertion of transcendence must end the poem as thematic counterweight to all that has come before. Despite the line's lack of punctuation, the grammetrical and thematic break is absolute.

In fact, the effect of "breaking off" is so frequent and so marked in free verse generally, one might hazard that at midline or endline its prosodies require — even glorify — the classical device of aposiopesis, or the dash construction actual or implied. To notice the importance of this, and of other grammetrical strategies (for example, the high incidence of the present participle, and of self-embedding in sentences), one must assume the poet's own perspective at the beginning of the utterance. When one sees the evolving unity of the sentence as a range of choices — a progressive transition from indeterminate towards determinate meaning, "in the finding fortuitous, but once found, binding" (Tomlinson) — one becomes especially alert to the eventfulness of grammatical and metrical facts. And thereby one learns to identify the special way each element both displays and inhibits continuity: the free-verse stanza, for in-

46. *The Lice,* copyright © 1966 (New York), p. 48; originally appeared in the *New York Review of Books;* reprinted by permission of Atheneum Publishers.

stance, may resist continuity with tight unrhymed forms such as fully punctuated, end-stopped quatrains, or at the other extreme may seek pure transition with notional stanzas which are grammetrically "open" at either end. About the precise impact of the poem as a structure of relations there is much to learn if, registering the parts as at once exhibiting and resisting continuity, we can also understand the whole as both process and product.

To turn from the outer to the inner form of the genre is to develop a suspicion: what validates free verse is the voice. Where the term Eliotic, in criticism, has properly come to signify a sophisticated profusion of poetic selves in which the poet's true voice is rarely if ever heard, Whitmanic by opposition requires that we posit a speaking subject whose meaning we must construe. Not that he speaks the Wordsworthian and mythical "real language of men," or Williams' version of it, the "American idiom"; nor even that the true voice can be related in any simple or direct way to the author's personal identity. In the same sense in which "poems are not samples, but representations, of speech," the true voice is a virtual one, a "special aspect of the author's total subjectivity . . . so to speak, that 'part' of the author which specifies verbal meaning." [47] Robert Lowell admits that in the autobiographical free verse of *Life Studies* he "invented facts and changed things, and the whole balance of the poem was sometimes invented," yet despite this literal untruth "the reader was to believe he was getting the *real* Robert Lowell." [48] This reality, of course, is as much prosodic as thematic, to be judged not by mechanical syllable counts but by the criteria of effectiveness, expressiveness, and verbal nuance we apply to patterns of speech. Thus it is that the free-verse poet, flattening his rhythms and verging on prose, is, as Valéry said of Verlaine, "full of inequalities which bring him extremely close to the reader."

47. The first citation in this sentence is from Smith, *Poetic Closure,* p. 98; the second is from E. D. Hirsch, Jr., "Objective Interpretation," *PMLA,* 75, 4, pt. 1 (September 1960).
48. "Robert Lowell," *Writers at Work: The Paris Review Interviews,* 2nd ser. (New York, 1963), p. 349.

Lowell, Williams, Lawrence, Dorn, Adrienne Rich, Hugh
MacDiarmid, Merwin, James Dickey, Robert Bly, Olson, Duncan, Tomlinson, and a few other fine poets all create the illusion of a sincere and integral presence by that achievement of
conscious style which I should call a voice. This is a moral category which subsumes the inequalities of theme and rhythm, the
sensory allure and the physical weight of any poem which controls the torrent of language. Again, this poetry is not a collection of voices all more or less off key from an absent central
self, nor on the other hand is it limited by the identity of the
poet. Usually a voice recognizable as the poet's will be somewhere in range, as in Williams' *Paterson* (II.1), when he picks
up a snatch of conversation overheard in the park: "I bought a
new bathing suit, just / pants and a brassier" and as abruptly
turns to judge it: "among / the working classes SOME sort /
of breakdown / has occurred." [49] And Edward Dorn's own
voice runs just beneath the narrative line of jokes, parody, and
hip-talk in his magnificent *Gunslinger I & II* (1968–1969):

>   I is dead, the poet said.
>
>   That aint grammatical, Poet.
>
>   Maybe. However Certain it seems,
>   look, theres no reaction.
>
>   Shake him no more then!
>   requested the Gunslinger,
>   we'll keep him with us
>   for a past reference
>   Thus are his cheeks the map of days outworn,
>   Having plowed the ground
>   I has turned at the end of the row
>   a truly inherent *versus*
>   .daeha sa kcab emas eht si I ecnis
>
>   Thus, this poor individual
>   like all the singulars of his race

49. *Paterson,* copyright 1948 (New York); reprinted by permission of
New Directions Publishing Corporation.

came in forward and goes out sternward
and some distant starre flashes even him
an indiscriminate salute.[50]

Among other things *Gunslinger* is political: "about the war /
in, well you know where the war is," to quote Book II. With
Merwin's "The Asians Dying" (*The Lice*) and Robert Bly's
"Driving Through Minnesota during the Hanoi Bombings,"
Dorn's poem might conclusively document the prosodic patterns I have identified. But profoundly, apart from stylistically,
in these admirable poems — most political because most truly
inward — a public voice emerges from the private one to en-
large and dignify it. By the end of Bly's poem, the simple geographical contrast between Minnesota ("lakes just turning
green") and Hanoi ("the sufferings of the stringy-chested")
has become violent connection: "We were the ones we intended
to bomb! / Therefore we will have / To go far away / To atone
. . ." [51] Here the achieved voice, the deployment of long and
short lines and the carefully emotive use of the logical word
"therefore," gives that precision to indignation which Mezey's
poem against the Vietnam war, quoted above, does not command.

More detailed consideration of units on the rank scale larger
and smaller than the line, of the morality of voice, and other
phases of the subject, such as the mutual influence of free
and formal prosodies, must wait another occasion. If in the
course of the argument I have convincingly shown the poet to
be justified in removing prosodic obstacles between himself and
the fulfillment of the laws of his design, it should be possible to
conclude by forcing into the open the contradiction of "free
verse." So, accepting all the implications of the genre, I now
abjure my earlier agreement with Eliot's claim that "no verse
is *libre*." I have quoted Barthes as saying "writing as Freedom
is . . . a mere moment," but must now complete my citation
with the crucial sentence omitted earlier: "But this moment is
one of the most explicit in History, since History is always and

50. *Gunslinger Book II*, copyright 1969 (Los Angeles); reprinted by
permission of the author and Black Sparrow Press.
51. *The Light Around The Body*, copyright © 1967 by Robert Bly; reprinted by permission of Harper & Row Publishing Corporation.

above all a choice and the limits of this choice." In this sense, all Lawrence's most extravagant claims about the inner form of free verse, with its "insurgent naked throb of the instant moment," the need for prosodic laws to "come new each time from within," are perfectly true. All traditional verse, by accepting a formal, prescribed rhythm, accepts at least partial anonymity. The poet who chooses to write formally, who wants the "ring of authority," is abandoning some of his identity to an abstract conception of the poem. Writers of free verse are committed to a project of self-exploration or, less often, self-exposure, which makes its own demands on their language but which implies a more open, visionary, generous life.

There are indeed times when freedom as a moral category must be conceived as willing bondage, but there are other times when freedom will hardly seem itself if it must be defined solely as the negation of order and limit. Such times of choice, maximum uncertainty, and genuine autonomy (prosodic as well as ethical) will be the explicit moments of the literary avant-garde, and eventually these moments will tend to anticipate tradition. In this way free verse has become the major alternative mode of writing during the past century. If there was a reaction against it with Auden and others in the 1930's, there is at present an almost overwhelming reaction to the reaction, which may be viewed either as a resurgence of the avant-garde prosodic impulse or as yet another vigorous renewal of the ancient, though undervalued, tradition of English accentualism. Graham Hough and J. V. Cunningham have argued that free verse is a detour from the traditional English versification; Yvor Winters has attempted to show its technical, and moral, degeneration. But as Renato Poggioli points out, modern art is often attacked for "denying those cultural ideals it never intended to serve," and its condemnation *"en bloc* by way of the concept of *degeneration"* is mere "pathological prejudice." [52] It is, I imagine, dismaying to come to terms with a massive deflection in English versification if it calls into question one's ingrained beliefs about the kingly presence of poetry at the apex of the hierarchy of types, lording it over churlish prose. To describe a range of

52. *The Theory of the Avant-Garde* (Cambridge, Mass., 1969), pp. 157–158.

free verse styles from the most continuous to the most abrupt and dismembered, one must revise one's conception of patterning and deal with units of unfamiliar size and weight — a task which will unsettle anyone greatly impressed with the authority of past achievement in American and especially English poetry. So those retrenching critics and poets who appeal to the inflexible authority of poetry are very properly threatened. The most difficult thing is to confront the literary fact with only the chance rightnesses of one's own unaided sensibility.

II. Twentieth-Century Valuations Reconsidered

G. K. HUNTER

T. S. Eliot and the Creation of a Symbolist Shakespeare

The most influential new movement in twentieth-century criticism of English poetry — the criticism which begins with Pound and Eliot and passes (through Richards and Empson) into the hands of the "New Critics" in America and the "Scrutiny" Critics in England — can be seen to be closely associated with the most powerful movement in the poetry of the same time. The domestication of French Symbolism in Yeats and Pound and Eliot and Stevens demanded a new set of literary priorities; it required the upgrading of the "Image" — Hulme says that "images in verse are not mere decoration, but the very essence of an intuitive language" (*Speculations* [Kegan Paul, 1924], 2nd. ed. p. 135) — and the downgrading of explicit and describable subject matter. Recent discussion of the critical movement has tended to speak of it in terms of a general shift in philosophical temper. Certainly the drift of thought can be described as anti-Cartesian, the content / form dichotomy in criticism being equated with the body/soul or matter/spirit one in metaphysics; and at least one of its principal figures, I. A. Richards, was explicitly concerned to find a philosophic basis for criticism, of such a kind that the pursuit of a paraphrased or abstracted content would no longer be respectable. But this philosophic side of the movement seems to me to have received too much attention. The instinctive reforming of boundaries which appears in the fairly haphazard critical statements of poets and artists writing at least a decade before Richards may offer less precision to the historian of ideas, but I suspect that it gives a more typical diagram of the way in which general critical attitudes come to be formed.

Eliot argued in "Tradition and the Individual Talent" that each new work of art alters the tradition it joins, by making us revalue the works that precede it. But Eliot was not willing to let his criticism work in quite so insidious a way; he sought deliberately to alter the landscape of the past by dynamiting some old reputations and building up others. The map of English literary history that the Romantics had drawn (for the similar purposes of their own time) was no longer useful. Not only did it fail to mention Yeats, Pound, Eliot; it did not even mark the highway as moving in their direction. A new road had to be designated the superhighway, a new tradition canonized. The general features of the new road are well known: it was drawn to bypass the now irrelevant capital cities of Spenser, Milton, Wordsworth; it gave importance to the forgotten area of the Metaphysicals; Ben and Samuel Johnson, Dryden, and Pope found themselves in an improved situation; Shelley, Swinburne, Tennyson, and the Georgians moved to the suburbs of displeasure. But what of Shakespeare? Too large to be ignored, too great to be dismissed, Shakespeare seemed also too antipathetic to be accommodated inside the Symbolist aesthetic.

From many points of view Shakespeare's mode of poetry seems to be at the opposite pole from that of *L'Après-midi d'un faune, Le Cimitière marin, Sunday Morning, Ash Wednesday,* or *Byzantium.* It is rhetorical, easily intelligible in general drift, powerfully expressive of large, extroverted emotions, unconcerned with the details or velleities of the poet's private emotional state, content to echo generalized assumptions about religion or patriotism and to stimulate a fair number of stock responses. He works along the line of an easily paraphrased content, and invites our response (in approval or condemnation) to men and women with clearly defined characteristics and lifelike social relationships. If Symbolism is concerned (as Arthur Symons said it was) with the attempt "to evade the old bondage of rhetoric, the old bondage of exteriority" (*The Symbolist Movement in Literature* [1899], p. 8), then Shakespeare would appear to be anti-Symbolist.

In what may be called the heroic age of English Symbolist criticism (the late teens and the twenties) Shakespeare does not figure much in the critics' remaking of the map. When he does appear he is usually passed off with some degree of petulance or enmity. This was the period in which Eliot was writing his brilliant essays on the Metaphysicals and on Elizabethan drama, and in which he displayed an almost obsessive concern with the categories and limitations of poetic drama. These would seem to be concerns which would lead directly to a confrontation with Shakespeare; but this is, in fact, avoided.

Only two essays in this creative phase of Eliot's criticism are explicitly concerned with Shakespeare, the *Hamlet* essay of 1919 and the 1927 essay "Shakespeare and the Stoicism of Seneca." The latter is a very interesting attempt to deal with what was obviously a central problem for Eliot, as it had been for Santayana and others, that Shakespeare's "philosophy" is so secondhand and (it is implied) so second-rate, compared with the great exemplar, Dante. Eliot commits himself in this essay to the opinion that "I have as high an estimate of the greatness of Shakespeare as poet and dramatist as anyone living; I certainly believe that there is nothing greater." Nonetheless the essay seethes with an ill-concealed irritation about all critical positions that may be adopted in relation to Shakespeare:

I propose a Shakespeare under the influence of the stoicism of Seneca. But I do not believe that Shakespeare was under the influence of Seneca. I propose it largely because I believe that after the Montaigne Shakespeare (not that Montaigne had any philosophy whatever) and after the Machiavelli Shakespeare, a stoical or Senecan Shakespeare is almost certain to be produced. I wish merely to disinfect the Senecan Shakespeare before he appears. My ambitions would be realized if I could prevent him, in so doing, from appearing at all. (*Selected Essays* [Faber & Faber, 1932], pp. 128ff)

He refuses to accept the positions of Middleton Murry or Wyndham Lewis or Lytton Strachey. But he finds them preferable to the positions of Coleridge or Swinburne or Dowden, in the sense that new errors are preferable to old errors. Error seems to be all that he sees available: "there are very few generalizations that can be applied to the whole of Shakespeare's work" (*ibid.,* p. 131).

Insofar as the hypothesis of Seneca's influence is applied to Shakespeare it seems purely destructive of what has traditionally been supposed to be the grandeur or effectiveness of his work. The famous passage in which Eliot describes Othello "cheering himself up" in his final speech is presented as if it is praise: "I do not believe that any writer has ever exposed this *bovarysme,* the human will to see things as they are not, more clearly than Shakespeare" (*ibid.,* p. 131). But the praise undercuts the whole mode of the play — as is made more crudely obvious in F. R. Leavis' extension of Eliot's perception in "Diabolic Intellect and the Noble Hero." One is reminded that Eliot had said in a footnote to the *Hamlet* essay of eight years earlier, "I have never by the way seen a cogent refutation of Thomas Rymer's objections to *Othello.*"

The *Hamlet* essay itself is a much more forthright attack on Shakespeare. Eliot had here the stalking-horse of J. M. Robertson's disintegration of *Hamlet,* and behind this he could shoot the arrows of his discontent. One can see the advantage to Eliot of Robertson's wholesale attribution of the machinery and theatricality of the play to other hands, for this enables him to say: "We find Shakespeare's *Hamlet* not in the action, not in any quotations that we might select, so much as in an unmistakable tone which is unmistakably not in the earlier play" (*ibid.,* p. 145). What is left after the Robertsonian deductions, the "unmistakable tone," brings Shakespeare's work within the orbit of the Symbolist aesthetic; for unmistakable tone is what unifies the "tone poems" of the Symbolists. It brings Shakespeare's *Hamlet* into direct comparison with the Hamlet of Eliot's poetic model, Laforgue. And in these terms "the play is most certainly an artistic failure." If what is Shakespearian in *Hamlet* is, as Robertson says, "Utter sickness of heart, revealing itself in pessimism [which] is again and again dramatically obtruded as if to set us feeling that for a heart so crushed revenge is no remedy" (*The Problem of "Hamlet"* [Allen & Unwin, 1919], p. 73), then Eliot is justified in assuming that "the Hamlet of Laforgue is an adolescent; the Hamlet of Shakespeare is not, he has not that explanation and excuse" (*Selected Essays,* p. 146). The play in this case lacks a unifying focus, a symbol. Such is the burden of Eliot's celebrated complaint that Gertrude fails to provide an "objective correlative." The function of a symbol is to mediate and "objectify" the emotion which attaches to it; Gertrude fails in this for both Hamlet and Shakespeare: she is neither the Freudian mother nor the aesthetic symbol. Another way of saying the same thing is to point out that she is not the Amy of *The Family Reunion.* It is a pity she should be thought of as trying to be.

More positive light on Eliot's attitude toward Shakespeare is cast by the general essays on poetic drama he was writing in this period. He had been seeking, it is clear, to formulate a notion of poetic drama that would liberate him from the degenerate Shakespearian tradition which turned up in the plays of Tennyson or Browning or Swinburne, or in the more recent work of Stephen Phillips — plays in which the poetry is a padded overlay applied to a dramatic structure already sufficient in its prose meaning. The enemy here is not the degenerate poetry but, as for Arthur Symons and other Symbolist critics, the assumption that the prose meaning is the essential core of the poetic presentation: "The great vice of English drama from Kyd to Galsworthy has been that its aim of realism was unlimited" (*ibid.,* p. 111). "Unlimited" here means not contained by any "form or rhythm imposed upon the world of action" (p. 112), not controlled by any consistent stylization or convention: "Shakespeare like all his contemporaries was aiming in more than one direction . . . It is essential that a work of art should be self-consistent, that an artist should consciously or unconsciously draw a circle beyond which he does not trespass . . . an abstraction from life is a necessary condition to the creation of the work of art" (p. 111). Art defends its autonomy from the standards of the real world (the desirability of heroines, the just-like-me quality of heroes) by the strictness of its stylization. And lacking this discipline, "a play of Shakespeare's and a play of Henry

Arthur Jones's are essentially of the same type, the difference being that Shakespeare is very much greater and Mr. Jones very much more skilful" (p. 114).

What is meant by "the limitations of art" is, I think, well expressed by the plays of another Symbolist poet writing at the time these pronouncements were being made, W. B. Yeats. Yeats's "plays for dancers," derived from the highly stylized "noble plays of Japan," represent a mode cleanly separate from that of Henry Arthur Jones. Yeats had of course anticipated Eliot's discontent with a poetic drama tied to "the daily mood" and, like him, objected to the sense of dramatic possibilities presented by journalist criticism:

One dogma of the printed criticism is that if a play does not contain definite character, its constitution is not strong enough for the stage, and that the dramatic moment is always the contest of character with character. In poetical drama there is, it is held, an antithesis between character and lyric poetry, for lyric poetry — however much it moves you when read out of a book — can, as these critics think, but encumber the action. Yet when we go back a few centuries and enter the great periods of drama, character grows less and sometimes disappears, and there is much lyric feeling.

("The Tragic Theatre" [1910], in *Essays and Introductions,*
[Macmillan, 1961], pp. 239ff)

Against the practices of the modern stage Yeats summons the image of a "Byzantine" art: "ideal form, a symbolism handled by the generations, a mask from whose eyes the disembodied looks, a style that remembers many masters that it may escape contemporary suggestion" (p. 243). Yeats's rhapsodic critical style hardly allowed him to formulate a general attitude toward Shakespeare. He recognized great moments (Timon's death) but he did not approach the larger problem of accommodating the actual plays to Byzantium. And his own plays are too far from Shakespeare to suggest any connection; they are too exotic in mode and too remote from any conceivable public.

The only play by Eliot which bears a direct relationship to these Symbolist ideals is *Sweeney Agonistes* (1926), the only play he wrote in the period when he was formulating the attitudes outlined above. The fact that the conventions of *Sweeney*

Agonistes are derived from a popular area of entertainment should not lead us to suppose that Eliot has abandoned the purism of the Symbolist aesthetic. Bernard Bergonzi has pointed out to me a revealing comment on the music hall made by Eliot in 1921. Writing his "London Letter" in the *Dial* for June 21, Eliot speaks of Ethel Levey, "our best revue comedienne . . . She is the most aloof and impersonal of personalities: indifferent, rather than contemptuous, towards the audience; her appearance and movement are of an extremely modern type of beauty . . . she plays for herself rather than for the audience." Eliot's admiration for the music hall is obviously close to his admiration for the Russian ballet. Both demonstrate artistic impersonality in an art form which is screened from the destructive disorder of real life by rigid or ritualized conventions. *Sweeney Agonistes* is of course a fragment; but it seems unlikely that Eliot could ever have developed it into an easily accessible structure. It is typical of the Symbolist aesthetic that what is defined is the mask, the lyric mode, the circle of art, the unmistakable tone; what is undefined is the developing interest which might hold an audience in a theatre. Before Eliot wrote his first generally performable play (*Murder in the Cathedral*, 1935) he had modified — and we might think he had to modify — his sense of the aesthetics of the theatre and his attitude to Shakespeare.

In the Dante essay of 1929 we hear that "we do not understand Shakespeare from a single reading, and certainly not from a single play. There is a relation between the various plays of Shakespeare, taken in order; and it is a work of years to venture even one individual interpretation of the pattern in Shakespeare's carpet" (*Selected Essays,* p. 245). Two new approaches to Shakespeare appear here together. One is the idea of the oeuvre, the whole life's work, which gives Shakespeare a weight comparable to Dante's. The other is the concept of "the figure in the carpet," the sense of a unifying pattern below the level of explicit statement, so woven into the texture of the work that it cannot be extracted, but which need not disrupt a surface realism.

Both these ideas appear again, considerably developed, in the preface which Eliot wrote for G. Wilson Knight's *The Wheel of*

Fire (Oxford University Press, 1930), an essay central to any view of Eliot's Shakespeare criticism. Here he explicitly disavows the "pure prejudice" which had led him in the 1927 "Shakespeare and the Stoicism of Seneca" to deny philosophical interest to Shakespeare. He corrects his earlier assumption by pointing to "the pattern below the level of 'plot' and 'character' " with which Wilson Knight's "interpretation" is concerned. The rag-bag surface philosophy of the Elizabethans can in fact be defended by invoking Henry James's figure in the carpet: "they do seem, the best of Shakespeare's contemporaries, to have more or less faint or distinct patterns" (*The Wheel of Fire*, p. xiii). One play, however, he says of *The Revenger's Tragedy,* "does not make a pattern . . . by work of art I mean here rather the work of one artist as a whole" (p. xv). There is also, we should notice, a switch of special attention to a new area of Shakespeare. The force of Wilson Knight's work (as of another book which anticipated him, Colin Still's *Shakespeare's Mystery Play*) is most obvious when we group the "last plays" together, and then perhaps it is felt in *Pericles* above all. The "important and very serious recurrences of mood and theme" (p. xvii) give to "these strange plays" a meaning which is not at all discursive, but which is similar in its impersonal and nonrealistic mode to the "meaning" presented by a Symbolist poem. Eliot's own *Marina* (1930) reflects the same sense of the Symbolist potential of *Pericles*. *Marina* is not only concerned with the discovery of life and meaning at the end of search, but with the knowledge that such "discovery" involves forgetting no less than remembering, the realisation of a pattern which has always been there but which can never be isolated from the experience and given abstract formulation:

> I made this, I have forgotten
> And remember . . .
> Made this unknowing, half-conscious, unknown, my own.

Pericles' recovery of the pattern which had always been there might almost serve as a symbol of Eliot's discovery of the Symbolist Shakespeare who had, in a sense, always been there.

The revaluation of the last plays as Symbolist masterpieces is one of the great achievements of twentieth-century Shakespeare criticism. But the mode of criticism which discovered the pattern of the last plays could not stop at this point. *The Wheel of Fire* is concerned with "Shakespeare's sombre tragedies," and it outlines a mode of reading which can be applied to all the plays. What Wilson Knight calls "interpretation" derives from a more or less visionary response to the whole of the artist's work, the "dominating atmosphere" of the plays rather than the mechanics of plot or character. At this level of response one's attention is guided by "a direct personal symbol growing out of the dominating atmosphere"; to seek to resolve this vision into logic or motivation is the Bergsonian error of seeking to stop the process in order to look at its working. Wilson Knight's reconstruction of the plays is not along the lines of the "temporal" structures of Ibsenite dramaturgy, but in the "spatial" terms of Eliot's "patterns below the level of plot and character," where all the material is simultaneously present, as that of an Imagist poem is said to be. These patterns have come increasingly to be understood as made up of recurrent imagery and thematic interests. Shakespeare criticism has, since the thirties, been increasingly concentrated on this point. Of course factors other than the Symbolist concern for aesthetic autonomy are involved. The Freudian and post-Freudian demonstration of man's pattern-making capacities, at levels well below the conscious, pushes criticism in the same direction. But it is interesting to note how dominant the Symbolist concern has become. When Caroline Spurgeon prepared her card index of Shakespeare's imagery, it seems to have been her primary aim to discover hidden truths about the mind of Shakespeare rather than the image-structures of his plays. But so strong was the desire to find that Shakespeare's plays were Symbolist, like Noh plays — at least as Pound described Noh plays, "gathered about one image" — that her work was at once taken over for aesthetic rather than biographical purposes. Cleanth Brooks has remarked: "perhaps her interest in classifying and cataloguing the imagery of the plays has obscured for her some of the larger and more important relationships. At any rate . . . she has realized only a part of the potentialities of her discovery" (*The Well Wrought Urn* [Reynal & Hitchcock, 1947], pp. 30ff). The larger and more important

relationships that Brooks refers to are those that might be judged
to support and unify the plays.

The concentration on imagery is only the most obvious part
of a new concern with poetry as the essential element in a
Shakespeare play. But Eliot did not dwell on his perception long
enough to develop this point. He was already, in his Harvard
lectures of 1932–33 (printed as *The Use of Poetry and the Use
of Criticism* [Harvard University Press, 1933]), moving to new
explorations of his interests, and these bring him still closer to
the actual theatre and the facts of social communication: "The
ideal medium for poetry, to my mind, and the most direct means
of social 'usefulness' for poetry, is the theatre" (p. 153). This
means some compromise with those old enemies of the Symbolist position, the "discursive" elements, plot and character;
but eventually unification by "unmistakable tone" inside "the
circle of art" is not irremediably lost: "In a play of Shakespeare
you get several levels of significance. For the simplest auditors
there is the plot, for the more thoughtful the character and conflict of character, for the more literary the words and phrasing,
for the more musically sensitive the rhythm, and for auditors of
greater sensitiveness and understanding a meaning which reveals
itself gradually" (p. 153).

In these terms Shakespeare's plays are rather like Eliot's own
plays, a point made obvious by the passage following. Both
authors accept a theatrical mode already available in contemporary entertainment (in Eliot's case the drawing-room comedy,
in Shakespeare's the revenge play, the romance, and so on). But
the real power lies not in the inherited mode but in "something
else," in "a pattern below the level of plot and character": "The
genuine poetic drama must, at its best, observe all the regula-
tions of the plain drama, but will weave them organically . . .
into a much richer design" (introduction to *The Wheel of Fire*,
p. xviii). Shakespeare is now "the rarest of dramatic poets, in
that each of his characters is most nearly adequate both to the
requirements of the real world and to those of the poet's world"
(*ibid.*, p. xviii).

Eliot seems to be concerned, in this phase of his criticism, to
find a way of describing Shakespeare which will make his plays
anticipations of the yet unwritten *Family Reunion* and *Cocktail*

Party. He is thinking in terms of an actual society and an actual theatre, not in terms of analyses which will take the reader through the text of a Shakespeare play. Here the mainstream of modern Shakespeare criticism has failed to follow him. For, as they have succumbed to the Symbolist image of Shakespeare, critics have moved further and further away from a language appropriate to the theatre. Wilson Knight has, throughout his life, been deeply involved in theatrical enterprises, but his mode of "spatial" interpretation belongs especially, perhaps exclusively, to the student's *reading* of a text, comparing different effects of minute detail, going backwards to check relationships. In the New Criticism the plays have become poems, approachable by the method now considered particularly appropriate to poems — close stylistic analysis.

It is a further point that most critics who have dealt in this revaluation of Shakespeare have been concerned with pedagogic method. Eliot was not. He remained content to use the Symbolist vocabulary of "meaning," "pattern," even "secret" without defining what these implied about particular plays. Others have felt the need (for the sake of their pupils) to be more precise. If what unifies plays is a pattern below the level of the explicit, one is likely to be asked to show this pattern in operation, to trace or define it, and even to say what it tells about the content of the play. Those who refuse this demand are likely to seem evasive; those who succumb to it probably betray the aesthetic they derive from. For the aesthetic Image does not "stand for" a meaning, it only evokes it. If the critic is too explicit he will hear that "generations have known this about Shakespeare without card-indexing his images"; if he is more evasive he will be told, "these patterns are not really there; they are not in the play; they are only in the over-heated brain of the critic himself." This latter has been a common response to Wilson Knight; for Knight has on the whole avoided anything other than the vaguest outline of a system. He himself has said: "The finest commentary will always leave the work of art more mysterious than it was before" (*Essays in Criticism,* III [1953], p. 390). His sense of the need to avoid abstraction from the work itself led him to write: "An imaginative interpretation will always be interwoven with numerous quotations. By the number of such quotations all interpretation must, to a large extent, be judged" (*The Imperial Theme* [Oxford University Press, 1931], p. 19). But he has himself indulged very little in the detailed reading that this would seem to imply.

L. C. Knights, Derek Traversi, John Crowe Ransom, and Cleanth Brooks have sought to avoid both abstraction and realism and what, on the other hand, might be thought the irresponsibility of Wilson Knight by a more purely inductive method. In *How Many Children Had Lady Macbeth* (Gordon Fraser, 1933), L. C. Knights describes the ideal procedure:

How should we read Shakespeare? We start with so many lines of verse on a printed page which we read as we should read any other poem. We have to elucidate the meaning (using Dr Richards's fourfold definition) and to unravel ambiguities; we have to estimate the kind and quality of the imagery and determine the precise degree of evocation of particular figures; we have to allow full weight to each word, exploring its "tentacular roots," and to determine how it controls and is controlled by the rhythmic movement of the passage in which it occurs. In short, we have to decide exactly why the lines "are so and not otherwise." As we read other factors come into play. The lines have a cumulative effect. "Plot," aspect of "character," recurrent "themes" and "symbols" — all "precipitates from the memory" — help to determine our reaction at a given point . . .
    (reprinted in *Explorations* [Chatto and Windus, 1946], p. 16).

Such an inductive approach seeks to protect the play's explicit subject matter from extra-aesthetic responses, by starting at the point of maximum aesthetic engagement and only subsequently taking up the discursive elements. But it is very doubtful if a *play* can be so protected. Even when we only read it — and this is the only kind of response with which Knights is concerned — it is doubtful if close attention to lyric-length passages will by itself take us very far. We rely on stage directions, on our past experience of the real theatre, on the counterpointing of the silent figures against the speaking ones, to tell us what is intended, what kind of listening is appropriate. Otherwise we shall never come from the texture of the trees to the shape of the forest. F. R. Leavis offers an interesting parallel attempt to deal inductively with characters. In his essay "The Criticism of Shakespeare's Late Plays" (1942) he tries to defend his preference for Florizel and Perdita by pointing out that "Florizel and Perdita are not merely two individual lovers; they are organic elements in the poetry and symbolism of the pastoral scene, and the pastoral scene is an organic part of the whole play" (*The Common Pursuit* [Chatto and Windus, 1952], p. 181). This is however very much an ex post facto induction; it defends the critic from the charge of deserting his system; but it does not correspond to anyone's process of exploring a play, in the theatre or even at home.

The antitheatrical prejudice of the New Critics stems not only from their desire to work, or seem to work, inductively, but also from their tendency to think in terms of the oeuvre. This habit has sometimes been presented as a method of rescuing plays which might be thought failures when considered in isolation, such as *Pericles,* or *All's Well* or *Timon of Athens.* The rescue is, however, a somewhat double-edged process. Inevitably a critical consensus working in this way widens the gap between any performance of a play (and what a theatre critic might say about it) and its literary criticism. It also, I suspect, gives rise to greater directorial tyranny over the very plays it is claiming to rescue. Since what the critics have had to say often seems irrelevant to any theatrical possibilities, the theatre has been left to fashion-crazed inventiveness. The plays have been made "good" (that is, successful) by methods that have as little to do with the structure of the play as have the critical efforts to extract its "significance." Shakespeare has had to pay a high price for admission into the Symbolist club.

On the other hand this may be the inescapable price for admission into the modern world. Opposition to the Symbolist Shakespeare has been vociferous, but it has hardly been successful in projecting an alternative that seems more than reactionary. The historical approach to Shakespeare does not escape the charge that its historiography belongs to the nineteenth century. Stoll and Schücking clearly believed that they were escaping from the subjective sentimentality of Victorian attitudes to character into an objective and "real" world of Elizabethan dramaturgy. But of course they were doing nothing of the kind; the emphases of their "Elizabethan" world are their own, and often designed in antithesis to what they dislike in their own real world. The final standards they apply are those of their own time, and in particular of their own theatre. Shakespeare's "primitive" dramaturgy is set in a pattern of progress towards a "modern" dramaturgy, which is in fact only that of the late nineteenth century. Now, in the age of *Endgame* and *The American Dream,* the theatre of illusion no longer seems a relevant norm for measuring Shakespeare's skills. The theatre of Schücking's "episodic intensification," of surface brilliances rather than psychological depths, is no longer a historical supposition, but rather a social reality; and in this light it looks very different, not at all primitive, not in the least folksy.

The relationship of Eliot to the other critics discussed in the second half of this essay is rather interesting. At one point (in the *Hamlet* essay of 1919) Eliot takes up a position close to that of Stoll. But whereas Stoll remained fixed in the same polemical attitude throughout his long critical life, Eliot displayed an artist's flexibility and uncommitedness. He moved through a series of attitudes and responses, and virtually invented the twentieth-century Shakespeare in a collection of asides. The academic and systematic critics are still largely engaged in dotting the i's and crossing the t's of what he said in the early thirties. And even at that time he was picking up another, more theatrical, phase of Shakespeare criticism. Certainly the current state of this trade could do with a more theatrical bias. Perhaps even now we may catch up with Mr. Eliot's further creative insights and reduce those too to system and teachability.

JOSEPHINE MILES

Twentieth-Century Donne

What did Donne give to English poetry in the twentieth century? To my youthful recollection, it was the *bracelet of bright hair about the bone,* so bright that bedazzlement for many years kept me from recognizing what else was in the poetry. Merritt Hughes said we kidnapped Donne for our own purposes; he thought we were drawn to Donne's skepticism; rather, as I remember, we were drawn to his sense, his "direct sensuous apprehension of thought" as Eliot put it, at the same time that we welcomed, over against Whitman, the tensions of that thought. With him, we might have our cake and eat it too. Now as I read Donne I marvel at what I did not read before, the simplicity and extremity of his conceptual construction, which few in the twentieth century have been capable of or even aspired to. Our cake is scarcely his. But the "scarcely" is worth exploring.

A characteristic poem by Donne proposes an excess, by superlative or imperative, then negates the excess. It makes an argument with many subordinate clauses and thus many verbs and logical conjunctions like *but, if, though, yet.* Its essential content is conceptual — adjectives of value like *good, bad, false*, nouns of abstractions, *thing* and *nothing*, terms of *fear*, *time* and *death*; verbs of interaction, not only *telling* and *thinking*, but *giving* and *taking*, *finding* and *keeping*. Such characteristic structure and substance differ from that of other "metaphysical" poets, seventeenth century or modern, by extremes of usage: far more verbs and connectives than for anybody else, far less concretion than for most others, a far more persistent pattern of poetic construction. Call him dramatic or dialectic or rhetorical or meditative or psychological and you get nuances of a complex whole which is not after all so complex in its persistent repetition. We see it in short, familiar form in "Song," the imperative *Goe, and catche,* and *Ride* carrying toward the negative of *a woman true, and faire,* and then the conditional *if* and contrastive *yet*:

> If thou findst one, let mee know,
>   Such a Pilgrimage were sweet;
> Yet doe not, I would not goe,
>   Though at next doore wee might meet,
> Though shee were true, when you met her,
> And last, till you write your letter,
>   Yet shee
>   Will bee
> False, ere I come, to two, or three.

The conclusion *Yet, doe not* is supported by its set of concessive hyperboles. The concrete terms like *starre, foot, wind, haires* are illustrative, not substantive. The actions are characteristically discursive — *go, tell, teach, find*. The concepts are the central thematic material, in *things invisible, ten thousand days and nights, nowhere, a woman true, and faire.*

From the beginning of *Songs and Sonnets* to the end of *Divine Poems*, and even in the longer, more complex poems, proceeds the explicit countering of concepts in extremes: *Send home my long strayd eyes,* (Yet keep them), *Send home my harmlesse heart* (yet keep it), *Yet send me* back my heart and eyes." So it is in "Witchcraft": "My picture drown'd in a transparent teare, / But now I have drunke thy sweet salt teares." In "The Broken Heart" the intense heart breaks, "Yet nothing can to nothing fall." And the contrast is central in "A Valediction:

Forbidding Mourning": "Dull sublunary lovers love / But we by a love so much refin'd." In "The Triple Foole," the consciousness is of verse itself: "Griefe brought to numbers cannot be so fierce, / For, he tames it, that fetters it in verse. / But when I have done so, / Some man, his art and voice to show, / Doth Set and sing my paine."

The extremes of "Lovers Infinitenesse" are balanced, like the vivid counter in "The Prohibition": "Take heed of loving mee, / Take heed of hating mee, / Yet love and hate mee too." [1] In "Batter my Heart," the strong imperative verbs, the concept of making new, the sense of truth, all are bound by the recurrent *buts*.

This essential counterstructure with its concomitant vocabulary of concept is missing from much poetry of both Donne's contemporaries and ours. Herbert, Vaughan, and Marvell far less than Donne used exceptive or negative structures, and far fewer verbs, connectives, abstractions. Sometimes, famously, the parallels are great. When, for example, the quatrains of Marvell's "The Definition of Love" are compared with Donne's similarly squared-off "A Feaver," "The Extasie," or "The Undertaking" — *But yet thou canst not die . . . But as all severall soules containe . . . But he who lovelinesse within Hath found . . .* there is a similar strong sequence:

> III—And yet I quickly might arrive
> Where my extended Soul is fixt,
> But Fate does Iron wedges drive,
> And alwaies crouds it self betwixt . . .

> VII—As Lines so Loves *oblique* may well
> Themselves in every Angle greet:
> But ours so truly *Paralel*,
> Though infinite can never meet.

These stanzas with their further Donnian vocabulary of *so divine a thing, extended Soul, jealous Eye, two perfect Loves, Loves whole World, some new Convulsion, so truly Paralel,* and

1. For the structure, see Thomas O. Sloan, *QJS*, 48 (1962), pp. 38–45. Other good examples are numbers 53, 63, 64, 65, 69; and among the Holy Sonnets 171, 173, 174, 175, 178, 180, 190, 193.

so on, make a fine metaphysical poem. Yet it is one as rare for Marvell as many in Cowley's *Mistress* are rare for Cowley. That is, in addition to the Donnian metaphysics in which most seventeenth-century poets to some degree participated, making Donne by their assent their extreme leader, there were other modes which they used though he did not. The figure of factor-correlation .91 shows how nearly complete was Donne's sharing of main terms with his contemporaries; so high a correlation makes for negative correlations with other groups — for the varied Classical qualities of the Jonson-Dryden tradition, for the biblical-aesthetic of Milton, Marvell, Waller, Sandys with their highest correlations only in the .70's. Only a few bracelets of bright hair for Donne, then, and only a few like Herrick's "Blossomes, Birds, and Bowers," Vaughan's clouds and wings, Marvell's garden grass. The sensory beginnings of "Twicknam Garden" and "A Nocturnall" are rare for Donne, as are the *bright, fair, sweet, rose, stone, grow, feel, sing, shine* of his confrères — no one of which, however, anywhere near, met his power of inclusive leadership.[2]

Not long in the seventeenth century after Donne did the essential metaphysical vocabulary survive in the poetry of his followers; and not much in the poetry of his twentieth-century followers did it return. As it was a language of conceptual evaluation, it was a poetry of thought and exchange, of anxious weighing, of oppositions and subordinations. The eighteenth century discarded most of this language, even so poetically prosperous a term as *good*, using *sad* for *bad*, and *hope* for *fear*, and *rise* and *fall* for *give* and *take*. The nineteenth century then picked up part of the past, but put it in such a new context that it was often unrecognizable. Note for example Byron's satiric return to *good*, Wordsworth's to *poor*, the pre-Raphaelites' to *time* and *death*, Hopkins' to *keep*. The most strongly metaphysical vocabulary in the nineteenth century in both content and structure was Swinburne's, with his *death, face, sun, tear, year*; how vividly then we may feel the sense of sea-change. The more truly

2. See my *Eras and Modes*, rev. ed., University of California Press, Berkeley, 1964; *Style and Proportion*, Little, Brown, Boston, 1967; and essay in *Computer and Literary Style*, ed. Jacob Leed, Kent State University Press, Kent, Ohio, 1966.

metaphysical is supposed to be Browning, but his adaptations are general — as in *good, sun, thing, world* — in psychological process.

Did the Donne of 1912 bring back a richer metaphysical substance for the poets of the new era, the late nineteenth century and later? Their tone was sensuous, the language full of colors and material objects, with only an implication of concept. Of major sensuous terms, Donne offered only *sun*, and this he used more for its relations than for its qualities. Apart from the personified "busie olde foole," the sun was chiefly maker of shadow, marker of time. Donne's contribution would be basically through the shape of thought carrying his chief concepts, his thought of bad and good, false and true, life and death, thing and nothing, give and take, a poetry which would rely upon these forces and counterforces.

Death and its variations persist for Lawrence, Sitwell, Owen, Graves, Auden, Barker, Jennings, Gunn; less for the Americans, Eberhart, Rukeyser, Lowell, Rothenberg. The language of thing and nothing is of Yeats, Auden, Ridler, Jennings, and Graves and strong in America. The language of time lessens for all but a few like Auden, Crane, and Warren. Truth and value are explicit in Lawrence, Muir, Auden, Ridler, Robinson, Eliot, Williams, Frost, Cummings, Jeffers, Eberhart, Warren.

As for Donne's logical vocabulary, his terms of connection, there are few moderns to follow him. Connectives as a whole have declined in poetry, and especially the logical ones of disjunction, concession, exception, explanation in which, even in Donne's own time, no other poet was so strong as he. Essentially, the *but*, the *if*, the *though* define his poetry's nature. At best in modern poems this nature works at half his strength: the *but* in Robinson, Sitwell, Auden; *if* in Robinson, Lawrence, Eliot; *because* in Yeats and Eliot; *therefore* in Graves; *though* and *yet* in Crane, Sitwell, Jennings. For locational prepositions, on the other hand, modern poets are far stronger: Dylan Thomas' *in,* twice Donne's; Sitwell's *of* and *on,* three times his.

When in *Primitivism and Decadence* Yvor Winters wrote an analytical survey of structural methods of American poetry, along with "the method of repetition" and "narrative," "pseudo-reference," "qualitative progression," and others he proposed "the logical method" as "simply, explicitly rational progression from one detail to another: the poem has a clearly evident expository structure." [3] He referred to seventeenth-century metaphysical poets for its use and misuse. But his very description is surprisingly scant: what sorts of logic, what kinds of connections are to be found? For many metaphysical poets, a simple additive sequence is logical enough. For Donne, the pattern is more fixed, clear, characteristic in its conditional and contrastive forms: the *if* or *though* of hyberbole; *but*, *yet* of counterthought. It may be suggested that the sonnet form itself is influential; maybe, but other sonneteers are not so argumentative, and Donne himself argues also in other forms.

To garland the Donne tradition as the chief seventeenth-century tradition, in some important ways distinct from classical and biblical, is to garland a highly special and limited tradition in the twentieth century — that of the poetry of concept countered by concept, the true yet false, good but bad, thing though nothing of the metaphysical.

Our greatest modern metaphysical poet, if we are to move from this center, is W. B. Yeats. Yeats and Donne agree in more than half their chief terms, and steadily in adversative structures. Chiefly they differ in values and actions of persons, Donne's negatives not matched by Yeat's *ancient, old, young, child, mother, dream, call, cry, sing. The Tower*'s first poem begins with a negative, moves to a *therefore* for its positive. So also in the three sections of *The Tower* itself. In *Meditations*, subordinate *buts* yet support cumulative conclusions; *give, place, turn away* do the work of logical disjunctives; "But O! ambitious heart . . . It had but made us pine the more." "Nineteen Hundred and Nineteen" begins with its negative "Many ingenious lovely things are gone" and continues "Now days are dragon-ridden," working by contrasts, not disjunctions. Then, finally, "But is there any comfort to be found?" or again, "A sudden blast of dusty wind . . . But now wind drops . . ." The contrast, one sees, is between two views of time, *then, but now*, a shift in motion, a pressure in the cycle of vision rather than an alternative.

3. Arrow ed., New York, 1937.

> Much did I rage when young,
> Being by the world oppressed,
> But now with flattering tongue
> It speeds the parting guest.[4]

Often, as in "A Man Young and Old," the connective *and* can work for its opposite, because the added materials themselves make the contrast.

The flickering perspectives of Eliot's Prufrock, on the other hand, are joined by *ands*, not argued; he is trying to convince nobody. The crucial negative is an exclamatory No! The ending verb is *drown*. Other phrases — "My self-possession gutters . . . with smell of steaks in passageways . . . submarine and profound . . . his dry and passionate talk" combine or fuse disjunctions. In "Gerontion" the old man's "thoughts of a dry brain in a dry season" are given more semblance of argument than Prufrock's, but sardonically: "I have lost my passion: why should I need to keep it / Since what is kept must be adulterated?"

The phrase *But Doris* in "Sweeney Erect" satirizes the *buts* of the metaphysical quatrain poem. In "A Cooking Egg" the *But where is the penny world I bought?* come closer, and closer yet the mock logic of "The Hippopotamus" and the triumph in "Whispers of Immortality" of

> And even the Abstract Entities
> Circumambulate her charm;
> But our lot crawls between dry ribs
> To keep our metaphysics warm.[5]

That's not Donne's story, that "No contact possible to flesh / Allayed the fever of the bone"!

In *The Waste Land*, "*respondebat illa: ἀποθανεῖν θέλω*." (I want to die). In this land, wish is no argument. "I will show you

4. "Youth and Age," by W. B. Yeats, in *The Collected Poems of W. B. Yeats,* copyright 1928 by the Macmillan Company, renewed 1956 by Georgie Yeats; by permission of the Macmillan Company.

5. From "Whispers of Immortality," by T. S. Eliot, in *The Complete Poems and Plays,* 1952; by permission of Harcourt Brace Jovanovich, Inc.

fear in a handful of dust. Fear death by water . . . But / O O
O O that Shakespeherian Rag — . . . But if Albert makes off, it
won't be for lack of telling . . . But at my back from time to
time." And elsewhere: " — For Thine is the Kingdom . . . Because I do not hope . . . Pray for us . . . Although I do not
hope . . . Let my cry come unto Thee. But to what purpose
/ I do not know. Words, after speech, reach / Into the silence."
The detail of the pattern is movement.

The 1934 *Poems* of Auden vigorously return to us the metaphysician: the concepts, the fear, the exceptive central turn in
the poem.

I — *Yet wear no ruffian badge.* II — *But waking sees.* III
— *Nor even is despair your own.* IV — *But poised between.* V
— *But now.* VI — *But not.* VII — *But should the walk.* VIII
— *But of no use.* IX — *But what does it mean.* XI — *But sel-
dom this.* XIV — *But in between.* XVI — *But thinking so.*
XVII — *But this was never.* XVIII — *But here.* XX — *Yet
there's no peace.* XXIII — *But we in legend not.* XXIV — *Yet
glory is not new.* XXV — *There is no change of place.* XXVI
— *But happy now.* XXVII — *But the answer.* XXVIII — *But
their ancestral curse.*

Throughout XX, for example, the tensions of concept, the
archetypal face, fear, these tears, and years all round upon
the turn "Yet there's no peace."

> Fear, taking me aside, would give advice
> "To conquer her, the visible enemy,
> It is enough to turn away the eyes."
>
> Yet there's no peace in this assaulted city
> But speeches at the corners, hope for news,
> Outside the watchfires of a stronger army.[6]

The turns of concept in Auden, for which see also the sonnets
"In Time of War," are less of argument, more of atmosphere
than in Donne; the whole step toward modernity is taken in
the assortment of sensuous imagery, which we then tend to read

6. This quotation (from poem XX in *Poems,* 1934) and the next (from
"As I walked out one evening") are in *Collected Shorter Poems 1927–
1957,* 1966, by W. H. Auden; by permission of Random House, Inc.

back, far too richly, into Donne. But the skeleton of unease, which says to the poet over and over, this way it is, yet not fully, not wholly, not really, not metaphysically, persists and provides the bond between centuries.

In the *Collected Poems* of 1945 the first and simplest of ballads runs

> As I walked out one evening . . .
> I heard a lover sing . . .
> "Love has no ending" . . .
> But all the clocks in the city
>   Began to whirr and chime:
> "Oh let not Time deceive you,
>   You cannot conquer Time."

And the epigraph to the volume is:

> Whether conditioned by God, or their neural structure, still
> All men have this common creed, account for it as you will: —
> The Truth is one and incapable of contradiction;
> All knowledge that conflicts with itself is Poetic Fiction.

This is the fiction-making of the metaphysician. Cummings recognizes it too:

> if you can't sing you got to
> die and we aint got
>
> Nothing to die,come on kid
>
> let's go to sleep[7]

This is the metaphysical language if not the structure of Cummings' *50 Poems* (1939). And this is even the structure in "anyone lived," and "i say no world," and "these people so-called" and many more.

7. This quotation and the next two are from poems 3, 5, and 16, by E. E. Cummings, in *Poems 1923–1954;* by permission of Harcourt Brace Jovanovich, Inc.

                                                    We're
                                    alive and shall be:
                                                    . . . but we've
                                    such freedom such intense digestion so
                                    much greenness only dying makes us grow.

In "proud of his scientific attitude" the logical connectives are
present and sardonic. *Which but*) is a turning point in "mrs."
And then again the beautiful

                        until out of merely not nothing comes
                        only one snowflake(and we speak our names

    Robinson Jeffers had not seemed to me metaphysical, Don-
nian, except as he shared the Random House bindings of the
1930's; yet he makes the basic turn of thought, in *Such Counsels*
and earlier.

                        Men suffer want and become
                        Curiously ignoble; as prosperity
                        Made them curiously vile.

                        But look how noble the world is,
                        The lonely-flowing waters, the secret-
                        Keeping stones, the flowing sky.
                                            ("Life from the Lifeless")

For the Greeks the love of beauty, for Rome of ruling; for the
    present age the passionate love of discovery;
But in one noble passion we are one.
                                            ("Shine, Republic")

        But the innocent and credulous are soon corrupted.
                                            ("The Coast Road")

                        But for each man
There is real solution, let him turn from himself and man to love
    God.
                                            ("Going to Horse Flats")

                                                    Because only
            tormented persons want truth . . .
        Not a man sinning, but the pure holiness and power of God.
                                            ("Theory of Truth") [8]

More usually considered, accepted or rejected, as metaphysical have been the poems of Wallace Stevens. In *Transport
to Summer* (1947):

> It is here, in this bad, that we reach
> The last purity of the knowledge of good.
>
> The crow looks rusty as he rises up
> Bright is the malice in his eye . . .
>
> One joins him there for company,
> But at a distance, in another tree.

*. . . But this book . . . And not yet to have written a book . . .
These are real only if I make them so . . .*

> One might have thought of sight, but who could think
> Of what it sees, for all the ill it sees?
> Speech found the ear, for all the evil sound,
> But the dark italics it could not propound.
> And out of what one sees and hears and out
> Of what one feels, who could have thought to make
> So many selves, so many sensous worlds,
> As if the air, the mid-day air, was swarming
> With the metaphysical changes that occur,
> Merely in living as and where we live.
>
> But see him for yourself. / The fictive man. . .
>
> There is one dove, one bass, one fisherman.
> Yet coo becomes rou-coo, rou-coo. How close
> To the unstated theme . . .

Fully concerned with the power of imagination and the creating of the fictive man, Stevens is less concerned with the metaphysical counter. But when as conscious artist he seriously turns

8. From *The Selected Poetry of Robinson Jeffers,* 1937; by permission
of Random House, Inc.

to the metaphysical mode, he uses it so carefully that he defines
it for us: the paradoxes, the conditional, and then the turn,
But suppose, and the return to language and concept, as in
"Connoisseur of Chaos" — "If all the green of spring was blue,
and it is" —

IV

A. Well, an old order is a violent one.
This proves nothing. Just one more truth, one more
Element in the immense disorder of truths.
B. It is April as I write. The wind
Is blowing after days of constant rain.
All this, of course, will come to summer soon.
But suppose the disorder of truths should ever come
To an order, most Plantagenet, most fixed . . .[9]

The metaphysical order admired and praised by the poets
and critics of the next generation reached less poetic expression
than one might expect. Robert Penn Warren is by far the
strongest because he can face and make use of negatives; he
can except and deny as well as add. His early version has now a
familiar literary ring, as in "Kentucky Mountain Farm."

Now on you is the hungry equinox,
O little stubborn people of the hill,
The season of the obscene moon whose pull
Disturbs the sod, the rabbit, the lank fox,
Moving the waters, the boar's dull blood,
And the acrid sap of the ironwood.

But breed no tender thing among the rocks.
Rocks are too old under the mad moon,
Renouncing passion by the strength that locks
The eternal agony of fire in stone.

Then quit yourselves as stone and cease
To break the weary stubble-field for seed;
Let not the naked cattle bear increase,

9. These quotations are from "No Possum" and "Connoisseur of
Chaos," by Wallace Stevens, in *The Collected Poems of Wallace Stevens*,
and the last stanza of "Esthetique du Mal," by Wallace Stevens, in *Transport to Summer*, 1947; by permission of Alfred A. Knopf, Inc.

Let barley wither and the bright milkweed.
Instruct the heart, lean men, of a rocky place
That even the little flesh and fevered bone
May keep the sweet sterility of stone.

More vividly new is "Insomnia," from "Tale of Time":

Come,
Crack crust, striker
From darkness, and let seize — let what
Hand seize, oh! — my heart, and compress
The heart till, after pain, joy from it
Spurts like a grape, and I will grind
Teeth on flint tongue till
The flint screams. Truth
Is all. But

I must learn to speak it
Slowly, in a whisper.
Truth, in the end, can never be spoken aloud,
For the future is always unpredictable.
But so is the past, therefore

At wood's edge I stand, and,
Over the black horizon, heat lightning
Ripples the black sky. After
The lightning, as the eye
Adjusts to the new dark,
The stars are, again, born.

They are born one by one.[10]

A long view back over five centuries of English poetic usage
shows certain main strands in the pattern. These can be given
traditional names: certain temporal groupings can be seen to
have great power, so that "eighteenth-century poetry" can be a
meaningful phrase; certain groupings across time can be given
conceptual titles like "classical" and "romantic." The term

10. Quotations from "Kentucky Mountain Farm," and "Insomnia" in
"Tale of Time," by Robert Penn Warren, in *Selected Poems New and Old
1923–1966* (New York: copyright Random House, Inc., 1966); reprinted
by permission of the publisher.

"metaphysical" has a clear seventeenth-century focus — an extension from, say, Wyatt through Sidney and Donne to Cowley — and then also a modern application, strong after 1912 and 1921. Especially, through the words of T. S. Eliot, attention fell upon Donne. What seventeenth-century metaphysical, what Donnian traits could be useful to the present? A true metaphysical complex, aside from small tokens, would need to include the following: a concern with the range of concepts, of truth and falsity, good and bad, what is and what is not. Thus a concern with death as with life, thus things and nothings as well as people, thus time in relation to space, thus human give and take, thus fear as well as love. Thus also an exceptive and limiting structure, not merely *and* but *but* and *yet,* with implicative *ifs* and concessive *thoughs* — not a balanced but a subordinating structure, not a weighing of alternatives and *either-or,* but an ebullient setting forth and then a check, a back and forth relation between heaven and earth, *ought* and *is.* The propositional structure asserts life *but* the actuality of death, the power of spirit *but* the power of body, the absurdities *but* the moderations of human existence.

By such criteria, the twentieth-century metaphysicals are not just the ones we might guess; not the Fugitives so much as the cosmic metaphysicians like Cummings and Jeffers and the younger Rukeyser, Wilbur, Rothenberg. Eliot, and many in the south, cared about a sort of fusing figure as an extension of symbolic mind; the modern metaphysicals, rather, maintain the subordinating view.

It might be asked how one so involved in the special thought processes of his time as Stein, Tuve, Leishman, Potter, and many others have shown Donne to be can have a strong effect in another century. Should it not be the classicists, the seekers of steady norms, who must recur, as indeed they seem to do, from one cultural context to another? How can a scholastic serve the twentieth century? By touching, I think the new need of the poets to think about their new cosmology, their new learning. Classicism and romanticism accepted, elevated, subjectivized the natural world; what the twentieth century needed was to grasp a whole new natural world brought in by the new learning, a new outer and beyond and other and double. The central focus on sense-impression made by imagism and symbolism did not much allow for discursive exploration; one needed to think about, know about, as well as observe, the new phenomena. So *new* itself is an important word for metaphysical time, and the *something-nothing* of speculation, and the *life-love-death*, *giving-taking* of human response.

The modern critics stressed less what they found new in Donne than what they found familiarly their own, the "imagery" and feeling. In his authoritative edition of 1912, Grierson countered Courthope's old-fashioned emphasis on quaintness and ingenuity with his own on depth of wit.

"Alike in his poetry and in his soberest prose, treatise or sermon, Donne's mind seems to want the high seriousness which comes from a conviction that truth is and is to be found. A spirit of scepticism and paradox plays through and disturbs almost everything he wrote, except at moments when an intense mood of feeling, whether love or devotion, begets faith, and silences the sceptical and destructive wit by the power of vision rather than of intellectual conviction." This is a romanticizing of Donne, even though Grierson wisely observes that "not much of Donne's poetry is given to description";[11] Yeats, too, romanticizes in response to Grierson, "the more precise and learned the thought, the greater the beauty, the passion." What is wise is the attention to the guidance of thought. Over against "direct sensuous apprehension of thought" and "sensibility which could devour any kind of experience" one needs to remember the seventeenth-century emphasis on concept as in Sir Aston Cokayne's guidance of 1658:

> Be metaphysical, disdaining to
> Fix upon anything that is below.[12]

Donne's own, "To the Countess of Bedford," says:

11. *The Poems of John Donne,* 2 vols., Oxford University Press, London, 1912, II, x, xiii, xxix, li.
12. Edward LeComte, *Grace to a Witty Sinner,* Victor Gollancz Ltd., London, 1965, p. 228.

Beeing and *seeming* is your equall care,
And *vertues* whole *summe* but *know* and *dare*.

And, as Grierson quotes "The Anniversarie," (*Poems of Donne*, p. xxix):

In this low forme, poore soule, what wilt thou doe?
When wilt thou shake off this Pedantery,
Of being taught by sense, and Fantasie?

To be, to know, to dare are the merits — and they are verbs — not the false forms of sense and the illusory impressions of appearance. The power of sense for Donne worked as loving apprehension susceptible of thought.

Some other modern critics, Cleanth Brooks, for example, have emphasized Donne's power of thought as power of dialectic and paradox. A paradox seems contrary to normal categories yet conveys a hidden truth, an acceptable reversal such as that it is better to be poor than rich or foolish than wise; that an extreme, foolish act is the same as its opposite extreme; that order can be reversed, as by Jonson's *Silent Woman*. A paradox takes many forms. For nineteenth-century Browning, as W. D. Shaw says, it meant multiple points of view; conflicts and internal contradictions meant inner growth,[13] union by reverting to and releasing the world. Donne's negatives were different — in his sense of the wrong of overcommitment, whether Ovidian or scholastic. I do not think it is so much the complexity of Donne's arguments that is important for us to note as it is their basic recurrent structure, their simple balancing upon a counterpoint. He was no stylistic systematist, as he said himself: "I ever thought the study of [law] my best entertainment and pastime, but I have no ambition nor design upon the style." Rather, his own character and feeling in relation to the pressures of his day, the sense of building up and excess, and then the sense of counterbalancing truth gave him his steady style in poetry and prose as well: "I leave a scattered flock of wretched children, and I carry an infirm and valetudinary body, and I go into the mouth of such adversaries as I cannot blame for hat-

13. *The Dialectical Temper,* Cornell University Press, Ithaca, 1968.

ing me, the Jesuits, and yet I go." [14] Grierson is right when he
says (*Poems of Donne*, II, i), "Effort is the note which predominates." Donne's is the poetry of effortful articulation of
thought; it is spelling out of problems, analyzing of motives and
situations, a learned exploring of extremes of the planes of
existence now and hereafter, of the cosmos below and above.

Rupert Brooke, Walter de la Mare, Elinor Wylie, Dylan
Thomas, the Fugitives, many more have been interested in
Donne in the twentieth century and found in him some clue to
poetic value. But few I think have tried for or achieved that
combination of values which makes for a whole likeness rather
than a scattering of likenesses. The favorable reviews of the
1912 edition and of the Hayward 1929 edition in *Athenaeum,
Spectator, Nation* and elsewhere made little sense of what
sense Donne might make for a new time. The power was
Eliot's, Williamson's, Theodore Spencer's suddenly to verify the
vogue. But much of the glamour of what we felt to be Donnian
belonged rather to Herbert or Marvell or Vaughan, to the more
aesthetic mode which shared affinities with symbolism. So students during a half century of "close criticism" have puzzled
over the true nature of the metaphysical mode they were seeing
essentialized in Donne, alien in most ways to their own. Poets
like Robinson and Ransom, with strong metaphysical vocab-
ularies and structures, nevertheless so often combined them with
nineteenth-century terms and narrative sequences that the effect was special. Intellectual Tate and Kunitz, like Eliot, thought
in progressions more than counterforces. Pound, Williams,
Moore, Crane, Roethke, Lowell even less could be looked to;
they were of a different tradition.

For the young poets writing in the second half of this century,
Donne's direct whole effect is minimal. Thom Gunn and Elizabeth Jennings make some strong connections; in America
after Warren and Rukeyser, there are a few like Rothenberg
with their sense of *death* and *sun*, *telling* and *thinking*, Snyder
and a few with *time*, McClure, Mezey, and a few with *thing* and
nothing. Their combining into structures of effortfully articulated argument is rare. I'd like to see, but do not expect to, a

14. Quoted by Mary Clive in *Jack and the Doctor*, Macmillan, London, 1966, pp. 95, 44.

new poetry of metaphysics come into being in which, as in
Donne, the process of thought is the shaping force of the poem,
not a fusion but an articulation of thought giving shape to feeling: thought-feeling rather than felt-thought.

But meantime, in single contemporary poems, curious ghosts
emerge. The long lyric "Fear" by W. S. Merwin[15] is a twentieth-
century metaphysical poem for us; it keeps the essentials of
language and attitude and moves them up through nineteenth-
century romanticism via Eliot and Cummings into the present
day. Fear as a metaphysical emotion in making its connection
with the unknown suggests two worlds. Merwin addresses it
much as Donne addressed fear or death, as an inner presence,
even in name.

> **Fear**
> there is
> fear in fear the name the blue and green walls
> falling of and numbers fear the veins that
> when they were opened fear flowed from and
> these forms it took a ring a ring a ring

The blue and green walls are by now I hope recognizable,
like the bracelet of bright hair, as appurtenances of the modern.
They develop in this poem through clusters of specifics that are
characteristically twentieth-century poetic, in the *rain falling,*
the *grass-green alley, glass giants, shoes, shadows, song, silence,*
parents, house, stone, forgetting, remembering, mouth, loves,
small door, the bird feather by feather, hair, edge, building, the
long crying, cold lights, star, from the beginning. At the same
time, across the loosely constructed sentences in their loosely
four-beat lines moves a metaphysical structure and reference,
a proceeding by concept and even argument, in

> fear into fear and the hatred and something
> in everything and it is my death's
> disciple leg and fear no he would not
> have back those lives again and their fear as
> he feared he would say but he feared more he

---

15. Originally in *The New Yorker;* from *The Carrier of Ladders,*
Atheneum, New York, 1970; © W. S. Merwin.

        did not fear more he did fear more
        in everything it is there a long time.

Key terms, *thing, death, life, time*; key conflicting formulations.
Then also

            fear etcetera water fire earth air
            etcetera in everything made of
            human agency or divine fear is
            in the answer also

And, more ritually,

                            but fear
    says logic follows . .
    hearts smoke in the gusts on earth as it is
    in heaven with the sentence beginning
    before the heavens were or the earth
    had out of fear been called and any began . . .
    and shall I couple heaven when the fear
    shall fear and those who walked in fear shall see
    fear their very form and being for
    their eyes shall be opened it was going
    on in everything and I forgot but if you
    stand here you can see . . .
    I'm telling you I'm asking you I'm dying . . .
    the next I said fear come on you it's you
    I'm addressing . . .
    mean there is you fear me fear but you
    must not imagine fear through which the present
    moves like a star that I or that
    you either clearly and from the beginning
    could ever again because from the beginning
    there is fear in everything and it is
    me and always was in everything it
    is me

Carrying Eliot and Cummings — even Olson, as in the shift
in the final line breaks — farther than they might wish to be
taken into a blur of past and present, Merwin makes a portmanteau journey with his fear. It is almost as if the metaphysical
structure began faintly but then, under the influence of its cru-

cial abstractions, strengthened its adversary tone of logic; the
modern abolishment of punctuation called up an older need for
connections, and to the early *ands* accrue more *ifs* and *buts* than
one might have expected at the onset of "fear in the name the
blue and green walls." Be the bracelet of bright hair as it may,
the survival of the skeleton of exceptive and adversative concept
in a poem such as this seems a wonder worth remark, a suggestion of the surviving power of Donne's thought in the twentieth century.

STEPHEN ORGEL

Affecting the Metaphysics

For modern readers the term metaphysical can be applied to poetry in two ways. First, and most simply, it can categorize a group of poets; and I intend initially to ignore the question of what the term is conceived to imply and what similarities it is assumed to define. The basic group for us consists of Donne, Herbert, Vaughan, Marvell, Crashaw, though sometimes Crashaw is redefined as baroque rather than metaphysical — and sometimes other poets are added to the core. In this sense, the term has the same sort of critical value as "romantic" in "romantic poetry": it is relatively neutral. The two are not precisely analogous, since romantic describes more a period than a special group of poets, but the point is that no implications of quality or judgment are included; the term is a critical convention. Such a question as "Are there any romantic elements in Pope?" would require a certain amount of defining before the term became usable. In fact, we tend not to use "romantic" in this way, and the question as it stands is meaningless; the response would have to be, "How are you using romantic?" But we do use "metaphysical" in this way, asking questions like "Are the Shakespeare sonnets metaphysical?" and here it is clearly less neutral as a critical term. To find metaphysical elements in *Astrophil and Stella* is somehow to redeem it. We take the metaphysical in one sense to be normative in poetry, and in another to be the characteristic of all good poetry. So it seems a reasonable critical pursuit for Reuben Brower to look for metaphysical elements in Pope and for Michael Putnam to look for them in Catullus.

Metaphysical poetry is largely the creation not of its poets but of its critics. When we ask what it is, or even how we know such a movement existed, we find ourselves confronting not a clearly defined body of verse, but a critical tradition beginning with Dr. Johnson and polarized by T. S. Eliot. It is this tradition that we must come to terms with if any real sense of the poetry is to be possible. We may start with a curious fact in the history of criticism: from the time "metaphysical" was first formulated as a critical term its definition has remained relatively constant, but the list of poets whom critics regarded as metaphysical has varied wildly from generation to generation.

Discussions of metaphysical poetry since the time of Dr. Johnson have tended to regard the basic question as one of definition: what quality is it that unites poets as obviously disparate as Donne and Vaughan, Herbert and Marvell, and at the same time distinguishes them from, say, Sidney and Pope? Dr. Johnson found the term a convenient way of describing certain qualities of style that he did not, on the whole, admire; a century and a half later T. S. Eliot used it to define certain qualities of intellect that he very much admired. The fact that between these two poles of criticism a radical change in taste had taken place is, for our purposes, less important than the fact that the whole problem is a peculiarly modern one and largely irrelevant to any concerns of the poets themselves. To speak of metaphysical poetry as if it constituted a historical category — a clear break with (or a clear development of) Elizabethan poetry — is itself historically unsound. On the other hand, the term has obvious value, often noted, as an index of the modern consciousness, defining at various times elements that we do or do not wish to emulate in the verse of the past.

The history of the term is a convenient place to begin. In the seventeenth century, metaphysical was used to mean contemplative or speculative, complex, concerned with the nonphysical or supernatural. Insofar as it could be applied to poetry at all, it characterized only the subject matter of a poem. The beginnings of its modern usage, to define a particular group of poets or a recognizable style, are barely found in the seventeenth century at all. William Drummond of Hawthorndon, Ben Jonson's friend, complained of a new type of poetry growing up around 1630: "In vain have some Men of late (Transformers of every Thing) consulted upon her [poetry's] Reformation, and endeavoured to abstract her to *Metaphysical* Idea's, and Scholastical Quiddities, denuding her of her own Habits, and those Ornaments with which she hath amused the World some Thousand Years." [1] Unfortunately, it is not clear whom Drummond has in mind. Possibly Donne, who (Jonson had told Drummond) "for not being understood would perish," though Drummond's vague terms are equally applicable to essentially conservative writers like Chapman or Fulke Greville. Of the poets familiar to us as metaphysicals, only Donne had appeared by 1630. Herbert's *The Temple* was published in 1633, but the description seems less appropriate to him.

Dryden, at the end of the century, makes metaphysics the specific point of an attack on Donne: "He affects the metaphysics, not only in his satires, but in his amorous verses, where nature only should reign; and perplexes the minds of the fair sex with nice speculations of philosophy, when he should engage their hearts, and entertain them with the softnesses of love." [2] Here again it is the speculative and complex nature of the subject matter that is considered indecorous. But Dryden's usage, like Drummond's, is quite casual; *metaphysical* has not yet become a category of criticism. This is important, because the Dryden passage is always cited as relevant to Dr. Johnson's usage.

Johnson in 1779 first attempted to analyze the qualities of "a race of writers that may be termed the *metaphysical poets*"; his *Life of Cowley* is the starting point for our sense of Donne and his followers. Like Dryden, he deplores Donne's tendency to

1. *The Works of William Drummond of Hawthorndon* (Edinburgh, 1711), p. 143.
2. "Discourse Concerning the Original and Progress of Satire" (1693), in *Essays,* ed. W. P. Ker (Oxford, 1900), II, 19.

affect the metaphysics, but he is also concerned with the qualities of style produced by this cast of mind and thereby creates one of the great *topoi* of modern criticism: "Wit, abstracted from its effects upon the hearer, may be more rigorously and philo-sophically considered as a kind of *discordia concors;* a combina-tion of dissimilar images, or discovery of occult resemblances in things apparently unlike. Of wit, thus defined, they have more than enough. The most heterogeneous ideas are yoked by vio-lence together; nature and art are ransacked for illustrations, comparisons and allusions . . ." [3]

We could start by objecting that this account will not distin-guish the metaphysicals from any other Renaissance poets, and that Dr. Johnson has simply made a vice of what any Renais-sance handbook would have urged on the aspiring poet as a virtue. But this is really beside the point. Johnson knew little about Renaissance poetry; he was writing about Cowley as the heir of Donne, and for these two poets the description is accu-rate enough. What should give us pause, however, is the list of metaphysical poets with which Johnson concludes. Correctly ob-serving that the style was influenced by Italian poetry, he cites as its two English inaugurators Donne and, of all people, Ben Jonson. "Their immediate successors," by which he means those seventeenth-century poets who were still being read in the eighteenth century, "were Suckling, Waller, Denham, Cowley, Cleveland, and Milton." [4] And of these he finds only Cowley, Cleveland, and, marginally, Milton practising the metaphysical style.

Clearly Johnson's definition of the metaphysical style will cover a multitude of sins. What it will not cover is precisely what modern criticism has tried to place beneath it: everything we admire most in the poetry of the seventeenth century, everything that has seemed to us the expression of a radical and unified sensibility on which we have undertaken to model our own. The poets we find central to the tradition after Donne — Herbert, Vaughan, Crashaw, Marvell — are not even mentioned in John-son's list, presumably because he considers them too unimpor-

3. *Lives of the English Poets,* ed. G. B. Hill (Oxford, 1905), I, 20.
4. *Lives,* I, 22.

tant. Whether or not he would consider them metaphysical poets there is no way of knowing.

The designation of these poets as the major figures in a recognizable school derives from a critical attempt to isolate and define the components of a certain kind of wit the model for which is the Donnian conceit. The school, that is, is a phenomenon of modern criticism, and it is important to realize how closely involved it is specifically with a particular modern sensibility. Dr. Johnson made a fair start at defining metaphysical wit, yet when he surveyed the range of the seventeenth century, he saw quite a different group of metaphysical poets from ours. There is nothing anomalous in this: criticism is as much what we bring to poetry as what we get out of it, and our response to poetry — something inherent in us, not in the art — is what makes it valuable for us. But we must beware of mistaking our responses for historical data; the act of criticism must allow us to distinguish our own minds from the objects they consider. It is easy to be objective about Dr. Johnson, whose attitudes are sufficiently unlike ours to place him at a comfortable distance. But we are in collusion with Eliot; his seventeenth century has been ours, and for us the dissociation of sensibility and the sensuous apprehension of thought have had less the status of critical perspectives than of historical facts.

Let us for the moment set aside the term metaphysical and consider how a contemporary reader would have regarded poetry like Donne's. To do this is not to imply that we ought to respond to it in the same way, even if we could; but considering the verse in its own context should help to clarify what we bring to a reading of Donne, the nature of our own expectations and assumptions. The best work on this sort of question is still Rosamond Tuve's *Elizabethan and Metaphysical Imagery,* which, despite its age, remains enlightening and relevant. Good poetry for our age has had to be both intellectual and sensuous, compressed, directly expressive of experience or emotion. We even like to say that a good poem *is* an experience. That Donne's poetry possesses these qualities to a remarkable degree is undeniable; yet the aesthetic of his own time never claimed self-expression as a function of poetry, found in elaboration as great a virtue as in compression, and prized what we feel as sensuousness for its ornamental qualities. We can understand such an aesthetic producing *The Faerie Queene* and the Elizabethan love sonnet; but Donne seems to us to have rung the knell of all that — a radical intellect who, almost alone, transformed the character of English poetry.

And yet by Elizabethan standards Donne has most of the traditional virtues. He is better than most of his contemporaries but different from them only in the sense that every excellent poet excels in his own way. He is, in fact, less of an innovator than Sidney — whom he resembles, moreover, in respects that are very difficult to perceive from where we stand. Thomas Carew, indeed, describes him in terms that Sidney would have been happy to see applied to himself:

> The Muses garden with Pedantique weedes
> O'rspred, was purg'd by thee; The lazie seeds
> Of servile imitation throwne away;
> And fresh invention planted . . .[5]

Elegies are not the place to look for objective judgments; but it is not the accuracy of the perception that is relevant here, only its terms. Donne's friend Ben Jonson, classicist and conservative as a poet, found only in Donne's rhythmic techniques a break with tradition, which he duly deplored. The simile that seemed so startling and far-fetched to Dr. Johnson, whereby distant lovers were compared with the two feet of a compass, would have appeared elegant and ingenious to a Renaissance reader and therefore perfectly decorous. It would have also seemed perfectly familiar in type (though no less pleasing for that), since it was precisely the sort of image that filled the very popular books of devices and emblems of the period. The compass was a standard emblem of constancy; in this case Donne's originality consisted in his special application of traditional materials. Nor was this particular image new to verse; Donne could have found it in a madrigal by Guarini published in 1598:

> You'le aske perhaps wherefore I stay,
> Loving so much, so long away,

5. "Elegie upon the Death of . . . Dr. John Donne," ll. 25ff.

> O doe not thinke t'was I did part,
> It was my body, not my hearte,
> For like a Compasse in your loue,
> One foote is fix'd and cannot mooue,
> The other may follow her blinde guide
> Of giddy fortune, but not slide
> Beyond your service, nor dares venture
> To wander farre from you the Center.[6]

What this means is, obviously, not that Donne is not "original," but that we tend to look in the wrong places for what is original about him. The things that have been most startling to readers since the eighteenth century — the far-fetched comparisons, the synthesis of disparate materials — are in fact the least new. What is new is the intelligence, the sensitivity, the extraordinary command of language and emotive detail: what is new, in fact, is what is new about every great poet. The curious thing is that, while we do not feel it an insult to the reputation of, for example, Pope to remark his obvious and conscious relation to a tradition, we do feel that Donne's excellence is somehow bound up with his newness, uniqueness, destruction of tradition.

If Donne's age felt that compasses were appropriate comparisons for statements about lovers, then the age clearly had a different notion of decorum from Dr. Johnson's or ours. But it also had a different notion of the nature and function of imagery; this is worth considering in some detail, since so much of what we recognize as metaphysical wit has to do with its imagery. The term *image* can be used in two ways: first to mean a picture, second to mean any of a variety of kinds of figurative language. It is very important to be clear about which of these two usages is operating at any given moment in a critical discussion of the nature of metaphysical imagery. To begin with the first, the relation between verbal statements and pictorial representations in the Renaissance was much closer and more direct than it has been since the eighteenth century. Every picture was a symbol: pictures might be prized for their sensuous qualities, but their significance lay in their meaning, which was invariably con-

6. The English translation is by Carew and quite literal. The original is reprinted in Rhodes Dunlap's edition of Carew's *Poems* (Oxford, 1949), p. 272.

ceived in symbolic or allegorical terms. The image was thus a
way of expressing in a visual fashion a basically verbal meaning. Here is Lovelace, retrospectively describing the situation
at the beginning of a new era:

> Not as of old, when a rough hand did speake
> A strong Aspect, and a faire face a weake;
> When only a black beard cried Villaine, and
> By *Hieroglyphicks* we could understand.
> When Chrystall typified in a white spot,
> And the bright Ruby was but one red blot;
> Thou dost the things *Orientally* the same,
> Not only paintst its colour, but its *Flame:*
> Thou sorrow canst designe without a teare,
> And with the Man his very *Hope* or *Feare;*
> So that th'amazed world shall henceforth finde
> None but my Lilly ever drew a Minde.[7]

Why the Renaissance should have wished so intensely to express verbal meanings visually is a complex question capable of a
variety of answers. The desire crystallized around the recognition that hieroglyphs were the oldest language and therefore
presumably closest to the sources of ancient wisdom. This assumption suited well with both the age's love of intellectual obscurity and complexity and with its elitist tendencies: to unlock
the wisdom of the past one needed a key, which only the learned
few might have. It also meant that the Renaissance viewer looked
at a picture differently from the way we do, past its aesthetic
qualities to what it was about, which was usually far from obvious. To take a simple and famous example, the device of the
great Venetian publisher Aldus was a dolphin twined about an
anchor, its motto *festina lente,* make haste slowly; the energy of
the dolphin is stayed and secured by the constancy and gravity
of the anchor. Such devices and the more elaborate emblems,
images with their mottos and poems, were immensely popular
and influential throughout the Renaissance. Donne's compasses
look a great deal less eccentric in this context; they are simply
the emblem without the picture. Indeed, the first emblem writer,

7. "To . . . Mr Peter Lilly" [Lely], *Poems,* ed. C. H. Wilkinson
(Oxford, 1953), p. 58.

Andrea Alciati, in the first edition of his famous *Emblemata* (1531), defines an emblem as an epigram that describes a picture, a verbal image.[8] The emblem is *only* the epigram for Alciati, and the book was not intended to include illustrations. The pictures were added by Alciati's German publisher, and though they became standard they were always conceived as ancillary; the *meaning* of the form was verbal, the picture was an illustration or expression of the meaning. Quarles, Wither, and occasionally Crashaw supply pictures for their emblematic poems; Herbert's shaped poems relate image and word even more intimately, and many of his other poems are emblems according to the strict, original definition. The important point here is that the picture is entirely a function of the word; it is the verbal element that is basic. Alciati's publisher was simply illustrating pictorial epigrams.

At the same time, it should be observed that except for perhaps Herbert and Crashaw, expression in the poets we think of as metaphysical tended to develop *away* from the emblem. Donne tends to *break down* his emblems by analyzing or analogizing them, or even more directly by translating them into dramatic contexts. Herbert and Crashaw are probably the exemplary figures in English for our purposes. For example, Herbert makes the church floor, static and patterned, a subject for moralization; and "The Weeper" is essentially a set of commentaries on a given picture. For such poets the typographical emblem, such as Herbert's "Altar" or "Easter Wings," should be a logical next step; yet these are Herbert's only shaped poems, and there are none at all by Crashaw. The strictly pictorial aspects of emblematic poetry held little interest for either writer.

The overtly emblematic poets, moreover, like Quarles and Wither, tend to allow the "metaphysical" aspects of their poems to be conveyed simply by the picture or, more precisely, by the subject matter. The accompanying verse may be *about* unexpected juxtapositions or disparate ideas yoked together, but this does not produce anything we would call metaphysical in the poem itself. In fact, contemporary English emblem writers tend

8. For a detailed discussion of Alciati's use of the term, see H. Miedema, "The Term *Emblema* in Alciati," *Journal of the Warburg and Courtauld Institutes,* 31 (1968), 234ff.

to conceive of the meaning as the motto or epigram, and of the accompanying poem as directly interpretive and moralistic; thus on the whole they avoid the highly conceited and complex style.

The Renaissance interest in images, then, is still in the strictest sense verbal. "Whosoever loves not Picture," said Ben Jonson, "is injurious to Truth and all the wisdom of Poetry." [9] But the general interest in images is also an aspect of a larger and opposite movement the philosophical standards of which were set by Platonists and the enemies of which were Aristotelians. Renaissance Platonism is too complex a phenomenon to be summarily characterized; but the aspects of it that are relevant to this discussion are its tendency toward mysticism and the occult, and the fact that in dealing with the relation of the mind to external reality it stressed not language and syntactic structures but forms and Platonic ideas, and these it invariably conceived as images. It was in the service of neo-Platonism that hieroglyphics were first expounded. To us the movement appears hermetic and its concerns arcane. In its own time it seemed a way of finally confronting the true nature of reality. Petrarch, attacking Aristotelian scholastic philosophers, says: "They have forgotten things, and grown old among words." [10] *Things* were real; the word to a Platonist only stood for a thing, or image, or idea; and with this went a conviction that everything could be represented pictorially or schematically. "The Conceits of the mind are Pictures of things," said Jonson in *Timber*.[11] Cowley went a vast step further in the ode *To the Royal Society*. He says in praise of Bacon,

> From Words, which are but Pictures of the Thought,
>   (Though we our Thoughts from them perversely drew)
> To things, the Minds right Object he it brought,
> Like foolish Birds to painted Grapes we flew;
> He sought and gathered for our use the True;
> And when on heaps the chosen Bunches lay,
> He prest them wisely the Mechanick way,

9. *Discoveries,* in *Ben Jonson,* ed. C. H. Herford and P. and E. Simpson, VIII (Oxford, 1947), p. 610, l. 1522.
10. "De Contemptu Mundi," dialogue I, in *Opera* (Basel, 1581), II, 336.
11. *Discoveries,* in *Jonson,* VIII, 628, l. 2128.

Till all their juyce did in one Vessel joyn,
Ferment into a Nourishment Divine,
The thirsty Souls refreshing Wine.[12]

Along with the vulgarization of Platonic imagery and the introduction of mechanics to explain what is "real," Cowley's world
consists exclusively of things and pictures of things, either of
which the mind contemplates. Language is left behind with the
perverse errors of the Dark Ages.

The conviction exemplified here, that there is a direct relation between pictures or objects and thought and that words are
really nothing, was institutionalized in the work of the French
sixteenth-century logician Petrus Ramus.[13] Intellectually medi-
ocre and philosophically trivial, Ramus nevertheless became the
single most influential philosopher of the age by providing what
was essentially a short-cut to learning. Declaring that rhetoric
(or dialectic) was the basis of all knowledge, he developed a
technique for dichotomizing and schematizing information that,
simplistic as it was, rendered the universe comprehensible to any
schoolboy. Ramist dichotomies and schemes appear to us arbitrary, irrelevant, or slightly mad, though the principle behind
them remains unquestioned: we still believe that the best way
of explaining something is to draw a diagram of it. Ramism
provides the rationale for the natural impulse of Alciati's German publisher: to supply pictures for a text is merely the standard way of conceptualizing abstractions.

Seen against this background, the pictorial aspects of poetry
lose a good deal of color. Consider the following purple passage
from Sidney's *Apology:* "*Poesie,* therefore, is an Art of *Imitation* . . . that is to say, a representing, counterfeiting, or figuring forth: to speak Metaphorically, a speaking *Picture,* with this
end to teach and delight." [14] To begin with, the only thing here

12. *Poems,* ed. A. R. Waller (Cambridge, Eng., 1905), pp. 449–450.
13. The most important discussion of Ramus's work and significance
is that of Walter J. Ong, S.J., *Ramus, Method and the Decay of Dialogue*
(Cambridge, Mass., 1958).
14. *Prose Works,* ed. Albert Feuillerat (Cambridge, Eng., 1912), III,
9. Feuillerat's diplomatic reprint of the inaccurate Q1 is still, unfortunately, the standard edition, and I cite it for convenience. But I have
adopted the universally accepted pointing of Q2 in placing a comma,
rather than a period, after "Metaphorically."

that directly suggests images is the phrase "a speaking *Picture*," which Sidney explicitly says he is using metaphorically; he distinguishes it from the literal terms "representing, counterfeiting, or figuring forth." Clearly, Simonides' famous definition of poetry as a speaking picture is more of a commonplace, and its ubiquitous application in the Renaissance of less significance, than we have been taught to believe. Modern criticism has regularly interpreted it to mean that poetry should be pictorial, but the phrase for the sixteenth century had no such intention. On the simplest level, poetry is a speaking picture because that is what all language is: "Words," says Cowley, "are but Pictures of the Thought." To the extent that the definition takes account of poetry's specialness, it is a speaking picture because it joins the image and the word, the fiction and its meaning.

Poetry, then, was first a form of language. We tend to see it as a form of experience, and to be impatient of its claims as rhetoric; but the art of rhetoric was central to the practice of the Renaissance poet, who was classed not with the painter or composer (essentially artisans) but with the orator. Imagery, then, had a different status; and here we come to the second definition of the term. Images in poems were not pictures but rhetorical devices, and they were analyzed by contemporary critics not in terms of their sensuous qualities but of their use in the verbal or oratorical structure of the poem. This is important because it is easy to assume, as much recent criticism has done, that the Renaissance Platonist's concern with ideas, and the Ramist's with schemes, resulted in an emphasis on pictures as opposed to or as better than words, and in a consequent emphasis on imagery in poetry. Thus E. H. Gombrich in an extremely important and very misleading article, "Icones Symbolicae," [15] observes that for the Renaissance mind pictures came closer to representing Platonic ideas than anything else in the sensible world, and therefore that truth condensed into a visual image is nearer absolute truth than truth conveyed in words. Gombrich then, without distinguishing between images as pictures and images as rhetorical tropes, goes on to cite Tasso for sup-

15. *Journal of the Warburg and Courtauld Institutes*, 11 (1948), 163–192.

port. In his essay on heroic poetry, Tasso justifies the use of
elaborate poetic imagery by an appeal to the hermetic emblematic tradition descending from Dionysius the Areopagite, explaining that to move readers by images is nobler than to teach by
demonstrations. The poet's images, then, are really Platonic
ideas because they are images of intelligible, not sensible
things.[16]

Aside from Gombrich's confusion of the two senses of
imagery, the thesis is vitiated by the fact that this is not what
the Tasso passage says. The word that Gombrich takes to mean
"images" is *immagini,* and it is Aristotle's term "fictions": whatever is imagined in the poem — not poetic conceits merely, but
the characters, the story. Moreover, though it is true that Platonic psychology (and, for that matter, Aristotelian psychology)
maintained that the mind *knows* by conceiving images, Platonic
ideas were not conceived as pictures in any such simple and
direct way. Indeed, pictorial representations — the "painted
chair" of Herbert's "Jordan I" — are explicitly rejected by Platonic philosophy. Socrates' position in *The Republic* can be
briefly summarized as follows: the craftsman who makes a bed
is imitating the ideal bed in the mind of god. A painting of a bed
is thus only an imitation of an imitation, a double lie "catching
the sense at two removes," as Herbert says. Of course Socrates'
thesis is vulnerable in a number of ways, and the fact that nobody in the dialogue attacks it merely testifies to Plato's lack of
interest in the visual arts. Glaucon might have replied, for example, that the artist represents the ideal bed, not the real one,
and so is coming closer to truth than the craftsman; but nobody,
even in the Renaissance, undertakes to defend pictures by claiming they are Platonic ideas. Ficino's emphasis on visual experience is powerful and broad, but it does not involve any interest
at all in paintings.

The stress on ideas-as-images in Renaissance poetry is misleading insofar as it tends to concentrate discussions of Renaissance poetry on its imagery as an aspect of its Platonism or
Ramism. (Miss Tuve goes astray here mainly because she
tended to treat images out of context, as discrete entities, and

16. *Ibid.,* 174.

only then to ask how they relate to the larger structure of the poem, thus adding to her critical vocabulary that terrible word "relatableness.") Renaissance poets tended to think of images as tropes or rhetorical figures, that is, as verbal structures. But we think of them as *visual* structures. Hence, a powerful charge in Eliot's attack on Milton is that his imagination was verbal rather than visual. So it was. But a seventeenth-century critic would have been very puzzled by the assumption that this was a defect.

Poetry, then, is rhetoric for the Renaissance, a form of *argument*. The most direct heir of the Renaissance tradition in the eighteenth century is not the writer of odes following Jonson, nor the occasional lyricist echoing Herrick and the Cavaliers, but Pope. And images and metaphors are parts of arguments, for Donne and Herbert as for Sidney or Jonson. When Sidney attacks love sonnets on the grounds that they would not persuade a mistress of anything,[17] he is assuming that poetry is rhetoric and that its function is therefore to persuade. We have seen Dryden as late as 1693 making the same assumption when he complains that Donne "perplexes the minds of the fair sex . . . when he should engage their hearts." If we took the implications of this seriously, it would clarify a good deal that is now obscure about Renaissance poetry, whether metaphysical or not. The function of poetry, both Sidney and Dryden, a hundred years apart, assume, is not to express the feelings but to move or persuade the reader or listener. The crucial feelings involved, the emotional experiences to which the poem must be true, are those of the reader, not the poet.

So initially, at least, it will help if we can see Donne as a *grand rhétoriqueur* rather than as a romantic being true to his sensations, translating thought into sensuous images or action, as Eliot saw him. Language *is* action for Donne, as for all Renaissance poets, but in a different sense, the sense in which language is action for the orator: it is power and control over his audience. The age took this very seriously; we do not. We praise Donne's command of scholastic logic, without observing that the logic of his poems is almost invariably specious. There are perfectly good reasons for an orator or a logician to construct

17. *Works,* ed. Feuillerat, III, 41.

false arguments; but we cannot get at them unless we are aware from the beginning that what Donne is doing is constructing arguments.

In fact, there is little in Renaissance critical theory beyond the basic and continuing assumption that poetry is rhetoric that helps us understand the development of Donne's style. This will seem less striking if we recall Sidney's accurate, unhappy observation that English writers were not interested in writing according to the rules of the best literary theory, or indeed according to any theory at all. English Renaissance poetry, much more than that of the continent, was a pragmatic art; hence the proliferation of handbooks like Puttenham's and Webbe's and the comparative dearth of essays like Sidney's.

Eliot's famous essay did undertake to treat metaphysical verse in a historical context. "The Metaphysical Poets" is the locus classicus for a complex of modern commonplaces about poetry: that to be good it must be sensuous and a direct expression of the feelings but also highly intellectual and the index of a unified sensibility. "Racine or Donne looked into a good deal more than the heart. One must look into the cerebral cortex, the nervous system, and the digestive tracts." [18] "Intellectual" poetry, by which Eliot says he means poetry conceived as experience, is good; "reflective" poetry — poetry *about* experience — is bad. The models for the former are Donne and Lord Herbert of Cherbury, for the latter Tennyson and Browning: "Tennyson and Browning are poets, and they think; but they do not feel their thought as immediately as the odour of a rose. A thought to Donne was an experience; it modified his sensibility. When a poet's mind is perfectly equipped for its work, it is constantly amalgamating disparate experience; the ordinary man's experience is chaotic, irregular, fragmentary. The latter falls in love, or reads Spinoza, and these two experiences have nothing to do with each other, or with the noise of the typewriter or the smell of cooking; in the mind of the poet these experiences are always forming new wholes" (p. 247).

All poetry, then — or perhaps Eliot means only all "real" poetry — is metaphysical by definition, "constantly amalgamating disparate experience." Doubtless it is vain to inquire how

18. *Selected Essays* (New York, 1932), p. 250.

the critic is to know whether or not a thought has modified a particular poet's sensibility. But the real critical problem would be whether the poet's thought, expressed in the poem, modifies the *reader's* sensibility; Eliot remains curiously aloof from this sort of question. He is writing, in fact, not as a critic, not even as a reader, but as a poet; and his primary interest is not in Donne's poetry at all, but in Donne's mind. He finds there all the qualities toward which he aspires in his own poetry, and the identification is complete.

Eliot's account of metaphysical poetry appears to have considerable breadth. To justify it, however, he had to be carefully selective. The essay first appeared in 1921 as a laudatory review of Grierson's anthology, *Metaphysical Lyrics and Poems of the Seventeenth Century*. But Eliot's list of metaphysical poets differs almost as significantly from Grierson's as it does from Dr. Johnson's: Eliot's is "Donne, Crashaw, Vaughan, Herbert and Lord Herbert, Marvell, King, Cowley" (p. 250). But to Grierson, Thomas Carew figures as largely as Marvell and receives as much space as Lord Herbert and King combined; Milton receives only slightly less; Lovelace and Suckling each have as much as Lord Herbert or King. Clearly Grierson's metaphysicals are not Eliot's.

To account for the difference between Renaissance poetry and that of Tennyson and Browning, Eliot proposed a theory that rapidly took on the status of a historical fact:

In the seventeenth century a dissociation of sensibility set in, from which we have never recovered; and this dissociation, as is natural, was aggravated by the influence of the two most powerful poets of the century, Milton and Dryden. Each of these men performed certain poetic functions so magnificently well that the magnitude of the effect concealed the absence of others. The language went on and in some respects improved; the best verse of Collins, Gray, Johnson, and even Goldsmith satisfies some of our fastidious demands better than that of Donne or Marvell or King. But while the language became more refined, the feeling became more crude. The feeling, the sensibility, expressed in the *Country Churchyard* (to say nothing of Tennyson and Browning) is cruder than that in the *Coy Mistress* (p. 247).

This crudeness, Eliot insists, is the result not of a mere difference in excellence, but of a historical process. "It is something which had happened to the mind of England." Such an assertion comfortably justifies our finding certain aspects of Renaissance culture more interesting than the culture of succeeding centuries, but as a critical theory it has a fatal flaw: it depends entirely on its choice of examples. There is nothing in the argument to prevent us from rewriting the final sentence to read as follows: "The feeling, the sensibility, expressed in 'The Epistle to Dr. Arbuthnot' (to say nothing of Blake and Hopkins) is cruder than that in 'The Weeper.'" There is nothing unfair about this revision; indeed, the historical claims of the passage positively demand it. But given such a conclusion, the theory looks a good deal less persuasive.

This is not to say that nothing happened in the intellectual history of the seventeenth century, or that the poetry of succeeding centuries is indistinguishable from that of the Renaissance. But what happened is not something that will allow us to talk about crudeness of sensibility as if it were a historical phenomenon. The development of empirical science was a product of, and it demanded, new ways of conceiving external reality. The two poets most sensitive to the radical aspects of seventeenth-century thought, Donne and Milton, responded in diametrically opposite ways. Donne's famous complaint in *The First Anniversary* that "new philosophy calls all in doubt" may be an index of his extraordinary awareness; but the feelings generated in him by that awareness are neither inevitable nor justified, logically or dramatically. Ben Jonson perceived this when he told Donne that if the poem "had been written of the Virgin Marie," rather than of the thirteen-year-old daughter of his patron, "it had been something." [19] The same disproportion between the facts and the feelings is observable in much of Donne's work. This is not a fault, but it *is* a characteristic. Donne's dismay at the appearance of new stars might be contrasted with the excitement of Milton's allusion to "the Tuscan artist" Galileo in *Paradise Lost* (I.288).

The intellectual revolution of the seventeenth century trans-

19. "Conversations with Drummond," in *Ben Jonson,* ed. C. H. Herford and P. Simpson, I (1925), 133, l. 45.

formed poetry, as it did all aspects of intellectual endeavor. Indeed, it changed the notion of what constituted a valid statement about reality. When the essential unity of the universe could be taken for granted, before new philosophy called all in doubt, anything could be defined by showing how it resembled something else. Even the most far-fetched likenesses expressed a truth, since the unity of widely disparate parts of reality was thus asserted. But the new science required distinctions: to define a thing, we assert its uniqueness. Metaphor, which proposes the identity of different things, then ceased to express a relation that could be conceived as in any way real; it was instead "poetic" or fanciful. A firm boundary quickly arose between scientific or rigorous thought and poetic or imaginative thought — taking off from the apostle of empirical science, Bacon, in the second book of *The Advancement of Learning.* The distinction between these two kinds of thought was based not, as it sometimes had been in the Renaissance, on utilitarian grounds, but on a far more indulgent principle. Dr. Johnson *defends* the faulty logic of Pope's *Essay on Man* by saying that philosophical rigor is not appropriate to poetry.

The transformations of thought were profound; the easiest landmarks of the transition are probably Hobbes's preface to Davenant's heroic poem *Gondibert* and Thomas Sprat's *History of the Royal Society,* each of which undertook to define the proper limits of language in the new age. We may, that is, take the age's own testimony as evidence of the effects of new modes of thought on language. But describing this transition as a "dissociation of sensibility" is only to confuse the issue. What happened in the seventeenth century did not make poetry worse or sensibilities cruder, but it did radically alter the status of poetry as an intellectual pursuit for both poet and reader. Eliot's perception of how far poetry had moved from the center of the intellectual life of English culture is perfectly accurate; but his longing for an age when to think was also automatically to feel and experience is in the strictest sense sentimental. His is a vision that still directs much of our critical energy, even in reaction to it.

Thus even the most cogent modern argument against the notion of a seventeenth-century dissociation of sensibility, Frank

Kermode's in *The Romantic Image,* suffers from its inability to take the whole discussion out of Eliot's terms. Kermode observes that the peculiar modern mystique of metaphysical poetry is built around a determination to see the crucial element in poetry as its imagery:

> It seems to me much less important that there was not, in the sense in which Mr. Eliot's supporters have thought, a particular and far-reaching catastrophe in the seventeenth century, than that there was, in the twentieth, an urgent need to establish the historicity of such a disaster. And the attempt to answer the question why there should have been takes us back to the Image. The theory of the dissociation of sensibility is, in fact, the most successful version of a symbolist attempt to explain why the modern world resists works of art that testify to the poet's special, anti-intellectual way of knowing truth. And this attempt obviously involves the hypothesis of an age which was different, an age in which the Image was more readily accessible and acceptable. When, in fact, the poets and aestheticians of the Image turn their attention to history, it is in search of some golden age when the prevalent mode of knowing was not positivist and anti-imaginative; when the image, the intuited, created reality, was habitually respected; when art was not permanently on the defensive against mechanical and systematic modes of inquiry.[20]

This is obviously right. The trouble is that instead of correcting the balance, it overturns the scales. Kermode is primarily interested in seeing Eliot as an agent of the international symbolist conspiracy, hence Eliot's very perceptions become suspect. So while it might seem perfectly reasonable to argue that the dissociation of sensibility is a misinterpretation of a perfectly valid perception, Kermode is unwilling to allow Eliot to have been responding to anything real at all — other than the needs of symbolist theory, of course. But surely something *did* happen in the seventeenth century; and in a most extraordinary passage this is precisely what Kermode is at some pains to deny. Eliot's term, he says, is "quite useless":

> It will not do to say that it is partly true, or true in a way, as some people now claim. A once-for-all event cannot happen every few

20. New York, 1957, p. 143.

years; there cannot be, if the term is to retain the significance it has
acquired, dissociations between the archaic Greeks and Phidias, between Catullus and Virgil, between Guido and Petrarch, between
Donne and Milton. As a way of speaking about *periods* the expression is much less useful than even "baroque." At its worst, it is merely
a way of saying which poets one likes, and draping history over
them (p. 146).

If this is anything more than a heavyhanded way of objecting
to the exclusiveness of Eliot's terminology, it is nonsense. Something *did* happen to Greek sculpture between the archaic Greeks
and Phidias; and observing it has nothing to do with which of
them one likes better. It is the unacknowledged moral inferences
— that the seventeenth century is "better" than the eighteenth,
that the best poetry is religious, that a particular modern sensibility is the single standard by which all others are to be
judged — that Kermode ought to be objecting to, not the perception.

But a historically oriented view, however accurate its sense of
detail, may leave one equally uncomfortable. Thus Joseph
Mazzeo finds a context for the practice of metaphysical poetry
by examining a good deal of continental poetic theory advocating
the virtues of complex conceits and abstruseness of style and
subject.[21] Clearly something about this must be right; *concet-
tismo* and *marinismo* must in some way be developments parallel
to what Donne and Herbert and Crashaw are doing — and in the
case of Crashaw, at least, the influence is quite direct. But this
requires us to think of Donne as writing poetry that was program-
matically obscurantist. He *might* have done so: is this what Ben
Jonson was objecting to when he told Drummond that Donne
"for not being understood would perish"? Hardly. The idea that
poetry, as an expression of the highest wisdom, should be obscure to limit it to the understanding of the learned was, as we
have seen, good neo-Platonic doctrine and more or less explicitly
endorsed by Jonson himself, along with Chapman and many
others. Documents in the case are Jonson's *Masque of Blackness*
and Chapman's *Shadow of Night* — deliberately, programmati-

21. "A Seventeenth-Century Theory of Metaphysical Poetry" and
"Metaphysical Poetry and the Poetic of Correspondence," in *Renaissance
and Seventeenth Century Studies* (New York, 1964), pp. 29–59.

cally obscure and intellectually elitist. There is no evidence that Donne was writing in this way, or that Jonson was accusing him of doing so, or that he would have disapproved if Donne *had* done so. The sort of thing Jonson found abstruse in Donne was the rationale for *The Progress of the Soul,* which Donne had to explain to him. The complexity of Donne's imagery, the enormous range of allusion and the continual relating of disparate kinds of experience, bespeak an intense and wide-ranging intellect; but there is nothing hermetic about the mind. The imagery, however complex, is never abstruse: on the contrary, Donne is always elaborately explaining it. The energy moves toward inclusiveness, not exclusiveness.

Where, then, does this leave us? The reason no theory of metaphysical poetry has proved adequate is that "metaphysical" really refers not to poetry, but to our sensibilities in response to it. All such theories are thus profoundly time-bound, concerned with why we feel more strongly about certain qualities of verse at a given moment than about others; and to take this into account, a theory of metaphysical poetry would have to be able to change as tastes change. The readjustment we now seem to require comes precisely from a change in taste. We are more interested in large forms than Eliot, who was primarily attracted to the lyric and to lyric aspects of the drama. Late Shakespearean plays are meaningful to us less in relation to metaphysical poetry than to a much larger and deeper — and historically oriented — symbolic tradition. Symbolic and rhetorical forms attract us generally; allegory interests us more than it did Eliot; we are less exclusively responsive to the virtues of compression in poetry and more alive to the older virtue of elaboration. Ironically, we have become in many ways more the traditionalists than was Eliot.

Where this leaves us is, I hope, back with the poetry. What we find as critics in works of art is largely determined by what we are looking for, and it is one of the functions of criticism to make us look again and again at works of art in ways that are valid but untried. The history of criticism is itself a history of literature, of the continuing response of the intellect to the creations of its past. The moral is only, to recapitulate, that we must beware of taking our responses for historical data; we must be able to distinguish our minds from the objects they contemplate.

DAVID KALSTONE

Conjuring with Nature: Some Twentieth-Century Readings of Pastoral

> . . . the sunlight has never
> heard of trees: surrendered self among
> unwelcoming forms
> A. R. Ammons, "Gravelly Run"

Renaissance critics were disappointed not to find pastoral among the "kinds" of literature Aristotle had discussed.[1] Imagined as one of the oldest and purest forms, it proved to be a late, Alexandrian invention, product of a sophisticated society, drawing for its styles upon epic, lyric, drama, and philosophical dialogues, and capable in later years of entering into combinations as promiscuously as Polonius suggests: "pastoral, pastoral-comical, historical-pastoral, tragical-historical, tragical-comical-historical-pastoral." In English literature, the eclogue nourished and was absorbed into lyric, dramatic, and narrative forms less easily classifiable and, in many cases, more complex than their Greek and Roman antecedents. Successive rediscoveries have preserved the power of pastoral but questioned, explored, and transformed its nature. Marvell and Milton, its

1. Thomas G. Rosenmeyer, *The Green Cabinet: Theocritus and the European Pastoral Lyric* (Berkeley, 1969), p. 4.

greatest seventeenth-century practitioners, became so because
they were also its most formidable and illuminating critics; as
much could be said for Wordsworth, Coleridge, and Keats in
the nineteenth century, or Frost and Stevens in our own. Our
expectations for the form should, in a sense, begin by understanding those of the poets who use it. When a contemporary
like A. R. Ammons speaks of the enterprise as that of the "surrendered self among unwelcoming forms," [2] his wry submissiveness hopes for something in pastoral performance, even as
it fails. Or in Wallace Stevens' words

> From this the poem springs: that we live in a place
> That is not our own and, much more, not ourselves
> And hard it is in spite of blazoned days.[3]

The note of dispossession is common to modern pastoralists.
Yet the impulse ("the poem springs"), the effort to assume the
role of pastoral singer, remains and rewards. A poem as bleak
as Frost's "Desert Places" may help us understand why:

> Snow falling and night falling fast, oh, fast
> In a field I looked into going past,
> And the ground almost covered smooth in snow,
> But a few weeds and stubble showing last.
>
> The woods around it have it — it is theirs.
> All animals are smothered in their lairs.
> I am too absent-spirited to count;
> The loneliness includes me unawares.
>
> And lonely as it is that loneliness
> Will be more lonely ere it will be less —

2. "Gravelly Run," reprinted from A. R. Ammons, *Corsons Inlet*
(copyright © 1965 by Cornell University), by permission of Cornell
University Press.

3. *The Collected Poems of Wallace Stevens* (New York, 1954),
p. 383. Quotations of Stevens' verse from *The Collected Poems of Wallace Stevens* and *Opus Posthumous* are reprinted by permission of Alfred
A. Knopf, Inc., and Faber and Faber, Ltd. (copyright 1936, 1942, 1947,
1952, 1954 by Wallace Stevens; copyright © 1957 by Elsie Stevens and
Holly Stevens).

A blanker whiteness of benighted snow
With no expression, nothing to express.

They cannot scare me with their empty spaces
Between stars — on stars where no human race is.
I have it in me so much nearer home
To scare myself with my own desert places.[4]

The trick of the poem is in the way it crystallizes both a vision and a power of expression. Beginning without the ceremony of a complete sentence, it takes in the scene with sidelong glances. By the end, defiant address has replaced the urgent and rapid notation of phrases, participles, breathless repetitions. Undesignated fears ("The woods around it have it — it is theirs") are to a degree mastered by more emphatic vocabulary and phrasings: *smothered, absent-spirited, unawares* (with its double syntax), *a blanker whiteness of benighted snow.* With this last phrase — its strong pun and heightened exposure of fear — the traveller seems to separate himself and to resist engulfment in a world "with no expression, nothing to express." The escape he wins comes out in *his* expression, in the bravado mustered by the final stanza — whose message, not at all reassuring, is delivered in a tone with something of the definite, the clarified, about it. "I have it in me so much nearer home" is a way of locating fears. The encounter with nature wakens a counterpower.

My point is that the poem has a clarifying or restorative force which, however ironically viewed, has always been associated with pastoral. The notion of the mind in the act of composing itself (Stevens' "poem of the act of the mind") may be especially modern,[5] but the means — the poet performing in or against a landscape — is not. It may be that, in Pater's phrase, in such landscapes "life itself is conceived as a sort of listen-

4. From *The Poetry of Robert Frost,* ed. Edward Connery Latham (copyright 1936 by Robert Frost; copyright © 1964 by Lesley Frost Ballantine; copyright © 1969 by Holt, Rinehart and Winston, Inc.), reprinted by permission of Holt, Rinehart and Winston, Inc., and Jonathan Cape, Ltd.
5. Reuben A. Brower, *The Poetry of Robert Frost* (New York, 1963), p. 92.

ing"; or it may be, as in "Desert Places" that the engagement of poet with setting is more active or more problematic. The French critic Roland Barthes makes a clear separation between earlier literature which assumes "that Nature . . . can be possessed, that it does not shy away or cover itself in shadows, but is in its entirety subjected to the toils of language" and modern poetry which gives its readers a "closed" nature, one of "fragmented space, made of objects solitary and terrible, because the links between them are only potential." [6] These distinctions are challenging ones in trying to think about modern writers — Frost and Stevens, notably — as heirs to a pastoral line. How does a genre which has its roots in that earlier world and its comfortable assumptions (nature is comprehensible) provide energies for poets who do not share those assumptions? Or, to phrase the question for critics, how can we be flexible and accurate enough to connect different kinds of pastoral verse — classical, Renaissance, Romantic, modern — doing justice to the vitality of the enterprise, rather than seeing it as a dead form, restricted to eclogues and dwindling into aristocratic masquerade? What follows is a sample argument, one way of viewing modern critical efforts and recent pastoral poetry. I talk principally about two twentieth-century critiques of pastoral, suggest how they have altered or enlarged our view of earlier pastoral and how that historical effort helps us to read and judge some pastoral performances of our own day.

It would be only a slight exaggeration to say that the most valuable and alert writings on pastoral in the past thirty-five years have been footnotes to Empson[7] — acting on his hints, unravelling confusions, stung into disagreement by his broad construction of pastoral or by his playing fast and loose with the history of the genre. If there is any single book which deserves to be as influential as *Some Versions of Pastoral,* it is Thomas G. Rosenmeyer's recently published *The Green Cabinet: Theocritus and the European Pastoral Lyric,* a book all the

6. Roland Barthes, *Writing Degree Zero,* trans. Annette Lavers and Colin Smith (New York, 1968), pp. 49–50.
7. William Empson, *Some Versions of Pastoral,* 2nd ed. (London, 1950).

better because Empson's writing has forced the author into tactful disagreements which help him see the importance of his subject. In some ways Empson and Rosenmeyer are at opposing poles. Rosenmeyer argues, with some justice, that Empson draws upon only "the most developed and the most differentiated products of the tradition." [8] His own effort is to restore our sense of what the first pastoral poet, Theocritus, was like; and how his achievement, far from being merely a forerunner of the pastoral lyric was — like Homer's in epic — one of its finest examples, coming to be accepted "as pointing the orientation" of what was to follow.[9] What Rosenmeyer leaves unsaid about later pastoral is almost as important as what he chooses to say; like accounts of old settlements, his makes us aware at every point of how different we are. His book helps us, for example, to see Empson's effort in perspective, as a modern one creating and exemplifying a taste for the complex in pastoral — an effort which parallels the ventures of twentieth-century poets to reclaim, if only partially, the resources of the genre. Like Frost's oven-bird, the question that we frame "in all but words / Is what to make of a diminished thing."

For all their differences, in method as well as attitude (Rosenmeyer is much less latitudinarian in what he calls pastoral), both these critics avoid the trivializing notion that pastoral is principally a genre of escape or of nostalgia for the past. They both assume that in the hands of the great practitioners of the genre, pastoral is not merely a bundle of preferences: country is better than city, gardens better than streets. Both are concerned with the active engagement of the singer or poet in a landscape: with the resources it offers to the spirit, the roles it allows him to take, the play of voices it allows him. Rosenmeyer makes it very clear that nostalgia for the Golden Age, though known to the Greeks, was quite a distinct strain, separate from the world of the Theocritean shepherd, and that pastoral did not come to include Golden Age themes until Roman poets took it up.[10] "The pastoral is not concerned with history, or the sequence of evolutionary stages. Its time is here and now;

8. Rosenmeyer, *The Green Cabinet,* p. 17.
9. *Ibid.,* p. 30.
10. *Ibid.,* p. 223.

its attention is to what is best in man, not to what he can do
at one time or another." [11]

The remark about pastoral and history brings us to the brink
of Rosenmeyer's disagreement with Empson, but the stress on
performance, on what is immediate and available to the spirit
in a pastoral world is one which Empson would understand
and one to which his own criticism returns again and again.
"Theocritus' herdsmen are free men . . . attempting to express what is in their hearts, at an hour [noon] when nature
least interferes with their freedom. Yet the awareness of the
anger of Pan is there; not the self-abasement before a divine
master, but the knowledge that the noon hour is a short-lived
thing; beyond it there are motions and passions that engulf
otium, and never cease to threaten the balance" (pp. 76–77).
Rosenmeyer sees the *Idylls* as embodying Epicurean values:
an appreciation of momentary pleasures, simplicity, a companionable rivalry and appreciation of song. Above all, Theocritus
is free of the subjectivity of earlier lyric styles, closer to the detachment of the epic from which he borrows the hexameter line
and a paratactic style which "tends to achieve its successes by
showing rather than telling. It presents a bird's-eye view of
characters in action rather than an intimate exploration of motives and impulses" (p. 15). There are few moments of self-
assessment; Polyphemus, awkward and frustrated in love, appears much less reflective than his descendant, Virgil's Corydon.
Endangering emotions — passion, fears for the dead — are held
in equilibrium by their place in singing contests and as part of
the ceremonial though momentary fellowship in song.

Even with the songs of frustrated love . . . the pretended musical-
ity makes the song take on the aspect of an aria . . . In the case
of the pastoral, which is recited rather than sung, the internal fiction of musical delivery makes the music a part of the lyric substance. It sets up a buffer that makes a direct identification much
more difficult . . . This saves us from losing ourselves and over-
indulging in private wrongs . . . Pastoral suffering, like pastoral
joy, calls for applause rather than pity or fear. The appreciation is
that of the connoisseur, not of the bewitched sympathizer (p. 152).

11. *Ibid.,* p. 220.

Much of what we take for granted in pastoral was at the beginning only a minor strain: the figure of the solitary singer, for example, becomes much more prominent in Renaissance and Romantic verse. Only three of Theocritus' pastorals are "solos." The norm is the fellowship of two, "the joint enterprise of like-minded men" (pp. 154–155). Whether in affectionate rivalry — tempered by the forms and demands of the singing contest — or the give and take of appreciative dialogue, the poems match "perceptive beings in a nexus of friendship and equality" (p. 157).

Society, in such a case, is not "all but rude to this delicious solitude." The shepherds enjoy their own sociability; and nature — another shock to the postclassical sensibility — is conceived primarily as a backdrop for this freedom and exercise of companionship. Characters belong to their surroundings but do not scrutinize them; the herdsman is not in the romantic sense a disciple of nature.[12] Natural detail is kept to the minimum, the simple props of the *locus amoenus:* trees, a clearing, a fountain or brook. Nature is neither elaborately described (just enough to suggest its free atmosphere) nor is it elaborately symbolic. "The Greek landscape is setting, background, not trope" (p. 196).

Rosenmeyer's book is full of such tonic insights and reminds us how transformed or even, to use Stevens' phrase, "far-fetched" our own versions of pastoral have become. It is here, of course, that he takes sharpest issue with Empson, criticizing his relish in complicated handlings of landscape and singling out Empson's account of the Eden of *Paradise Lost*. That account, from *Some Versions of Pastoral,* is an instructive one. Empson comments on the lines:

Thus was this place,
A happy rural seat of various view:
Groves whose rich Trees wept odorous Gums and Balm,
Others whose fruit burnished with Golden Rind
Hung amiable, Hesperian fables true,
If true, here only, and of delicious taste.

12. *Ibid.,* pp. 183–185.

The whole beauty of the thing is a rich nostalgia, but not simply for a lost Eden; sorrow is inherent in Eden itself, as Johnson found it in *L'Allegro,* and that the trees are weeping seems to follow directly from the happiness of the rural seat. The trees that glitter with unheeding beauty and the trees that weep with prescience are alike associated with the tree of knowledge; the same Nature produced the *balm* of healing and the fatal *fruit* . . . The melancholy of our feeling that Eden must be lost so soon, once attached to its vegetation, makes us feel that it is inherently melancholy. These are the same puzzles about the knowledge, freedom, happiness, and strength of the state of innocence, but applied to the original innocence of Nature . . .

One reason for the force of Milton's descriptions of Eden is that these contradictory ideas can be made there to work together.[13]

The careful response to "wept odorous gums and balm," as well as Empson's own phrasing of "trees that glitter with unheeding beauty," reveal how deeply and why Empson is engaged by landscape which, unlike Theocritus', *can* be taken as trope, nature presented in complex ways and seen from different angles. He attributes to Milton the view that "the human creature is essentially out of place in the world and needed no fall in time to make him so." The argument — whether Empson's Milton is the true one — will continue like Jarndyce and Jarndyce. My concern here is not to arbitrate, but to notice Empson's special sensitivity to views prominent in twentieth-century pastoral literature: that we are in a sense intruders in nature; that the direct restorative power of pastoral is not ours; and that we must hear in it discordant tones and see in complicated landscape both what restores the spirit and what endangers that restoration. This Empson demonstrates over and over in nuances of his readings of sixteenth- and seventeenth-century verse. The past fifteen years have been rich in books on Milton, correcting Empson's history, his view of doctrine, his iconography, his sense of seventeenth-century literary conventions and disputing what they claim as his willful opinions of Milton's God and Satan. Nevertheless, as with the recent flood of critical books on Marvell, even cautious critics have been liberated

13. Empson, *Some Versions of Pastoral,* pp. 186–187.

by the questions Empson asked;[14] they have been made aware
of the problematic nature of the literature of that period and of
the intricate adaptations Milton and Marvell had to make in
order to revive and recreate traditional forms.

There is more at stake, of course, than descriptions of nature. At the beginning of the twentieth century W. W. Greg
published his pioneering study, *Pastoral Poetry and Pastoral
Drama,* which treated the genre as if it consisted only of "pure"
pastorals: eclogues and pastoral plays like *Aminta* and *Il Pastor
Fido.* Empson's book frees us (too much, some would argue,
turning to his discussion of *Alice in Wonderland*) by calling attention in its opening chapters to the double plots, those strange
hybrids of pastoral and heroic or historical themes which test
one genre against the other. Whether or not these mixed genres
are, as Rosenmeyer argues, alien to true pastoral style, writing
pastoral in the "comparative mode" begins with Virgil, in whose
eclogues politics are (the phrase is Rosenmeyer's) "the ever-
present condition without which the pastoral fiction could not
last." [15] In Theocritus, politics are "marginal, conveyed via images and passing references that allow small glimpses of the
realities ringing the bower." With Virgil the elements which
endanger song are felt from the very start and shadow even the
gestures and vocabulary which Virgil assigns his shepherds.
In the first eclogue, which contrasts one shepherd saved by, one
victimized by, politics, Meliboeus has lost his secure place in the
pastoral world and must leave, along with other shepherds, the
lands he has long cultivated and grazed; Tityrus, his companion
in song, has managed to save his bit of land, presumably by ap-
pealing to the same political force which has exiled Meliboeus.

Meliboeus describes Tityrus as he lies under a spreading
beech:

nos patriam fugimus: tu, Tityre, lentus in umbra
formosam resonare doces Amaryllida silvas.

14. See, for example, Christopher Ricks, *Milton's Grand Style*
(Oxford, 1964); Anne D. Ferry, *Milton's Epic Voice* (Cambridge, Mass.,
1963); Joseph Summers, *The Muse's Method* (Cambridge, Mass., 1962);
and Stanley E. Fish, *Surprised by Sin* (New York, 1967).
15. *The Green Cabinet,* p. 214.

> We are outcasts from our country; you, Tityrus,
> at ease beneath the shade, teach the woods to
> re-echo "fair Amaryllis." [16]

Lentus in umbra: at ease beneath the shade. Twenty lines later that adjective recurs, robbed of some of the secure repose it seems to offer the pastoral singer. Tityrus is describing Rome, where he has gone to see the "god" who has heard his suit:

> verum haec tantum alias inter caput extulit urbes,
> quantum lenta solent inter viburna cupressi.

> But this one has reared her head as high among all other
> cities as cypresses oft do among the bending osiers.

A word which has had special resonance for the singer, *lentus,* associated with his freedom and song, suddenly takes on a wider dependency. Tityrus, with his tone of awe and gratitude, is not meant to be raising such questions, but the reader sees his simile as a kind of flawed glass. Those bending osiers, so harmlessly overshadowed by cypress, speak obliquely of the place of shepherds in relation to Rome. Prepared by Meliboeus' misfortunes to think of Rome's encroaching force, as well as its power to rescue, the reader finds a bristling question in Tityrus' bucolic comparison. There is a similar *frisson* when Meliboeus imagines his "kingdom" (*mea regna*) reduced by "godless soldiers" in some future years to a few ears of corn. The single word *regna* spans meanings as sadly separate as are the shepherd's dreams of independent power from the reality of imperial sway over his land of song. Before our eyes, as in the changed meaning of *lentus,* pastoral gestures and landscape become trope; the shepherd is forced to make explicit what is only implicit in Theocritus, that the land both is and is not his kingdom. The contrasting fates of Virgil's two shepherds raise delicate questions about history, about the incursions of power or the possibility, strong for Tityrus, stronger yet for the speaker

16. Virgil, Eclogue I, 4–5, *Eclogues, Georgics, Aeneid,* trans. H. T. Rushton Fairclough (Cambridge, Mass.; Loeb Classical Library, 1932). See also, Michael Putnam, *Virgil's Pastoral Art* (Princeton, 1970).

of the fourth eclogue, that imperial prosperity may favor pastoral liberty.

Virgil's charged comparisons were the forerunners of similar mirrorings in English Renaissance poetry and in the interlocking double plots of pastoral drama and romance.[17] The implied pressures of history, of society and of heroic obligation measured against pastoral freedom and prosperity, provide energies for English writing at least through the Horatian epistles of Pope. It is here really that Empson becomes engaged by pastoral: at the point where access to its powers is threatened or called into question by history. He provokes us to look again — though he himself has not explored these examples in detail — at the dovetailed heroic and pastoral plots of *The Faerie Queene* and Sidney's *Arcadia* or at the interplay of pastoral dream and Augustan reality in the satires of Pope. He provokes us as well to look at works in which human weakness, private vicissitude endangers pastoral freedom — those common treacheries of egotism and desire like Eve's temptation in *Paradise Lost,* or Leontes' jealousy or Marvell's delicate and comic examples of sinning — all of which dramatize ways we cut ourselves off from the natural temper of pastoral.

For better or worse, critics since Empson have been particularly alive to the notion of a threatened or encircled pastoral world, its emblem perhaps the retreating visions of Prospero or the vanishing Graces of Colin Clout, frightened at the approach of Calidore the Knight of Courtesy. What might have been dismissed as bucolic episode has drawn detailed appreciation and is seen as bound up with larger ventures, larger dramatic structures. Prospero's masque in *The Tempest,* Perdita's pastoral feast (which Shakespeare added when turning *Pandosto* into *The Winter's Tale*): such scenes perform the traditional function of pastoral; they offer visions of power over nature or of a simplicity of demeanor quite apart from the jaded distinctions of court, the corroded insight of Leontes, or the treacheries of Antonio and Sebastian. Yet the plays which surround such pastoral moments etch out the special conditions

17. Walter R. Davis, "A Map of Arcadia: Sidney's Romance in Its Tradition," in Walter R. Davis and Richard A. Lanham, *Sidney's Arcadia* (New Haven, 1965), esp. pp. 7–44.

under which their innocence and freedom can be felt to be true. Caliban and his roisterers will lope into view; Polixenes will threaten to scratch out Perdita's beauty with briers.

I am especially concerned with pressures that come to be felt in pastoral lyric. Sidney's steely attention to the problem in the *Arcadia* provides one vivid Renaissance example of how far pastoral had come since Theocritus. His Greek princes visit Arcadia, with all its traditional harmony and its piping shepherds and yet, for some five hundred pages, stand oddly apart from it. Sidney makes extraordinary stylistic adjustments: the Theocritean elements, eclogues sung by Arcadian shepherds, are set off as *intermezzi* or interludes between the books or "acts" (as Sidney called them) of the romance; they provide momentary respite but are almost dwarfed by the drama of heroic obligation and the "fall" from heroism into pastoral love. The princes remain spectators at the pastoral feasts, and even those exercises, once enjoyed, are revealed with the rapidity of a transformation scene to be corrosive: "In these pastoral pastimes a great number of days were sent to follow their flying predecessors, while the cup of poison (which was deeply tasted of this noble company) had left no sinew of theirs without mortally searching into it." [18] When the princes assume the robes and roles of pastoral singers to engage in singing contests Sidney must, with some stiffness, devise a separate pastoral style for them, one which counters pastoral ease and takes nature *only* as trope, a style in which the symbolic or metaphorical side of the shepherd's role cannot be forgotten. Musidorus, wooing his Pamela, must interpret his costume for her in a relentless and hypnotic lyric: "My sheep are thoughts . . ." and must explain to himself what can, in a hero's eyes, only be viewed as a blemish: "Come shepherd's weeds, become your master's mind: / Yield outward show, what inward change he tries / . . . Helpless his plaint, who spoils himself of bliss." [19] Sidney's is the extreme example, a tense denial of the connection between heroic responsibilities and pastoral restoratives.

18. *The Complete Works of Sir Philip Sidney,* ed. Albert Feuillerat, 4 vols. (Cambridge, Eng., 1912–1926), I, 145.
19. *The Poems of Sir Philip Sidney,* ed. William A. Ringler, Jr. (Oxford, 1962), pp. 39, 13.

It focuses difficulties which other writers of pastoral lyric were to feel and problems which draw critics to, say, Sidney, Spenser, and Marvell rather than to Drayton, Herrick, William Browne, or the poems in *England's Helicon.*

For students of the pastoral lyric Marvell has provided some of the most enticing examples; the past five years have seen a greater concentration of books on his poetry than ever before.[20] Apart from the accidents of critical fashion — it may be simply his "turn" — there are, as in the case of Sidney, strong reasons why Marvell should engage our attention at this particular time. He seems to be on the threshold of modern poetic problems, and yet because of his extraordinary wit and poise he never needed to feel them as such. Rosalie Colie speaks of Marvell's "poetry of criticism," [21] an apt term for the Mower poems or "Upon Appleton House" or "The Nymph Complaining." A wariness about pastoral lyric pervades his poetry, so that even in the simplest poems the chance to exercise the Theocritean mode is accepted in only the most guarded ways. Damon the Mower sings what might well be a fetching classical lament.[22] It owes a lot to the Corydon of Virgil's second eclogue and to the Polyphemus of Theocritus. And yet, beneath his delectable boasts and his imaginative visions —

> Nor am I so deformed to sight,
> If in my scythe I lookèd right;
> In which I see my picture done,
> As in a crescent moon the sun

— there is a pristine though attractive egotism which allows him to feel the identity of nature and his own thoughts. The narrator, from the outside, sees beyond the swagger to the fact that he is "depopulating all the ground." This is no longer a shepherd-lover singing a pastoral song; and in the brilliant substitution of mower for herdsman Marvell embodies most clearly

20. See, for example, Rosalie L. Colie, *My Ecchoing Song* (Princeton, 1970); J. B. Leishman, *The Art of Marvell's Poetry* (London, 1966); Ann E. Berthoff, *The Resolved Soul* (Princeton, 1970); Harold Toliver, *Marvell's Ironic Vision* (New Haven, 1965).

21. *My Ecchoing Song,* pp. 3–9.

22. *The Poems and Letters of Andrew Marvell,* ed. H. M. Margoliouth, 2 vols. 2nd ed. (Oxford, 1952), pp. 41–44.

the self-deceptive powers of mythmaking about one's place in
nature. When Damon makes his half-jesting, half-grim discovery at the end of the poem ("For Death thou art a Mower
too"), in a sense his occupation's gone; he cannot simply be
restored to pastoral tasks. Whatever clarity of vision those lines
offer, they also suggest a separation from nature which Damon
in his braggadocio and disarming wooing of Juliana had never
been led to suspect.

Marvell's critical sense makes it difficult for him to find a satisfactory pastoral mask, a satisfying role which does not destroy
as it creates in nature. One thinks even of "The Coronet," where
he tries to substitute sacred for erotic song and where

> Alas I find the Serpent old
> That, twining in his speckled breast,
> About the flowers disguised does fold,
> With wreaths of fame and interest.[23]

Not always, but very often, Marvell sees the pastoral speaker
as by nature an intruder. For him, as for Milton, pastoral is
part of a fallen world whose richness nourishes an essential
fiction-making activity. He is rarely — except in "The Garden"
— fully at rest with pastoral's recuperative powers. He tests
one stance after another: the nymph lamenting over her dead
faun, who makes of pastoral materials a self-cherishing monument; Damon's complaint; or the exploring poet of "Upon
Appleton House," with his complicated attempts at satisfaction
in different pastoral theaters. Marvell relishes pastoral song and
yet remains wary of "the surrendered self among unwelcoming
forms." Conscious of our intrusions — what we try to *make*
of nature — he can go on to invent lyrics in which true pastoral
recreation often seems to elude him.

It is an odd literary achievement. Odd because the restless-
ness or wariness I have described does not seem to destroy the
pleasure Marvell takes in reviving certain conventions, like the
one behind Damon the Mower's lament. If Damon is deprived
of his pastoral recreation, if the nymph is imprisoned by her
pastoral complaint, the reader in each of these cases is not. Pre-

23. *Ibid.*, pp. 14–15.

cisely by showing up the limits of their points of view, by giving them up as literary hostages, Marvell is able to restore what engaged him in Virgil and Theocritus: the power of pastoral fictions both to express and to temper our cravings, our fantasies, our desires. He anticipates the condition which came to govern modern pastoral, the human figure as an intruder, a kind of Polyphemus at large in the natural world. But he does not share the related notion that by virtue of our intrusions we are almost excluded from the pleasures of pastoral fiction.

It is a long way from the momentary assurance of Marvell's "green thought in a green shade" to Stevens' momentary exultation in a scene from which he excludes himself almost entirely:

> Today the air is clear of everything.
> It has no knowledge except of nothingness
> And it flows over us without meanings,
> As if none of us had ever been here before
> And are not now: in this shallow spectacle,
> This invisible activity, this sense.

I take these lines, from "A Clear Day and No Memories," [24] as representative of a particular kind of modern sensibility; in such poems we become the "intensest" spectators in order to claim even a momentary sense of nature's relation to mind. Part of the task of the poem, as in much of Stevens and Frost, is to convince us that the hostility, the changeability of nature is itself within the grasp of the imaginer. Empson, looking at literature of the past, shares that perspective: "The feeling that life is essentially inadequate to the human spirit, and yet that a good life must avoid saying so, is naturally at home with most versions of pastoral." [25] Roger Sale is right to see *Some Versions of Pastoral* as "a history of literary responses to disintegration." [26] It seems to me that much of modern pastoral verse answers to that same urgency and attempts to reclaim the nat-

24. Wallace Stevens, *Opus Posthumous,* p. 113.
25. *Some Versions of Pastoral,* p. 114.
26. "The Achievement of William Empson," *Hudson Review,* 19 (1966), 382.

ural world through a series of difficult poetic treaties, self-defi-
nitions against or by means of landscape.

   In "A Clear Day and No Memories" Stevens' lines, one after
another, appear to bar us from the scene they summon up. A
series of denials (*clear of everything, except of nothingness,
without meanings, as if none of us*), they end by conferring an
understanding we were never led to expect. If one thinks of
Marvell, of Milton, of Virgil and the Theocritean pastoral, this
modern pastoral performance seems to win its powers in
oblique and guarded ways. The poet can be said to be *in* a
landscape only in a diminished sense. Not only is he isolated,
but he remains a spectator and, by virtue of that, an intruder
as well. As Stevens puts it in "Notes Toward a Supreme Fiction":

> The blue woman looked and from her window named
>
> The corals of the dogwood, cold and clear,
> Cold, coldly delineating, being real,
> Clear and, except for the eye, without intrusion.[27]

The special recreations of pastoral performance are achieved,
as it were, from outside, as the repeated and qualified triumphs
of Frost and Stevens remind us. Yet the provisional, propitiat-
ing tones which the intruder's role forces upon them lead to
dazzling examples of the residual powers of pastoral.

   Helen Vendler has commented on Stevens' landscapes, his interest not in the solidity of nature but in the fluency of weather,
as if recognizing that it is the medium, the lens of vision which
is important rather than what is at any given moment seen.[28]
"A Clear Day and No Memories," for all its exclusions, gathers
the observer into the scene at the moment when he is most sub-
missive to the conditions of change, indeed, at the moment
when he seems least present. The air

> flows over us without meanings,
> As if none of us had ever been here before
> And are not now . . .

   27. *Collected Poems*, pp. 399–400.
   28. *On Extended Wings: Wallace Stevens' Longer Poems* (Cambridge,
Mass., 1969), p. 47.

The spectator, however reduced, is made to seem, in an implicit metaphor, like the very wind and moving air; he lacks the body of "having been here before" or of "being here now." There is some grammatical sorcery here: the unobtrusive shift from subjunctive to indicative (*are,* not *were*) and from the third-person denial (*none of us*) to an implied first person (we *are*). The poem closes with that fluent presence which is always a victory in Stevens: "in this shallow spectacle, / This invisible activity, this sense." *This sense:* the expression, seemingly vague, refusing a more specific name, has its penumbra of affirmative meanings. It counters the faintness of "shallow spectacle" by turning the scene into something distinctly felt (through the senses) and by the implied identity of a pun, something comprehensible, that is, making sense. Like the wooing poet at the end of "Notes Toward a Supreme Fiction" he emerges "pleased that the rational is irrational."

Stevens, by his questions, qualifications, paradoxes, and attempts to give multiple names to experiences (*shallow spectacle, invisible activity, sense*) can suggest the richness, the changeability, the quirks of the natural world he is trying to discover and reclaim. To find the right tone, the right air of affectionate submissiveness is part of the secret: "Fat girl, terrestrial, my summer, my night": "I call you by name, my green, my fluent mundo." One might say of him what Reuben Brower says of Frost: the "consciousness that he is playing a high game — as poet and worshipper — in the presence of nature" is what is most modern in Stevens.[29] "It is the human that is the alien, / The human that has no cousin in the moon." [30] By calling attention to the limits of vision, by making his affirmations conditional or guarded, he can still call up or imagine some of the traditional freedom of pastoral.

It is clear from the example of Stevens, as it might be from studying a poet otherwise as different as Frost, that modern pastoral draws its energies from exercises of the eye and ear, from explorations rather than companionable song. What is discovered lacks the hospitable qualities of the Theocritean bower;

29. *The Poetry of Robert Frost,* p. 89.
30. Stevens, *Collected Poems,* p. 328.

song gives way to those minute adjustments of voice, rhythm, and syntax through which setting is perceived. It is in this latter connection that I want to talk about description, the actual arrangement of physical detail. I take my final example from a poet of a later generation than Frost and Stevens: Elizabeth Bishop, whose handling of landscape seems almost a consequence of theirs, the role of cautious spectator reinterpreted in a new, more understated poetic style.

Miss Bishop is praised, justly, for her "eye," and her poems have, by comparison with Stevens' landscapes, a surface closer to toneless presentation of physical detail. There is an air of making very modest claims, of not pressing for symbolic meanings, and of not — as Frost often does — deliberately pressing against them. If Frost's verse is often "about the very uncertainty of vision," [31] Miss Bishop appears to take this for granted in her absolute submission to the scenes she describes. It is fair to say, as one can of Stevens' reminders of human intrusion, that her very submissiveness becomes a way to reclaim the nature from which her speakers are excluded.

Set among the poems of her last separate volume, *Questions of Travel,* is a very important story, "In the Village," which gives one version of that feeling of homelessness. The tale reaches back to a Nova Scotia childhood, that of a young girl glimpsing her mother, who is just back from a sanitarium.

A scream, the echo of a scream, hangs over that Nova Scotian village. No one hears it; it hangs there forever, a slight stain in those pure blue skies, skies that travellers compare to those of Switzerland, too dark, too blue, so that they seem to keep on darkening a little more around the horizon — or is it around the rims of the eyes? — the color of the cloud of bloom on the elm trees, the violet on the fields of oats; something darkening over the woods and waters as well as the sky. [32]

Memories of the mother's scream echo through scenes which are also rich, strong recollections of village life and of a child's country comforts. "In the Village" was intimately related to the

31. Brower, *The Poetry of Robert Frost,* p. 91.
32. From *Questions of Travel* (copyright © 1965 by Elizabeth Bishop), reprinted by permission of Farrar, Straus and Giroux.

travel poems among which it was set — the darker side of their serene need to reclaim "the elements speaking: earth, air, fire, water." That particular necessity lies behind one of Miss Bishop's finest poems, "At the Fishhouses," set, as the story was, in Nova Scotia. It opens with an intense, lengthy description:

> Although it is a cold evening
> down by one of the fishhouses
> an old man sits netting,
> his net, in the gloaming almost invisible
> a dark purple-brown,
> and his shuttle worn and polished.
> The air smells so strong of codfish
> it makes one's nose run and one's eyes water.
> The five fishhouses have steeply peaked roofs
> and narrow, cleated gangplanks slant up
> to storerooms in the gables
> for the wheelbarrows to be pushed up and down on.
> All is silver: the heavy surface of the sea,
> swelling slowly as if considering spilling over,
> is opaque, but the silver of the benches,
> the lobster pots, and masts, scattered
> among the wild jagged rocks,
> is of an apparent translucence
> like the small old buildings with an emerald moss
> growing on their shoreward walls.
> The big fish tubs are completely lined
> with layers of beautiful herring scales
> and the wheelbarrows are similarly plastered
> with creamy iridescent coats of mail,
> with small iridescent flies crawling on them.[33]

Like one of Stevens' pastorals, Miss Bishop's is a scene almost without a spectator, the speaker comically unwelcome in an air which smacks of another element and which makes her eyes water and her nose run. She slowly exposes the scene, present tense, with a tempered willingness to let it speak for itself in a kind of declarative simplicity. Things *are;* things *have.* The

33. From *The Complete Poems* (New York, 1969), p. 72 (copyright © 1969 by Elizabeth Bishop), reprinted by permission of Farrar, Straus and Giroux, and of Chatto and Windus.

lone fisherman, a Wordsworthian solitary, is faded into the
scene, his net "almost invisible," his shuttle "worn and polished," his "black old knife" with a blade "almost worn away."
The dense opening description — deliberately slow, fifty lines
of the poem — is in all details of sight and sense and sound
intended to subject us to the scene, to draw us deeply into it.
"The five fishhouses have steeply peaked roofs / and narrow,
cleated gangplanks slant up . . .": even the insistent conso-
nants and the doubling of adjectives force those words apart
and force us to dwell on them, as if to carve out some certainty
of vision. We are to become what the speaker claims for herself later in the poem: "a believer in total immersion." From
that immersion a pattern gathers, unhurried but there: present,
for example, in the odd half-rhyme of *codfish* and *polished* or
in the unassuming repetition of *iridescent*. The wheelbarrows
are "plastered / with creamy iridescent coats of mail, / with
small iridescent flies crawling on them." The crudeness and
delicacy of these details are made to appear strokes of the same
master, of the landscape's age-old subjection to the sea, to the
caking, the plastering, the lining, the silvering-over which turns
everything to iridescence or to sequins at the same time as it
rusts them, wears away, erodes.

In its fidelity to setting — to what is both jagged and
strangely jewelled — the poem accumulates the sense of an
artistry beyond the human, one that stretches over time, chisel-
ing and decorating with its strange erosions. The human enterprise depends upon and is dwarfed by the sea, just as the fish-
house ramps lead out of and back into the water:

> Down at the water's edge, at the place
> where they haul up the boats, up the long ramp
> descending into the water . . .

Precisely by imagining these encircling powers, the speaker
wins some power over them. This is her largest gesture, reflected in some smaller moments of propitiation: offering a cigarette to the fisherman, and with odd simplicity singing Bap-
tist hymns to a moderately curious seal, true creature of that
"element bearable to no mortal." Behind them — or more to

the point, "behind us" — as if left behind in human history "a
million Christmas trees stand / waiting for Christmas." This
"believer in total immersion," through her patient wooing or
conjuring, finally wins a certain elevation of tone, though it is
a vision, in a twice-repeated phrase, of the sea "cold dark deep
and absolutely clear."

> The water seems suspended
> above the rounded gray and blue-gray stones.
> I have seen it over and over, the same sea, the same,
> slightly, indifferently swinging above the stones,
> icily free above the stones
> above the stones and then the world.
> If you should dip your hand in,
> your wrist would ache immediately,
> your bones would begin to ache and your hand would burn
> as if the water were a transmutation of fire
> that feeds on stones and burns with a dark gray flame.
> If you tasted it, it would first taste bitter,
> then briny, then surely burn your tongue.
> It is like what we imagine knowledge to be:
> dark, salt, clear, moving, utterly free,
> drawn from the cold hard mouth
> of the world, derived from the rocky breasts
> forever, flowing and drawn, and since
> our knowledge is historical, flowing and flown.

The poet returns knowledge to concreteness, as if breaking it
down into its elements ("dark, salt, clear . . ."). The speaker
herself seems drawn into the elements: at first jokingly in the
fishy air which makes the nose run, the eyes water; then in the
burning if one dips one's hand, as if water were a transmuta-
tion of fire that feeds on stones. The absorbing and magical
transformations of earth, air, fire, and water make it impossible
— and unnecessary — to determine whether it is *knowledge* or
the *sea* which is "derived from the rocky breasts / forever."
With a final fluency she leaves her declarative descriptions behind and captures a rhythm at once mysterious and acknowledging limitations: "flowing and drawn . . . flowing and
flown." Her earlier submission to the scene has prepared the

way for a momentary freedom in nature; the poem realizes
one of Stevens' promises, "refreshes life so that we share / For
a moment the first idea." From its Theocritean beginnings as a
variety of communal song and performance (such was the
fiction the poem maintained), pastoral becomes an effort at
limning out private discoveries. Miss Bishop's poem is one example of how completely landscape has taken over the substance of such poems and how it can assume an individualizing
force. The poet, now more spectator than singer, recognizing
dependencies, measures his mind against and by means of natural detail. This is the conjuring which appears to satisfy another modern pastoralist, A. R. Ammons in "Gravelly Run":

> I don't know somehow it seems sufficient
> to see and hear whatever coming and going is,
> losing the self to the victory
>   of stones and trees,
> of bending sandpit lakes, crescent
> round groves of dwarf pine:
>
> for it is not so much to know the self
> as to know it as it is known
>   by galaxy and cedar cone,
> as if birth had never found it
> and death could never end it.

That final *as if* is the illusory power of pastoral.

PAUL J. ALPERS

The Milton Controversy

Despite a good deal of critical sniping at Milton in the 1920's, the Milton controversy can be said to have begun with F. R. Leavis' essay "Milton's Verse," the first fully developed argument against his preeminence in English poetry. This essay was published in *Scrutiny* in 1933 and appeared in Leavis' book *Revaluation* in 1936. In the same year, T. S. Eliot published a brief and trenchant polemic under the diffident title "A Note on the Verse of John Milton." [1] Both Leavis and Eliot attacked certain weaknesses, as they saw them, in the verse of *Paradise Lost* — impoverishment of sensory experience, exploitation of sound and rhythm for their own sake, a consequent relaxation of alertness and intelligence. Though they concentrated on Milton's verse, they suggested severe criticisms of such matters as structure, dramatic action, and characterization, and these criticisms were developed in A. J. A. Waldock's book *Paradise Lost and Its Critics,* published in 1947. All these writings are challenging in both the social and intellectual senses; nevertheless, Milton's

1. *Essays and Studies,* 21 (1936), 32–40. Reprinted as "Milton I" in *On Poetry and Poets* (New York: Farrar, Straus, and Cudahy, 1957), pp. 156–164.

defenders did not rise to the challenge. Fifteen years after Waldock's book — a period which saw an unprecedented volume of publication on Milton — Christopher Ricks began his *Milton's Grand Style* by observing: "Certainly it is true that the twentieth-century attacks on Milton's style have not been directly and satisfactorily answered. Equally certainly, the Miltonists' praise of Milton has not gone very far towards showing what exactly is good about the style of *Paradise Lost*." [2] Thirty years after Leavis' essay, Ricks at last provided the kind of answer it required, one that pays scrupulous attention to the arguments it is meeting and that proceeds by detailed analysis of passages of verse. Ricks's book is a model of disinterested criticism — fair and patient (almost to a fault) and continually illuminating about Milton's verse itself. William Empson, reviewing the book, praised it for "refuting a line of talk which has been influential for a generation . . . Dr. Leavis," he rightly said, "can no longer say he has never been answered." [3]

Good as it is, however, Ricks's book does not give a sufficiently comprehensive or searching answer to Leavis' and Waldock's criticisms of *Paradise Lost*. One reason for this is that he was dealing, as Empson's remarks suggest, with an exacerbated social situation. Why should it have been thirty years before Dr. Leavis could no longer say he has never been answered? Largely because there was a sense in most academic circles that the anti-Miltonists were to be either ignored or snubbed. Even well-meaning writers accepted the notion that it is better to stay out of nasty quarrels. A good many "answers" to Dr. Leavis therefore do not mention his name. These tactics sometimes remind you of the ostrich and sometimes of Milton's God. They created a dispiriting situation, which was well described by John Peter, writing in 1952:

To shy away from an argument is not to win it and, more important still, is bound to leave the bewildered onlooker (that is, the student) in a greater state of bewilderment than ever. Yet in a matter like this no one has a stronger right than the student to be considered. Having watched several groups of students . . . torn this way and

2. Oxford: Oxford University Press, 1963, p. 1.
3. *New Statesman*, August 23, 1963, p. 230.

that in their attempts to form an estimate of Milton, I am convinced that unless the argument is allowed to run its course, unless it is persevered with responsibly and in the open, it can be of no use to them. If it is allowed to go underground they are left only with a dim sense of taboos and smouldering resentments and may easily conclude, in self-defence, that the assessment of this poet is an improper activity, something that decent people don't talk about.[4]

Ricks's task, then, was as much social as intellectual, and the social situation affected his sense of Leavis' argument. John Peter acutely remarked that Milton's defenders seemed to write "not from any vital concern about the poetry, but from a desire to vindicate the individual, John Milton, as though he were a personal friend." [5] It is equally true that Leavis and his followers, whose tempers and arguments were not improved by the slighting of their views, tended to treat Milton as a personal enemy. For this reason, I think, Ricks devoted himself to refuting that one of Leavis' arguments that is, so to speak, most personally abusive of the poet — the argument that "cultivating so complete and systematic a callousness to the intrinsic nature of English, Milton forfeits all possibility of subtle or delicate life in his verse." [6] This statement is not *merely* abusive: it is precise enough in its formulation to have provoked some of Ricks's most attractive and convincing analyses. But its hostile intent explains why Ricks conceived his task as first and foremost to demonstrate that John Milton could write English well.

Leavis' case, however, is more powerful than it appears in Ricks's book. As a case against Milton it has been sufficiently answered. But as an argument about the nature of Milton's verse, Leavis' essay points to some fundamental truths with which Ricks does not adequately deal. To begin with, let us examine the description of Eden in Book IV, a passage which has an important place not only in the poem, but also in the Milton controversy. It is the passage of *Paradise Lost* that Leavis singles out for adverse comment, yet Ricks does not mention it at all,

4. "Reflections on the Milton Controversy" in *A Selection from "Scrutiny,"* ed. F. R. Leavis (Cambridge, Eng.: Cambridge University Press, 1968), I, 197.
5. *Ibid.,* 20
6. *Revaluation* (London: Chatto and Windus, 1936), p. 53.

presumably because he feels he cannot defend it. But it is important and characteristic enough that we can say we must be able to justify it if we are to justify Milton's style.

> And now divided into four main streams,
> Runs diverse, wandering many a famous realm
> And country whereof here needs no account,
> But rather to tell how, if art could tell,
> How from that sapphire fount the crisped brooks,
> Rolling on orient pearl and sands of gold,
> With mazy error under pendant shades
> Ran nectar, visiting each plant, and fed
> Flowers worthy of Paradise which not nice art
> In beds and curious knots, but nature boon
> Poured forth profuse on hill and dale and plain,
> Both where the morning sun first warmly smote
> The open field, and where the unpierced shade
> Embrowned the noontide bowers: thus was this place,
> A happy rural seat of various view.
>
> PL IV. 233–247 [7]

Leavis says of these lines: "As the laboured, pedantic artifice of the diction suggests, Milton seems here to be focussing rather upon words than upon perceptions, sensations or things . . . In this Grand Style, the medium calls pervasively for a kind of attention, compels an attitude towards itself, that is incompatible with sharp, concrete realization; just as it would seem to be, in the mind of the poet, incompatible with an interest in sensuous particularity. He exhibits a feeling *for* words rather than a capacity for feeling *through* words." [8] I think these observations are true but that, far from entailing a condemnation of the passage, they enable us to see just why it is so good. Our first task is to go through the passage and see what is engaging Milton's attention if "sharp, concrete realization" is not.

For Leavis, Milton's medium calls attention to itself in the bad social sense, as if unwittingly to distract the reader from what

7. I use the text edited with excellent notes by Alastair Fowler in *The Poems of John Milton*, ed. J. Carey and A. Fowler (London, 1968), in the Longmans Annotated English Poets series. Spelling is modernized, but punctuation of the seventeenth-century copy text is retained.

8. *Revaluation*, pp. 49–50.

it cannot do. But if one looks at the beginning of this passage, it is evident that Milton is drawing attention to his medium in a quite different way — one that is fully compatible with alert intelligence and an exploitation of all the resources of language. As the poet turns to describing Eden, the phrase "if art could tell" explicitly raises the question of whether the merely human skills of poetry are sufficient to his task. Hence Leavis is right to discern an element of "pedantic artifice" in "sapphire fount," "crisped brooks," and "orient pearl." The point clearly is the attempt to match the reality of Eden by verbal artifices that man has developed in the course of describing innumerable ideal (and literally artificial) gardens. But there is more to these phrases than conscious artifice, for the terms do have a potential truth to them. "Sapphire" is a regular epithet for the sky, and Sidney speaks of "sapphire-coloured brooks";[9] a fount is a natural source. So the sapphire fount could be direct natural description, just as one could say that the brooks of Eden really did run on pearl and gold.[10] One would still agree with Leavis that Milton is focusing upon words rather than things, but the element of descriptive truth in the words shows that he is concerned with vital problems of human apprehension.

Speaking of this passage, Leavis says: "If the Eighteenth Century thought that poetry was something that could be applied from the outside, it found the precedent as well as the apparatus in Milton." [11] But Milton grasped these locutions and rhythms from within. With the enjambment — "With mazy error under pendant shades / Ran nectar" — the verse becomes more physically responsive, as it describes nourishing action instead of static visual detail. So secure is the effect that we can now leave "nice art" behind and participate in the workings of "nature boon." But we enter Eden this way precisely by means of the

9. See *OED*. Sidney's phrase occurs in the poem "What Tongue Can Her Perfections Tell?" (line 27) and is a locution for the veins in the landscape of the mistress' body. The poem is in Book II, chap. xi, of the *New Arcadia* and appears in Ringler's edition of Sidney's *Poems* as OA 62.

10. On this point see Fowler's learned note. He cites Genesis 2:11–12 and the commentators on it.

11. *Revaluation*, p. 51.

poetic art to which Milton drew attention at the beginning of the
passage. The rhythmical devices do not simply support the descriptive force of "ran," "visiting," "fed," and "poured forth."
They also enact one of the most important word-plays in the
poem, that on the phrase "mazy error." One is self-consciously
aware, as Ricks has pointed out, that the word here has only its
Latin meaning of "wandering," not the moral meaning that came
in with the Fall.[12] The metrical devices, by enacting the innocent meaning, enable us to participate in it. There is, it seems, a
great deal that "art can tell." Ten lines after the poet uttered
this qualifying phrase we have been made, for the moment, inhabitants of Eden. Note the importance of word order and line
division in "Both where the morning sun first warmly smote /
The open field." "First warmly smote": we feel the sun shining
down on us rather than merely observe it shining elsewhere.
Similarly the next detail, "and where the unpierced shade / Em-
browned the noontide bowers," assumes that we are engaged in
the normal cycle of a pastoral day — working in the open fields
in the morning and seeking the shade to rest at noon. Though
we began by looking at Eden from the outside, we are now at
the center looking around us — "a happy rural seat of various
view."

As we look out on the various view, Milton does not attempt
— as Leavis is perfectly right to say — to realize a world.
Rather, he uses the series of scenes to explore, in a more intensified way, the problem of what human art can apprehend of
Eden. The first two scenes range between the exotic and the simple, the artificial and the natural, and thus are a sort of com-
pendium of ideal landscapes:

> Groves whose rich trees wept odorous gums and balm,
> Others whose fruit burnished with golden rind
> Hung amiable, Hesperian fables true,
> If true, here only, and of delicious taste:
> Betwixt them lawns, or level downs, and flocks
> Grazing the tender herb, were interposed,
> Or palmy hillock, or the flowery lap

12. *Milton's Grand Style* (see note 2 above), p. 110.

> Of some irriguous valley spread her store,
> Flowers of all hue, and without thorn the rose.

Various rhetorical devices suggest the presence of human art: the explicit artifice of the groves, the reference to Hesperian fables, the way word order and lineation support the meaning of "were interposed" and "spread her store." These effects are relatively straightforward. The next description engages us with exceptional intimacy and point:

> Another side, umbrageous grots and caves
> Of cool recess, o'er which the mantling vine
> Lays forth her purple grape, and gently creeps
> Luxuriant.

"Umbrageous grots and caves" is sufficiently external, but "of cool recess" suggests our entry into them.[13] Our sense of physical participation is increased by the concrete activity cf "mantling," the personifying of this activity in "Lays forth her purple grape," and the intimate sensuousness of "gently creeps." All this is a preparation for "Luxuriant," which genuinely surprises us — first by its forcible enjambment, which is not grammatically required, and then by the fact that the word is isolated at the beginning of the line. The point, as such, is very much like that of the word play in "error": one is forced to recognize that a morally suspicious word is innocent here. What is new is the intimacy of our involvement, the intensity of the discrimination imposed. "Mazy error" involved self-conscious intellection; "luxuriant" draws upon all our sensuous and appetitive participation in the preceding description and forces us to experience two sides of our nature, almost in the manner of a moral choice. It is very much to the point that Milton learned to write this way from the most famous and ambivalently involving artificial paradise in English poetry, Spenser's Bower of Bliss.

13. "Recess" in the seventeenth century meant "the act of retiring, withdrawing" (*OED* 1) and "retirement, seclusion" (2b). Under the latter definition *OED* cites "Faire Parks or Gardens . . . being onely places of recesse and pleasure" (1645) and "Ev'ry neighbouring Grove / Sacred to soft Recess and gentle Love" (Prior, 1709).

In the next scene, the art which has so exploited our suscepti-
bilities reaffirms its power to control the visionary landscape:

> mean while murmuring waters fall
> Down the slope hills, dispersed, or in a lake,
> That to the fringed bank with myrtle crowned,
> Her crystal mirror holds, unite their streams.

These lines display Miltonic syntax and word order with a vengeance. The main verb phrase, "unite their streams," is produced
so as not only to surprise, but also to increase the sense of difficulty in the passage. The effect occurs not simply because the
main verb comes pressing upon the verb of the relative clause,
but also because we were scarcely aware that a main verb was
necessary or appropriate. Up to this point we took "In a lake"
and the rest as simply dependent on "fall," so that the grammatical turn directly mimes the attribution of positive activity to the
streams — *uniting*, rather than merely falling in one direction
instead of another. There is a corresponding sense of paradox
and difficulty in the image presented: we are made to see, in a
single moment of apprehension, an artificial stillness as a union
of living waters. These effects are more than a tour de force, because their difficulty has its basis in the tension the lines maintain between artistic control and one's sense of physical participation. The responsiveness with which we follow the "murmuring waters" makes us take the holding of the mirror as an action
of the personified lake, with "to the fringed bank" indicating the
limits reached by its waters. On the other hand, these lines,
coming after the description of the mantling vine, give us a sense
of being external observers. "Dispersed," which could have
powerful psychological suggestions in a false paradise, is
hemmed in here by the descriptive "down the slope hills" and
the alternative "or in a lake." From this point of view, we look
into the mirror, which is held "to the fringed bank" in the sense
that Hamlet says art holds the mirror up to nature. The syntactic
difficulty in the last line corresponds to a reversal in the experiences of participation and control. Our identification with the
waters attains the stillness of the "crystal mirror," while as exter-

nal observers we are suddenly called upon to participate in the uniting of the streams.

In these last two scenes, the poet's artistic resources are not merely a matter of craft and tradition. They have been directly identified with man's own mental resources, his abilities to participate, apprehend, conceive. Milton summons all these capacities for the climactic final passage:

> The birds their choir apply; airs, vernal airs,
> Breathing the smell of field and grove, attune
> The trembling leaves.

The pun on "airs" is the most notorious in the poem, and Empson has done it full justice: "The airs attune the leaves because the air itself is as enlivening as an air; the trees and wild flowers that are smelt on the air match, as if they caused, as if they were caused by, the birds and leaves that are heard on the air; nature, because of a pun, becomes a single organism." [14] Having traced the problem of artifice through the whole passage, we can see how fitting and how grand it is that the poet should achieve this apprehension by means of a pun. The effect is due not simply to a double meaning, but to all Milton's resources of poetic language. The power of the pun comes from the tone of wonder in "airs, vernal airs," and the fusion of meanings and experiences in the utterly simple line "Breathing the smell of field and grove." The intensity of our engagement is what it was in the lines about the mantling vine and the crystal lake, but the scene itself is the open field, smitten by the morning sun, where we first felt ourselves to be inhabitants of Eden.

Instead of the explicit artistry, controlled and controlling, of the preceding lines, Milton has restored a sense of ease and responsiveness. The pun on "airs" therefore seems not to proceed from the poet's wit, but to release meanings and harmonies inherent in the word itself. But these meanings are released because of the poet's art, which is acknowledged in the concluding lines:

14. *Some Versions of Pastoral* (London: Chatto and Windus, 1935), p. 157.

> airs, vernal airs,
> Breathing the smell of field and grove, attune
> The trembling leaves, while universal Pan
> Knit with the Graces and the Hours in dance
> Led on the eternal spring.

We do not end in the role of true inhabitants of Eden. For us, the partaking of "vernal airs" means not the daily round of Adam and Eve, but a vision of eternal spring. The poet's mind and our minds most fully manifest their powers when classical myths, which before were simply shadows of biblical truths — fables that were "if true, here only" — now become living presences. We are persuaded of their presence because of our participation in innocent nature in the preceding lines, but when the figures appear before us, they are engaged in the human artistic activity of dancing.

The passage as a whole shows remarkable power and self-awareness; yet at the same time it does answer to Leavis' description of Milton's verse. This is the reason, I think, that Ricks did not attempt to defend it. Ricks himself says that he shares Leavis' criteria of dramatic realization,[15] and he therefore chooses to analyze only passages that reveal the nature and implications of characters and situations. For example, he is only able to defend Milton's similes when they either show correspondences to the dramatic situation or when they meet a rather narrow criterion of intentional disparity. He has no way of dealing with similes that leave the narrative to explore general aspects of man's fate and nature. When such issues are in question, he always treats them in terms of foreshadowing or recalling events in the poem. Since the phrase "if art could tell" has no status in the narrative action of the poem — just as Pan and the Graces do not — a positive analysis of this passage would not, I think, come naturally to him. By the same token, Ricks does not seem to respond naturally to some essential verbal devices. On the important subject of rhythm, all his examples come from speeches in which characters sustain sentences by way of heroic assertion. When the effect is not dramatic or mimetic — as when the rhythm

15. *Milton's Grand Style*, p. 9.

plays out the innocent meaning of "error" — it seems to escape him. To acknowledge such an effect, we must recognize the virtue in what Leavis assumes is a vice — that Milton reveals a feeling *for* words, as opposed to a desire to apprehend sensuous particularity *through* words.

More important than Ricks's lack of sympathy with particular effects is the fact that he can give us no means of following this passage as a whole. He tries to answer Eliot's charge that Milton's "syntax is determined by the musical significance, by the auditory imagination, rather than by the attempt to follow actual speech or thought." [16] But he does not tell us what Milton's syntax and rhythms do attempt to follow. Quite the contrary, he seems to accept Eliot's criteria, because his defence of Milton's syntax consists of showing how often it makes for effective speech or is expressive of actions, perceptions, or situations. He therefore cannot explain why a passage like this keeps going on: compare his unhappiness with digressive similes, or his exemplifying sustained rhythms only in speeches. Consider a particular moment: "gently creeps / Luxuriant; mean while murmuring waters fall . . ." The syntax here produces a very intense engagement: after the density and complexity of "luxuriant," we are moved, at a metrically unexpected point, to a wholly new phenomenon. The temporal meaning of "mean while" is important to the effect, but it has less to do with a scene or an action than with what our minds are being forced to take in and control. This can be called absolute, as opposed to mimetic, syntax. It is not that Ricks would not appreciate the force of such a turn, but that he provides no terms for understanding it. I think we should speak of conjunctions and rhythms like these as rendering movements of the mind, and in the rest of this essay I shall try to explain and justify the principle on which such a passage unfolds. For the moment, let us observe that our truest guide to it is not Ricks's attempt to meet Leavis' positive criteria, but such hostile remarks of Leavis' as: "The pattern, the stylized gesture and movement, has no particular expressive work to do, but functions by rote, of its own momentum, in the manner of a ritual." [17]

16. *On Poetry and Poets,* p. 161
17. *Revaluation,* p. 46.

Let us therefore return to Leavis and try to understand his
rooted antipathy to Milton. This can best be done by turning
to one of the classic problems of the Milton controversy: Milton's influence on later English poetry. Eliot made this a main
point in his attack on Milton. "Milton's poetry," he said, "could
only be an influence for the worse, upon any poet whatever." [18]
In Eliot's hands this issue was always something of an evasion,[19]
but for Leavis it had great force and significance. Leavis' main
concern was not the eighteenth-century imitators who keep bob-
bing up in the Milton controversy, but the Victorian poetic tradition and the stultifying notions of the poetical that it passed on
to the twentieth century. In this tradition, as Leavis saw it, Milton had an essential part:

[Tennyson] like Milton, had other than musical preoccupations; he
aspired to be among "the great sage-poets of all time." In the ease
with which he reconciled the two bents we see the Miltonic inheritance — as in the readiness with which the nobly-phrased statement of "thought" and moral attitudes in sonorous verse . . . was
accepted as the type of serious poetic expression . . .

For [Arnold], poetry . . . differs from prose . . . in not imposing any strict intellectual criterion. The inferiority, in rigour and
force, of the intellectual content is compensated for by nobility,
sonority and finish of phrasing. But the compensating cannot be
clearly distinguished from a process that combines exaltation and
an effect of heightened significance with an actual relaxing of the

18. *On Poetry and Poets,* p. 157.
19. Even so frank an attack as the sentence just quoted left room for
saying that Milton could be called great "when we isolate him, when
we try to understand the rules of his own game" (*ibid.,* p. 164). By the
same token, when Eliot "retracted" his views in 1947 and said that poets
could now profit from the study of Milton, it seems to have been a way
for him to manage some unambiguous praise — something more whole-
hearted and acceptable than his praise of individual passages for such
merits as "the happy introduction of so much extraneous matter" or "a
kind of inspired *frivolity.*" These remarks will not be found in *On Poetry
and Poets* because "Milton II" in that volume omits the passages in which
they occur in Eliot's original lecture — talk about evasion! The complete
text of the lecture is in James Thorpe, ed., *Milton Criticism* (New York,
1950); the quoted phrases are on pp. 327, 328. The complete texts of
both Eliot's essays on Milton have been published in *Milton: Two Studies*
(London, 1968).

mind, so that the reader, though conscious of an intellectual appeal, doesn't notice any need for compensation.[20]

Whether or not Milton is justly blamed for deficiencies in Victorian poetry, it is clear that Leavis is concerned with fundamental relations between the poet's mind, his experience, and his art — or, to look at it from the reader's point of view, between the pleasures of poetry and actions and qualities of the mind.

By the same token, Leavis' rejection of Milton comes from an understanding and revaluation of some major critical attitudes. His watchwords echo vital nineteenth-century praises of Milton, which he rejects precisely because he grasps the nature of their life, their imaginative impulse. For example, one of his slogans, if you will, is that in Milton one must salute character rather than intelligence: "For character he indisputably has: he massively is what he is — proud, unaccommodating and heroically self-confident . . . In these passages, where he seems 'to be giving of his own substance,' we have the clear marks of Milton's failure to *realize* his undertaking — to conceive it dramatically as a whole, capable of absorbing and depersonalizing the relevant interests and impulses of his private life. He remains in the poem too much John Milton, declaiming, insisting, arguing, suffering, and protesting." [21] What is this but a true grasp and defensible evaluation of Coleridge's praise? "In the *Paradise Lost* — indeed in every one of his poems — it is Milton himself whom you see; his Satan, his Adam, his Raphael, almost his Eve — are all John Milton; and it is a sense of this intense egotism that gives me the greatest pleasure in reading Milton's works. The egotism of such a man is a revelation of spirit." [22]

Or consider Walter Bagehot's well-known essay on Milton published in 1859. Much of the essay sounds like a preliminary version of Waldock's book. "The defect of *Paradise Lost* is that, after all, it is founded on a *political* transaction." "Milton had in such matters [the nature of the Trinity] a bold but not very sensi-

20. *The Common Pursuit* (London: Chatto and Windus, 1952), pp. 29–31.
21. *Ibid.*, pp. 23, 25. The contrast of character and intelligence is more stridently asserted in *Revaluation*, p. 58.
22. "Table Talk," August 18, 1833, in *Table Talk and Omniana* (Oxford, 1917), pp. 267–268.

tive imagination." "The source of the great error which pervades
Paradise Lost" is that "Satan is made *interesting*." [23] And so on
through the familiar complaints that it was disastrous to make
God argue, that the good angels are insipid, that Adam is tedious, that the last two books are dull. But what is Bagehot's conclusion after all this?

There is no difficulty in writing such criticisms, and, indeed, other
unfavourable criticisms on *Paradise Lost*. There is scarcely any book
in the world which is open to a greater number, or which a reader
who allows plain words to produce a due effect will be less satisfied
with. Yet what book is really greater? In the best parts the words
have a magic in them; even in the inferior passages you are hardly
sensible of their inferiority till you translate them into your own
language. Perhaps no style ever written by man expressed so adequately the conceptions of a mind so strong and so peculiar; a manly
strength, a haunting atmosphere of enhancing suggestions, a firm
continuous music, are only some of its excellences. To comprehend
the whole of the others, you must take the volume down and read
it, — the best defence of Milton, as has been said most truly, against
all objections.[24]

Compare Leavis on Eliot's remarking some visual inconsistencies in *Paradise Lost*: "These criticisms seem to me unanswerable, though, properly understood, they amount to more than
criticism of mere detail — unanswerable, unless with the argument that if you read Milton as he demands to be read you see
no occasion to make them . . . Such things escape critical recognition from the responsive reader as they escaped Milton's —
and for the same reason: response to the "Miltonic music"
(which, therefore, they don't disturb) *is* a relaxation of atten-
tiveness to sense." [25]

It would be easy enough to say that Bagehot is being insincere or evasive. We might feel a similar suspicion of Victorian
hypocrisy when Arnold rehearses a series of objections like Bage-

    23. *Literary Studies,* ed. R. H. Hutton (London, 1879), I, 207, 208,
210.
    24. *Ibid.,* p. 217. The last sentence refers to a remark by Hazlitt, cited
by Ricks, p. 26.
    25. *The Common Pursuit,* pp. 15–16.

hot's but then finds that the saving grace of *Paradise Lost* is its
"unfailing level of style." [26] But Leavis' implicit point about
Victorian Miltonism is precisely that it *is* sincere — that just as
Tennyson and Arnold believe in the poetry they are writing, so
Bagehot and Arnold are pursuing the critic's task as Arnold
defines it:

> This is the sort of criticism [Addison's *Spectator* papers on *Paradise
> Lost*] which held our grandfathers and great-grandfathers spell-
> bound in solemn reverence. But it is all based upon convention, and
> on the positivism of the modern reader it is thrown away. Does the
> work which you praise, he asks, affect me with high pleasure and
> do me good, when I try it as fairly as I can? The critic who helps
> such a questioner is one who has sincerely asked himself, also, this
> same question; who has answered it in a way which agrees, in the
> main, with what the questioner finds to be his own honest experi-
> ence in the matter, and who shows the reasons for this common
> experience.[27]

What alarms Leavis is that in Bagehot's and Arnold's "honest
experience" the grand style indeed compensates for all the deficiencies they find in *Paradise Lost*.

All this is said partly to defend the vitality and integrity of
Leavis' criticism — it seems to me that he himself has performed
the critic's task as Arnold defines it — and partly to argue that
he must be answered in as fundamental a way as possible. Let
us now return to the passage we analyzed and ask what are the
conditions of our finding pleasure and interest in it? Consider the
last lines:

> while universal Pan
> Knit with the Graces and the Hours in dance
> Led on the eternal spring.

We did not observe before how poignant is the use of the past
tense in "Led," reminding us that this vision, which had seemed
so present, is indeed a thing that is past, is now present *only* as a

26. "A French Critic on Milton" in *Mixed Essays, Irish Essays, and
Others* (New York, 1883), p. 200.
27. *Ibid.*, p. 186.

vision. To understand the conditions of our apprehending such a stroke, let us compare a similar moment in Keats' "Ode to a Nightingale":

> Thou wast not born for death, immortal Bird!
>   No hungry generations tread thee down;
> The voice I hear this passing night was heard
>   In ancient days by emperor and clown:
> Perhaps the self-same song that found a path
>   Through the sad heart of Ruth, when, sick for home,
>   She stood in tears amid the alien corn;
>   The same that oft-times hath
>   Charmed magic casements, opening on the foam
>   Of perilous seas, in faery lands forlorn.
>
> Forlorn! the very word is like a bell
>   To toll me back from thee to my sole self!

Here, too, one is brought to recognize that an intensely present vision is not a reality; and in Keats, as in Milton, this recognition stems from and reinforces the poet's awareness of his own human nature. In Keats both the moment and the whole poem assume what Leavis and, I think, most readers consider the normal conditions of poetry. The poem depends on and is rooted in — though it does not, of course, merely record — experience in the ordinary sense — sensory experience of the world outside and internal experiences of thoughts, feelings, desires, psychological states. By the same token, the unfolding of the poem in time is directly analogous to that of ordinary experience: earlier moments in the poem have consequences, later moments depend on and develop the full dramatic experience of earlier moments. The images of Ruth and the magic casements develop experiences and recognitions of the preceding stanza:

> Now more than ever seems it rich to die,
>   To cease upon the midnight with no pain,
>   While thou art pouring forth thy soul abroad
>   In such an ecstasy!
>   Still wouldst thou sing, and I have ears in vain —
>   To thy high requiem become a sod.

The bleakly final last line draws out the consequences of identifying song with ecstatic consummation. The crucial recognition of the poem — that full identity with the nightingale's song would be death for the human poet — comes by means of intense experience: we recall the dense and luxuriant sensory appeal of the stanza before this. The images of Ruth and the magic casements are dramatic in the sense that they are imagined as the ways in which an individual human being deals with the experiences registered and evaluated up to this point in the poem. They attempt — for example in the nostalgia of the image of Ruth — to acknowledge the recognitions of the preceding stanza while maintaining as much as possible of the otherworldly loveliness of imaginative experience. This comes out clearly in the clinching phrase "faery lands forlorn." "Forlorn" is here made to support the aura of enchantment, partly by echoing the glamorous danger of "perilous seas," partly by the echoing sounds (f-r-l) that make it seem to go naturally with "faery lands." But this word too has consequences, and they are developed by the poet's own dramatic apprehension of the word he has just produced.

Now let us ask what produces the word "Led" in Milton's passage and the sudden recognition it brings. We may feel a necessity as compelling as in Keats's poem, but its nature and manifestations are very different. In Keats the necessity is that of dramatic consequence — the feeling and thinking mind acknowledging the force and direction of what it has felt and expressed most intimately. One can see how the "Ode to a Nightingale" would deserve one of Leavis' most honorific epithets, "exploratory-creative." But in Milton's passage, the necessity that we speak of Pan and the Graces in the past tense comes not from something freshly perceived and discovered, but from something we knew all the time: that Eden is gone and that the classical myths are false. This truth, far from being achieved in the dramatic manner of Keats's poem, has already been flatly stated in the lines about the "Hesperian fables true / If true, here only."

An "exploratory-creative" use of language is what you would expect from a poet who said that life is a vale of soul-making. By contrast with the individual and dynamic view of man implied in this remark, Milton's view of human nature is fixed, objective, and general. He had no less strenuous and in a sense dynamic a view of life than Keats. But he thought that men's souls, though individual in one sense, all have the same nature and the same relation to the world and its creator. Hence he characteristically speaks of spiritual effort as the restoration of something definable and once objectively present. In *Areopagitica* he describes man's intellectual efforts as the search for the mutilated limbs of the once whole body of Truth. In *Of Education* he says: "The end then of learning is to repair the ruins of our first parents by regaining to know God aright." The description of Eden is explicitly an attempt to regain the paradise we have lost by means of the creative powers we now possess. And the promise held out to man at the end of the poem is that he can achieve a "paradise within."

An awareness of Milton's objective and, if you will, dogmatic sense of truth usually leads to views of the verse like Leavis'. Yet in some ways Milton's view of human nature liberates his verse. Whereas Keats, respecting the concrete nature of ordinary experience, assumes that sensory experience is at least prior in time and that a poem's temporal development is dramatic, Milton, with a more static and abstract view of man, feels free to range among various phenomena, all of which are equally human realities to him. Earlier, the sense of physical participation in these lines was mentioned:

> Ran nectar, visiting each plant, and fed
> Flowers worthy of Paradise which not nice art
> In beds and curious knots, but nature boon
> Poured forth profuse on hill and dale and plain.

It would be quite wrong to show these lines to Leavis as if they met his criteria. Why, he would ask, did Milton not write

>   fed
> Flowers worthy of Paradise, which nature boon
> Poured forth profuse . . .

Leavis' criteria are summed up in his favorite word "realize," the double meaning of which — "to render concretely" and "to be aware of the nature of" — contains in his view an inherent connection. In reply it can be said that for Milton "being aware of the nature of" can easily involve turning from one level of experience to another. But this in itself is too static a view, suggesting both that "levels of experience" are fixed counters and that one combination of these counters has as much validity in Milton's eyes as any other. Precisely what troubles Leavis about Milton's verse is that he cannot discern what constraints it acknowledges, what sense of reality it holds itself responsible to. (This is the difficulty modern readers feel with *The Faerie Queene*; what has been described here, in fact, is the side of Milton that has the strongest affinities with his master, Spenser.) To answer these questions, it is not enough to say that Milton's view of reality made him free to add the remark about "nice art" in the lines we are considering. A positive explanation must be given of the dynamics of these lines, so that we can say, borrowing one of Leavis' favorite words, that the added words have their own kind of "rightness."

If we ask, as we do in the "Ode to a Nightingale," how these words follow upon — that is, how are they the consequence of — what precedes them, there is, as Leavis rightly discerned, no very positive answer. The proper question is rather: what do these words add to what precedes and what follows? First, by engaging us in a moral rejection of "nice art," they give point and challenge to the preceding phrase, "worthy of Paradise." The challenge is to conceive what this phrase can mean if we acknowledge that art as we know it is unworthy. What may have seemed a conventional hyperbole is made to intimate the full dimensions of the puzzles we must all feel in imagining an original state of innocence. In addition, the moral rejection of "nice art" makes one identify with the moral qualities of "nature boon." It could be said that the personification of nature is intensified, but nature does not become an externalized mythological figure in the eighteenth-century manner. The intensification is entirely a matter of our apprehending the meaning of nature's bounty, that it corresponds to modes of feeling and acting that we find in ourselves and value for ourselves. Here again a whole range of considerations about nature and human nature opens

— and these among the most ambitious and fruitful that concerned Renaissance thinkers and artists.

These lines show how active is the reader's participation in Milton's verse. In verse dramatically conceived, it is of the essence that the reader maintain his identity and therefore a certain distance from the poet and the experience the poet realizes. When a poet interrupts a description of flowers to say they are worthy of paradise, we say that he seems to be telling us what to think, imposing his views on us. This is a familiar complaint about Milton's verse. Waldock, for example, distinguishes between "the level of demonstration or exhibition" and "the level of allegation or commentary." [28] He assumes that demonstration has a greater validity than commentary, because he thinks the poet's task is to render an external reality which the reader is able to observe, enter, and judge as an independent individual. But the separation between poet and reader cannot be maintained if we, in Leavis' phrase, "read Milton as he demands to be read." The interjected phrase "which not nice art / In beds and curious knots" engages one's understanding of the surrounding phrases both by its meaning and by its occurrence as part of a continuing movement of the mind. Syntactically, it occurs in a "not" construction that requires an answering "but." The rhythms continue the run-on effects that had engaged our responses in the preceding lines. The effect is not of being talked to by someone else, but of coming to certain awarenesses about oneself.

Having mentioned Waldock, I want to look more directly at the aspect of the Milton controversy represented by his book. Waldock's central complaint about the poem is that the official viewpoints represented by God, his angel spokesmen, and the poet speaking in his own voice contradict and are never made accountable to the feelings and attitudes aroused by what is seen of the characters and situations when they are dramatically presented. Such objections are of a piece with Leavis' remarks about Milton's failure to realize a situation, and they confirm what Leavis has always claimed, that the issues about verbal de-

28. *"Paradise Lost" and Its Critics* (Cambridge, Eng.: Cambridge University Press, 1947), p. 78.

tails in *Paradise Lost* involve the largest problems of the poem. But no one has attempted to deal with Leavis' and Waldock's objections together. Waldock himself did not connect his arguments with a view of Milton's style: he felt that Milton got into so much trouble because, writing before the age of the novel, he was naive about the problems of narrative. Ricks deals only with verbal detail and mentions Waldock only once; on the large issues of the poem he is satisfied with platitudes, as Empson's review rightly objected. It is Empson himself to whom we might look for a comprehensive dealing with Leavis and Waldock. But *Milton's God* bypasses stylistic matters, because Empson is intent on showing that Milton was willing to imagine the story of the Fall down to every detail of action and motive. Hence he treats every detail of the poem as a narrative detail; he even expounds the poem in the chronological order of events and not in its own temporal sequence. By re-imagining *Paradise Lost* this way, Empson conveys its scope, claims, and difficulties more adequately than any other critic. But his central principle of reading seems to me wrong: "Anything which lets you off attending to the story ends up by making you feel the poetry is bad." [29] Though the insight and grandeur of *Milton's God* are due to Empson's own sticking to this principle, no other reader could repeat the process with the same results. An admiring reviewer justly called the book "Empson's novel." [30]

All the problems Waldock raises cannot be dealt with here. But we can indicate how Milton's style, as described thus far, engages the issues of the poem rather than riding roughshod over them.[31] Waldock complains bitterly about the passage describing Satan perched on the tree of life:

29. *Milton's God* (London: Chatto and Windus, 1961), p. 99.
30. Roger Sale in the *Massachusetts Review,* 3 (1962), 598–600.
31. The best study of the way Milton's style engages the issues of the poem is Stanley Fish's *Surprised by Sin: The Reader in "Paradise Lost"* (New York, 1967), an implicit answer to Leavis but one that never addresses his arguments and objections to Milton. Fish pays a great deal of attention to Waldock and in a sense does what I do with Leavis: agrees with Waldock's observations and turns them into positive virtues. Anyone who has read Fish will see the similarity in our approaches to Milton, especially our attention to "the reader in *Paradise Lost.*" My analyses of specific passages continually imply disagreement with Fish

                                                on the tree of life
        The middle tree and highest there that grew,
        Sat like a cormorant; yet not true life
        Thereby regained, but sat devising death
        To them who lived; nor on the virtue thought
        Of that life-giving plant, but only used
        For prospect, what well used had been the pledge
        Of immortality. So little knows
        Any, but God alone, to value right
        The good before him, but perverts best things
        To worst abuse, or to their meanest use.

                                                        IV.194–204

"What a fall is here!" exclaims Waldock. "Here, surely we may
say, the poem reaches one of its really low spots, here is manipulation with a vengeance. Satan perched on his bough, neglecting
his opportunities, put to incidental, momentary use as a sort of
illustration to a trivial homily! This is Sunday-school-motto
technique. It was mean of Milton to use his Satan so." [32] Waldock thinks any categorical moral interpretation is a denial of
dramatic life — in the reader as well as in the character, for he
clearly considers Satan and the reader to be equally "manipu-
lated" by Milton here. But making moral judgments is not in
itself illegitimate, and the judgment in this case is a reasonable
one: from the beginning, Satan has said that he seeks to destroy
Eden purely for the sake of vengeance. If we find him impressive
and heroic in the first two books it is because of qualities like
steadfastness and courage, not because we think his purposes are
any different from what Milton says they are here. The antipathy
Waldock feels for this passage would only be reasonable if Milton's moral judgment were delivered in the spirit attributed to
him by Leavis: "He reveals everywhere a dominating sense of
righteousness and a complete incapacity to question or explore
its significance and conditions." [33]

---

on the great Miltonic subjects of human freedom and spiritual capacity;
but the subject of this essay prohibits my giving Fish's arguments the
kind of attention and counterargumentation they deserve.
    32. *"Paradise Lost" and Its Critics*, p. 87.
    33. *Revaluation*, p. 58.

But suppose we now think of ourselves not as external observers of a dramatic action, but as participants in the series of words that the poet unfolds. Simply by thinking of the words as normal reflection and contemplation about Satan and not as thrusts aimed *at* him, we see that Waldock has mistaken the tone of

>   nor on the virtue thought
> Of that life-giving plant, but only used
> For prospect, what well used had been the pledge
> Of immortality.

There is a sense of pathos in these lines: we recognize the loss that Satan has sustained because we ourselves have sustained it. We now see that the phrase "what well used had been the pledge / Of immortality" refers to ourselves as well as to Satan. The tree of life and the tree of knowledge are closely associated in the myth of the Fall, and it is for us that the tree of life would have been the "pledge of immortality" — Satan is immortal already. The lines are not morally obtuse or objectionable, precisely because Milton has not made himself or us immune to the criticism they contain. And this is confirmed by the lines immediately following:

>   So little knows
> Any, but God alone, to value right
> The good before him, but perverts best things
> To worst abuse, or to their meanest use.

Waldock despises these lines because he assumes that Milton is identifying himself with God, in a smug, homiletic manner. Quite the contrary, the lines mean just what they say: that no creature, only God himself, can always and truly discern the good. The management of the passage, and particularly the open-ended meaning of "well used," keeps vitally alive the major issues of the poem. "Value right / The good before him" beautifully states what Adam and Eve must do, and the line division brings out implications that engage the sense just felt of "paradise lost." "Value right" is isolated by the line ending so that it gets full weight as an absolute spiritual act. Hence "the good before him" has a strong specifying force — it defines what is to be valued — and thus suggests how easy right valuing was in Eden, and how challenging it turned out to be and is now.

To judge from their other analyses, both Empson and Ricks would say that "well used" refers not only to Satan but also to Adam and Eve. I think we must go further to say that the style directly includes us in the spiritual situations it recounts. After all, the point of this story is that it is our story too. This is clear when we ask of the following lines the question "What does this add to the passage?"

>   yet not true life
> Thereby regained, but sat devising death
> To them who lived; nor on the virtue thought
> Of that life-giving plant . . .

That is, suppose Milton had written

> Sat like a cormorant, and only used
> For prospect, what well used had been the pledge
> Of immortality.

Written this way, "well used" would refer only to Satan and to Adam and Eve. The additional lines draw out the significance of the tree for the Christian reader in all times and places. "Nor on the virtue thought / Of that life-giving plant" has meaning for the reader if he simply reflects on what the words mean, and frees himself from thinking that all spiritual matters in this poem are to be revealed by demonstrations to the senses. And since Milton has just compared Satan to the hireling clergy who climb into the church, like the thieves in the parable of the good shepherd, there is also a moral challenge in "sat devising death / To them who lived": compare the clergy starving their sheep in *Lycidas*.[34]

Critics and readers have often noticed the excursiveness of Milton's style; for Leavis this is a sign of its failing to be respon-

34. Fowler, in his note on the passage, says: "Anyone guilty of greedy rapaciousness might be called a cormorant, but the term was especially often used of 'hireling' clergy."

sible to a coherently conceived mind or a concretely realized world. It should be clear by now that the unfolding of Milton's verse does not render the dramatic development of a mind, but rather its steady contemplation of truths, attitudes, traditions, locutions — all the immense store of man's accumulated recording of his wisdom and experience. In a brilliant metaphor, Hopkins' friend R. W. Dixon said that Milton's style is "a deliberate unrolling as if of some vast material." [35] It is truly breathtaking to see how Milton, after apparently reaching an endpoint in this passage, maintains an issue in all its life and intensity simply by returning to the narration:

> Beneath him with new wonder now he views
> To all delight of human sense exposed
> In narrow room nature's whole wealth, yea more,
> A heaven on earth.   IV.205–208

These seem like conventional locutions, but Milton secures their fullest meaning. The exclamation of our wonder, "A heaven on earth," was Adam's literal experience, and our partial capacity to identify with Adam validates the truth in the hyperbole. At the same time, we are aware of the meaning of the phrase for Satan, for whom "heaven on earth" sums up his bitter envy of man. But the line I particularly want to point out is "To all delight of human sense exposed." It is perfectly straightforward and ordinary; there are no difficulties for an editor to untangle; indeed, it could be omitted and its loss not noticed. But think what it adds at this point, how vitally it continues our engagement with the issues of the preceding passage — how much the phrase, simply by its plain and obvious meaning, bears witness to our ability in some way to perceive "the good before us." How right Empson is to speak of Milton's capacity to "screw a moral case up tight." And we once more see how Milton's mind, as Empson says, was working on very central matters for the Renaissance and Western civilization.

The theme of sensory delight has already been developed in an earlier passage of Book IV, part of which will be my final illustration of the strength and adequacy of Milton's poetic re-

35. Quoted by Ricks, p. 102.

sources. After the first description of paradise, Milton describes
Satan's approach to it:

>   and of pure now purer air
> Meets his approach, and to the heart inspires
> Vernal delight and joy, able to drive
> All sadness but despair: now gentle gales
> Fanning their odoriferous wings dispense
> Native perfumes, and whisper whence they stole
> Those balmy spoils. As when to them who sail
> Beyond the Cape of Hope, and now are past
> Mozambic, off at sea north-east winds blow
> Sabean odours from the spicy shore
> Of Arabie the blest, with such delay
> Well pleased they slack their course, and many a league
> Cheered with the grateful smell old Ocean smiles.
>
>   IV.153–165

Arnold Stein's commentary on this passage shows what a modern critic looks for in Milton's verse: "No matter how luxuri-
ously, and innocently, the description seems to wander, it never
ceases to explore the drama of Satan's consciousness." For example: "The breezes . . . significantly reflect Satan's mind.
They tell 'whence they stole / Those balmie spoiles.' And so they
. . . betray Satan's intended crime as the 'first grand Thief,' and
anticipate Satan's own language when he says that man has been
endowed 'With Heav'nly spoils, our spoils.' " [36] Stein does what
Empson, Ricks, and a host of other commentators do: he looks
for correspondences with the narrative action. As we should be
prepared to see by now, there is more to the passage than this.
Milton speaks not of Satan's heart, but of *the* heart — that of
any creature. In the first six lines both moral statement and sensuous description engage our capacities directly, so that we are
not merely observing Satan but, as in the last passage, defining
ourselves in relation to him. Angels may merely observe and
judge Satan's spiritual plight; for us it brings out the unique
tragedy of despair, the one sadness to which created nature can-

36. *Answerable Style* (Seattle, Wash.: University of Washington Press,
1953), pp. 58–59.

not minister. Coming on the heels of the lush description that precedes, the lines so engage the reader's assent that, given the lineation and word order, he can scarcely separate "despair" from "all sadness." There but for the grace of God go I, he may well say. But Milton's emphasis here is less on our dependence on God than on our capacity to use his gifts to us. As always in Milton this is a challenge as well as an invitation, and both elements are felt in the phrase "stole / Those balmy spoils," which hints, as Stein says, at Satan's designs. But it *is* a rich and seductive locution for a bit of natural loveliness: it is not mere exotic luxury, for these are "native perfumes." The phrase first engages our sensory responsiveness and yearning; second, its dubious terms bring out an inherent ambivalence in our own exotic imaginings and the poetry we create for and out of them; finally, the likeness to Satan's aims brings out the constant possibility that one side, the worst side, of our nature can engulf the other and "pervert best things / To worst abuse, or to their meanest use."

Ricks likes to quote the eighteenth-century critic Jonathan Richardson, who said: "Whoever will possess [Milton's] ideas must dig for them, and oftentimes pretty far below the surface." [37] But in a way this is misleading advice, though Ricks himself follows it with great sense and tact. Certainly what is inadequate about Stein's comment is that he is able to discern only what is beneath the surface. The surface itself Stein describes in the following terms: "Then there is the luxurious epic simile, traditionally digressive, wantoning in rich description, with much lingering on the conventional magic of name and phrases." [38] Q.E.D., Leavis might well say. But of course this is the impression readers have always had of Milton's similes. What I think we are now able to do is show how these obvious surface workings of the verse engage one's attention and intelligence in such a way that they are continuous with the obscure and difficult points that develop, extend, and complicate them. Thus the simile does not, as in Stein's account, simply comment on Satan's passing the Cape of Hope and slackening his course. It continues the work of the opening lines by making us apprehend, in the

37. Quoted in *Milton's Grand Style*, p. 69.
38. *Answerable Style*, p. 59.

most powerful and intimate ways, our relation to Satan. We are indeed in the same boat with him — a fact we feel the more strongly since several earlier passages have compared Satan to heroic and enterprising voyagers.[39] The question is whether we are "beyond the Cape of Hope" in the sense that Satan is, whether "Arabie the blest" is as ironic for us as for him. The likenesses between ourselves and Satan — our situation as fallen creatures, the likeness between our heroic enterprises — suggest the possibility that these other likenesses are so. But the simile asserts they are not, or need not be, because as we smell the spicy breezes we slack our course in a way that Satan cannot. The fullness of the verse makes us, like the sailors in the simile, "with such delay / Well pleased." We experience a moment of liberation from the need to arrive anywhere or to do anything to exploit the place we have reached. These verses suspend us — as, in Milton's view, we are suspended in every detail and aspect of our lives — between Adam and Satan. Adam, our great parent, is the innocent creature for whom the goodness of creation is manifested everywhere with equal fullness, just as we and the sailors experience the pleasures of Arabia Felix diffused over the whole ocean. Satan, our grand foe, is the pure fallen creature, defining himself by his fallen nature — "Evil, be thou my good" — whose gratifications are so thoroughly identified with his own goals, purposes, and actions that he literally cannot be himself when he is passive and receptive. Perhaps this is the last curse of his ingratitude: that he is cut off from "all delight of human sense," that he cannot be "cheered with the grateful smell."

The last line of the simile does something with which we should now be familiar: it endows a conventional poeticism with all its human meanings. The reader is of course aware that this is a piece of mythologizing. To turn a literal ocean of "many a league" into a creature is to acknowledge that doing justice to this special moment necessitates, in Bacon's definition of poetry, submitting the shows of things to the desires of the mind. And yet the fiction is almost felt to be true. "Cheered with the grateful smell" simply registers our experience, and since the men on shipboard can have this experience at any point on the ocean —

39. See II.636, 1017, 1043.

the phrase "many a league" first seems to refer to them — it can be attributed to the ocean itself without hyperbole. For a moment the verse lures us into seeing not simply earthly gardens, but the whole creation as a shadow of Eden — even a primeval figure like old Ocean, whom we might imagine to be kin to the Chaos and old Night through whose realms Satan has just voyaged.

Milton's verse harmonizes simplicity and complexity in ways that scarcely seem possible to poets who follow him. The frankness, range, and human reality of the Arabia Felix passage make the exoticism of the "Ode to a Nightingale," the Hebrides stanza of Wordsworth's "To a Solitary Reaper," or "The Comedian as the Letter C" seem specialized, no matter how intensely felt and understood. For certain modes of verse, Milton has the godlike quality that one senses in Shakespeare. He had, in relation to the materials and traditions, the very locutions and commonplaces of western poetry, that negative capability that Shakespeare had in relation to and their affairs. When he coined this phrase, Keats had in mind Shakespeare's attitude towards men and life; but I think what it now conveys is a sense that these poets are inexhaustible. As God himself is supposed to, they seem to work in conscious possession of all their knowledge and of all their purposes; yet conscious control in them seems not to entail the exclusions, limitations, and choices it normally does. With such poets we particularly need to learn from each other, and, as Christopher Ricks has shown, from critics of the past. Studying and writing about the Milton controversy, I have been reminded of the biological law that ontogeny recapitulates phylogeny. It is an irony of the Milton controversy that what should have been a dialogue was warfare, and that Milton's image of the search to restore truth to her wholeness was not ours. But of course Milton's own behavior in controversy was very different from this image, so that however much one regrets the atmosphere of the controversy, one at least has the consolation of poetic justice. There is also this consolation in contemplating the Miltonic isolation and sense of rectitude with which Dr. Leavis has insisted on holding Milton to the highest standards, as he sees them, of integrity in style. Bitter as has been Leavis' feeling about the whole affair, I think he has fundamentally done honor to Milton and to criticism. To the extent that his critics were content with partial and local victories, they have been untrue to the scope and singlemindedness of the work they were defending. I hope I have demonstrated the kind of integrity Milton's style has. And I hope that henceforth we Milton critics can emulate the humanity and largeness of the poem we love, and not the worst side of the man who wrote it.

THOMAS R. EDWARDS

Visible Poetry: Pope and Modern Criticism

It was only ninety years ago that Arnold pronounced Dryden
and Pope "classics of our prose." In 1880 Shaw was twenty-
four, Yeats fifteen, Joyce two years unborn and Lawrence five;
as Arnold suspected, a new literary age was dawning, one that
would find his view of the Augustan poets no more congenial
than many of his other views. But modern criticism was shaped
by the need to answer Arnold, and our idea of Pope owes more
than we like to admit to the Arnoldian terms it rejects.

The terms themselves are of course almost embarrassingly
vulnerable: "Are Dryden and Pope poetical classics? Is the historic estimate, which represents them as such and which has
been so long established that it cannot easily give way, the real
estimate? Wordsworth and Coleridge, as is well known, denied
it; but the authority of Wordsworth and Coleridge does not
weigh much with the younger generation, and there are many
signs to show that the eighteenth century and its judgments are
coming into favor again. Are the favorite poets of the eighteenth century classics?"

Few others abide our question as meekly as Dryden and
Pope, that is; but in fact these questions are rather feeble. The

favorite poets of the eighteenth century were not Dryden and
Pope at all, but Homer, Shakespeare, and Milton, Arnold's and
everyone's favorites; and it is a slippery logic that would make
the high estimate of the Augustans both a "long established"
piety and an irritating fad of an impertinent new age. Yet if
both "the historic estimate" and "the younger generation" have
the suspicious rustle of the straw-man, still, our answers to
Arnold on this matter have led to confusions of our own, not
least the assumption that he spoke for an "official" Victorian
culture unanimously insensitive or hostile to the Augustans. He
himself assumed no such thing — his tone is defensive, if bellig-
erently so.

Victorian taste resists casual definition — there was so *much*
of it — but Arnold's age was of several minds about Pope.[1]
Arnold himself was restating a standard eighteenth-century
view: that of, for example, Joseph Warton's insistence that
"ethical poetry" like Pope's, however excellent of its kind, was
of a lower order than the poetry of Shakespeare, Spenser, and
Milton.[2] (Johnson's defense of Pope tacitly conceded the
point.) What Warton was saying in the 1750's Wordsworth was
still saying in the 1830's: "if the beautiful, the pathetic, and the
sublime be what a poet should chiefly aim at, how absurd it is
to place these men [Dryden and Pope] amongst the first poets
of their country! Admirable are they in treading their way, but
that way lies almost at the foot of Parnassus."[3] (In the same
remark, however, he admitted that "to this day I believe I could
repeat, with a little previous rummaging of my memory, several
thousand lines of Pope.") This historic estimate was memorably summed up, a decade before Arnold's remarks, by a
Victorian belles-lettrist improbably named John Dennis, in
whom Pope's Appius indeed lived on in softer forms of passion:
"He has written none of the verses which children love, nor
any lines which grown-up people care to croon over in mo-

1. Useful collections of critical opinion about Pope, from his time to
ours, are *Discussions of Alexander Pope,* ed. Rufus A. Blanshard (Boston: D. C. Heath, 1960), and *Critics on Pope,* ed. Judith O'Neill (London: Methuen, and Coral Gables: University of Miami Press, 1968).
2. Warton, *Essay on the Genius and Writings of Pope* (1756, 1782);
see Blanshard, pp. 3–13, and O'Neill, p. 13.
3. *Letters of the Wordsworth Family,* quoted in Blanshard, p. 29.

ments of weakness or sorrow. [No Touchstones, in fact?] In his works the wit o'ertops the poetry, the intellect gets the better of the heart, and thus he wins admiration from his readers rather than affection." [4]

But of course there was another line on Pope kept alive in appreciative remarks by Byron, De Quincey and others, the line taken by Thackeray in *The English Humourists* (1853):

In considering Pope's admirable career, I am forced into similitudes drawn from other courage and greatness, and into comparing him with those who achieved triumphs in actual war. I think of the works of the young Pope as I do the actions of young Bonaparte or young Nelson. In their common life you will find frailties and mean-nesses, as great as the vices of the meanest men. But in the presence of the great occasion, the great soul flashes out, and conquers tran-scendent. In thinking of the splendour of Pope's young victories, of his merit, unequalled as his renown, I hail and salute the achieving genius, and do homage to the pen of a hero.[5]

This sees Pope less as poet than as Representative Man, but Thackeray's "admirable career" at least has more generous in-tentions than Wordsworth's "admirable are they in treading their way," Dennis' "admiration . . . rather than affection," Arnold's own "admirable for the purposes of the high priest of an age of prose and reason." And an even higher heroic tone was being taken by Swinburne in the same year "The Study of Poetry" appeared:

And what a spirit it was! how fiery bright and dauntless! . . . It rouses the blood, it kindles the heart, to remember what an indomi-table force of heroic spirit, and sleepless always as fire, was inclosed in the pitiful body of the misshapen weakling whose whole life was spent in fighting the good fight of sense against folly, of light against darkness, of human speech against brute silence, of truth and reason and manhood against all the banded bestialities of all dunces and all

4. John Dennis, "Alexander Pope," in *Frazier's Magazine* (May 1870), quoted in Oscar Maurer, "Pope and the Victorians," *University of Texas Studies in English, 1944* (Austin, 1945), p. 214.
5. Quoted in Blanshard, p. 43.

dastards, all blackguardly blockheads and all blockheaded black-
guards, who then as now were misbegotten by malignity on dulness.[6]

One sees what Arnold had to contend with. Yet it was convenient for the twentieth-century estimate of Pope, in its beginnings
in Bloomsbury, to take Arnold's estimate as representing the
nineteenth century in toto. Lytton Strachey and Virginia Woolf
admired the feeling rationality of Pope and his contemporaries
— what Strachey, who aspired to it himself, appreciatively
called "civilization illuminated by animosity" [7] — largely because it so neatly rebuked the muddle of high principles, pom-
posity, and aggressive coarseness of taste in the Victorian ancestors they were so anxious to live down. In the charming
prank she called a biography of Pope, Edith Sitwell put the
new mood with characteristic verve:

A large section of the public has not yet recovered from the cold,
damp mossiness that has blighted the public taste for the last fifty or
even sixty years; and to these people, Pope is not one of the greatest
of our poets, one of the most loveable of men, but a man who was
deformed in spirit as in body . . . This general blighting and withering of the poetic taste is the result of the public mind having been
overshadowed by such Aberdeen-granite tombs and monuments as
Matthew Arnold — is the result, also, of the substitution of scholar
for poet, of school-inspector for artist.[8]

One loves Pope in order to punish those one does not love, and
the famous deformities make the preference all the more cruel
— "What can such a nice girl see in him?" poor Arnold is im-
agined jealously asking. Bloomsbury does to public taste, in
Arnold's name, what Arnold in his day did to public taste in
Pope's name.

Now if compelled to choose, which of us would not prefer
Arnold's "culture" to Lytton Strachey's "civilization," even if
it meant losing Pope? High seriousness is at least serious, if
rather high. But the idea of such a choice is a nice historical

6. Swinburne, "A Century of English Poetry," *Fortnightly Review*
(October 1880), quoted in Blanshard, p. 57.

7. Lytton Strachey, *Pope* (Cambridge, Eng., 1925), quoted in O'Neill,
p. 24.

8. Edith Sitwell, *Alexander Pope* (London, 1930), quoted in O'Neill,
p. 24.

irony — Arnold wins the argument, in effect, by establishing
the terms in which even Pope's better champions, outside
Bloomsbury, show that he loses it. For Eliot and Pound,
though their main stakes were elsewhere, Pope could be invoked to show a "hard" sensibility that measured the softness
of a received and debased tradition. (If Pope, of all people, was
good, then Milton, Shelley, and Tennyson were really out of
luck.) For Empson, whose *Seven Types* in 1930 gave him more
attention than anyone except Shakespeare and put him to some
of the best "close reading" he's received, Pope was excellent
proof of the complexity of motive good poetry reveals. For
Leavis, Pope carried the healthy seventeenth-century "line of
wit" farther than Eliot's scheme allowed, while embodying a
positive integrity of culture and imagination that later ages
would try to vulgarize or destroy. For American "New Critics"
like Brooks and Tate, Pope demonstrated the "anti-Platonic"
energy of wit and paradox. For Geoffrey Tillotson Pope showed
the validity of "period" conventions of style we had forgot how
to understand; for Maynard Mack he showed the rhetorical
operations of the neoclassical genres, especially satire; for Reuben Brower he showed how poetry is made of other poetry,
particularly the classical poets Pope's age felt in their brains as
we feel Joyce and Eliot in ours; for a current generation of
scholar-critics he shows how poetry contains the stuff of intellectual history, the philosophical, religious, political, and economic assumptions of an age. For Marshall McLuhan (to end
a tiring list with a bang) the *Dunciad* gives a true account of
how Gutenbergian typography detaches words from their meanings and ushers "the polite world back into primitivism, the
Africa within, and above all, the unconscious."

This summary is of course cavalier and superficial; the study
of Pope has been one of the finest achievements of our age of
critical redefinition. Yet that achievement is significantly col-
ored, and inhibited, by Arnold's terms. We deny that Pope was,
in Arnold's sense, the high priest of an age of prose and reason
by substituting for "prose and reason" qualities more to our
taste — and to Arnold's, some of them. We find "imagination"
in the wit of his imagery, organizational control rather than
pedantry in his allusions, moral and metaphysical seriousness

in his "social" attitudes and ironies; in general he serves as a
useful corrective to a too narrow idea of poetry. Quite so, these
findings are right — yet in effect we may only have redefined
"prose and reason" as *something better* for Pope to be the high
priest of, some other state of mind and culture he positively and
masterfully can represent.

Our age understands more than Arnold about the nature of
Pope's materials, the expressiveness of his poetic "prose" and
the issues at play beneath the surface of his "reason"; but I
doubt that we have sufficiently asked whether his *relation* to
those materials is priestlike. Does our approval of Pope mean
as much as it seems to? Do we read him for pleasure as we do
other great poets? Do students find him as exciting as we tell
them they should? Do teachers fight and scheme to teach him as
they do to teach Shakespeare, Blake, Yeats, Chaucer, Milton,
Wordsworth? In short, does Pope occupy minds today as something more than a little treasury of marvelous passages, and of
brilliant exegetical moments in the masters of modern criticism?
We can "analyze" his verse beautifully, appreciate his relation
to his culture ancient and modern, see how the genres contributed to his art; but have we really grasped the pleasures, and
the difficulties, of his poems as whole literary experiences?

I want to suggest that Pope's perspective on his own "civilization," what Arnold meant by prose and reason, was in its
own way no less questioning and skeptical than Arnold's perspective on his, or ours on our own. And Pope's perspective is
implicit in his way of organizing his materials, in the demands
his "extensive" kind of poetry makes on the mind as one reads.
My example will be Epistle II of the *Essay on Man,* a poem
which, more than Pope's others, presents itself as reasoned, sequential discourse and seems to deny itself the digressive excite-
ments of satire. Here Pope is as close as he ever gets to talking
like a high priest, an official spokesman who knows the answers
and aims to tell the truth for his reader's own good. Though
sequential interpretation can be tedious, it may be useful to look
through the Epistle part by part, to see what its way of pro-
gressing suggests about Pope's relation to his own poetic art.[9]

9. My reading of Epistle II is much indebted to Maynard Mack's introduction and notes to the "Twickenham" edition (London: Methuen,

Epistle II begins memorably with the great "glory, jest, and riddle" passage, which from its location both summarizes the attack in Epistle I on "Presumptuous Man" for failing to apprehend the implicit order in creation and establishes the ground for what follows, the account of passion's role in human experience:

> Know then thyself, presume not God to scan;
> The proper study of Mankind is Man.
> Plac'd on this isthmus of a middle state,
> A being darkly wise, and rudely great:
> With too much knowledge for the Sceptic side,
> With too much weakness for the Stoic's pride,
> He hangs between; in doubt to act, or rest,
> In doubt to deem himself a God, or Beast;
> In doubt his Mind or Body to prefer,
> Born but to die, and reas'ning but to err;
> Alike in ignorance, his reason such,
> Whether he thinks too little, or too much:
> Chaos of Thought and Passion, all confus'd;
> Still by himself abus'd, or disabus'd;
> Created half to rise, and half to fall;
> Great lord of all things, yet a prey to all;
> Sole judge of Truth, in endless Error hurl'd:
> The glory, jest, and riddle of the world!

Maynard Mack's notes for these eighteen lines in the "Twickenham" edition run to more than a hundred lines of small type, with dozens of references to Pascal, Montaigne, Hooker, Milton, Robert Gould, Bezaleel Morrice, and other thoughtful worthies. Pope was well aware of the ethical traditions behind him, and Mack admirably explains the relation of Epistle II to the philosophical design of the whole poem. Yet that design seems more coherent in Mack's exegesis than it does in reading

---

and New Haven: Yale University Press, 1950), from which I quote the poem. I should say, too, that my way of thinking about Pope draws upon Robert Martin Adams' idea of "open form" (see his *Strains of Discord* [Ithaca, N.Y.: Cornell University Press, 1958]); upon Richard Poirier's idea of literature as "self-performance" (see his essay in this volume and his book *The Performing Self* [New York: Oxford University Press, 1971]); and upon D. J. Greene's " 'Logical Structure' in Eighteenth-Century Poetry," *Philological Quarterly*, 21 (1952), 315–336.

the poem; in this passage one feels a complexity of attitude that derives from the "background" but that also expresses a particular, dramatically "located" state of mind which the ideas themselves don't wholly account for.

That confident, magisterial first couplet seems to settle things — now that we know our proper study, all should be well. Yet what follows is unsettling. We are the pitifully confused thing we should study; and how can it hope to study itself? The antithetical, oxymoron-ridden verse patterns emphasize man's isthmian place in the creation, the terrible paradoxes of his nature — our nature. But once "Man" becomes "he," a third person both poet and reader can stand aside from, the paradoxes seem not to be personally menacing problems but the substance of a familiar and intelligible human situation. The contradictions in man's nature, that is, become material for speculative conversation — this is the voice of someone who "talks that way" and with whom we can thus be fairly comfortable, though (like Rosenkrantz and Guildenstern listening to "what a piece of work is a man") we risk something by assuming we know how to take such a message from such a voice.

But the rather abrupt rise of sarcasm in the following attack on speculative intellect — "Go, wondrous creature! mount where Science guides" — disturbs the reader's new-found composure. We can accept the general proposition that man is an absurd mixture of jarring natures, we've heard *that* before, but it hurts when intellectual heroes like Newton and Boyle (to say nothing of Plato!) — men we admire and are proud to claim as fellow creatures — are put to ridicule. And indeed the indulgence in an exhilarating Juvenalian, or Swiftian, animus ("Go, teach Eternal Wisdom how to rule — / Then drop into thyself, and be a fool!") does yield to a kind of control:

> Superior beings, when of late they saw
> A mortal Man unfold all Nature's law,
> Admir'd such wisdom in an earthly shape,
> And shew'd a NEWTON as we shew an Ape.   (31–34)

This puts Newton in his place, but it's not simply a ludicrous place. It makes some sense to value apes for their surprising and

charming resemblances to us, and there's some comfort in hearing that "superior beings" aren't wholly unlike us in their pleasures. If Newton thinks the universe centers upon him, then the
lines are a terrible affront; but if he understands (as Pope wants
us to do) that the creation is a design of overlapping hierarchies
in which apes, men, and superior beings have a mutual relation
that shames none of them, he will find the remark as compli-
mentary as it is satirical and limiting.

The point is that this opening section is made up of movements and countermovements of feeling, false starts, interrup-
tions, and collisions. The poetic mind that examines man's isthmian nature also demonstrates it in its own noticeable shifts of
emphasis and outlook. Elsewhere in this volume Paul J. Alpers
speaks of the "seamless" effect of Milton's blank verse, one's
sense that new material grows out of what has gone before
without evident transitions or connections, like a tapestry endlessly unrolling before the eye. Pope's couplet verse, here and
elsewhere, works quite differently — passages are being arranged
as we watch, visibly put together for maximum effect like pieces
of furniture in a large room, or like ideas in the Lockeian mind.
(Even the self-containment of Pope's couplets suggests that
"parts" are being arranged, that the verse moves not through
"organic" growth but through a conscious and even ostentatious
"art.") This is not, of course, mere "interior decoration," but the
process of a poetry that confesses and makes a virtue of the uncertain, provisional nature of its own effects. The making of a rational doctrine — what Pope's prose "Arguments" for the four
Epistles try to convey[10] — is as much upset as advanced by a
moment like the Newton-ape passage, which is less a contribution to the "thought" of the poem than a cue to a properly complex response to it, a response that in a way is also a resistance
to the thought.

I am suggesting that Pope's is an art that makes visible its
own difficulties in achieving structural coherence and doctrinal

10. The "Arguments" of Epistles I–III were added to the "corrected"
edition of Epistle I but not printed in the first editions of these epistles
(see Mack, "Twickenham" edition, p. 9n.) This suggests that the "Arguments" were afterthoughts, not really evidence of working to a coherent
plan.

clarity. Epistle II shows him trying to accommodate doctrine to moral imagination, by finding and releasing elements in the traditional psychology of reason-and-passion that could support his own interest in irrational energy without sanctioning utter mindlessness. From Newton he moves rather abruptly to "Self-love" and "Reason" as the defining terms of isthmian self-awareness. It is not an exciting stretch of poetry, but in his analogies for self-love — the spring of motion in the mind's clockwork (59–60) without which human life would be only a vegetable cycle (63–64), a kind of mental eyesight that takes short but intense views (71–76) — one can at least see him searching for the best that can be said for unregulated passion, and the verse finally does wake up a bit:

> In lazy Apathy let Stoics boast
> Their Virtue fix'd; 'tis fix'd as in a frost,
> Contracted all, retiring to the breast;
> But strength of mind is Exercise, not Rest:
> The rising tempest puts in act the soul,
> Parts it may ravage, but preserves the whole.
> On life's vast ocean diversely we sail,
> Reason the card, but Passion is the gale;
> Nor God alone in the still calm we find,
> He mounts the storm, and walks upon the wind.
>   (101–110)

As usual when the issue crystalizes into an object, a human embodiment of error like the lazy Stoic, Pope gets down to poetic business, here that of finding and sustaining a tone feelingly vigorous enough to support the claims being made for the value of passionate activity.

The culminating analogy for the relation of Reason and Passion comes here, and it stresses the difficult complexity of their interaction:

> Passions, like Elements, tho' born to fight,
> Yet, mix'd and soften'd, in his [God's] work unite:
> These 'tis enough to temper and employ;
> But what composes Man, can Man destroy?
> Suffice that Reason keep to Nature's road,

> Subject, compound them, follow her and God.
> Love, Hope, and Joy, fair pleasure's smiling train,
> Hate, Fear, and Grief, the family of pain;
> These mix'd with art, and to due bounds confin'd,
> Make and maintain the balance of the mind:
> The light and shades, whose well accorded strife
> Gives all the strength and colour of our life.   (111–122)

Reason, God's "work," operates on the passions like a painter mixing and modifying his colors, creating balance out of elements that would glaringly clash if no such composing art held them in accord. The analogy was commonplace in ethical theory, and one sees why. Where the writer or musician in effect makes something of nothing — the words or sounds he "creates" are not the paper and ink he uses — the painter organizes what already exists. The finished painting is only the paint he began with, though wonderfully modified by what he has done with it. The passage says quite directly that such an ethical "art" is possible and desirable. Our life *can* be beautiful if we let reason exercise its composing powers. The conventionality of the terms — "fair pleasure's smiling train," "the family of pain" — does seem tacitly to confess that such an art ends in virtual cliché, like allegorical painting: the balanced mind isn't very novel or glamorous. But "the strength and colour of our life" ends the passage with a hopeful touch of vividness and affirmation.

But the Epistle is less than half finished, and this resolved mood is shadowed by the pages yet unturned, the lines we know remain to be read. Incompleteness was hinted at by "confin'd" and "strife," the rhyme words that may not be entirely appeased by their echo in "mind" and "life." (The rhymes indeed make us remember, not forget, the tension implicit in "balance.") And the next passage, though it begins with assured delight in a work compatible with the art of reason ("Pleasures are ever in our hands and eyes"), soon runs into a challenging qualification: "All spread their charms, but charm not all alike" (127). Minds are not regular and uniform; receptivity to the objects of rational pleasure differs from man to man, and in each man one "master Passion" lurks, "like Aaron's serpent," to crowd out the other passions that should be part of the balanced whole. "The ruling passion is the manifestation of God's power," says the "Twickenham" note on Aaron's serpent, but as "Man" we consider the allusion as much from the viewpoint of Pharaoh and his magicians — it's an unnatural mystery that shakes our belief in the dignity of our own powers — as from Moses' and God's viewpoint. And this return to uncertainty is confirmed by lines 133–144, where the "lurking principle of death" in the youngest and healthiest constitution is the figure for the ruling passion, "the Mind's disease" which, fed by imagination, concentrates in one spot the "vital humour" that should nourish the whole psychic economy. The "dang'rous art" (143) of imagination subverts the art of reason and we are back on the dark isthmus, in the chaos of thought and passion we supposed the analogy with art had transformed into "the balance of the mind."

This seems to be the crux of the ethical problem. Reason, which should control and guide natural impulse into integration of the self, seems in practice only a grim judge condemning our folly without helping us overcome it: "What can she more than tell us we are fools?" (152). Epistle II manfully seeks a positive answer, but Pope's art in effect shows that it really has no answer — that the reason of the ethical poet, the authority by which he condemns bad men and praises good ones, is always provisional and ad hoc, an unprovable instinct that acts powerfully in negative modes but is virtually helpless to accomplish its purpose of satiric correction. To tell the rational truth about Sporus, Cibber, Atticus, Atossa, or Timon is to punish them so severely as to fix them in their defiant antipathy to truth and nature; and all the Men of Ross in the world won't lead them back to virtue's paths once Pope's reason has pronounced sentence upon them. In practice we either rationalize our vices into self-justification or conceive a horror of self from which there's no exit into positive, active virtue (153–160).

In short, the isthmian mood returns in the middle of Epistle II in a form that strikes closer to home than the large ethical commonplaces we admired but were so well able to bear in the opening lines. The verse of the middle sections is quieter, more abstract and discursive, than the high rhetoric earlier; but if anything this makes the mood harder to resist, less "placeable" as poetic or philosophical mannerism. Even so, Pope works hard at mitigating this dark idea of reason's practical impotence. "Nature" is invoked (161–174) as authorizing a view of reason as "no guide, but still a guard"; all men are at least consistent in their individual passionate fixations, though the consistency may be trivial or pathetic and ultimately self-defeating:

> Thro' life 'tis follow'd, ev'n at life's expence;
> The merchant's toil, the sage's indolence,
> The monk's humility, the hero's pride,
> All, all alike, find Reason on their side.

Reason is simply that which transmits natural energy into usable social forms; like delicate fruits grafted on "savage stocks . . . the surest Virtues thus from Passions shoot, / Wild Nature's vigor working at the root" (183–184) as anger is transformed to "zeal and fortitude," avarice to "prudence," pride and shame to "Virtue" (chastity), and so on. Reason is less a faculty than a disposition of mind, a channel through which passion flows and, in its passage, is purified into "civilized" behavior — virtue comes, as it were, not from repression but from sublimation.

Pope tries hopefully to see the passivity of reason both as transformational medium and as the instrument that measures the resulting differentiation between "negative" impulse and "positive" virtue: "This light and darkness in our chaos join'd / What shall divide? The God within the mind" (203–204). Yet this couplet sums up a passage (195–202) on the virtuous potential of villainy that seems very precarious (Nero and Cataline are so established in their evil roles by history as to make the thought that they *could* have been good seem empty theorizing — "Nero reigns a Titus, if he will," but he won't, he didn't) and from the metaphor of sorting out emerges a new and less hopeful appeal to the mixing of effects in painting:

> Extremes in Nature equal ends produce,
> In Man they join to some mysterious use;
> Tho' each by turns the other's bounds invade,

As, in some well-wrought picture, light and shade,
And oft so mix, the diff'rence is too nice
Where ends the Virtue, and begins the Vice.   (205–210)

These lines are a kind of miniature of the larger movement of
the poem. The positive claim for the "mysterious use" of extremes is made; but what follows dwells not upon the use, the
achievement of "balance," as above, but the mystery, in four
lines of concession that pull against the hopeful commonplace.
Here painting signifies not integration of opposites but the impossibility of telling light from shade, virtue from vice, in a
well-made picture or human character. As usual, Pope's dialectic moves away from synthesis when it seems to have been
achieved — it unresolves what had seemed settled. Though we
(addressed as "Fools!") are immediately warned that we know
very well the difference between vice and virtue (211–216), this
stubborn common sense appeals not to reason but, as the
"Twickenham" note says, to an "intuitive" apprehension that
vice and virtue exist and are different. We get so used to our
own vices as to think them less dreadful than our neighbors'
(217–230), but this is only because custom and self-interest
film over the ugliness we naturally recognize at first sight.

This section of the epistle seems a jumble of claims, conces-
sions, and qualifications that is almost impossible to follow as
"argument." But we miss the point, I think, if we simply judge
Pope a bad philosopher and the poem therefore faulty. Rather,
in Pope's very visible difficulty in reconciling the ethical doc-
trines philosophers offer us, something significant is expressed.
A poet's mind lets us see what it is doing — making poetry
out of lumps of philosophy that resist becoming poetry. The
mind that can't quite resolve these ideas into coherent unity is
a recognizably human one, by no means immune to the weakness and error it finds in the mind of "Man." Whatever we
make of the argument, we can follow the ethical poet's refusal to ignore or sentimentalize human folly as it struggles
against his determination to salvage from the chaos some basis
(almost any will do) for continuation of life within that chaos.
The qualification and redirection of points, the shifts of tone and
mood, express not mere confusion but a visible and meaningful

dissatisfaction with what one can say, what one has said, about the nature of moral consciousness. Pope shares some of Eliot's understanding of the hopelessness, and the absolute necessity, of philosophical poetry, where each attempt at truth is

> a new beginning, a raid on the inarticulate
> With shabby equipment always deteriorating
> In the general mess of imprecision of feeling,
> Undisciplined squads of emotion.[11]

Pope's view of "emotion" is less austere than this, but despite its assertive moments the general tone of the *Essay on Man* is anything but confident and cheerful. Not the substance of a doctrine, but the activity of trying to formulate it satisfactorily — and only partly succeeding, and knowing that the success is only partial — is what Pope most powerfully expresses.

The making of poetry out of resistances to one's own doctrinal impulses is especially clear and impressive in the last section (VI) of Epistle II. In a long passage (231–260) Pope first seems to arrive at the goal, a mood (if not a coherent argument) that sums up and turns to positive account the hesitations and contradictions that have accumulated. All men are virtuous *and* vicious in idiosyncratic ways, but "HEAVEN's great view is One, and that the Whole" — God counteracts our weakness by assigning to each man the "happy frailty" that suits his station. The "glory, jest, and riddle" formula is converted into terms that seem to answer and resolve it — "[Heaven] builds on wants, and on defects on mind, / The joy, the peace, the glory of Mankind" (247–248) — and Pope goes on to praise Society as the gift of heaven that puts passion and weakness into a reciprocal play that serves all needs:

> Wants, frailties, passions, closer still ally
> The common int'rest, or endear the tie:
> To these we owe true friendship, love sincere,
> Each home-felt joy that life inherits here:
> Yet from the same we learn, in its decline,

11. T. S. Eliot, "East Coker"; from *Four Quartets,* by T. S. Eliot (New York: Harcourt Brace Jovanovich, 1943), quoted by permission of the publishers.

> Those joys, those loves, those int'rests to resign:
> Taught half by Reason, half by mere decay,
> To welcome death, and calmly pass away.   (253–260)

There is still a half-turn ("Yet from the same . . .") from positive to qualifying negative, but the dying fall delicately makes death seem a necessary and acceptable completion of "life." The Epistle could end here.

But of course it doesn't, and the thirty-four concluding lines are astonishing in this context — as well as being, independent of context, one of Pope's finest pieces of poetry. "Half by Reason, half *by mere decay*" recalls something the analysis of reason and passion has largely obscured, the biological imperative, so to speak, that shadowed the opening lines but had little part in the ethical speculations that followed. Life reconciles you to the self you are — such has been the Epistle's hopeful burden — but the result looks different from another perspective:

> The learn'd is happy nature to explore,
> The fool is happy that he knows no more;
> The rich is happy in the plenty giv'n,
> The poor contents him with the care of Heav'n.
> See the blind beggar dance, the cripple sing,
> The sot a hero, lunatic a king;
> The starving chemist in his golden views
> Supremely blest, the poet in his muse.   (263–270)

Happiness may indeed compensate for our deficiencies, but a world of dancing blindmen, singing cripples, drunks and madmen convinced of their own heroic grandeur, obsessed alchemists and "inspired" poets, is no happy prospect to the rational reader. This is the world of Swift's "Digression on Madness," the world of the misers in *To Bathurst* who starve themselves to fatten their bank accounts, the world of the poor compulsive scribbler in *Arbuthnot* who "lock'd from Ink and Paper, scrawls / With desp'rate Charcoal round his darken'd walls," the world of nonsense that oozes from the inner sanctuary of Dulness herself:

> Hence the Fool's paradise, the Statesman's scheme,
> The air-built Castle, and the golden Dream,

> The Maid's romantic wish, the Chymist's flame,
> And Poet's vision of eternal fame.   (*Dunciad,* III.7–12)

Such happiness heartbreakingly feeds on delusion and suffering, and the visionary intensity of Pope's "See" mixes rapt fascination with an almost unbearable pitying wisdom — *this* is what heaven offers to make our isthmian lot endurable!

At this moment it is hard to value the doctrinal point, that passionate self-deception is God's way of allowing man to live at all. Once you know what Pope knows in these lines, their consoling power mostly disappears. He does try to regain the "philosophical" perspective:

> See some strange comfort ev'ry state attend,
> And Pride bestow'd on all, a common friend;
> See some fit Passion ev'ry age supply,
> Hope travels thro', nor quits us when we die.
>
>   (271–274)

But the terms and implications clash with the doctrine. That persistent "Hope" is what sustains the Dunces, the obsessed women of *To a Lady,* the lost souls at the end of *To Cobham* whose hopeful deaths merely re-enact the compulsive follies that ruined their lives. "Some *strange* comfort" is not said by someone who takes much comfort in it himself, and while "a common friend" tries to mean a mutual, impartial one, it comes close to meaning an indiscriminate one, notoriously available to all like a common alehouse or a common whore. (A friend who's everyone's friend seems no friend at all; and of course the antecedent for all this is *Pride.*) And what follows offers strange comfort indeed:

> Behold the child, by Nature's kindly law,
> Pleas'd with a rattle, tickled with a straw:
> Some livelier play-thing gives his youth delight,
> A little louder, but as empty quite:
> Scarfs, garters, gold, amuse his riper stage;
> And beads and pray'r-books are the toys of age:
> Pleas'd with this bauble still, as that before;
> 'Till tir'd he sleeps, and Life's poor play is o'er!
>
>   (275–282)

Jaques' "strange eventful history" of the ages of man[12] is seen
here with more compassion but equal melancholy; for Pope
"Life's poor play" defines man less as actor than child, indulged by "kindly" nature and unable to grow up to put away
childish things. Again, the voice that speaks knows better, yet
can't really insist on its superior wisdom — we have not been
reconciled to the isthmian state but made to feel its inadequacy
and folly even more poignantly.

And this discontent, what the poem vows to talk us out of,
is not appeased but further exacerbated by the final reappear-
ance of the analogy with painting, which now stresses the illusory quality of the attitudes that sustain us:

> Mean-while Opinion gilds with varying rays
> Those painted clouds that beautify our days;
> Each want of happiness by Hope supply'd,
> And each vacuity of sense by Pride:
> These build as fast as knowledge can destroy;
> In Folly's cup still laughs the bubble, joy;
> One prospect lost, another still we gain;
> And not a vanity is giv'n in vain;
> Ev'n mean Self-love becomes, by force divine,
> The scale to measure others wants by thine.
> See! and confess, one comfort still must rise,
> 'Tis this, Tho' Man's a fool, yet GOD IS WISE.
>
> (283–294)

The doctrine is adequately preserved — man's folly proves God's
wisdom in giving comforts even to foolish creatures. But the
final couplet is imaginatively less "final" for coming after such
a vision of human futility. To see and confess one's folly requires that one be wise enough to recognize it as folly and desire something better — yet according to the poem that desire
is itself foolish. The difficult argument leads back to its begin-

12. As well as echoing *As You Like It* and other analogues mentioned
in the "Twickenham" notes, the passage is almost an anthology of moments from *Macbeth* that stress Macbeth's terrible sense of the banality
of "life": "for, from this instant, / There's nothing serious in mortality;
/ All is but toys" (II.3, 92–94); "After life's fitful fever he sleeps well"
(III.2, 23); "Life's but a walking shadow; a poor player, / That struts
and frets his hour upon the stage, / And then is heard no more" (V.5,
24–26).

ning, the dark isthmus from which both mainlands are always poignantly visible but unattainable. Still, if the proper study is circular and frustrating, the proper student, the reader, has learned something. He now can see what is left unsaid by pronouncements about The Human Condition; he knows that "philosophy" as doctrinal product matters less than the activity of trying to produce it, the continual redefining and shifting of emphasis required to think seriously about the case.

When one asks what post-Arnoldian criticism of Pope has not sufficiently taken account of, so simple a matter as the poems' length comes to mind. The Horatian imitations, for example, are all longer than their originals, on average more than fifty percent longer; and if some of the excess is due to the relative prolixity of an uninflected language, still, English isn't that much wordier than Latin, and the concision of Pope's couplet English is proverbial. It is rather startling to realize that the *Dunciad* is longer than "Prufrock," *The Waste Land, Ash-Wednesday* and *Four Quartets* combined, and even the shorter major poems run to several hundred lines. And the scale is not supported by the devices one expects in long poems. No full-length story is told, at least not in any direct and efficient way; the perspectives of history or allegory are incompletely developed when they figure at all; there is, apart from *Eloisa to Abelard*, no intensive representation of a particular consciousness "personally" involved in its own experience. (The voice in *Arbuthnot* and the other "personal" satires is at least as much "the satirist" as he is "Pope.") It is usually hard to grasp the connection between a passage in Pope while reading it and a significant whole order of progression in the poem. There seems something provisional, potentially alterable, about the arrangement of parts; and of course Pope often did write "parts," passages that would later be fitted into poems, and many of his best works were rewritten, rearranged, added to or cut down, as second thoughts suggested new possibilities.

The lengthiness of the poems makes him a nuisance to anthologists, who must either print inferior shorter poems, truncate several of the masterpieces, or print one or two major poems in entirety and so exclude other aspects of a richly various body

of work.[13] And the anthologists' problem is in a way our critical problem too, since even learned readers mostly possess the
poetic tradition as a kind of big personal anthology of favorites
into which short poems fit better than long ones unless the latter are broken up into storable and retrievable "beauties." Pope
belongs in that anthology, and prominently, but the great moments fit better than the poems. Or, if one abandons the anthology and gets down to work on Pope himself, it is easier and
tidier to transform long and relatively "unstructured" works into
a synthetic order made of selected passages, which when released
from the whole context are more available for one's purposes —
image tracing, genre definition, allusion hunting, intellectual
historiography, whatever it is we "do." These things are worth
doing, they help us to understand Pope as Arnold or even
Johnson couldn't; but our sense of parts may interfere with an
understanding of whole poems.

My account of Epistle II of the *Essay on Man* may roughly
suggest a way of thinking about what Pope's long poems are like.
By this account, the poem is a collection of moments assembled
to cast light on or even interfere with each other. Some of the
moments are memorable in themselves, others tend to fade when
the eye leaves the page. And their order may seem tentative and
logically loose — we remember what we remember not as a progressive, unfolding design but as a complex overlaying of conflicting attitudes and feelings that are not perfectly governed
by the poem as formal object or generic instance. *The Rape of
the Lock* is a well-made poem, perhaps Pope's most brilliant
"design"; yet one remembers better the moments of excessive
intensity — the sad and curiously useless wisdom of Clarissa's
speech, for example, as it picks up earlier, glancing suggestions
of the futility and pathos of merely "social" existence — than the
splendid moments that grasp and place social details in the
teasingly ironic main picture. The *Essay on Criticism* rehearses
the standard neoclassical literary dicta, but only (as Empson
shows) through jokes about Wit confessing that the kind of

13. Even Dryden is easier: in the space required by *Arbuthnot* alone
one could fit *Mac Flecknoe,* "To Dr. Charleton," "To the Memory of
Mr. Oldham," and "A Song for St. Cecilia's Day," with room left over
for one of the great Prologues and a cynical love song or two, thus
"representing" Dryden well enough.

writer Pope is, while superior to the mere witlings who mostly make up the world of poetry and criticism, is yet from the perspective of truly great writers, the Ancients, rather small potatoes; what the Rules don't teach is finally more important than what they do. The *Essay on Man* and the *Moral Essays* represent a struggle between an ethical theory and a particular awareness of vice and folly that the theory can't quite take care of; the *Epistle to Arbuthnot* and the *Epilogue to the Satires* dramatize the virtual impossibility of reforming uncivilized behavior with the resources of civilized irony; the *Dunciad* is so confusing in plot and action because it is so insistent and thorough in detail, because the "myth" of Dulness can't wholly accommodate the passion of Pope's response to actual dunces or his fascination with the processes of degeneration that his "civilization" compels him to abhor.

Pope's poetry, that is, has less (though less is not nothing) to do with the neoclassical qualities of formal order, reasoned argument, logical coherence of parts, urbanity of manner, than we have tended to suppose. His verse is more than a way of presenting the data and skills of "Augustan" literary culture. I am convinced that the poems are not harmonious, resolved wholes, and that they are none the worse as poems therefore. They don't make sense taken as narrative or discursive orders like *Paradise Lost* or *The Prelude*; they do make "dramatic" sense only if one conceives of wit and poetry and Pope in terms that do more than turn the tables on Arnold. The past changes as we change, obviously, and the twentieth century might want to think Pope more like Eliot and Pound and the Stevens of the longer poems than like Milton or Wordsworth. If we think of his as a "visible" art — one that depends on recognizing and participating in logical and emotional discontinuity, juxtaposition of contradictory tones and moods, imperfect adjustment of feeling to convention — we might understand and enjoy him better.

So large and vague a suggestion of course solves nothing; I mean only to suggest that our view of Pope may be too comfortable, that his poems pose more difficulty than they seem to. One doesn't want to have to put on an imaginary periwig to read him, coming to him only by forgetting who and where we really are. On the other hand, too much "relevance" is worse than none at all — Pope is not *simply* a "modern" poet, and we must see and respect his differences from us because they are what he has to teach us. His poetry is not just a collection of fine passages, yet it really won't do to claim for it the "thematic" or "structural" or "imagistic" integrity we have invented to describe Shakespeare or the novelists or the lyric poets. He is more than the drawing-room wit his enemies think him, yet views of him as Swinburnian hero or McLuhanesque pivotal mind run into his own skeptical amusement about such pretentions even in himself. If he was in some sense a Christian poet, his religious moments usually sound like rhetorical devices; and his beliefs, such as they may have been, don't strongly bear on the subjects and moods his poetry takes as its imaginative province.

It may be better to accept these contradictions than to try to resolve them, seeing him as an artist imperfectly convinced that his own art worked, or that any human art could achieve its highest intentions. In the poems assertion and denial, positive hope and worldly skepticism, visibly confront and criticize each other. Progressive design turns back on itself questioningly, so that "endings" are usually inconclusive or despairing, as in *To Bathurst,* the *Epilogue,* or the *Dunciad.* Or, when the positive note is struck, as at the end of *The Rape of the Lock,* the *Essay on Man, To Burlington,* or *Arbuthnot,* one at least recognizes that it has been hard earned, that something has had to be left out to make the final major chord feasible. This is not to claim for him some tragic sense of life, only a wonderful power of perceiving the limits of secularized imagination and of letting *us* see that he sees them.

Modern criticism has excellently told the main truth about Pope, that he is a poet, that the great moments are fully imagined, complex, rich in evoked feeling, mature in moral intelligence. But the criticism is most useful and interesting when it asks how the poems render a mind at work — Empson and Brower are especially helpful here — and as yet it hasn't taken this direction often and fully enough. We know a great deal about Pope's "civilization," the cultural materials, ideas of personal style, and assumptions about literary manner and intention out of which he made poems. But it is not the mere possession of ideas and techniques, but possessing them in particular, potentially unstable ways that defines his civilization, which remains open to its discontents, the difficult possibilities its official tenets and assumptions tend to exclude. If he believed in prose and reason, it was because they were impossible; if he was a high priest, his sermons show his awareness that the church might fall on him at any moment. In a way, as Arnold saw, he was the wrong man to have taken on the task of realizing in English the shape and substance of what his age took to be the "classical" state of mind; in another way, that very wrongness is what makes his poems so compelling and potentially so congenial to the twentieth century, if — as of course I have failed to do, too — it can ever get Arnold out of its head.

F. R. LEAVIS

Wordsworth: The Creative Conditions

That Wordsworth is a great poet seems to me certain. That he was in the nineteenth century, and still in my childhood, a very important influence — such an influence as only a great poet could be — is, I think, unquestionable. I haven't, all the same, read any account of the nature of the influence that I found satisfying, and I myself couldn't be glib (or shall I say fluent?) about it. But then, here we have a major critical datum: the greatness itself is hard to give a satisfying account of.

Let me state the spirit of my own critical approach. If Wordsworth is a great poet, then one ought to be able to urge convincingly that he should be current — that is, known, frequented and appreciated among the cultivated — now. I think this is true in respect of every great writer — every writer whom one sincerely and actively believes to be great. Great literature has its life in the present, or not at all. Where there is so much claiming permanent value, inert concurrence in conventional valuations and reputations is to be challenged: they get in the way of life.

There is too much of the merely conventional; perhaps it will

First appearance of this essay was as the Bicentenary Lecture at the University of Bristol.

be said that there is too much literature. Most certainly it can
be said with indisputable justice that there is too much Wordsworth. You can't tell a student to look through his copy of the
Wordsworth in the Oxford Standard Authors and mark the
poems that in his opinion are worth going back to. There are
nine hundred small-print double-column pages. Wordsworth had
a long life, and, though he didn't finish his great philosophic
poem, he went on indefatigably practising his art. There are
those acres of sonnets, and a great deal else. That formidable
mass of printed paper contains things we wouldn't be without, as
well, no doubt, as things we should have called memorable if we
had ever found them.

There is a consensus, of course, that the great Wordsworth,
the Wordsworth of decisive creativity, is the Wordsworth of a
very limited phase of his life, and that the triumphantly innovating poet lost his drive early. But what *was* the great Wordsworth? What can we say by way of defining his innovating
power, its importance, and the nature of his originality?

These questions are not easy to answer — which doesn't mean
that they shouldn't be asked. It means rather that the effort at
answering will be a profitable one: it is the critic's business, and
I, as is fairly widely known, believe in the critic's business. If I
make such obvious points it is in order to express, not only my
sense of the difficulty, but my conviction that while, in the nature
of the case, no neat formulations worth having will be found,
the complexities of a real answer will immensely enhance the
critical value of the judgment that the Wordsworth of decisive
creativity was the Wordsworth of a limited phase of his life.
Critical value: I am interested in explanations and genetic accounts only insofar as they enable one to appreciate more intelli-
gently and fully the creative achievement and to realize the importance of the poet. And this is the point at which to adduce
the criticism of Wordsworth I have found most use for. It is
Shelley's in "Peter Bell the Third" (1819).

Shelley's commentary there on Wordsworth is, in its way,
fellow to Eliot's on Donne and his school in the essay on "Metaphysical Poets." In it Shelley shows that he has turned on Wordsworth the intensity of interest and critical intelligence that one
poet turns on another from whom, he perceives, he has some-

thing essential to learn. What is so significant is the nature of
the emphasis. Here are four stanzas from Part the Fourth:

> He had a mind which was somehow
>   At once circumference and centre
> Of all he might or feel or know:
> Nothing went ever out, although
>   Something did ever enter.
>
> He had as much imagination
>   As a pint-pot; — he never could
> Fancy another situation,
> From which to dart his contemplation,
>   Than that wherein he stood.
>
> Yet his was individual mind,
>   And new created all he saw
> In a new manner, and refined
> Those new creations, and combined
>   Them by a master-spirit's law.
>
> Thus — though unimaginative —
>   An apprehension clear, intense,
> Of his mind's work, had made alive
> The things it wrought on; I believe
>   Wakening a sort of thought in sense.

In the next stanza, as the opening lines intimate, he returns
to his adverse and limiting criticism —

> But from the first 'twas Peter's drift
> To be a kind of moral eunuch

— returns, since no one reading can have failed to note the un-
sympathetic element. As the "unimaginative" brings out, what he
means by the first two stanzas is that Wordsworth hadn't a
Shelleyan imagination. Shelley, in fact, is registering his perception of the differences between himself and Wordsworth. The
stanzas, with those extra two lines added, touch decisively on
the two differences that come out when one looks at almost any
three or four lines of the other. Wordsworth seems static; poised
above his own centre, contemplating; Shelley always moving
headlong — eagerly, breathlessly, committed to pursuing his

centre of gravity lest he should fall on his face. The two lines
from the stanza I don't quote in full give the characteristic tem-
perature difference — Shelley always seems to *have* a tempera-
ture — the effect is given by the pervasiveness in his verse of
erotic suggestion, overt or implicit. Naturally he finds Wordsworth subnormal — cold, frigid; and, however unfair he may be,
he does point to a Wordsworthian characteristic I shall have to
refer to later on as very important. There is in Wordsworth a
notably un-Shelleyan absence of suggestions of embracing, ca-
ressing, fondling — of erotic warmth — in the habit of sensibility expressed in his verse. I mean, this is what you note when
you make the comparison and ask what lies behind the tempera-
ture difference. I don't endorse the implications of Shelley's way
of registering the difference.

He does register the difference — the differences. And let me
here make an observation about the nature of influence — influence as, in the important kind of case, it is exerted by one
great poet upon another; or rather, about the way in which the
beneficiary of "influence" *is* influenced. It will be largely a matter of its being brought home to him how different he is — in
what ways he is different, and so having his sense of his own
essential idiosyncrasy, his own expressive need, sharpened. Of
course, if there had been only difference, Shelley wouldn't have
been drawn to read Wordsworth with that devoted intensity;
and what draws him he states with significantly felicitous precision in the line of the passage that begins with "Yet." I will lead
up to it again so as to give the "Yet" its proper force:

> He had as much imagination
>   As a pint-pot; — he never could
> Fancy another situation,
> From which to dart his contemplation,
>   Than that wherein he stood.
>
> Yet his was individual mind

There you have it; there you have what made Wordsworth
decisive for the later poets of the Romantic period. They were
very different from one another, and from Wordsworth; what
they had in common was the need to escape — positively —

from the habits and conventions of expression handed down to them by the eighteenth century. These made the expression of "individual mind" impossible; they laid all the emphasis on "social." What is meant by this is a matter for discussion. For the present purpose, meaning enough, I think, will be conveyed to make *this* worth saying: Wordsworth's success in expressing creatively an intensely and profoundly individual sensibility gave later contemporary poets the impulsion they needed.

I recall here an observation of T. S. Eliot's. He says of "certain poets" of the eighteenth century: "They had not the consciousness to perceive that they felt differently, and therefore must use words differently." Shelley in "Peter Bell the Third" arrives at an essentially kindred formulation in paying *his* tribute to Wordsworth's genius; I will quote the stanzas leading up to the formulation I have in mind. I shall so, while bringing out with what responsiveness Shelley had frequented Wordsworth, ensure that the brief formulation has a suitable charge of definitive suggestion; for, like Eliot's, it has its focus on words — the use of words — and "word," in respect of the question what the object it points to, or evokes, *is,* is a disconcertingly elusive word: some intimation of what Shelley registers as the purpose, or spirit, of Wordsworth's "using" helps. Here, then, is "Peter Bell the Third," Part the Fifth (Peter, of course, is Wordsworth, and the "subtle-souled psychologist" is Coleridge):

> Among the guests who often stayed
> Till the Devil's petits-soupers,
> A man there came, fair as a maid,
> And Peter noted what he said,
> Standing behind his master's chair.
>
> He was a mighty poet — and
> A subtle-souled psychologist;
> All things he seemed to understand,
> Of old or new — of sea or land —
> But his own mind — which was a mist.
>
> This was a man who might have turned
> Hell into Heaven — and so in gladness
> A Heaven unto himself have earned;
> But he in shadows undiscerned
> Trusted — and damned himself to madness.

He spoke of poetry, and how "Divine
    it was — a light — a love —
A spirit which like wind doth blow
As it listeth, to and fro;
    A dew rained down from God above;

A power which comes and goes like dream,
    And which none can ever trace —
Heaven's light on earth — Truth's brightest beam,"
And when he ceased there lay the gleam
    Of those words upon his face.

Now Peter, when he heard such talk,
    Would, heedless of a broken pate,
Stand like a man asleep, or balk
Some wishing guest of knife or fork,
    Or drop and break his master's plate.

At night he oft would start and wake
    Like a lover, and began
In a wild measure songs to make
Of moor, and glen, and rocky lake,
    And on the heart of man —

And on the universal sky —
    And the wide earth's bosom green —
And the sweet, strange mystery
Of what behind these things may be
    And yet remain unseen.

For in his thought he visited
    The spots in which, ere dead and damned,
He his wayward life had led;
Yet knew not whence the thoughts were fed
    Which thus his fancy crammed.

And these obscure remembrances
    Stirred such harmony in Peter,
That, whensoever he should please,
He could speak of rocks and trees
    In poetic metre.

For though it was without a sense
    Of memory, yet he remembered well
Many a ditch and quick-set fence;

Of lakes he had intelligence,
  He knew something of heath and fell.

He had also dim recollections
  Of pedlars tramping on their rounds;
Milk-pans and pails, and odd collections
Of saws and proverbs; and reflections
  Old parsons make in burying grounds.

But Peter's verse was clear, and came
  Announcing from the frozen hearth
Of a cold age, that none might tame
The soul of that diviner flame
  It augured to the Earth:

Like gentle rains, on the dry plains,
  Making that green which late was gray,
Or like the sudden moon, that stains
Some gloomy chamber's window-panes
  With a broad light like day.

For language was in Peter's hand
  Like clay when he was yet a potter . . .

There you have it. Shelley as critic of Wordsworth is, to use Eliot's word, the "practitioner." I won't now examine the felicities of his evocation of the great poet who mattered so much to him; the point that takes the stress at the moment is that Shelley's commentary comes to a close — which is the kind of conclusion the "For" makes it — in this:

For language was in Peter's hand
  Like clay when he was yet a potter . . .

I am reminded of another dictum of Eliot's; it comes from the same essay: "Sensibility alters in everybody, whether we will or no; but expression is only altered by a man of genius." Wordsworth, for Shelley — for his younger contemporaries in general — was the genius who had triumphantly "altered expression," thus making it possible for *them* to achieve the means of expressing their own distinctive sensibilities. I'll not now discuss, either, the relation between "sensibility" as referred to in the sentence of Eliot I quoted — in what sense is there a period sensibility?

— and the "sensibility" of that last phrase; but it would repay some inquiry in seminar conditions. Meanwhile there is no problem that need hold up discourse.

The Wordsworth of the period of "decisive creativity," to take up the phrase I threw out, is the Wordsworth who earned the tribute paid him in "Peter Bell the Third" (a tribute the more impressive for being accompanied by severe adverse and limiting judgments). That period, in 1819, is already well in the past. The defining formulation I've just given doesn't enable us to set an end date to the great creative phase, but it does help us to think perceptively about the oddity of the creative Wordsworth represented by the early decline. The point of that, as I've said, wouldn't be that it satisfied an itch for "explanation" as such, but that it led to a better perception of the nature of his genius and so to a fuller realization of the value of what he achieved.

When in the 1920's I heard Herbert Read, as Clark Lecturer, defining his approach to Wordsworth, his subject, I reflected (very relevantly) that the oddity I've just referred to is not merely that Wordsworth started to decline as creative power early, but that he started to be a poet late. This latter fact is the odder because if ever a young man was early convinced that he was a poet by vocation it was William Wordsworth. He was so determined to be a poet that he refused — his neglect amounted to that — to acquire the professional qualifications for earning a living. He was born in 1770. The first work that tends to justify his sense of vocation, and actually it justifies it transcendently, is "The Ruined Cottage."

I can't think that anything he had written before would have been found to show much promise of the writer's turning out to be a great poet, an original genius, if the fact of his later demonstration that he *was* one hadn't been there among the data the critic or scholar started with. But "The Ruined Cottage" is an utterly convincing creative achievement. Jonathan Wordsworth, writing about it in his recent book *The Music of Humanity,* adduces me as having said that it is Wordsworth's greatest poem. When I wrote about it, thirty-five years or so ago, the accepted datum was that Wordsworth wrote it in 1795–96 — a datum that made me recall a phrase from "Tradition and the Individual

Talent": "he who would continue to be a poet after his twenty-fifth year" — it being the "Romantic" idea of the poet that Eliot is glancing at (critically). The date for the original drafting given now is 1797–98, which gives us a Wordsworth who was beginning to be a poet in his twenty-eighth year.

I reflected on the late start as I listened to Herbert Read forty-five years ago because, though he was discussing the significance of the early decline, he made no reference to the complementary fact — which, it seemed to me, ought, where significance was in question, to be thought of as essentially complementary. He was intent on providing an explanation of the early decline: the petering-out of the triumphant creativity celebrated, we have seen (I think it should be a locus classicus), by Shelley. Since I was alive in the 1920's and coeval with Read, and knew something of his work, I could have forecast the terms of his explanation. The discoveries of Harper and Legouis about the affair with Annette Vallon were then quite recent. Further, the invocation of Freud by nonspecialist intellectuals had become a familiar, though still "modern," practice in the cultivated world. Read explained the case of Wordsworth in terms of Annette and the illegitimate daughter. Wordsworth, the argument goes, was tormented by guilt over this surrender to passion and over the consequences of it, and, after a betraying attempt or two to deal with passion and guilt in poetry, closed down on passionate love and eliminated it from the world of his creative interests; that is, repressed in his own life what is represented by the theme. The inevitable result was the petering-out of his creativity.

Read, you perceive, might have adduced Shelley in support; at any rate, he doesn't reject as I do the implications of "But from the first 'twas Peter's drift / To be a kind of moral eunuch." For I think Shelley, in a very Shelleyan and self-ignorant way, was wrong there (the whole passage amounts with related things in the poem to a very drastic privative judgment). And where Herbert Read's explanation is concerned I stand by the reply I made so long ago in written criticism: his theory, invoking as it does repression, is obviously false — demonstrably so, I'm inclined to say. Repression, surely, would manifest itself in an avoidance of the explicit theme and an oblique and disguised insistence by the repressed "interest," or vital potency, on its clandestine

presence. Actually Wordsworth showed not the slightest tendency to shy away from the theme of erotic passion. On the contrary, strikingly uninhibited utterances are reported of him (they
may reasonably be called characteristic) — utterances that are
quite inconceivable in a repressed man, or in what Shelley meant
by "moral eunuch" and "solemn and unsexual man." The "coldness" that Shelley registers as contrasting with the sensibility
expressed in his own poetic texture certainly means that Wordsworth was a different kind of man from Shelley. There is nothing
at all to suggest that it indicates repression or unsexual solem-
nity; it goes with the fact that creativity in Wordsworth is impelled by the pressure of deeply and intensely experienced preoccupations — emotional problems that are at once personal and
impersonal (that is, moral) — in relation to which erotic passion plays only a minor part.

And this brings me to "The Ruined Cottage," the poem in
which the creativity that earned the tribute paid by Shelley
manifested itself with such convincing power, manifested itself
for the first time, superlatively. "The Ruined Cottage" as it appears in the collected poems is incorporated in Book I of *The
Excursion*. I had almost said, constitutes Book I; but in the
form in which we have it there it has been much extended. The
original completed poem, or what may reasonably be taken as
that, can be found in the book by Jonathan Wordsworth that I
have mentioned. If you compare it with Book I of *The Excursion* you will see at once, even without considering the other
data produced by Mr. Wordsworth, how he comes to be discussing another poem, "The Pedlar," amalgamation with which
gives us (this is substantially the case) the text we now read as
the opening of *The Excursion*. I, for my purposes here, shall
refer to and quote from the text that is accessible in the Oxford
Standard Authors. I shall do that, not merely because Book I of
The Excursion is so accessible, but because I think that the form
in which "The Ruined Cottage" ought to be current — ought in
general to be read.

My reasons will come out as I explain the view of "The
Ruined Cottage" that Mr. Wordsworth doesn't actually endorse,
and my reasons for holding it. My reasons are an account of the
conditions of — the conditions behind or implicit in — this

supreme initial manifestation of the great poet's creativity; that
it *is* a supreme manifestation Mr. Wordsworth agrees. My account lays an essential emphasis on the significance of the dramatic mode of presentation that, in an obvious way, distinguishes
"The Ruined Cottage" from "Michael," that other poetic classic
on the theme of "silent suffering" and one which, I think, is considered to be the more characteristically Wordsworthian. And
there is, indeed, a sense in which "The Ruined Cottage" may be
said to be *not* characteristic: its essential distinction is to have
a disturbing immediacy that makes it, in its major way, unique.
That distinction, the poignant disturbingness, is inseparable from
the mode of presentation — from the fact that, while the tale
is told by the Pedlar, the poet himself (William Wordsworth)
is so insistently and effectively a presence for us that the sensibility *we* share is felt as very personally his.

Let me illustrate. The Wanderer (as the Pedlar is called here)
visits the Cottage at a time when "two blighting seasons" and
"the plague of war" have brought desolation on it. Margaret's
husband, Robert, who — stores running out — has tried in vain
to get work, hasn't yet left home, and behaves with the profoundly disturbing oddness of a man reduced to impotent despair:

> "One while he would speak lightly of his babes,
> And with a cruel tongue: at other times
> He tossed them with a false unnatural joy:
> And 'twas a rueful thing to see the looks
> Of the poor innocent children. 'Every smile',
> Said Margaret to me here beneath these trees,
> 'Made my heart bleed.' "
>   At this the Wanderer paused;
> And, looking up to those enormous elms,
> He said, " 'Tis now the hour of deepest noon.
> At this still season of repose and peace;
> This hour when all things which are not at rest
> Are cheerful; while this multitude of flies
> With tuneful hum is filling all the air;
> Why should a tear be on an old man's cheek?
> Why should we thus, and with an untoward mind,
> And in the weakness of humanity,

> From natural wisdom turn our hearts away;
> To natural comfort shut our eyes and ears;
> And, feeding on disquiet, thus disturb
> The calm of nature with our restless thoughts?"

The passage exemplifies the completeness with which, in this poem, in 1797–98, Wordsworth has suddenly achieved his "alteration of expression" ("expression is only altered by a man of genius"). I don't mean that it is comprehensively exemplary. In the body of memorable Wordsworthian poetry you can distinguish a remarkable range of styles or manners. But this is, very significantly, at the centre of the range; it gives us, in all its power, a poetic that represents, or manifests, an achieved major originality. We have here the great Wordsworth who is qualified to be a decisive influence. I must not attempt to discuss now the relation of Wordsworth's achievement of "altered expression" to the confused and ineffective, though not essentially unintelligent, arguments about Poetic Diction in the Preface; I will merely point to the obvious facts that the style of "The Ruined Cottage" is intensely Wordsworthian, *not* the language of humble and rustic life or trying to be, and not Miltonic, and that it couldn't for a moment be mistaken for Akenside.[1] It accommodates readily and naturally the representation of natural speech, sensitively rendered.

Take, for instance:

>   'Every smile,'
> Said Margaret to me here beneath these trees,
> 'Made my heart bleed.' "

The heart-piercing immediacy of that is brought out by the ensuing abrupt transition:

>   At this the Wanderer paused;
> And, looking up to those enormous elms,
> He said . . .

1. See Nichol Smith's preface to *The Oxford Book of Eighteenth Century Verse* (Oxford: Clarendon, 1926). He quotes (p. x) a dozen lines of blank verse, and says triumphantly: "Not Wordsworth, but Akenside."

What he says brings home to us that *his* heart is not now bleeding; for him the historical fact is "recollected in tranquillity." We note this, because the effect of "made my heart bleed," notwithstanding the past tense, is one of present intensity of feeling, present and disturbing. I am not making a criticism, but calling attention to the inner organic, the emotional moral-spiritual, structure or economy of the poem — on which its distinctive power depends. The avowed "I" and the Wanderer are both Wordsworth. The "I" is the actual Wordsworth, for whom, at this crucial moment of his creative career (indistinguishably, for him, of his life — his greatness as a poet is given in that identity), the thought of the poor woman's suffering is not a matter of "emotion recollected in tranquillity." The Wanderer, of whom we have been told, with the diagnostic verb italicized, "He could *afford* to suffer / With those whom he saw suffer," is the ideal Wordsworth he aspires, in an effort of imaginative realization, to be. So little can the actual Wordsworth achieve such assured tranquillity that he is tormented by a compulsion that makes him expose himself to the contemplating he can hardly endure. The compulsion, the whole complex state, is evoked for us in the consummate passage — dramatically immediate, surprising and inevitable — that follows on from where I stopped:

> He spake with somewhat of a solemn tone;
> But when he ended, there was in his face
> Such easy cheerfulness, a look so mild,
> That for a little while it stole away
> All recollection; and that simple tale
> Passed from my mind like a forgotten sound.
> A while on trivial things we held discourse,
> To me soon tasteless. In my own despite,
> I thought of that poor Woman as of one
> Whom I had known and loved. He had rehearsed
> Her homely tale with such familiar power,
> With such an active countenance, an eye
> So busy, that the things of which he spake
> Seemed present; and, attention now relaxed,
> A heart-felt chilliness crept along my veins.
> I rose, and, having left the breezy shade,
> Stood drinking comfort from the warmer sun,

> That had not cheered me long — ere, looking round
> Upon that tranquil Ruin, I returned,
> And begged of the old man that, for my sake,
> He would resume his story.

Any detailed commentary aimed at enforcing the judgment "con-summate" I threw out before quoting the passage I must, again, leave to a different occasion. But one can here observe the way in which the utter unattainableness for Wordsworth of the Wanderer's "easy cheerfulness" is brought home to us, and the significance of "In my own despite." The talk about "trivial things" can't hold him, the effort at self-distraction peters out, and the compulsion reasserts its power. Such is Wordsworth's emotional involvement that he is physically affected, and has to get up and stand in the sun, which "hasn't cheered him long" before he begs the old man that he will, "for my sake," resume the story.

When he says

> In my own despite
> I thought of that poor Woman as of one
> Whom I had known and loved

some who share Herbert Read's exegetical bent may exclaim: "Annette!" But there is nothing in the context, or in what is known of the biographical facts, to support such an interpretation. The Wanderer's comment further down the column is more to the point: " 'Tis a common tale, / An ordinary sorrow of man's life." It is the condition incident to human life in general, the condition made concretely present in the story of Margaret, that Wordsworth can't think of without profound emotional disturbance. And if we ask what is the traumatic experience behind the compulsion, we have the hint that gives it a name in the account of the Wanderer's advantages that, in Book I of *The Excursion,* precedes his tale:

> In his steady course,
> No piteous revolutions had he felt,
> No wild varieties of joy and grief.
> Unoccupied by sorrow of its own,

> His heart lay open; and, by nature tuned
> And constant disposition of his thoughts
> To sympathy with man, he was alive
> To all that was enjoyed, where'er he went,
> And all that was endured; for, in himself
> Happy, and quiet in his cheerfulness,
> He had no painful pressure from without
> That made him turn aside from wretchedness
> With coward fears. He could *afford* to suffer
> With those whom he saw suffer.

The point of this is that it reminds us — or conveys to us — that Wordsworth *had* suffered wild varieties of joy and grief; he *had* known piteous revolutions. We can't, in fact, help telling ourselves that he was prompted with that last word, "revolutions," by the great historic event concerning which he could testify later, in *The Prelude:* "Bliss was it in that dawn to be alive, / But to be young was very heaven." He was not volatile — he was very different from Shelley; but he committed himself in that spirit to the revolutionary cause. Earnest, responsible, and loyal by nature, he identified himself with the Revolution, and the Revolution developed in the way it did. He witnessed, close at hand, hopes frustrated, suffering entailed upon the innocent and helpless, and diverse kinds of human deterioration, he being very young. His own innocent assumptions and his exalted faith were brutally questioned by actualities; the Revolution, in the accepted phrase, devoured its children; his own country declared war on revolutionary France; and after no great passage of time France invaded Switzerland, the home of liberty.

That chapter of Wordsworth's history is well enough known. Back in England, he eludes for a while the close confident knowledge aspired to by the modern biographer. Certainly he suffered a moral and emotional crisis; the haunting question was, how could he reconcile himself to life? When we find him again, living in the country, he has — tacitly, at least — come to one decision: he has renounced the centres and activities of political man and "the storm / of sorrow barricadoed evermore / within the walls of cities." And drawing on memories and habits of childhood and boyhood, he is bent on identifying the desired emotional-moral balance ("equipoise," the Wanderer calls it) with a devotion to "Nature" — something which the student of Wordsworth has to try to define.

But the trauma is there; even if it were possible in the country to escape the spectacle of that "wretchedness" from which the Wanderer does *not* "turn aside with coward fears," the "painful pressure," the compulsion to "feed on disquiet," is there. The urgent personal problem is what Wordsworth is wrestling with in "The Ruined Cottage"; his preoccupation with technique, "poetic diction," versification, as he writes and ponders, identifies itself in his mind — and his fingers — with that. It is by reason of the inner "pressure" during his "wrestle with words and meaning" that (if you add the after all well-grounded conviction of his that a poet was what he was meant to be) he achieves, in that poem, his "alteration of expression." "The Ruined Cottage," essentially representative of the major Wordsworth as it is, is unique; it is the one poem of that kind — that vital equivocalness, that kind of tense equipoise — in his *oeuvre*. Of course, he wrote much other poetry; poetry in various ways vitally Wordsworthian, building up the body of work that, in its diversity, made him a major presence, a living force and an influence. But the decisive "alteration of expression," the release of creativity, is achieved in "The Ruined Cottage"; the conditions of the achievement are so clearly manifested in it that we can say: "Wordsworth becomes a great poet here."

He had solved his personal problem for good, in the sense that there are (I think) no signs later in his work of the "painful pressure" that had, as the Wanderer puts it, made him "feed on disquiet." In the nature of the success, however, he had not solved for good his creative problem, the problem of being a poet. The evoked Wanderer, plainly enough, is no more a poet potentially than he *is* one in his serene actuality. It was because the Wordsworth of 1797 was so different that he longed to be the Wanderer.

The "equipoise" of "The Ruined Cottage," then, is *not* the "equipoise" that Wordsworth attributes to the Wanderer. Its poignant livingness unsays any promise of finality, of permanence, the poem may seem to offer — to say which is to point to the peculiar poetic vitality of the poem, even while we note, knowing of course what is to happen, the poet's strong impulse towards the Wanderer's state. He can't hold this tense and difficult poise very long.

What, with no relapse, he settles down to is, in that phrase of his from the 1800 Preface, "emotion recollected in tranquillity," and, what goes with it, "natural wisdom." This latter phrase is of course from "The Ruined Cottage," where it is associated with and supported by others — "natural comfort," for instance, and "the calm of nature." Heaven forbid that I should be thought to be suggesting that there can be any simple comment on that Wordsworth. He is often a great poet. If I were faced with undertaking a critical discourse on that theme I might very well start from a passage which, in the close of "The Ruined Cottage," he attributes to the Wanderer. Though, as the vibration tells us, it *belongs* to "The Ruined Cottage," it has an essential relevance to the theme of the tranquil Wordsworth:

> Why then should we read
> The forms of things with an unworthy eye?
> She sleeps in the calm earth, and peace is here.
> I well remember that those very plumes,
> Those weeds, and the high spear-grass on that wall,
> By mist and silent rain-drops silvered o'er,
> As once I passed, into my heart conveyed
> So still an image of tranquillity,
> So calm and still, and looked so beautiful
> Amid the uneasy thoughts which filled my mind,
> That what we feel of sorrow and despair,
> From ruin and from change, and all the grief
> That passing shows of Being leave behind,
> Appeared an idle dream . . .

Judgments about that passage taken in isolation cannot, of course, be secure or final; we have seen how complex the emotional-moral situation registered in the poem is. But we can make some comments on manifest potentialities.

"She sleeps in the calm earth, and peace is here" — if we are to distinguish between the Wordsworth of the poem and the Wanderer, that is the Wanderer. But then, the Wordsworth we know *includes* the Wanderer; and further, we can say that, in terms of "The Ruined Cottage," both parts in the dialogues (if that is the right description of the relation between the two personae) are to be heard in this passage: "and looked so beautiful / Amid the uneasy thoughts which filled my mind" — that is unmistakably the young, troubled Wordsworth. And *his* presence in the distinctive vibration of the passage counters the complacent potentialities of "She sleeps in the calm earth, and peace is here." We feel the troubled Wordsworth in the emphasis on "here." The Wanderer has helped him to that; and there *is* a sound wisdom in the Wanderer's admonitions: life has to be lived. There *is* a refusal to accept that can be reasonably stigmatized as "feeding on disquiet." But no simple formulation, no easily summarizable doctrine, can be adequate to the human state — which is what the poem implicitly says.

I don't suppose that Wordsworth *intended* irony when he italicized the "afford" in "He could *afford* to suffer / With those whom he saw suffer"; but when we come to it in the account of the Wanderer we inevitably see irony, for we know Wordsworth's own history. As he achieved the longed-for equipoise, and the equipoise became more and more assured, he became more and more the Wanderer. I repeat, everyone admiring Wordsworth's genius must recoil from the idea of simplifying in an account of it. "The Ruined Cottage" is unique, but between it (that is, the state out of which it issues) and the lapse of creativity we have poetry (more diverse, I think, than gets due recognition) that makes him the classical presence for us he is — or ought to be. But that there *was* a lapse of creativity no one disputes.

One can see the movement that way in the characteristic Wanderer-Wordsworth phrase (not, actually, from "The Ruined Cottage"), "natural piety." It would be hard to determine and fix the "nature" of "natural" in an excluding definition, and "piety" is a word that becomes of great importance to Wordsworth as — time doing its work — the equipoise settles into security (and security, remember, is on the way to inertness). There is nothing insincere or censurable, so far as I can see, in his development into the Tory Anglican. One can see the movement that way in the Christian explicitnesses he worked in when he turned "The Ruined Cottage" into Book I of *The Excursion*

— one follows on from where I stopped and completes the sentence:

> all the grief
> That passing shows of being leave behind
> Appeared an idle dream that could maintain,
> Nowhere, dominion o'er the enlightened spirit
> Whose meditative sympathies repose
> Upon the breast of Faith.

Though these Christian explicitnesses obviously don't belong, there is nothing obtrusively and offensively insincere about them: the transition was so easy for Wordsworth.

It was natural that, as in his reaction against the idea of revolution he fostered his equipoise, he should think of the village church as a focus of piety, and there could be no incongruity, no sharp separation, between that piety and the religious apprehensions that came to him among the mountains and in the presence of nature. But his poet's sensibility, his creative organization, a matter of painful growth, was *not* focused upon the village church. And when, with his gift of piety, he had arrived at affording to suffer with those whom he saw suffer as easily and securely as the Wanderer did, there wasn't much to save his creativity from lapsing into habit, or the Wanderer's philosophic calm. It had lost its intransigence. It had lost, that is, its creativeness

CHRISTOPHER RICKS

The Twentieth-Century Wordsworth

"He has no style." It would be a mistake simply to identify the nineteenth-century Wordsworth with Matthew Arnold's Wordsworth,[1] but Arnold did succeed in limning the poet with intense recognisability. Twentieth-century criticism has mostly been better at engaging with one half of Arnold's Wordsworth than with the other. Much recent criticism has been a challenge to one aspect of Arnold's subtle abnegation: "The Wordsworthians are apt to praise him for the wrong things, and to lay far too much stress upon what they call his philosophy." The academic study of English literature has since seen to it that there are even more Wordsworthians; the best of them have convincingly vindicated "what they call his philosophy." But the other half of Arnold's Wordsworth has proved less amenable. "Wordsworth's poetry, when he is at his best, is inevitable, as inevitable as Nature herself. It might seem that Nature not only gave him the matter for his poem, but wrote his poem for him. He has no style."

To the twentieth-century critic, such a way of speaking is both defeatist and obscurantist — Arnold, we hope, must rather

1. "Wordsworth" (1879), *Essays in Criticism,* 2nd ser. (1888).

have meant that Wordsworth had no "style." But the twentieth-
century Wordsworth — the distinctively so — will not stand out
with cogent clarity until a more coherent and delicate understanding of Wordsworth's style has been achieved. True, there
is much more by way of aperçu and local felicity than one might
think, but insights into style nevertheless remain scattered and
sparse in comparison with all the other varieties of exegesis which
have been devoted to Wordsworth. So it seems worthwhile to
try to redress the balance by marshalling from recent criticism
some related suggestions and thinking where they lead.[2]

In his fine and capacious book *The Egotistical Sublime*, John
Jones suggests — one page before he comes to an end — a
whole dimension of Wordsworth's stylistic achievement.

> Clothed in the sunshine of the withering fern
> *(The Prelude* VI.11, 1850) [3]

"Clothed in sunshine" is easy: so is "clothed in the withering fern."
But "clothed in the sunshine of the withering fern" is odd, its oddness resting in "of," and the different kinds of work it has to do.
One might say that the word is ambiguous; but this would be a perverse way of expressing it, since the block-impression of the phrase
is clear, even without knowing its history [that is, the history of the
variants]. We admit "of" as we admit others of Wordsworth's busy
prepositions: in their degree they are the stride of his thought.[4]

Mr. Jones's point is acutely vivid, and I have no intention of
condescending to it if I say that I should like to have heard more
from him — by way of an imaginative tactful unpacking — about
"the different kinds of work" which *of* is doing in that line; his
point feels right and suggests much, but it doesn't perhaps help
us sufficiently through the initial stages of thinking about such
nuances. It could have stood a bit more spelling out; as could the
general claim that Wordsworth's prepositions are "busy" (at

2. I discuss some other aspects of Wordsworth's style in "Wordsworth:
'A Pure Organic Pleasure from the Lines,'" *Essays in Criticism,* January
1971.

3. Quotations from *The Prelude* are of 1805 unless otherwise noted;
The Prelude, ed. E. de Selincourt, rev. H. Darbishire (1959).

4. *The Egotistical Sublime* (London: Chatto and Windus, 1954), p.
206.

what, exactly?); as could the general question of the relationship between such busy prepositions and the whole Wordsworthian endeavour.

Again, there is a delicate aside by Jonathan Wordsworth in *The Music of Humanity,* his excellent study of "The Ruined Cottage."

> She is dead,
> The worm is on her cheek, and this poor hut
>
> (103–104)

"Margaret, already dead, loses not her 'vital qualities' but her humanity itself: the word 'on' especially ('The worm is *on* her cheek'), reduces her almost brutally to an object." [5] Another busy preposition; again a critic's drawing to our notice something which carries strong conviction; but again a feeling that the force, and even the full meaning, of the word *on* asks to be further pondered. One way of eliciting the further suggestiveness which Jonathan Wordsworth here divines would be to treat the clause for a moment as if it were an incomplete quotation: ". . . is on her cheek." What would ordinarily complete such a clause is an abstract noun such as pain or grief or care: "and care / Sat on his faded cheek" (*Paradise Lost* I.601–602). But Margaret is dead now; if she can still be preyed upon, it is at least no longer by pain or grief or care; what is on her cheek, the worm, is seen for precisely what it is — for good and ill — by a tacit comparison with those other ravages which had in life been on her cheek. Jonathan Wordsworth's suggestion, and it is a mark of good criticism that this should be so, is itself productive of suggestions. "Reduces her almost brutally to an object": that *almost,* which is surprising when you look at it, needs to be seen as occasioned by the compassion at that unmentioned pain or grief or care which had earlier been on her cheek.

That Wordsworth's prepositions may be richly paradoxical is brought out, too, in another central study, David Ferry's *The Limits of Mortality.*

5. *The Music of Humanity* (London: Nelson, 1969), p. 129.

Thou art a dew-drop, which the morn brings forth,
Ill fitted to sustain unkindly shocks,
Or to be trailed along the soiling earth;
A gem that glitters while it lives,
And no forewarning gives;
But, at the touch of wrong, without a strife,
Slips in a moment out of life.

("To H.C. Six Years Old")

"Does this mean he will die easily, that a child is more vulnerable to physical death than we are? Or does it mean that adulthood, maturity, is a kind of death? Both at once . . . The maturing of the child is only the measure of its distance from that world [the world of eternity], so that the line could be reasonably construed as 'slips in a moment *into* life' without changing the feelings involved in it at all." [6]

Finally, one might cite two observations by C. C. Clarke, whose *Romantic Paradox* is a spirited inquiry into Wordsworth's meanings.

Once again
Do I behold these steep and lofty cliffs,
That on a wild secluded scene impress
Thoughts of more deep seclusion;

("Tintern Abbey" 4–7)

"The formula 'Thoughts of . . .' is ambiguous: a possible meaning is that the thoughts are more secluded than the secluded scene. At any rate the thoughts are not only *about* deep seclusion, they are themselves deep and secluded." [7]

these thoughts did oft revolve
About some centre palpable, which at once
Incited them to motion, and control'd,
And whatsoever shape the fit might take,
And whencesoever it might come, I still

6. *The Limits of Mortality* (Middletown, Conn.: Wesleyan University Press, 1959), pp. 83–84.
7. *Romantic Paradox* (London: Routledge, 1962), p. 45.

> At all times had a real solid world
> Of images about me;
>
> *(The Prelude* VIII.599–605)

"When therefore the metaphor of the circle (*'About* some centre . . .') is covertly repeated ('. . . a real solid world Of
images *about* me') the reader tends to assume that the relationship between the images and the self, like that between the
forms and the thoughts, is not purely external: in other words
'about me' is not interpreted simply as 'outside and independent
of me' but also as 'centred upon me' and even perhaps, in some
sense, ' dependent upon me.' " [8]

Such critics as John Jones, Jonathan Wordsworth, David
Ferry, and C. C. Clarke, then, have rich and various things to
say about Wordsworth's "busy prepositions"; but in each case
what they have to say remains a valuable aside, unrelated. I
should like to move Wordsworth's prepositions to the centre —
or rather, to suggest that they are at the centre.

If as a poet you seek the simplest and most permanent forms
of language, you are bound to give special importance to prepositions and conjunctions — those humble fundamentals, *in, up,
and, but, of,* and so on. And if as a poet you are concerned
above all with relations and relationships, you are bound to
give special importance to those words which express relationships: prepositions and conjunctions. Their importance for
Wordsworth can hardly be overstated. A rather serious misreading is involved when a critic can say of the boating episode
(*The Prelude* I.372–427) that "he stole the boat, and felt the
terrifying presence of the mountain rearing up behind him." [9]
Not behind him; in front of him as he rowed away from it and so
brought more of it into view.

Wordsworth's poetry was to be "important in the multiplicity and quality of its moral relations." [10] His commitment was
to an exploration of all the most important relationships of man:
man to nature, man to society, man to family, man to God. The

8. *Ibid.,* p. 54.
9. Stephen Prickett, *Coleridge and Wordsworth: The Poetry of
Growth* (Cambridge, Eng.: Cambridge University Press, 1970), p. 122.
10. Preface to *Lyrical Ballads.*

humbly essential medium for all such relationships is the preposition. Moreover, Wordsworth's demand was for "a more permanent, and a far more philosophical language, than that which
is frequently substituted for it by Poets"; he could delight in
the fact that "the affecting parts of Chaucer are almost always
expressed in language pure and universally intelligible even to
this day." There is a sense in which prepositions constitute a
"more philosophical language"; more importantly, there is a
sense in which though all language changes, the language of
prepositions changes strikingly less than most. In expressing the
fundamental relationships of things, prepositions constitute a
bedrock, subject no doubt to change but to change of a geo-
logical slowness. Old and Middle English offer even to the ignorant the foothold of prepositions and conjunctions.

Take a famous line from "Tintern Abbey" and imagine it
as a puzzle for the compositor. "Felt in the . . . and felt along
the . . ." To be slotted in are the words *heart* and *blood*. The
expected placing would give: "Felt in the heart, and felt along
the blood," since the heart is static and the blood is diffused.
Indeed, elsewhere Wordsworth does give us "along the blood." [11]
Yet Wordsworth's line — so famous by now as to be exceptionally hard to see as what it is, rather like the plot of *Hamlet* —
is "Felt in the blood, and felt along the heart." The unobtrusive
surprise of the prepositions is a matter of our being tacitly aware
of how they might have been expected to figure; deploying them
this way round then enables Wordsworth to challenge the pre-
supposition that the heart is simply a place and the blood simply
diffused; the relationship between the heart and its blood is
seen to be more intimate, more mysterious, and more reciprocal
than that. The heart has no blood that is not coming from and
going to; the blood's coming and going are dependent upon the
heart; and this reciprocity, like that of the "affections sweet,"
can be subtly and touchingly signalled by interchanging their
prepositions. Helen Darbishire picked out this line in a brief note
on "A Phrase of Wordsworth's," [12] and she mentioned some
comparable uses of *along*: "Which, like a tempest, works along
the blood" (*The Prelude* I.612); "That flow'd along my dreams"

11. *The Prelude* I.612.
12. *RES*, 21 (1945).

(I.276). She was right to remark the mysterious power which "even such a workaday word as 'along' takes on" in Wordsworth. But she was too reluctant to investigate the mystery, and said nothing of the unexpectedness of the placing of *in* and *along,* and nothing of the *blood* and *heart* themselves.

The instance is a simple one, though its workings are not. Its simplicity may serve to build up a sense of those elementary or initial stages of critical thinking about Wordsworth's prepositions which John Jones overleaped. Marshalling such aperçus as his may entail a rather slower exposition of what is going on. A famous instance is the crucial distinction introduced by the innocent authority of the word *in* when Wordsworth hails that spirit

> Whose dwelling is the light of setting suns,
> And the round ocean and the living air,
> And the blue sky, and in the mind of man:
> ("Tintern Abbey" 97–99)

The spirit's dwelling is light, sea, air and sky; its dwelling is in the mind of man. One has only to replace "Whose dwelling is" by "Which dwells in" — wording which would occlude any such distinction — to see the narrow limits within which a crucial distinction may thrive. Crucial, and mysterious, since the spirit's dwelling place *in* the mind of man remains unspecified and perhaps unspecifiable: it doesn't dwell there, it dwells in there, as if the mind of man were the darkest and deepest of continents. One is reminded of De Quincey's feeling for a great Wordsworthian moment when

> a gentle shock of mild surprise
> Has carried far into his heart the voice
> Of mountain torrents;
> (*The Prelude* V.382–384)

"The very expression 'far' by which space and its infinities are attributed to the human heart, and its capacities of reechoing the sublimities of nature, has always struck me as with a flash of sublime revelation" (*Literary Reminiscences*).

In such a case the word *in* functions explicitly, albeit

strangely; that is, if you were translating the lines from "Tintern Abbey" you would have to render the plain stated difference of sense (which is something other than a poetic suggestion) between "Whose dwelling is x" and "Whose dwelling is in y." But the critic will need to deal too with suggestions and surmises. "Three years she grew in . . ." The ordinary pressures of "to grow in . . ." should lead one half consciously to expect the line to end with qualities: "Three years she grew in loveliness, goodness, femininity." But the line selects a different destination: "Three years she grew in sun and shower." A perfectly natural sequence; what she grew *in* was not qualities but circumstances. Perfectly natural; yet the poem's effect depends upon a sense of the other perfectly natural sequence which the line could well have followed.

> Footfalls echo in the memory
> Down the passage which we did not take
> Towards the door we never opened
> Into the rose-garden. My words echo
> Thus, in your mind.[13]

Wordsworth's line echoes down a passage which it did not, in the event, take. Yet we have no sooner put, however fleetingly, before ourselves some such possibility as "Three years she grew in loveliness," than a form of the word *lovely* surfaces in the next line:

> Three years she grew in sun and shower,
> Then Nature said, "A lovelier flower
> On earth was never sown . . ."

Are we about to speak of the qualities in which she grew, or of the circumstances in which she grew? The eventfulness of language makes its choice, but with quiet surprise, and with a sense of the alternative; moreover, we are then urged back into considering the relationship between qualities and circumstances. For is it not circumstances which foster qualities? We have only to replace "shower" with "drizzle" — "Three years she grew

13. Eliot, "Burnt Norton," *Collected Poems 1909–1962* (New York, 1963), reprinted by permission of Faber and Faber and Harcourt Brace Jovanovich, Inc.

in sun and drizzle" — to see that "sun and shower" aren't *just* circumstances, but are there because in describing circumstances they also suggest qualities of mind. The "sun and shower" are not simply climatic; they suggest inner weather, the changes and chances of this mortal life, the sunshine of happiness and the "shower" (not yet, not for the child, the chilling blasts of storm) of brief sadness. And such circumstances, such "sun and shower," naturally foster such a temperament, one which blends sun and shower in qualities of mind and heart. In short, the question of whether it was qualities or circumstances in which she grew is seen to resolve itself, and dissolve itself, into reciprocity. Geoffrey Hartman has said of surmises in poetry that "they revive in us the capacity for the virtual, a trembling of the imagined on the brink of the real." [14]

A preposition may be a small, sturdy word, but within Wordsworth's relationships it can create a trembling of the imagined on the brink of the real. "Though nothing can bring back the hour / Of splendour in the grass, of glory in the flower" ("Ode, Intimations of Immortality"). The characteristically Wordsworthian quality of that second line is not just a matter of its four prepositions, or of its beginning — as do so many of the great Wordsworth lines — with the word *of*. The line is saved from a merely illustrative repetition by the fact that its parallelism is subtly modified. For whereas "splendour in" remains precisely what it states, "glory in" cannot but be affected by the other sense, *to glory in*. So that within the line there can be heard the faint suggestion that "nothing can bring back the hour . . . of glorying in the flower." And whether the glory is something which is indeed within the flower or whether it is rather something which the perceiving eye works upon the flower, glorying in it — this question belongs with all those which so endlessly, and so rightly, fascinated Wordsworth: "Creates, creator and receiver both" (*The Prelude* II.273). Of course it is true (and here again one may think what it would be to translate these two lines) that there is no feasible ambiguity of syntax; Wordsworth has not created, as he might easily have done, a form of words in which *glory* might function equably and equally as either

14. *Wordsworth's Poetry 1787–1814* (New Haven: Yale University Press, 1964), p. 11.

noun or verb. The syntax is such that the stated sense must be that of *glory* as a noun parallel to *splendour*. Nevertheless a surmise, created by the momentary uncertainty as to the function of *in*, has flickered: the surmise that the unit might be *glory in* rather than the units being (1) *glory*, (2) *in the flower*.

It should now be easier to see why Matthew Arnold was right (though altogether unforthcoming) in selecting as Wordsworth's "own strong and characteristic line" the magnificent "Of joy in widest commonalty spread." [15] It is not just the sentiment to which Arnold might have drawn attention. Again, we have *of* at the head. Again, *in* is deployed with an apt suggestiveness. For the line cannot adequately be cast, though such is indeed the main sense, as "Of joy spread in widest commonalty." To put it in that way would be to destroy more than the rhythm. For it would abolish the flickering suggestion of "joy in" by which there is held momentarily before us the richly human need to joy in commonalty. The effect is of a superb compression which yet speaks paradoxically of the "widest commonalty," a compression by which the line economically but lavishly accommodates "Of joy in widest commonalty spread in widest commonalty." The widest commonalty is both what the joy joys in (what creates the joy) and what the joy acts upon (what the joy creates). Such joy spreads, both outwards and inwards, in the widest commonalty.

It therefore seems to me that a very important class of words has not had the attention it asks. Twentieth-century criticism of Wordsworth has done much by scrutinizing some of his crucial terms. Most notable is William Empson's study of *sense* in *The Prelude*.[16] Hugh Sykes Davies[17] has mined the word *impulse*. There is C. C. Clarke's *Romantic Paradox* on the related terms *image*, *form*, and *shape*; he had been anticipated in some minor respects by Ellen Douglass Leyburn, whose inquiry into "Recurrent Words in *The Prelude*" [18] singled out

15. From "The Recluse"; preface to *The Excursion*.
16. *The Structure of Complex Words* (London: Chatto and Windus, 1951).
17. "Wordsworth and the Empirical Philosophers," in *The English Mind*, ed. Hugh Sykes Davies and George Watson (Cambridge, Eng.: Cambridge University Press, 1964).
18. *ELH*, 26 (1949).

earth, being, object, forms, image, presence, intercourse, and *power.* But her belief that "the richness of [Wordsworth's] diction goes with the richness of his thought" may be misleading unless it takes a widely imaginative view of the forms that richness may take, and in particular of the rich possibilities of the humblest and apparently most insignificant of words. There is nothing about prepositions in Josephine Miles's *Wordsworth and the Vocabulary of Emotion* (1942),[19] and yet it might be claimed that his prepositions are central to his vocabulary of emotion. Moreover, Lane Cooper's indispensable *Concordance* (1911, reprinted 1965) lamentably lacks them. Some of Wordsworth's most important words are therefore unrecorded in the *Concordance*: not only the forms of the verb *to be,* but also the prepositions and conjunctions. It omits *and* and *but*; *at, by, for, from, in, of, on, to, up, with,* and so on; and it only partially lists *above, along, among,* and so on. Even those who feel that recent criticism (and not especially of Wordsworth) is often marred by niggling and by a lack of any sense of proportion may nevertheless feel that the attitudes of 1923 now seem altogether too rough and ready: Franklyn Bliss Snyder's account of "Wordsworth's Favorite Words" [20] was necessarily curtailing most drastically what it could hope to achieve when it announced, with round cheerfulness, that "In compiling such a list it would seem the part of wisdom to follow the practice of the Wordsworth Concordance and omit all reference to words which were omitted entirely from the Concordance, and similarly, to omit words represented by only partial lists. In the use of *and, I, but, is,* etc., there is but little significance." On the contrary, those four little words can be, and often are, of the greatest significance. The closing pages of *The Egotistical Sublime*[21] rightly insist that the Wordsworthian achievement is

an achievement shared . . . by the short words, the long words, and all the time and space of language. Shared, too, by language's humblest parts. "And," more frequent in Wordsworth than in any

19. Or in her discussion of Wordsworth in *Eras and Modes in English Poetry* (Berkeley and Los Angeles: University of California Press, 1964).
20. *JEGP,* 22 (1923).
21. Pages 206–207.

poet, is the preserver of extreme structural simplicity through hundreds of lines of *Prelude* narrative: if the ice is thin, the skating is light and swift. "And" helps to sustain the calm elevation of *Tintern Abbey:*

> And the round ocean and the living air,
> And the blue sky, and in the mind of man . . .

By its monotony, its insistence on the particular, "and" develops Wordsworth's expository style, in common with other words of modest function — "but," "thus," "therefore."

A simple instance would be to contrast the changed function and attachment of *with* in *The Prelude* I.466–467:

> *1805:*   And not a voice was idle; with the din,
> Meanwhile, the precipices rang aloud

> *1850:*   And not a voice was idle; with the din
> Smitten, the precipices rang aloud

Wordsworth was especially adept with, and committed to, the sequence by which a prepositional adverb (*up,* in *rose up*) is followed by a preposition. He sometimes pursued such sequences to the point of an authentic gracelessness, or perhaps one should say a graceless authenticity, and he fretted about whether the proportions of manliness to stutter were right. In "Michael" 455–456 the old man still ventures out after his disaster: "Among the rocks / He went, and still looked up upon the sun." The semistutter of "up upon" is piercing in its combination of dignity with precariousness;[22] a lesser poet would have ironed it out, in the interests of a simpler, more mellifluous grandeur. Wordsworth became that lesser poet: the fine line, which had stood from 1800 to 1827, was replaced in 1832 by "He went, and still looked up towards the sun," to be restlessly replaced in 1836 by "He went, and still looked up to sun and cloud." But beneath the fretting changes, the basic structure

22. Echoing an earlier pathos in "Michael" 350–352: "And in the open fields my life was passed / And on the mountains; else I think that thou / Hadst been brought up upon thy Father's knees."

remained: verb, prepositional adverb, preposition. The best version, the earliest, is that which most insists upon this structure by boldly juxtaposing "up upon."

Again and again this sequence is one of the hiding places of his power.

> Would leave behind a dance of images
> That shall break in upon his sleep for weeks
> > (*The Prelude* VIII.165)

> And, turning the mind in upon itself,
> Pored, watch'd, expected, listen'd; spread my thoughts
> And spread them with a wider creeping
> > (III.112–114) [23]

So simply lucid is Wordsworth's speech that it can constitute a temptation: we may not pay sufficient attention to the very words, since we are so confident of what they are saying. "And the whole body of the Man did seem / Like one whom I had met with in a dream" ("Resolution and Independence"). As we reflect upon *whom* there (*which*? does not "one" refer back to *body* rather than to *man*?), we are led to reflect upon relationships (whom/which problems) such as are central to the poem and to the mysterious thing-like humanity of the leech-gatherer. And the sequence "met with in," with the preposition following the prepositional adverb, is firmly characteristic, with a delicately hypothetical suggestion (the hypothesis faintly advanced and rescinded) such as might, with minimal change, quietly become: "And the whole body of the Man did seem / Like one whom I had met within a dream."

When Wordsworth borrows, he makes the borrowing his own by assimilating it to such a sequence. In his preface, de Selincourt cites Pope, *The First Epistle of the First Book of Horace Imitated* 39–40: "So slow th' unprofitable Moments roll, / That lock up all the Functions of my soul." *The Prelude* I.247–248 turns Pope to Wordsworth by creating the Wordsworthian

---

23. Donald Wesling writes excellently on the word *spread* here and its relation to Wordsworth's verse (*Wordsworth and the Adequacy of Landscape* [London: Routledge, 1970], pp. 18–19).

sequence "that now / Doth lock my functions up in blank reserve." And the *1850* revision lets that essential structure
stand: "that now / Locks every function up in blank reserve."
So it is possible to guess what it was that alerted de Selincourt [24]
when he deprecated this 1850 revision:

> Catching from tufts of grass and hare-bell flowers
> Their faintest whisper to the passing breeze,
> Given out while mid-day heat oppressed the plains.

"The voice of the authentic Wordsworth is more distinctly
heard in the delicate simplicity of the rejected lines:"

> Lay listening to the wild flowers and the grass,
> As they gave out their whispers to the wind.
>
> (*The Prelude* VI.231–232)

He does not say in what "the authentic Wordsworth" inheres;
I should like to suggest that one of the things which 1850 mis-
takenly abandons is the sequence "gave out . . . to." Such a
sequence — strange in that it manages to be both ubiquitous
and freshly potent — can be seen at work three times in a passage such as this:

> Hush'd, meanwhile,
> Was the under soul, lock'd up in such a calm,
> That not a leaf of the great nature stirr'd.
> Yet was this deep vacation not given up
> To utter waste. Hitherto I had stood
> In my own mind remote from human life,
> At least from what we commonly so name,
> Even as a shepherd on a promontory,
> Who, lacking occupation, looks far forth
> Into the endless sea, and rather makes
> Than finds what he beholds.
>
> (*The Prelude* III.539–549)

At which point one may turn to the heart of Arnold's Wordsworth:

24. Page lxi.

The right sort of verse to choose from Wordsworth, if we are to seize his true and most characteristic form of expression, is a line like this from *Michael* —

> "And never lifted up a single stone."

There is nothing subtle in it, no heightening, no study of poetic style, strictly so called, at all; yet it is expression of the highest and most truly expressive kind.

The instance is a triumphant one, and the triumph is Arnold's as well as Wordsworth's. But if the line is to be a talisman and not just a shibboleth, we need some sense of how it effects its high and true expressiveness. The immediate context says much:

> 'Tis not forgotten yet
> The pity which was then in every heart
> For the old man — and 'tis believed by all
> That many and many a day he thither went,
> And never lifted up a single stone.   (462–466)

The word *single* should send us back, to see through what contrasts of singleness and multiplicity the lines evolve. *Every heart* as against *the old Man; all* and *many and many a day* as against *he* and *a single stone*. The focus narrows to that singleness which is loneliness and integrity; from *every* and *all* and *many and many* down to *a single stone*.

But we may approach the line from another direction if we put a question whose pseudo-rigour might justly be thought of as flippant. Given that Wordsworth's language here is that of the utmost austerity and economy, is not the word *up* redundant? Might not the line just as well be "And never lifted a single stone"? Such a question is fatuous, but not because of an inappropriate intensity of scrutiny, not because it doesn't matter whether so small a word as *up* really earns its keep. On the contrary, the question is fatuous because the word *up* is here, for all its quietude, intensely active. For "Michael" is a poem which, with consummate naturalness such as never invites the suspicion of a disembodied symbolizing, sets *up* severely against *down*. Its opening is a tactful signpost:

> If from the public way you turn your steps
> Up the tumultuous brook of Green-head Ghyll,
> You will suppose that with an upright path
> Your feet must struggle; in such bold ascent
> The pastoral mountains front you, face to face.   (1–5)

Up, upright, ascent: they signal. Yet at the same time the word *suppose* assures us that all is not simply as it seems, and that a *but* is imminent.

The structure of the poem, from aspiration to dignified defeat, is implicit in three echoing lines. The first sentence of the poem gives us "Up the tumultuous brook of Green-head Ghyll"; the middle of the poem gives us, with balanced neutrality, "Near the tumultuous brook of Green-head Ghyll" (322); the final lines give us: "and the remains / Of the unfinished Sheep-fold may be seen / Beside the boisterous brook of Green-head Ghyll' (480–482). From *up*, via *near*, to *beside*.

The importance of the modest word *up* is evidenced in its placing: of its eleven occurrences in the poem, six are at the beginning or end of the lines. But a word like *up* derives its meaning from the contrast, implicit or explicit, with *down*. (The critic of Wordsworth must not fear, any more than did Wordsworth, the bathos of banality.) So it is at once surprising and apt that the word *down* comes only twice in the poem. Indeed, there are moments when the word seems to be crying out to get into the poem and yet is fended off with a firm dexterity:

>   For, as it chanced,
> Their cottage on a plot of rising ground
> Stood single, with large prospect, north and south,
> High into Easedale, up to Dunmail-Raise,
> And westward to the village near the lake   (131–135)

Rising, high, and *up* are one side of all this; yet with all that range of views, no view is *down;* instead the word *westward* supervenes where the word *down* might have been anticipated.

And the two instances of *down?* The first has its studied neutrality; its humdrum literalness protects the poem against the suspicion of symbolic coercion.

> Down from the ceiling, by the chimney's edge,
> That in our ancient uncouth country style
> With huge and black projection overbrowed
> Large space beneath, as duly as the light
> Of day grew dim the Housewife hung a lamp   (110–114)

That calm neutrality leaves everything clear for the great moment in the poem when the word *down* can figure as the saddening counterpart and contrast to all that rightly aspires:

> "Now, fare thee well —
> When thou return'st, thou in this place wilt see
> A work which is not here: a covenant
> 'Twill be between us; but, whatever fate
> Befall thee, I shall love thee to the last,
> And bear thy memory with me to the grave."
>   The Shepherd ended here; and Luke stooped down,
> And, as his Father had requested, laid
> The first stone of the Sheep-fold.   (412–420)

"Luke stooped down." He was to stoop yet lower. And it is that *down* which — in the company of all which contrasts with it — informs with pathos and gravity the small word *up* when later Michael "thither went, / And never lifted up a single stone."

Many of the most memorable of Wordsworth's prose apothegms cast themselves prepositionally:

a sinking inward into ourselves from thought to thought
                    ("Answer to Mathetes," *The Friend,* 1818)

I was often unable to think of external things as having external existence, and I communed with all that I saw as something not apart from, but inherent in, my own immaterial nature.
                    (Fenwick note on the "Immortality Ode")

Men who read from religious or moral inclinations . . . come prepared to impart so much passion to the Poet's language, that they remain unconscious how little, in fact, they receive from it.
                    (Essay, "Supplementary to the Preface," 1815)

And as for Wordsworth's critics, a cento of quotations from some of the best of them will show how natural it is for the critic's way of couching things to learn from the poet's own way. (The italics are theirs.)

Coleridge

Although Wordsworth and Goethe are not much alike, to be sure, upon the whole, yet they both have this peculiarity of utter non-sympathy with the subjects of their poetry. They are always, both of them, spectators *ab extra* — feeling *for*, but never *with*, their characters.   (*Table Talk* [1835], I.61–62)

Keats

[of Milton] He did not think into the human heart, as Wordsworth has done.   (Letter to Reynolds, 3 May 1818;
Forman's Oxford University Press ed.)

Clough

He is apt to wind up his short pieces with reflections upon the way in which, hereafter, he expects to reflect upon his present reflections.
("Lecture on the Poetry of Wordsworth,"
Prose Remains [1888], p. 315)

A. C. Bradley

[In Wordsworth] the arresting feature or object is felt in some way *against* this background, or even as in some way a denial of it.
(*Oxford Lectures on Poetry* [Macmillan, 1909], p. 131)

F. R. Leavis

If these "moments" have any significance for the critic (whose business it is to define the significance of Wordsworth's poetry), it will be established, not by dwelling upon or in them, in the hope of exploring something that lies hidden in or behind their vagueness, but by holding firmly on to that sober verse in which they are presented.
(*Revaluation* [Chatto & Windus, 1936], p. 174)

James Smith

But is it humanly possible to carry renunciation to the point which may be necessary? It is conceivable that other things should close in to such an extent upon a creature that, if he yields to them, any inner activity left is too insignificant to be called human.
("Wordsworth: A Preliminary Survey," *Scrutiny*, 7 [1938])

F. W. Bateson
[Of *She dwelt among the untrodden ways*] The reader begins by
looking *down* at the violet, and then *up* at the star, and in the process the two juxtaposed images form themselves into a single landscape . . . By manipulating his words, metaphors and symbols so
that they create the illusion of cancelling each other out, he was
able to suggest a more inclusive and a more rarefied meaning than
it was possible to express directly. But the poetry lay *between* the
words.
     (*Wordsworth: A Re-Interpretation* [Longman, 1954], pp. 33, 38)

W. W. Robson
He imposes conviction by means of that characteristic medium
through which we are made to see and judge all that Wordsworth
wishes us to see and judge . . . Wordsworth's personal need, his
demand for reassurance, issuing in that oddly inappropriate question
["How is it that you live, and what is it you do?"], is not so much
for a reassurance *from* the old Man as for a reassurance *about* the
old Man.
                    (Wordsworth's "Resolution and Independence,"
                    Interpretations, ed. Wain [Routledge, 1955];
                    Critical Essays [Routledge, 1966], pp. 124, 131–
                    132)

Hugh Sykes Davies
[On the word *impulse*] For him, it meant not an inexplicable eddy
within the human spirit, but a movement stirred in it from without.
     (*The English Mind* [Cambridge University Press, 1964], p. 155)

Geoffrey Hartman
[1] Everything that happens on this mountain [Snowdon] is de-
ceptive because everything leads beyond (though not away from)
itself.
[2] According to Wordsworth, the imagination of a child is, like
a Romance hero, in nature but not of it.
[3] The child grows from a stage in which it walks *with* nature, to
one in which it is in search *of* nature, and finally to a crisis when
nature no longer suffices. This crisis is overcome when it is seen
that Nature itself taught the mind to be free of nature and now
teaches the mind to be free of mind and mingle with nature once
more.

[4] The man who knows he has been strong *in* and *against* imagination.

[5] These spots are not only *in* time, like islands, but also creative *of* time or of a vivifying temporal consciousness.

> (*Wordsworth's Poetry* [Yale University Press, 1964], pp. 67, 75, 135, 146, 212)

Christopher Salvesen

Wordsworth is always much more aware of the *presence* of landscape, of its surrounding influence, than of any pictorial qualities it might have. His sense of being not merely related to it, but of being *in* it, part of it, precludes any very objective view.

> (*The Landscape of Memory* [Edward Arnold, 1965], p. 69)

Donald Davie

[On two lines from *Anecdote for Fathers:* "His head he raised — there was in sight, / It caught his eye, he saw it plain — "] The lines convey brilliantly how his eye flits across the weather-cock, returns to it, and then, seeing it will do for a pretext, focuses on it.

> ("Dionysus in *Lyrical Ballads*," *Wordsworth's Mind and Art,* ed. A. W. Thomson [Oliver & Boyd, 1969], p. 118)

All these critics see their insights take shape prepositionally, just as some of the best books on Wordsworth cast their titles alike: *The Limits of Mortality, The Landscape of Memory, The Music of Humanity.* Even one critic who on this occasion steps from the egotistical sublime to the egotistical ridiculous finds himself ending his account of Wordsworth with the customary turn of speech: "Wordsworth would be a comical figure except for the appalling fact that he has been preserved in amber (or something) by (and with) a good many scholars and critics for more than a century" (Yvor Winters, *Forms of Discovery* [Alan Swallow, 1969], p. 172). Even Max Beerbohm's famous caricature breathes an awareness of the Wordsworthian prepositions: *William Wordsworth in the Lake District, at cross-purposes.* The pressure there of *in* is enough to make *at* sound as if it ought to signify a location (at the crossroads, say); the implication is that "at cross-purposes" is a haunt of Wordsworth — as indeed it is. By mistitling the caricature (as

"Mr. Wordsworth at cross-purposes in the Lake District"),
Geoffrey Hartman[25] blunts Beerbohm's point. But then how
often Hartman has shown us the fineness of Wordsworth's point.
The twentieth-century Wordsworth? — there has been no
greater poet in the two centuries since he was born, and the best
recent criticism does justice with as well as to him.

25. *Wordsworth's Poetry,* p. 144.